THE ULTIMATE TIMELINE OF
WORLD HISTORY

-3000

3000-1000

1000-500

500-0

1-500

500-1050

1050-1250

1250-1450

1450-1560

1560-1650

1650-1770

1770-1815

1815-1850

1850-1900

1900-1920

1920-1939

1939-1945

1945-1970

1970-1989

1990-2010

American History

THE ULTIMATE TIMELINE OF
WORLD HISTORY

BARRON'S

SOLVING AND RESOLVING HISTORY

The study of the past is, by nature, "forensic," meaning it uses investigative skills to interpret events in order to construct the type of story that might stand up in court. Scientists—such as physicists, chemists, and biologists—can all create their objects of study in laboratories and experiment until they are sure of the cause of certain events. But, like a team of criminal investigators, historians arrive "at the scene of the crime" after it has occurred and cannot make it happen again. Whether the event is catastrophic (such as the volcanic destruction of Pompeii in 79 A.D.), or long and subtle (such as the decline of China's Ming empire in the 1500s), or worldwide and complex (such as the economic depression of the 1930s), there will be some evidence, including testimony—which may be reliable or unreliable. Skill, art, and intuition are required to reconstruct the event, and more skill and more art will be required to present a convincing story, consistent with all evidence, for students and other readers. And as in the case of a crime, the story is meaningful. But what is its meaning?

All cultures have shown an interest in the past. Unlike our families, homes, work places, food, or possessions, the past is not materially present. We take it on faith that many things in our surroundings were created before us, but we have no way to prove it. In the same way, none of us can prove, absolutely, that we existed before the present moment. We accept this lack of proof without going crazy, because we all agree that there is circumstantial evidence—evidence that has to be interpreted in order to relate it to an event, as contrasted to the proverbial "smoking gun" that leaves no doubt of its meaning—which can be accepted as credible evidence for the explanation of how we got here. Principles of evidence and logic allow us to have confidence in that explanation. We accept that there is a story somewhere that leads up to us, and suggests that after us will come something else. Even if we disagree about what the story is, we accept that a story exists.

The concept of a story—a narrative—is so essential to the understanding of history that the two words in English are actually the same. They derive from the Greek verb *historein*, "to inquire," which itself comes from an earlier root that is the source of words in many Indo-European languages for asking, discovering, perceiving, and narrating. Essentially, it is a reference to the first levels of knowledge: How do we know we existed before the present moment? Who made the world as we know it, and how? Why is each of us positioned as we are in our societies and in the wider world? If there is unhappiness and injustice, how were they produced, and how can they be remedied?

Among the many specializations in historical study, "world history" does something unusual. Whatever starting point world historians choose, they would like to tell a story that transcends every kind of local bias—whether personal, national, religious, or based on ethnicity or gender. They are looking for the story that all humanity shares. Its great events will be on the order of the emergence of agriculture; patterns of migration; climate change; the fundamentals of human travel and communication; the progress of scientific discovery; the impact of disease and genetic mutation; the integration of continental and ultimately global patterns of trade, finance, freedom, slavery, spirituality, secularism, and the arts. Actually, world historians want to know more than the evidence can tell them directly.

Beyond that, they want to learn how to make good guesses. They want to figure out details of daily lives of the past, for which we may have no diaries and no excavations. They want to understand the degree to which great physical forces, such as volcanic upheavals, or temperature fluctuations and even collisions between the earth and asteroids can change history. They want to fill in the blanks in understanding how culture changes human destiny and is changed by it. They want to reconstruct the causes of wars and of long periods of peace. But because they are human themselves, with particular histories of their own, they find the truly global story always a little beyond their reach. It is like the story of Achilles trying to overtake the tortoise. No matter how many times Achilles halved the distance between himself and the tortoise, he still had halfway to go. World historians find that they can keep cutting the distance between themselves and a truly worldwide vantage point in half, yet still have halfway to go. Nevertheless, the more they research, analyze, and test for coherence, the closer we get to a story that means something to us all.

In their great forensic enterprise, historians—particularly world historians—need certain tools. Some are tools of primary investigation—original documents from archives or personal collections, or material artifacts such as photographs, art works, or archeological discoveries. Using such tools to produce completely new evidence of the past is a primary task of many historians. Yet they must go beyond this. They must combine their own evidence with the evidence produced by historians past and present to change, improve, or deepen the story. They may find themselves retracing the steps of great early historians, such as the Greeks' Herodotus (484 B.C.–c. 425 B.C.) and Thucydides (460 B.C.–395 B.C.), or the Chinese historian Sima Qian (145 B.C.–86 B.C.), or the great medieval historian Rashid al-Din (1247–1318) in order to test past stories or add a new conclusion. They might find themselves disputing their own contemporaries regarding what causes what. And for these greater tasks they need tools of reference, primarily maps and timelines.

A timeline is basic to every story and every forensic investigation. Thinking of what we have said before about the challenges of globalizing the story, it is clear that the significance and challenges of a timeline are both very deep. Points in time, like points in space, are infinite. Even if we arbitrarily decide that a point in time is something like a day or a year (the units used by ancient chroniclers all over the world), about most points in time in the past we are completely ignorant. A timeline must capture not only the points of crisis and transformation that the evidence suggests, but also test the significance of each point—and each individual—against the global, inclusive context.

Equally important, a timeline is a visual presentation of the historical concept of simultaneity—all the things that are happening at the same time. Horizontally, we see the changes happening locally; vertically, we see the emergence of a world perspective, of limitless simultaneity. If you can imagine all the things happening right now, everywhere in the world, you understand the challenge of the timelines. Or, just to take the year 1492 as an example, Columbus was discovering the American continent as Spain was being recaptured from the Muslims, the great Persian scholar and poet Jami died, and Pope Alexander VI was beginning his very controversial reign. With this information, we build contexts that allow us to better understand the overall significance of events. The context is the framework over which the story is stretched, and the context is composed entirely of the elements selected, polished, and set into the timeline. A modern, comprehensive work such as *The Ultimate Timeline of World History* is essential to the forensic field kit of every historian, from the beginning student to the mature professional.

PAMELA CROSSLEY
Professor of History
Dartmouth College

2.4 mil. Early human ancestors produce the first **primitive stone tools**.

1 mil.–700,000 In Africa, **Homo erectus** learns to **control fire**, a decisive step in the cultural development from animal to human.

100,000 Prehistoric man produces the first **jewelry objects from stone and bones**.

50,000–30,000 First **primitive hammers** are produced **from hand axes**.

43,000 Humans make **sharp-edged blades from stone** and use them to produce **weapons** like **spear-throwers and harpoons**.

1.5 mil. Homo erectus creates **sharp-edged hand axes** which were used, among other things, to butcher prey.

450,000 The earliest known hearth is ignited in present-day Hungary.

400,000 Early man develops the **wooden spear**, the most important **weapon of the Mesolithic Age**.

100,000 Neanderthals develop **religious concepts of death**. They bury their dead in pits and provide them with ritual burial objects like jewelry or food.

32,500–30,000 The first cave paintings by Paleolithic people appear in Europe, Siberia, and Eastern Asia. The artists primarily depicted **Ice Age animals** in profile and in motion.

---

c. 6 mil. — c. 1 mil. — c. 100,000 — c. 50,000

---

6 mil. The first humanoids, the **australopithecine** ("southern ape"), emerge in Africa. They live in the trees and are vegetarian.

2.2–1.6 mil. Homo habilis ("handy man"), the first "real" human, develops from prehumans in East Africa. His physique resembles that of the ape.

1.8 mil. Hominids of the genus **Homo erectus leave Africa for the first time** and spread across Asia, verifiably as far as **China and Java**.

800,000 "Peking Man": Earliest verification of a species of Homo erectus in the region of present-day China.

120,000 **Modern man leaves Africa for the first time** and settles in present-day **Israel**.

60,000 The settlement area of the **Neanderthal** ranges **from Western Europe all the way to Iraq**. However, the Neanderthal population is **forced back** to the European continent **by modern man** in the coming millennia.

2 mil. **Homo erectus** ("upright man") develops in Africa and is **more intelligent and stronger** than his predecessors.

1.8 mil. The **Ice Age begins** on earth. The water level of the oceans sinks significantly.

90,000–35,000 In Egypt, the Nile begins flooding the area beyond its banks with fertile silt. The **annual flooding of the Nile** largely contributes to the later development of an **advanced Egyptian civilization**.

45,000/38,000 The first humans **reach New Guinea** and settle there.

43,000 The **Upper Paleolithic Age** begins in Eurasia. During the **last Ice Age**, large sections of northern and central Europe are covered with ice.

3 mil. The **australopithecine** develop the **ability to walk upright**.

2.4 mil. Homo rudolfensis, the **earliest known representative of the genus Homo**, emerges in present-day Kenya. The **upright-walking vegetarian** has a larger brain volume than prehumans and possibly already uses tools.

1.1 mil. "Java Man": Hominids of the species Homo erectus appear for the first time in present-day **Indonesia**.

600,000 **Archaic Homo sapiens**, the **direct ancestor of modern man**, lives in Africa.

70,000 **Modern man leaves Africa** over the water-deficient Red Sea and **populates the entire world in the following millennia**.

40,000–30,000 The first modern **humans** settle on the **Indian subcontinent**.

40,000–10,000 Modern humans are living in **caves or rock crevices**. As hunters and gatherers, their diet consists of **meat from animals, fruits, and berries**.

400,000 The **Neanderthal** develops out of Homo erectus in Europe. He is already capable of **speech**, lives from **hunting**, and develops complex **stone-working techniques**.

70,000 **First traces of human culture** can be found in the regions of present-day **Spain and Portugal**.

200,000 The **first knife-shaped tools** are predominantly produced from flint.

60,000/50,000 The first modern humans presumably already possessed a **complex language system for communication**. This is considered to be an important prerequisite for the development of hunting societies and cultural achievements **like painting or burials**.

125,000 Modern man lives in **nomadic tribes**. Men and women are presumably already practicing a **sexual division of labor**.

160,000 The anatomically modern man, the **Homo sapiens sapiens**, develops from **Homo erectus**.

40,000 **Modern man** appears almost **simultaneously in Europe and Asia** (China, Borneo).

40,000 The **total population** of humans in the world reaches scarcely **3.5 million**.

until 3000 B.C.

Who are we? Where do we come from? Not too long ago, the great questions about the origin of mankind had been the domain of philosophers and theologians. For people born and raised within the Judeo-Christian-Islamic tradition, it was considered an indisputable certainty that God had created mankind. It was not until the 19th century that the English naturalist Charles Darwin openly broke the taboo and placed the development of mankind within the context of the evolutionary history of nature. Since then, archaeologists and geneticists have scientifically substantiated Darwin's theory of the animal origins of mankind, based on a large number of skeletal finds. With the aid of modern technology, the development of modern, intelligent man and his proliferation around the world can now be reconstructed with ever-increasing accuracy. However, it was not until the invention of writing—a seminal cultural revolution—some 5,500 years ago, that people were able to document events and experiences and in doing so entered history themselves as actors.

Stages of evolution up to modern man

THE EVOLUTION OF HUMANS

The Prehuman
Between ape and human: the australopithecines are considered to be the first hominids that could walk erect.

The theory that humans share a common ancestor with apes, introduced by Charles Darwin in 1871, has been modified and supplemented, but is supported by modern biological research today. The first apes presumably evolved in Africa some 38 million years ago, from which the earliest hominids branched off **6 million years** ago. The australopithecine ("southern ape") is considered to be the first prehuman that appeared in eastern and southern Africa and developed the ability to walk upright about **3 million years** ago due to climate changes. This bipedal ape was a vegetarian, had a larger brain volume than a chimpanzee, and is believed to have used stone tools. The australopithecine died out a million years ago.

The First Humans
About two million years ago the first human, Homo habilis, appeared, who steadily expanded his abilities over the course of time.

The first representative of the genus Homo was Homo habilis, the "handy man." His brain volume was almost double the size than that of the prehumans. Then Homo erectus, the first early man, appeared in East Africa some **2 million years** ago, whose size and proportions were already similar to those of modern man. Homo erectus discovered the use of fire for warmth, cooking, and the protection against predators. He also refined the technology of stone tool making. About 1.8 million years ago, he migrated out of Africa. Due to depressed sea levels during the Ice Age, early man reached Europe and later Asia.

Neanderthal
The Neanderthal, named after a valley in Germany where his bones were first found, evolved 400,000 years ago from early man. However, he lost the competition in evolution to modern man.

The Neanderthal, who lived in Europe and western Asia, is undoubtedly the most famous primitive man. Compared to anatomically modern humans, he was more robust and possessed a larger brain volume than his predecessors. As a skilled and savvy hunter who could kill mammoths, the Neanderthal improved his technique of producing stone weapons and tools and probably wore clothing that was made of animal skins. Individual finds indicate proper stone workshops. The Neanderthal is also believed to have developed language skills as well as a religious imagination that required a certain capability of abstract thinking. How the Neanderthal died out 30,000 years ago—giving way to modern humans—is still uncertain.

Modern Man
The anatomical modern man—Homo sapiens sapiens—migrated to Europe about 40,000 years ago.

Today's modern man, Homo sapiens sapiens, evolved in Africa from the Archaic Homo sapiens, who, in turn, evolved from Homo erectus an estimated **600,000 years** ago. Homo sapiens sapiens was slimmer and a better runner than his predecessor. During the course of evolution, he developed superior cognitive capabilities. He constructed primitive dwellings and continued to live from hunting, at first. Modern man invented the spear, the bow, and the harpoon and set pitfall traps. He constantly improved his tools that allowed him, for example, to build boats from tree trunks. He also developed an aesthetic sense, attested to by jewelry and musical artifacts. Especially the cave paintings and petroglyphs—the oldest were created **32,500 years** ago—testify to an artistry that is impressive even today.

4500 In **Mesopotamia**, farmers use a **primitive plough** to prepare the ground for planting.

4000 **Burials** in the early Egyptian cultures give evidence of a nascent **belief in gods and an afterlife**.

4000 Around 4000, the **wheel** is invented independently in different parts of the world.

3500 The first **wheeled vehicles** appear in the region of the Black Sea.

3761 Beginning of the Jewish calendar: Based on biblical accounts, the **creation of the world** is traditionally calculated to be on the 7th of October, 3761 B.C.

3500 The pot-ter's wheel is invented in Meso-potamia.

3500 The presumably **oldest form of writing**, the cuneiform script, is invented in Mesopotamia. An abstract syllabary steadily emerges out of pure pictographic writing.

3200 **Corn cultivation** is practiced in **Central and South America**. Corn becomes the most important food of the region.

3000 **Hieroglyphs** develop in **Egypt**. The complex phonetic alphabet, originally based primarily on pictures, first became decipherable at the beginning of the 19th century with the aid of the Rosetta stone.

3000 The Egyptians produce **malt beer from germinated barley grain**. It is one of the main staples of the Egyptian diet. The Sumerians are considered to be the actual inventors of beer.

3000 The first primitive **lathes** made of wood are developed in **Egypt and Mesopotamia**.

3000 The **nail** is invented in Mesopotamia.

5000 **3000**

5500 Later than in the Near East, the dynamic process of **settlement formation** marks the beginning of the **Neolithic period in the region of Central Europe**.

5500 From Hungary, the earliest European agrarian culture spreads to central and southern Germany. It is named **"Linear Pottery culture"** after the decorations on pottery vessels.

5500–4000 In **Upper and Lower Egypt**, two **semi-nomadic cultures** (Badari and Faiyum A cultures) develop independently from each other.

5300 Clay tablets found in **Tartaria, Romania** possibly bear the **world's oldest known form of writing**, dated to around 5300 B.C. They have yet to be deciphered.

5000 The **Yangshao culture** spreads out in the region of present-day **central and northern China**. Painted pottery is a prominent feature of the first significant culture on Chinese territory. Burial objects indicate a high position of women in their society.

5000 For the first time, people settle along the coast of the **Mediterranean Sea**. There is evidence of pile dwellings or stilt houses down to around 900 B.C.

5000 The **first wet rice fields** are laid out on the territory of present-day **China**.

4800/4300 Evidence of large-scale **megalithic tombs** or dolmens is found on the territory of present-day **Ireland**, **Great Britain**, and **Spain**.

4700–4400 The **Rössen culture** develops in **western and central Germany**. It is known for pottery vessels decorated with double incisions.

4800–4000 The **Lengyel culture**, a successor to the Linear Pottery culture, primarily develops in the southeastern European region.

4500 The **Longshan culture** in **eastern China** begins to crystallize. Typical are their black ceramic vessels.

4300–3600 The **Michelsberg culture**, named after an excavation site in the southwestern region of Germany, develops in **Central Europe**. Characteristic are pottery vessels in the shape of a tulip.

4200–2800 **Funnelbeaker culture:** For the first time, a Neolithic agrarian culture arises in **northern middle Europe** and in **southern England**, where hunter and gatherer cultures persisted longer than elsewhere.

4000–3500 **Gold** and **silver** are being smelted in **Egypt** and **Mesopotamia**.

4000 The **domestication** and **breeding of horses** begins in **Eurasia**.

3900 The **first great city-states** with a high level of civilization and economy arise in **Mesopotamia** and in bordering **Elam**. Uruk develops into a major trading capital.

3800 The **first fortified farming settlements** are evident in **Western Europe**.

3700 First administrative techniques in Mesopotamia: **Stamp seals** and **control stamps** are introduced in the city-states of Mesopotamia to document property ownership, taxes, and duties.

3600–2900 The **Baden culture** flourishes in the territory of Austria. Groove-decorated pottery, clay wagon models, and copper jewelry are typical characteristics of this culture.

3600 A **temple economy** typical of the Mesopotamian city-states develops in **Uruk**. All powerful **priest-kings** centrally distribute the economic system's entire yield in the cult sanctuaries.

3400 Two **independent states** begin to develop in **Upper and Lower Egypt**.

3300 In **Europe**, people have **sophisticated tools and weapons** like copper axes and flint daggers.

3250 In 1991 a well-preserved **glacial mummy** of a man is found in the Ötztal Alps in Austria. The man, named **"Ötzi"** shortly after his discovery, lived in the time around 3250 B.C.

3200 There is evidence of **wine cultivation** in **Mesopotamia**. The necessary knowledge probably came to Mesopotamia from the Caucasus region.

3000 **Babylon**, at first a small and insignificant city-state, emerges in lower **Mesopotamia**.

3000 **Predynastic Period**: History's first territorial state is created around 3,000 B.C. with the **union of Upper and Lower Egypt**. Narmer is considered the legendary founder of the Egyptian empire and its first pharaoh. The Early Dynastic Period begins, however, with Pharaoh Aha around 3,000/2,950 B.C.

3000 The sundial is said to be simultaneously invented in **Mesopotamia** and **Egypt**.

3000 At the turn of the 3rd Millennium, the **Indus Valley civilization** develops in present-day Pakistan. Irrigation systems and an as yet undeciphered script testify to an advanced civilization.

3000 **Megalith cultures** develop independently of each other in many parts of the world around 3000 B.C. The typical structures of huge stones weighing several tons are often associated with **burial practices**. Megaliths can be found particularly in northern and western Europe, but also outside of Europe, for example, in Palestine, Syria, and also Korea.

35,000 The first musical instruments are **flutes** made from animal bones.

30,000 Ivory figures like the "Lion Man" indicate **early artistic expressions** of mankind.

30,000–25,000 Symbols scratched in stone found in **central Europe** possibly serve as the **first primitive calendar.**

25,000–20,000 Female statuettes like the **"Venus of Willendorf"** most likely serve as **cult fertility symbols.**

17,000/16,000 Hundreds of masterful **representations of animals** and symbolic arrow marks are painted on the walls of a cave in present-day southwestern France. Today, the **cave of Lascaux** is part of the world cultural heritage.

10,000 In many parts of the world, people start **burying their dead** in a fetal position termed a **crouch burial.**

10,000 Petroglyphs in a cave called **Cueva de las Manos** ("Cave of the Hands") are created 10,000 years ago in present-day Argentina.

8000 The first **clay tiles** are produced in **Anatolia and Palestine.**

8000/7000 The earliest known **wooden canoes** are made in northwestern Europe. **Sea-going ships** had probably already been developed ten thousand years earlier.

7000/6000 In the Near East fabrics are being worked into **clothing** on a primitive loom.

5000 In Mesopotamia and Egypt the first **water management networks for irrigating fields** are constructed.

 c. 25,000 — 9000

30,000 The first modern humans **reach the Australian continent by sea.**

30,000 Hunters and gatherers invent the **bow and arrow.**

30,000/20,000 The first **humans reach the American continent** by crossing the **Bering Strait.**

30,000 The **Neanderthal dies out** in Europe. Afterwards, modern man settles the whole of the European continent.

28,000 Finds near Sungir in Russia show how the people of the time lived **on the edge of the artic circle.** The reindeer hunters lived in dwellings made of bones and skins and followed clearly defined ritual burial practices.

25,000 Sandia Pueblo: The earliest known culture in **North America** develops in the southwest of present-day USA.

20,000 Paleo-Indians in North America are primarily living from the **hunting of bison.**

20,000 First settlements are evidently established in the **Andes region** around the present-day Peruvian city of Ayacucho.

18,000 First hunting cultures develop along the Nile.

15,000 The **first people permanently settle** in what is **later Mayan territory** in Central America.

13,000 The **Clovis culture** begins to spread out in North America. Their characteristic **spearheads** are among the most dangerous weapons of the Stone Age.

12,000/10,000 The **last Ice Age ends** in Eurasia. The climate in this part of the world gradually becomes warmer and wetter; the amount of forests increases significantly. Historians speak of the **beginning of the Mesolithic Age.** Humans still live as **hunters and gatherers.**

10,000 Paleoamericans settle in **Tierra del Fuego,** the southernmost tip of South America.

10,000/9000 By the time of the Mesolithic Age, the **dog** is presumably the **first animal to be domesticated.** Evidence from this period indicates that domestic dogs were buried in graves alongside humans.

9000 Neolithic revolution: Beginning in the Near East, humans start to become **sedentary** and **practice animal husbandry and agriculture.**

9000 Jericho, most likely the **oldest city in the world,** arises in the Near East, within the area of the **Fertile Crescent.**

9000 The **culture of big game hunters** spreads from North America through Central Mexico to South America.

9000 Göbekli Tepe (Potbelly Hill), perhaps the **oldest temple complex** in the world, is erected in southeastern Anatolia near the city of Shanliurfa. The religious function of this monumental stone structure has yet to be explained.

9000/8000 Between the 10th and 9th millennia B.C., **sheep and goats** are bred for the first time in the **mountain regions of the Near East.**

8000/7000 In the late 9th and early 8th millennia B.C., the **cultivation of potatoes and beans** begins in **South America.**

8000/7000 Pigs, chickens, and water buffalo are domesticated for the first time, presumably in the region of the Middle East.

8000 An estimated **5.5 million people** are living on the earth.

8000 The **earliest datable pottery culture** of the world develops during the **Jomon period** in Japan. The characteristic cord-pattern (jomon) of the ceramics gives the period its name.

7000 The **first early Neolithic settlements** arise in Mesopotamia.

7000 Sugarcane and bananas are evidently cultivated in **New Guinea.**

7000 The first known **farming and herding settlement** develops in South Asia, in **Mehrgarh,** within the territory of present-day Pakistan.

7000–4500 An **independent culture** develops in the territory of present-day **Hungary and Romania** named after an archaeological site in **Lepenski Vir,** Serbia. Typical are egg-shaped stone sculptures with piscine features.

"The only thing constant in life is change."

Charles Darwin, founder of modern evolutionary biology, 1809–1882

6500 Çatalhöyük, the first "metropolis" in the Near East, in which thousands of people are estimated to have lived, arises in Anatolia.

6500 Cattle are first domesticated in southwestern Anatolia.

6000 Village-like hilltop settlements of the **Halaf culture,** named after an excavation site of painted ceramic, Tell Halaf, develop in **present-day Iraq.**

6000 As a result of the **rising sea level,** the British Isles become separated from the European continent.

6000 Chalcolithic Period (Copper Age): Metallurgy begins in the Near East. Ores and metals, primarily copper at first, are mined and worked into useful objects.

5600–4800 The **Peiligang culture,** an early Neolithic group of communities and predecessor of the Yangshao culture, develops in the territory of northern China.

5400–4000 The **Ertebølle-Ellerbek culture** develops on the territory of present-day **Denmark and North Germany.** The people probably lived primarily on a diet of fish and mussels.

HISTORICAL EVENTS

"Out of Africa"
Even though early man left his home on the African continent, it was modern man who was able to permanently explore and conquer the world.

Populations of modern man migrated out of Africa for the first time some **120,000** years ago, and their traces can still be found in caves in present-day Israel. When the water level of the Red Sea was very low around **70,000 B.C.**, another group of modern men wandered from East Africa to the Arabian Peninsula. From there, they spread out all across Europe and Asia. By 20,000 B.C., when they also reached South America, they had practically settled every accessible part of the world. The diversity of today's humans should not belie their strong common roots. Genetic research has proven a great similarity in the genetic material of all non-Africans. They are all descendents of a few people who, in the distant past, had set out from Africa into the great unknown.

New weapons and the use of language made it possible for modern man (Homo sapiens sapiens) to expand his scope of activities.

America's Original Inhabitants
About 30,000–10,000 years ago, America became the last continent to be settled.

The "First Americans" originally came from East Asia. **30,000** to **20,000** years ago, members of nomadic hunter and gatherer societies found their way from Siberia to Alaska across a dry land bridge near the Bering Strait. Due to an abundance of food, Palaeo-Indians spread quickly over all of North, Central, and eventually South America, reaching Tierra del Fuego some **10,000** years ago. The skilled hunters killed mammoths, bison, and other big game. They belonged to the Clovis culture, named after the site in Mexico where their characteristic arrowheads and spear points were first discovered. Whether the members of the Clovis culture were the first Americans or not has become a matter of debate. The ancestors of today's Inuit did not migrate out of Siberia to Alaska until around **2500 B.C.**

While hunting wild animals, groups of nomads found their way from Siberia to North America.

Neolithic Revolution
The way humans lived changed decisively with the end of the last glacial period. Nomadic hunters became sedentary farmers.

With the end of the last Ice Age, **12,000** to **10,000** years ago, the earth's climate grew warmer and wetter. The accompanying changes in the flora and fauna radically transformed the way mankind lived and worked. People began to take up permanent residence in fixed settlements, cultivated plants, and domesticated animals to support themselves. They also invented new technologies like the firing of pottery. With a permanent residence came the development of an initial division of labor and thus more social differentiation. At the same time there was a rapid growth in population. The appearance of a steady economy based on breeding and agriculture at the start of the Neolithic Age took place around the world, but at different times. Whereas the Neolithic revolution was underway in the fertile valley regions of Mesopotamia and India by 9000 B.C., it did not reach central Europe until around 5550 B.C. and parts of northern Europe until 4200 B.C.

Division of labor, agriculture, animal husbandry, and production of pottery in the Neolithic Age

The First Cities
The first urban centers arose in the Near East in the favorable climate of the Fertile Crescent beginning in the 8th millennium B.C.

The first city-like settlements were founded in the fertile regions of Mesopotamia, whose remains speak of their developed cultural life. The oldest city in the world is generally considered to be Jericho, which was built around **9000 B.C.** and has been inhabited ever since. About 7000 B.C., a city wall was erected around Jericho, where as many as 2,000 people once dwelled. Among the earliest hilltop settlements in the Near East, the city of Çatalhöyük, located in southwestern Anatolia, is the most well-preserved today. During its heyday, around **6500 B.C.**, more than 7,000 people lived there crowded into clay brick houses that also served as a burial place for the dead. Around 5000 B.C., a culture developed in the south of present-day Iraq that lived in houses with multiple rooms. They also possessed a central administrative elite—an essential feature of early advanced civilizations. It was a forerunner of the first great city-states of the Sumerians that developed around **3900 B.C.** Uruk took a leading position among these city-states. Around 3200 B.C., some 20,000 people lived in Uruk, the first "major city" in history. In the center of the metropolis was a temple for the goddess Inanna. The city wall, built around 2500 B.C., was over five miles long.

The foundation of a tower is part of the remnants of Jericho's city wall.

The Invention of Writing

The cultural development of mankind experienced a quantum leap with the invention of Cuneiform writing by the Sumerians in the mid-4th millennium B.C.

The more complex the organizational structures in early communities became, the greater was the need to record and store information. In order to manage the increasingly complicated distribution of labor and goods, the Sumerians, sometime around **3500 B.C.**, became the earliest known culture to invent writing, and in doing so triggered a kind of early media revolution. Similar to Chinese writing and Egyptian hieroglyphics that appeared a little later, it was initially pictographs, scratched on small clay tablets, that were used to record matters

A Sumerian clay tablet with Cuneiform writing

such as the levies paid by farmers. Over time, the characters became more and more abstract. By 2500 B.C. a syllabary had developed, a system that allowed for the reproduction of all parts of the language. Now it was also possible to record the heroic deeds of the rulers and preserve them for posterity. It was with such first-hand accounts that the "history" of mankind first began in its truest sense. However, an actual alphabetic script made up of a limited number of letters was only developed by the Phoenicians around **1300 B.C.**

The ancient city of Mohenjo Daro was one of the most important settlements of the Indus culture.

The Indus Civilization

One of the earliest advanced civilizations developed around the Indus River basin at the close of the 4th millennium B.C.

There is evidence that people practicing agriculture and animal husbandry began settling along the Indus River in present-day Pakistan by 6000 B.C. The first advanced civilization on the Indian subcontinent, named after the ancient city of Harappa in northeastern Pakistan, did not develop before **3000 B.C.** The Indus or Harappa civilization entered its golden age in **2600**, when major urban centers began to thrive. Its inhabitants lived mainly from the cultivation of the fertile soil, evidenced by large granaries and a complex system of irrigation.

They were also engaged in trade with the Sumerians in distant Mesopotamia. However, their writing has yet to be deciphered. Typical are their rectangular houses of baked bricks and the geometric city layouts. In striking contrast to other early advanced cultures, there are no clear signs of kingship in form of monumental palaces or sacred structures. The members of this civilization appear to have been "middle class" farmers, artisans, and traders. The Indus civilization collapsed after 1700, presumably due to natural catastrophes.

Portraits of the founding emperors were carved in stone in the Chinese Province of Henan.

China's Origins

One of the oldest civilizations in the world was founded, according to myth, by the Three August Ones and the Five Emperors.

China was populated very early. Archaeological finds suggest that Homo erectus had arrived in the area that later became Beijing about **800,000 years** ago. By **5000 B.C.**, Neolithic communities of cattle herders and millet farmers settled along the great Yangtze and Yellow River that became known as the cradle of Chinese civilization. According to legend, the Three August Ones and Five Emperors, ruler gods with magical powers, played an important role in promoting Chinese culture, beginning with the Yellow Emperor (Huang Ti) whose reign commenced in **2674 B.C.** These semi-mythical emperors were stylized into the actual originators of Chinese culture who had taught the people such skills as medicine and agriculture. Emperor Yu, who is still honored by many for his success in controlling floods, is credited with having founded the Xia Dynasty around **2200 B.C.** The Shang Dynasty that began in **1500 B.C.** is the earliest recorded dynasty in China.

The Unification of Egypt

Legendary King Narmer unified Upper and Lower Egypt into history's first territorial state at the turn of the 4th millennium B.C.

In the Predynastic Period Egypt was divided into two independent kingdoms. There was Upper Egypt along the Nile's narrow river oasis in the south, and Lower Egypt in the north, where the Nile formed a great delta. According to later tradition, the first pharaoh, Narmer, unified the two regions around **3000 B.C.** after a long period of rapprochement and fighting. It is believed that he conquered the Nile Delta and made Memphis, on the border of Upper and Lower Egypt, his capital. Although recent archaeological finds reveal that other kings have periodically ruled over all of Egypt before Narmer came to power, the history of a unified country begins with Narmer. His successor, Aha, is considered to have been the founder of the First Dynasty around **3000–2950**. Therafter, each new pharaoh symboli-

cally re-enacted the unification of the two territories by being crowned with the White Crown of Upper Egypt and the Red Crown of Lower Egypt. The unity of Egypt was repeatedly in danger, especially in times of weak rulers or major threats from outside. On several occasions in the history of Egypt, the two parts were ruled by different dynasties.

Pharaoh Narmer, wearing the traditional crown of Upper Egypt, slaying an enemy

3000 With the domestication of plants, permanent settlements, and pottery making, conditions were met in **Mesoamerica and Peru** for the development of **advanced civilizations**.

3000 **Silk worm farming** evidently begins in **China** in the 3rd millenium.

3000 In **Egypt**, rolls of **papyrus** are being produced for writing material.

3000/2550 The **Sumerians** engage in "scientific" astronomy.

2782 The **365-day calendar** is presumably originated in **Egypt**. It divides the year into three seasons, each with four 30-day months, plus five extra days.

2700 The polymath, physician, and pyramid-builder **Imhotep** serves under the Egyptian pharaoh Djoser.

2600 In the **Indus River floodplain**, farmers begin to use the **plough**.

2600 The **Sumerians** use lyres, reed pipes, and drums as **musical instruments**.

2580 The **Cheops Pyramid** is erected at Giza. The world's largest pyramid is the only one of the **Seven Wonders of the World** still standing.

2572/2546 The **Great Sphinx** is built in Giza, Egypt. The original function of the lion figure with a human head has yet to be explained.

2500/2639 The cult of the **sun god Ra (or Re)** becomes dominant in **ancient Egypt**.

2500 The **culture and language of the Bantu** spreads beyond the border region of the present-day states of Nigeria and Cameroon to all of **central and southern Africa**.

3000 About **30 million people** are living on the earth.

3000 **Chinook society** emerges in the **Pacific northwest region of North America**. The Chinooks' livelihood comes from fishing, hunting, and gathering nuts, berries, and plant food.

3000 The city of **Memphis**, south of present-day Cairo, becomes the **first residence of the Egyptian pharaohs**.

3000 The **Minoan civilization**—named after the legendary King Minos—emerges on the Aegean island of **Crete** through an increase in immigration, presumably out of Asia Minor. During the Prepalatial Period, **ceramics and metal** are artistically crafted at different central sites.

3000/2950–2700 During Egypt's **Early Dynastic Period**—also called the **"Thinite Period"** after Thinis in Upper Egypt, the ancestral home and capital of the pharaohs of the first and second dynasties—**Egypt** develops into a strictly structured hierarchical, **centralized bureaucratic state** based on literacy.

2900 A **struggle for the supremacy of the region** begins between the various city-states in **Mesopotamia**. In the process, the cities of Uruk, Kish, Ur, and Umma, among others, repeatedly form alliances.

2800/2600 The **Bell-beaker culture**, named after the typical clay vessels found as **burial artifacts**, spreads out from the Iberian Peninsula all the way to Eastern Europe.

2750 In **Mesopotamia**, the city-state of **Kish gains supremacy**. Its kings found their own dynasty.

2700 The flowering of the Bronze Age **Cycladic culture** begins on the Cyclades, a group of islands in the **Aegean Sea**. It stands in close contact with the Minoan civilization.

2690 The **Old Kingdom in Egypt** begins with the coronation of **Pharaoh Djoser**. The country experiences its first political and cultural golden age.

2675 The legendary hero **Gilgamesh** wins the **independence of the city of Uruk** from the kings of Kish.

2696 The age of the **Three August Ones** and the **Five Emperors** begins in **China** with the Yellow Emperor (to 2205 B.C.). According to legend, the mythical **ideal rulers** are the founders of the Chinese civilization.

2640 **Imhotep** builds the **step pyramid of Saqqara** for the burial of the Egyptian Pharaoh Djoser.

2639/2598 **Snefru** founds the **4th dynasty** in Egypt and heads military campaigns against the Libyans and the Nubians.

2600 **Caral**, held to be **the oldest urban complex in the Americas,** is built in present-day **Peru** around 2600 B.C. Its **step pyramids** testify to a highly developed civilization.

2600 **Cheops** succeeds **Snefru** around 2600 B.C. as pharaoh of Egypt.

2600 Around 2600, important Indus cities in present-day Pakistan, like **Harappa** and **Mohenjo Daro**, are built with granaries, sanitary facilities, and sewer systems.

2500 The **Phoenicians** settle the costal region between **Syria and Palestine** and found city-states independent of each other.

2500 The **ancestors of the Inuit** migrate from **Siberia into Alaska**.

2600 In the **northwest of Asia Minor**, the building of the fortified settlement of **Troy** begins around 2600.

2500 The **Maya civilization** begins to develop in **Central America** on the peninsula of Yucatán.

2500 The **kingdom of Elam** emerges in the countryside of Chusistan, Iran's present-day Khuzestan.

2500 In Mesopotamia, **King Mesannepada** founds **Ur's first dynasty**. The royal tombs testify to a high cultural and economic standard.

2465 The period of the **5th Dynasty** in Egypt begins with Pharaoh **Userkaf's ascension to power**.

2457 In Mesopotamia, the **city-state of Lagash** under King Eannatum conquers all of Sumer and parts of Elam.

2375/2347 **Lugalzagesi**, king of the southern Mesopotamian city of **Umma**, subjugates all the Sumerian city-states and makes **Uruk** his capital.

2350 The **city of Ebla** develops into a political and economic hub in Mesopotamia.

2340 Under **King Urukagina**, up to 2,340 comprehensive **social reforms** are undertaken in Lagash.

2330 **Sargon of Akkad** wrests the whole of southern Mesopotamia from the Sumerian king Lugalzagesi and founds **Mesopotamia's first great empire**.

2300 **Sargon of Akkad** conquers and annexes the **city-state of Ebla**.

2347–2166 In Egypt, **Pharaoh Teti** founds the 6th dynasty (to 2166 B.C.).

2300–2100 The **last independent culture on the Cyclades** emerges (named Phylakopi I Group after a site on Melos).

2279 **Sargon of Akkad dies.** In his campaigns of conquest, he expanded his kingdom from **the Persian Gulf to the Mediterranean Sea**.

2250–2213 Under **Naram-Sin**, the **Kingdom of Akkad** reaches its maximum size after successful campaigns in East Arabia. He titles himself **"King of the Four Quarters."**

2200 The invading **Gutains destroy the Kingdom of Akkad.** They rule over the north of Mesopotamia.

2200 In China, the reign of the legendary **Xia Dynasty** begins.

2200 The **Úntice culture** proliferates in eastern **Central Europe** in the 23rd century B.C.

3000

2500

The First Empires
3000–1000 B.C.

The number of people rose dramatically with the further development of agriculture and animal herding. In the steadily enlarging settlements, the need for organization grew, and societies became increasingly more complex through specialization in priests, administrators, warriors, artisans, and farmers. The first advanced urban civilizations developed in fertile river valleys: in Mesopotamia along the Euphrates and Tigris, in the river oases of the Nile in Egypt, and around the Indus in present-day Pakistan. Priest-kings were often at the head of the societies, supported by literate officials who controlled trade and agricultural production. The first territorial state in world history, the pharaonic kingdom, developed in the isolated cultural region of Egypt. Numerous different city-states emerged in Mesopotamia; later the Assyrians and the Babylonians were able to expand their dominant positions.

Colossal statue
of the Egyptian
pharaoh
Ramses II

HISTORICAL FIGURES

Imhotep (c. 2700/2600 B.C.)
Architect, physician, and scholar: Imhotep, later accorded divine status, is considered to be history's first universal genius.

Little is known of Imhotep's personal life. His outstanding achievements in Egypt, however, have inscribed him forever in the memory of mankind. He was the first to build of stone on a monumental scale: the pyramids, whose size and grandeur are impressive even today. He designed the tomb of Pharaoh Djoser, constructed around **2700/2600 B.C.** at Saqqara, a 200-foot-high step pyramid. His own tomb is also thought to be located in the expansive complex of pyramids. But Imhotep not only distinguished himself as an architect. In addition, he advised Djoser on political issues and was named high priest of the sun god Ra in Heliopolis. He also made a name for himself as a physician. He is credited with the authorship of the oldest medical text, the *Edwin Smith Papyrus*. Imhotep was the first Egyptian "ordinary mortal" to have his status elevated in later times to that of a deity.

Sargon I of Akkad (died 2279 B.C.)
Sargon founded the first territorial state in Mesopotamia with the kingdom of Akkad.

Sargon's origins are shrouded in myth. He was supposedly of lowly birth, if not a foundling. His rise began in the service of the king of Kish. In **2330 B.C.**, Sargon overthrew his former lord, made Akkad the capital of Mesopotamia and began with the expansion of his realm. He first broke Lugalzagesi's dominance over the Sumerian cities in the south—and the defeated king was put on public display in a cage. Then Sargon won control over northern Syria. Building up his own bureaucracy served to guarantee central control of the state. He was the first to maintain a standing army. His kingdom had crumbled by **2200 B.C.**, but Akkadian remained the official language of Mesopotamia for over a thousand years.

Hatshepsut (died 1457 B.C.)
Egypt experienced a period of peace and prosperity under this female pharaoh.

Women in ancient Egypt always had relatively equal rights, and the wives of the pharaohs often held great influence. But Hatshepsut's career from model wife of a ruler to god-like pharaoh is unique. After the death of her husband in **1479 B.C.**, she first took over the regency of her underage stepson Thutmose III, then assumed the title of pharaoh and ruled the country single-handedly for twenty years. During her reign, Egypt experienced a golden age. The borders were secure and her trading expeditions into the legendary land of incense, Punt, brought Egypt great wealth. She had her successes immortalized in her terraced mortuary temple of Deir el-Bahari, one of ancient Egypt's most important buildings. After Hatshepsut's death, Thutmose III tried to erase all traces of her from collective memory—to no avail.

Tiglath-Pileser I (died 1077 B.C.)
Under his rule, Assyria rose again to become an important major power in the Near East.

By **1850 B.C.**, the Old Assyrian kingdom was already forming in the north of present-day Iraq around the city-state of Assur, which initially was under the dominance of the neighboring Babylonians and Hittites. From **1364**, the Assyrians expanded their position of power through brutally waged wars. The most important ruler of the Middle Assyrian period was Tiglath-Pileser I, who, after **1116**, led his military campaigns all the way to the Mediterranean and present-day eastern Turkey. He also forced the rich Phoenician trading cities to pay him tribute. In addition, the king excelled as a builder and a patron of the sciences. He had the first great library built and promoted the research of animals and plants.

1850 In Egypt, **pi** is determined to have the approximate value of 3.16.

1800 The **Epic of Gilgamesh** is written in Mesopotamia, **the first great epic in world literature**.

1850 With the ancient monument of **Stonehenge** in southern England, the most gigantic example of megalithic culture is created.

1792/1750 The **Code of Hammurabi**, the **most significant legal code of the Near East**, is compiled in Babylon.

1700/1600 The **Ebers Papyrus** is ancient Egypt's most important work about medicine.

1648/1645 The **Hyskos** introduce **horse breeding** and **chariots to Egypt**.

1600 The **Nebra Sky Disk**, found in Germany, provides evidence of the high degree of knowledge about astronomy of the time.

1400 The **Hittites** develop a **method of economically producing iron**.

1400 Scrolls of **parchment** are produced in **Egypt**.

1300 The **Phoenicians** develop the **first alphabetic writing system**, the basis for all European alphabets.

1279–1213 On the initiative of the Egyptian pharaoh **Ramses II**, the construction of a **canal to connect the Nile and the Red Sea** begins.

1250 The **citadel of Mycenae** in present-day Greece is enhanced with the addition of the famous **"Lion Gate."**

1200/1100 The **four-wheeled wagon** is invented.

1000 In Egypt, the first **gear drives** are used to generate energy.

1500 --- **1000**

1500 The earliest historically verifiable dynasty in **China**, the **Shang or Yin Dynasty**, reaches its peak. The hierarchically structured society is headed by kings or priests.

1500 Indo-European groups, the **Arians**, begin to **migrate into India**.

1500 The **Lapita society** emerges ranging from **New Guinea** to **Samoa** and **Tonga**.

1479–1457 **Hatshepsut**, as regent for her underage stepson, **Thutmose III**, virtually **rules over Egypt**. She eventually also assumes the title of pharaoh.

1458/1457 In **the first datable battle in world history**, the Egyptian pharaoh **Thutmose III** is victorious over a Syrian-Mittannian coalition at **Megiddo** and gains **sovereignty over Syria and Palestine**.

1450 The Minoan palace complex on **Crete** is presumably destroyed by natural catastrophes, leading to the **fall of the Minoan civilization**. Crete is conquered by Mycenaean Achaeans.

1400 Onset of the **golden age of the Mycenaean culture**: gigantic fortifications are constructed in Mycenae and Pylos.

1397–1388 During the reign of Pharaoh **Thutmose IV**, peace is concluded with the kingdom of **Mitanni**.

1390 Under King **Tushratta**, the **kingdom of Mitanni** is at the pinnacle of its power. He rules over parts of Mesopotamia, Syria, and Palestine.

1364 Middle Assyrian Kingdom: **Assuruballit I** becomes the new king in Assyria. His victory over the Hittites assures the **independence** of the weak kingdom of Mitanni.

1355/1350 The **Hittite Kingdom** becomes a major power in the Middle East under **Suppiluliuma I**. The king subjugates all of Asia Minor, penetrates into Syria, and wages successful wars, including against the kingdom of **Mitanni**.

1333–1323 The Egyptian pharaoh **Tutankhamun** relocates the capital back to **Thebes** and **rescinds Akhenaten's religious reforms**.

1335 The **kingdom of Mitanni collapses** under pressure from the Assyrians and Hittites.

1292/1290 **Ramses I** founds the **19th dynasty in Egypt**, heralding in the Ramesside period, lasting until 1070.

1279 **Ramses II** becomes the new pharaoh. He becomes one of the **most important builders** in Egyptian history.

1274 **Ramses II** fails in his attempt to seize northern Syria from the Hittites in the **battle of Kadesh**.

1259 In the **first known peace treaty** set out in writing, Ramses II and the Hittite king, Hattusili III, mutually **set the boundaries of Syria**.

1200 "Sea People" crush the **Hittite Kingdom** and settle in the Syrian-Palestine region.

1200 **Maize** spreads from **Mesoamerica** to the southwestern part of the present-day **United States**.

1116–1077 King Tiglath-Pileser I conquers Asia Minor to the Black Sea, thus **founding the Middle Assyrian Kingdom**.

1050 In China, **the Zhou topple the Shang rulers** and found the dynasty with their name.

1012 According to the Bible, **Saul** is the first king of **Israel**.

1351–1334 **Pharaoh Akhenaten** (formerly Amenhotep IV) dictates the **monotheistic worship of the sun god Aten**. He is supported by his wife, **Nofretete**. In order to break the power of the Theban priests, the **capital is moved to Akhetaten**.

2500 In **Mesopotamia**, glass is systemically produced for the first time.

2350 A **royal palace library** is established in the Lower Mesopotamian city of **Lagash** with over 30,000 **clay tablets**.

2500/2000 Early **Mayan** civilizations cultivate **maize** in Central America.

2130 Measurements, weights, and scales are known in **Mesopotamia**.

2200 Polished pottery and **metal working** evidently exists in the **Longshan culture** in China at the close of the 3rd millennium.

2100 Rice is cultivated in **China** with the help of **irrigation farming**. The technique quickly spreads to Southeast Asia.

2170–2025 During Egypt's First Intermediate Period, ancient **Egyptian literature** experiences its first bloom.

2048–2031 Ur-Nammu compiles the **first Sumerian legal code**.

2025/1976 *Kemit*, known as the **oldest textbook** in the world, is written in **Egypt**.

2000 On the island of **Crete**, the Minoan people construct expansive **palace complexes** in Knossos, Phaistos, and Malia.

2000 Mathematics develops into an autonomous science in **Babylon**.

1962 The biographical novel, the *Story of Sinuhe*, is written. It is considered to be a classic example of **ancient Egyptian literature**.

1956 The **White Chapel** is built in Thebes, present-day Karnak and Luxor. Karnak subsequently develops into Egypt's **largest temple complex**.

2000

2200 The **Andronowo culture**, often credited with having invented the chariot, emerges in **southern Siberia and Central Asia**.

2155 Social unrest and **revolts** in Egypt lead to the **collapse of the Old Kingdom**.

2120–2025 First Intermediate Period in **Egypt**: The 11th dynasty of Thebes reigns in the south; the 9th and 10th Heracleopolitan dynasties rule in the north.

2100 An **extensive network of trade routes develop** between central and southern Europe.

2060 King Gudea of Lagash subjugates the cities of Lower Mesopotamia.

2048 Ur-Nammu founds the **3rd dynasty of Ur**. He makes the city **Mesopotamia's political and cultural center**. UrNammu and his successors title themselves the "Lords of Sumer and Akkad."

2040 Egypt is once again united under **Mentuhotep II**, pharaoh of the 11th dynasty. The capital of the ensuing **Middle Kingdom** is Thebes.

2000 The **Italic People**, diverse groups of Indo-Europeans, migrate **over the Alps into Italy**.

2000 In Unteruhldingen, on Lake Constance, **lake pile dwellings** develop.

"Egypt was a gift of the Nile."
Herodotus, 5th century B.C.

2000 The **Thracians**, a group of Indo-European tribes, settle in the region of present-day northwest **Turkey and Bulgaria** (ancient Thrace).

2000 **Indo-Europeans** advance into the **Greek mainland** and mingle with the native cultures to form the Middle Helladic culture, a predecessor of the **Mycenaean culture**.

2000 The **transition** from the **Copper to the Bronze Age** begins in Europe.

2000/1700 According to Biblical tradition, **Hebraic nomads** under the leadership of **Abraham** migrate from Ur in Mesopotamia into **Palestine**.

1991 Pharaoh **Amenemhat I** founds the **12th dynasty in Egypt** and moves the capital from Thebes to el-Lisht in northern Egypt.

1956–1911/10 Pharaoh **Sensusret I consolidates Egypt** both politically and economically. He embarks on the construction of the **temple complex in Thebes** honoring Amun, who is elevated from being a local deity to Egypt's supreme state god.

1950 **Elamites and Amorites** crush the empire of the **3rd dynasty of Ur**. The land of the Sumerians again disintegrates into individual city-states.

1900 From out of the region of the Black Sea, the **Hittites penetrate into Anatolia** and establish their own culture.

1872–1853/52 Under the regency of **Pharaoh Senusret III**, the territory of the Middle Kingdom is expanded further along the Nile into southern **Nubia** (present-day Sudan).

1853–1806/05 Under **Pharaoh Amenemhat III**, the **oasis swamp of Fayum** is drained and made usable for agriculture.

1850 Old Assyrian Kingdom: The **city-state of Assur** in Upper Mesopotamia increasingly **gains in political importance** after the fall of the 3rd dynasty of Ur.

1830 The **Amorites**, a Semitic people, found their own dynasty in Babylon.

1800–1200 The **Carians**, originally from the Aegean, establish the small, independent **kingdom of Caria** in the southwest of Asia Minor.

1750–1717 Under **King Schamshi-Adad I**, the old Assyrian Kingdom temporarily becomes the **dominant regional power in Upper Mesopotamia**.

1728 First Dynasty of Babylon: After the Amorite king **Hammurabi** takes the throne, **Babylon** quickly rises to become **Mesopotamia's political and cultural center**.

1700 Natural catastrophes, combined with military misfortunes, lead to the gradual **decline of the Indus civilization** in northwestern **India**.

1695 The **Babylonians** conquer the important Sumerian city of **Mari** and assimilate it into their kingdom.

1686 **Hammurabi**, the founder of the ancient Babylonian empire, **dies**. Under his rule, the Babylonians unite practically all of **Mesopotamia**.

1648/1645 Second Intermediate Period: Equipped with modern chariots, the **Hyksos**, an Asiatic people, advance into Egypt and take over rulership of **a major part of the pharaonic kingdom**.

1600 The legendary **King Labarna** united the Hittite city-states in Asia Minor around 1600 and founds the **Old Kingdom of the Hittites**. In 1531, King Hattusili I ransacks Babylon.

1600 The **kingdom of Mitanni** emerges in **Upper Mesopotamia**.

1600 The **Arcaean culture**, an early Mycenaean culture, develops in the **Greek Aegean region**.

1600 The **Olmecs** develop an advanced civilization in present-day Mexico, which spreads out over vast areas of Central America after 800 B.C. and influences all following civilizations.

1550 After **expelling the Hyksos, Pharaoh Ahmose** of the 18th dynasty founds ancient **Egypt's New Kingdom**.

1531 The **Kassites**, originally from the area of modern-day Iran, penetrate into Mesopotamia and take **control of the Babylonian territories**.

HISTORICAL EVENTS

The pyramid of Giza in Egypt is the only one of the Seven Wonders of the World to survive.

Period of the Pyramids
Monumental testimonies to two advanced civilizations arose almost concurrently in both Egypt and South America.

The pyramids of Giza were built around **2580 B.C.** during the classical period of the Old Kingdom by the pharaohs Cheops, Chephren, and Mycerinus. Almost 480 feet high, the Cheops pyramid is the tallest of them. It is thought Cheops also commissioned the building of the Sphinx, whose exact function is not clear. The pyramids served as the tombs of the pharaohs. They were to be the "homes" of the dead rulers for all eternity, but also stood for the might of their kingdoms. Less well known are the pyramids of Caral that were built in Peru almost at the same time, around **2600 B.C.**, bearing witness to the earliest certifiable advanced civilization in the Americas. Located some 125 miles north of Lima are the ruins of a city in which perhaps 3,000 people of all classes once lived. Around the ruins are six pyramids, the largest being 59 feet high and 525 feet long.

Expansion of the Bantu
Around 2500 B.C., the culture and language of the Bantu began to spread to the east and west of their original area in West Africa.

The largest migration of people in the history of Africa had its beginnings in present-day Cameroon and eastern Nigeria. The development of new methods of cultivation led to a growth in population and at the same time made it possible to develop tropical regions for agriculture. Beginning in **2500 B.C.**, the Bantu gradually spread out in several waves over the whole of the southern half of the African continent. While doing so, they mixed with local groups—presumably for the most part peacefully—learned additional technologies and formed new societies and cultures. There is evidence of a first Early

Iron Age Bantu culture about **1000 B.C.** in present-day Uganda. After migrating to almost all of central and southeast Africa, eventually around 1000 A.D. the region of southern Africa was also settled from the east. To the present day, Bantu-speaking peoples make up the majority of the populations in most of the states of Sub-Saharan Africa. This diversity—there are over 400 ethnic groups—nicely corresponds to the original meaning of the word "Bantu." It means, pure and simple, "people."

A wooden figure from the Congo region set up for oath-taking ceremonies.

The Code of Hammurabi
The legal code of Hammurabi, the founder of the ancient Babylonian empire, is considered one of the most important texts of the ancient Orient.

Hammurabi was one of the greatest ruling figures of the early period in the Orient. He came to power in **1728 B.C.** in Babylon, at first expanding the initially insignificant city-state in the center of Mesopotamia into an empire that encompassed the whole of Mesopotamia through campaigns of conquest against, among others, Assyria and Mari. Domestically, he gave the country its first period of economic and cultural flowering. The famous Code of Hammurabi gives evidence that he sought to rule over his subjects according to the principles of law and justice. Discovered on a stele in 1901/02 the code consists of 282 legal provisions formulated in concrete if-then cases. For example, written in detail is how a royal official is to respond to theft or murder, or what the duties of a soldier or a tradesman are. Inheritance procedures are also precisely regulated by the code. To this day, the code is considered to be the most important systematic collection of laws of the Orient's early period, which remained authoritative down into the Neo-Babylonian period.

The stele with the text of the Code of Hammurabi, found in Susa in modern-day Iran.

Arrival of the Indo-Aryans
Ethnic groups belonging to the Indo-European or Indo-Iranian family of languages began to settle on the Indian subcontinent around 1500 B.C.

Natural catastrophes around **1700 B.C.** probably led to the collapse of the sophisticated Indus civilization. This opened the way for immigrants from the north. Starting in **1500 B.C.**, ethnic groups, primarily from present-day Russia, Central Asia, and Iran, made their way into the Indian subcontinent. It is presumed that the settling was a continuous process of the migration of smaller groups over a long period of time. The Rigveda, from around 1000 B.C. and part of the Vedes, the holy scripture of Hinduism, remains a major source. The texts draw a picture of a war-like, strictly hierarchical society that lived primarily from cattle raising. The immigrants—"Arian" means "noble"—considered themselves to be members of an elite culture in relation to the native population. They lived in tribal kingdoms, with ruler and ruled carefully kept separate. From this system, the caste system started to develop after **1000 B.C.** The caste system has marked the structure of Indian society to this day, despite having been officially abolished with the independence of India.

Their chariots made the Indo-Arians militarily far superior to their opponents.

Mycenaean-Minoan Cultural Sphere
In the 15th century B.C., the Mycenaean civilization replaced the leading Minoan civilization in the Greek Aegean region.

The first verifiable advanced civilization in the Greek region developed after **3000 B.C.** on the island of Crete. It is called the Minoan civilization after the legendary King Minos. Its center was the metropolis of Knossos. Its richly decorated palace complex had some 1,300 rooms; it is estimated that tens of thousands of people lived in the city, with its paved streets and water and drainage systems. The Mycenaean culture, which emerged on the Greek mainland between **2000** and **1600 B.C.** out of a mixing of immigrant Indo-Europeans and local inhabitants, was named after its most important excavation site, Mycenae. Citadels and fortifications give proof of a warrior-like social structure. The Mycenaeans, also called Achaeans, spoke an early form of Greek, as can be seen from the deciphering of written tablets. The

Palace ruins in Knossos give proof of the highly developed Minoan culture on Crete.

Achaeans occupied Crete, except for Knossos, around **1450 B.C.**, making the Mycenaean civilization the leading power in the Aegean until it was destroyed around **1200 B.C.** during the time of the migration of the "Sea Peoples." But the memory of the Minoans and Mycenaeans lives on in Greek myths like the epics of Homer.

Egyptian Cultural Revolution
Pharaoh Amenhotep IV, called Akhenaten, radically broke with all Egyptian religious traditions in the 14th century B.C. by introducing a monotheistic sun god cult.

The sun disc as symbol of Aten receiving the offerings of Pharaoh Akhenaten

When he came to power in **1351 B.C.**, Pharaoh Amenhotep IV began a period of revolutionary change in Egypt's political and religious life. Presumably to curtail the growing power of the Amun priesthood in the capital of Thebes, he and his co-regent and wife, Nofretete, promoted the cult revering the sun god Aten. In 1346 B.C., the pharaoh banned the cult of Amun and had its followers and undesirable officials persecuted. Aten was elevated to the sole state god. Amenhotep changed his name to Akhenaten, meaning "devoted to Aten." As a sign of the new beginning, he abandoned the royal court in Thebes and relocated to the newly founded Akhetaten, "horizon of the Aten," present-day Tell el-Amarna. The highly educated king also broke with all the conventions in the field of art. He promoted a new, realistic style, termed the Amarna style. Apparently the majority of the people opposed the reforms even during Akhenaten's lifetime. After his death in **1334 B.C.**, they were reversed and the court returned to Thebes. The attempt was made to erase all memory of the heretic king.

The Battle of Kadesh
In 1274 B.C., in the best documented battle in the history of ancient Egypt, Pharaoh Ramses II fails in his planned conquest of northern Syria.

Monumental structures like his rock temples of Abu Simbel have made Ramses II, who ruled from **1279 B.C.**, the most famous of the Egyptian pharaohs. But he was also a successful politician and general. During his 66-year rule he asserted Egypt's claim as a major power, primarily against the rising power of the Hittites, who threatened his empire on the northeastern borders of Syria. In this, Ramses also had luck on his side. In **1274 B.C.**, he marched a massive army in the direction of Syria and walked into an ambush near the town of Kadesh. The surprising appearance of an elite contingent of troops, who had earlier been rebellious, saved the Egyptians from a catastrophic defeat and allowed Ramses II an orderly retreat. In **1259 B.C.**, the Egyptians and the Hittites made peace in history's earliest surviving written treaty.

The Battle of Kadesh between the Egyptians and the Hittites ended undecided.

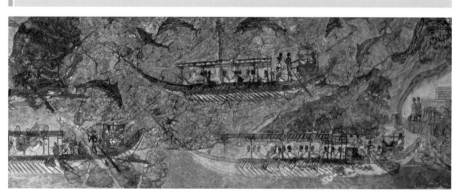
A fleet of war ships in a Minoan mural

The Migration of the Sea Peoples
The invasion of the "Sea Peoples" in the eastern Mediterranean led to sweeping territorial upheaval.

Around **1200 B.C.** there were intense migration movements in the eastern Mediterranean, during which ancient civilizations collapsed and new ones emerged. Sources from antiquity speak vaguely of pillaging "Sea Peoples," who for more than a century terrified the costal regions between Asia Minor and Egypt. Today their origins are presumed to be the Aegean and the western Mediterranean. Following the total destruction of the Mycenaean and Minoan cultures at the turn of the 12th century B.C., the Dorians settled in present-day Greece around **1000 B.C.** His-

torical Troy also seems to have perished in the storm of the "Sea Peoples." At the same time, the north Syrian trading center of Ugarit was destroyed and a short while later the Hittite empire in Asia Minor collapsed. Only with great effort was Egypt under Pharaoh Ramses III able to withstand the onslaught of the invaders. While the Philistines, who were one of the "Sea Peoples," settled along the coast of Palestine, the Israelites, according to Biblical tradition, founded their own kingdom in the interior in **1012 B.C.**

The First Empires

1000 The **Trundholm sun chariot**, an outstanding example of **Bronze Age** art, is produced in present-day Denmark around 1000 B.C.

1000 The oldest known work in Indian literature, a collection of sacred hymns called the *Rigveda*, is completed around 1000 B.C.

1000 In China, **Beijing** is mentioned for the first time as **Ki**.

950 In **Japan**, early **Shintoism** begins to emerge.

950 The Biblical *Song of Songs* is written around 950. Attributed to **King Solomon**, this love song marks the beginning of **Israelite literature**.

950 The **Phoenicians** begin producing purple dye from the banded dye-murex, a species of **sea snail**.

945 The **Chaldeans** use a coherent system of measurement, the **cubic foot**.

900 **Printing from copper plates** develops in **China**.

900 Small **temples**, usually **of wood**, are the earliest evidence of **Greek architecture**.

880 The **orgiastic cult of Dionysus** enters Greece by way of Phrygia.

878 The Phoenician **cult of Baal** begins to spread throughout **Israel**, which, according to the Bible, provokes the **opposition of the prophet Elijah**. The **monotheistic cult of Yahweh** develops in the confrontation with the religious concepts of neighboring tribes.

840 The **victory stele of King Mesha of Moab** bears one of the earliest historical references to the **people of Israel** outside the Bible.

1000 · · · **950** · · · **900** · · · **850**

1004 According to the Bible, **David** is the **new king of Israel**. By his death in 969, he has expanded his realm to the north and south and has made **Jerusalem** the country's capital.

1000 **Bantu**-speaking tribes spread further across **Central and East Africa**. Around the turn of the millennium, the Bantu people in present-day Uganda take over the mining of **iron ore**.

930 According to the Bible, the **kingdom of Israel is split** after the death of **King Solomon**. Jeroboam I becomes king of the northern kingdom of **Israel**; in the small southern kingdom of **Judah**, the dynasty of King David remains in power through Solomon's son, Rehabeam.

900 The **Indo-European Latins** settle in the **Tiber Valley** in central Italy, laying the groundwork for the emergence and spread of **Latin**, radiating from the ancient city of Alba Longa.

856–831 **Takelot II** reigns in **Egypt**. However, his realm is primarily limited to Upper Egypt.

836 The **Medes people** inhabiting present-day Iran are first mentioned by the Assyrians.

828 King **Menua** becomes king over the east Anatolian **kingdom of Uratu**.

1000 During the first millennium B.C., the **Chavin culture** in present-day **Peru** spreads out from the Andes to the Pacific coast.

"How much better to get wisdom than gold."

A quote ascribed to King Solomon

900 The invention of **iron metallurgy** is made in **Sub-Saharan Africa**.

853 The **kingdom of Kush** emerges in **Nubia**, present-day Sudan, which is culturally influenced by Egypt. The royal residence of the ruler is initially in **Napata**, later in **Meroë**.

814 **Phoenician settlers** found **Carthage** ("New City") in present-day Tunisia. Other bases are established in Spain and Sicily, which later are under the rule of Carthage. On their trading expeditions, the Phoenicians discover **Madeira** and the **Canary Islands** and go as far as the **British Isles**.

1000 During the first millennium B.C., tribes later called **Iberians** by the Greeks settle in present-day **Spain and Portugal**.

1000 The **Norton tradition**, a predecessor of today's **Inuit**, develops in West Alaska.

900 **Baasha** becomes the third **king of Israel**.

900 **Illyrian tribes** like the **Messapii** move down into Italy from the Adriatic coast in present-day Croatia and develop their own cultures, primarily in modern **Apulia**.

879 The **Assyrian king Ashur-nasir-pal II** inaugurates his new residence in **Kaluh** (Nimrud) in the north of present-day Iraq with several days of great festivities.

853 In the **Battle of Qarqar** on the Orontes, Shalmaneser III crushes **an anti-Assyrian coalition** of different local city-states.

1000 **Dorian Migration:** The Dorians, a **Greek tribe**, advance from the north into the Peloponnesian Peninsula, where they found the **city-state of Sparta**.

969 The Biblical King **Solomon** follows his father, David, to the throne. He erects the **first temple** in **Jerusalem**.

900 **Indo-European tribes** from the north settle in **central and southern Italy**. Among them are also the **Umbri**, who, like other Italic tribes, are later subjugated by the Romans.

860 King **Sardur I** founds the kingdom of **Urartu**, which later spreads over large parts of eastern Anatolia, western Iran, and the Trans-Caucasus.

850 The **Greek city-states** are ruled by kings. Around 700, the monarchies give way to **rule by nobility**, except in Sparta.

810 As regent for her underage son, **Semiramis** rules over the **Neo-Assyrian Empire**. She is also credited with the building of the **city walls and obelisk in Babylon**.

1000 The first important **city kingdoms** on **Cyprus**, like Salamis, Paphos, Kition, and Soloi, develop around 1000 B.C.

882/878 **King Omri** founds the Omride dynasty in Israel.

845 **Jehu** slaughters the Omrides and becomes king of Israel. He has the followers of the **Baal cult liquidated.**

1000 The **city-state of Damascus** in present-day Syria is in full bloom. It is ruled by kings of Semitic, Aramean-speaking tribes.

945 **Shoshenq I,** a Libyan and commander-in-chief of the Egyptian army, founds the **22nd dynasty in Egypt**.

926 The **Egyptians** under **Shoshenq I** invade Palestine and, according to the Bible, plunder **Jerusalem**.

871–852 **Ahab of Israel** wages war against the Arameans.

859 During his rule, **Shalmaneser III** expands the **Neo-Assyrian Empire** through a series of **campaigns** undertaken almost on a yearly basis until 824.

843 Assyrian sources mention the **Persian people** for the first time. Around 800 B.C., they settle in the present-day **Province of Fars** in the northwest of Iran.

841 In **China**, **King Li of Zhou** is driven from his capital by rebels.

800 The **Etruscans** displace the Villanova culture, until then dominant in **Tuscany**. They later expand their influence into the **Po Valley** to **Campania**.

The Birth of Antiquity

1000–500 B.C.

The first millennium B.C. was a time of change. The movement of migrating people and the spread of cultures and cultural technologies like metalworking changed many regions of the world permanently. Central America was dominated by the Olmecs, the Celts were spreading out in Central and Western Europe, the Etruscans settled in Italy, Greeks and Phoenicians colonized the Mediterranean area, and the Scythians, a horse people, pushed into the Middle East. In the Near East, the empires of the Assyrians, Babylonians, Medes, and finally that of the Persians followed each other in succession. Rome began to rise in the second half of the first millennium B.C., while some of the Greek city-states, the poleis, established an early form of democracy. These and other developments of Antiquity made Greece, and later Rome, the cradle of Western civilization. Also in China, which had as yet no unified state, Confucius laid the cornerstone for a social understanding and a concept of statehood that would later be influential far beyond China.

Sarcophagus of the Spouses (an Etruscan married couple)

HISTORICAL FIGURES

David (c. 1040–969 B.C.)
According to biblical tradition, King David united the tribes of Israel and created a vast empire.

To this day, David has a prominent position in the Judeo-Christian world. He is regarded as the ideal ruler, from whose lineage the future Messiah would proceed. But the figure of the king is only known from the Bible, and his historic authenticity is disputed. According to the Bible, David, who is thought to have been born in Bethlehem as a member of the tribe of Judah, began his rise in the army of King Saul, the first king of the Israelites. His victory over the Philistines, specifically over the gigantic Goliath, quickly made the youth famous. In **1008 B.C.**, he succeeded Saul as king. Supported by a private army, he subjugated all twelve tribes of Israel and created a unified state. In the end, his realm stretched from the Euphrates to Egypt. David also conquered the Canaanite city-state of Jerusalem, which he chose as the political and religious center of Israel. But it was his son and successor, Solomon, who erected the first temple to serve as the center of the cult of Yahweh.

Nebuchadnezzar II (c. 640–562 B.C.)
The Bible long determined the image of the king of the Neo-Babylonian Empire.

During his years as crown prince, Nebuchadnezzar had completed several successful military campaigns, such as his victory over Egyptian Pharaoh Necho II. After ascending to the throne in **605 B.C.**, he crushed revolts in Palestine; took Jerusalem in **597**, completely annihilating the city; and destroyed the state of Judah in **587**. He deported the population's upper class, sending them into "Babylonian exile." He brought growth and prosperity to his empire and transformed Babylon into one of the most magnificent cities of the Near East. The Ishtar Gate that opened up to the famous Processional Way, a massive ziggurat (Tower of Babel), and the legendary Hanging Gardens, were all constructed under Nebuchadnezzar.

Cyrus II the Great (c. 590–530 B.C.)
The successful warlord of the Achaemenid dynasty laid the cornerstone for the rise of the Persian Empire to a great power in Antiquity.

The son of Cambyses I became king of Persia in **559 B.C.** and established the supremacy of the Persians over the Near East in military campaigns. Cyrus freed himself from the Medes and in **550** subjugated his former overlords. In **546** he vanquished Croesus, king of Lydia, and absorbed his empire. A little later, the rest of Asia Minor fell into Cyrus's hands. His conquest of Babylon in **539** finally solidified Persia's status as a major power. Cyrus treated the peoples he subjugated humanely and was particularly tolerant in religious matters. For example, he allowed the Jews released from Babylonian captivity to rebuild their temple in Jerusalem. Cyrus fell in 529, presumably in the Middle East during a battle against the Massagetae.

Confucius (551–479 B.C.)
The teachings of the Chinese philosopher have to this day a defining influence on China's state and society.

Confucius, who came from a poor but noble family in the Chinese state of Lu, acquired a broad education and entered state service. He spent time as an official and minister, but later became a wandering teacher. After staying at the courts of different Chinese kingdoms, he returned to Lu. His teachings are compiled in the Five Classics. The goal of leading a correct life is to find harmony in the pivotal interpersonal relationships on the basis of loyalty, respect for others, and obedience. The nucleus of a hierarchical state based on these principles is the patriarchal family. Confucius's teachings became dominant in China centuries after his death in 479 and developed into the system of philosophy known as Confucianism.

688 Boxing competitions and chariot races take place for the first time at the Olympic Games.

660 In Egypt, a simple script for everyday use develops out of hieroglyphs.

650 In Nineveh, Assyria, a library is founded holding the largest collection of knowledge in the ancient Orient.

621 To prohibit blood feuds, Draco draws up a harsh (draconian) written penal code in Athens.

600 The first coins are minted in Lydia in Asia Minor. From there, the technology gradually spreads across the whole Mediterranean region.

600 Zoroaster is thought to have founded Zoroastrianism around this time, which is elevated to a type of state religion of the Persian kings after 550.

600 On the Greek island of Lesbos (Lesvos), Sappho composes the first famous love poems.

600 On the initiative of the Egyptian pharaoh Necho II, Phoenician seafarers supposedly were the first to sail around the African continent.

550 In India, the *Baghavad Gita* is produced in the 6th century, one of the sacred scriptures of Hinduism.

547 Thales of Miletus, an important pre-Socratic philosopher and mathematician, dies in Asia Minor. He is considered the father of natural philosophy.

510 The Cloaca maxima is built in Rome. The subterranean sewer system is still in use today.

525 The Greek philosopher Pythagoras of Samos begins developing principle laws of mathematics and geometry.

500 The Chinese philosopher Confucius presents the central principles of his ethics that remain influential to this day.

---

650 | **600** | **550** | **500**

700/600 Miletus, on the west coast of Asia Minor, develops into the political and cultural center of the Ionian League.

671 After securing his rule in Syria and Palestine, the Assyrian king Assurhaddon conquers Egypt to the Nubian border. The Neo-Assyrian Empire is at the zenith of its power.

664 Psamtik I becomes pharaoh of Egypt. In alliance with Lydia, and aided by Greek mercenaries, he drives out the Assyrians and unites the country. He allows Greek traders to found the city of Naucratis in the Nile delta.

660 According to legend, the empire of Japan is founded by Jimmu Tenno, a direct descendant of the sun goddess. In reality, the first emperor was probably not installed until 400 A.D.

657 Cypselus, a member of the ruling dynasty in Corinth, usurps power and institutes a tyranny.

652 The Scythians again invade Asia Minor; in alliance with the Assyrians, they make great territorial gains.

650 In Italy, the legendary Roman king Tullus Hostilius conquers Alba Longa, turning Rome into the hegemonic power in Latium.

646 Elam in southwestern Iran is conquered by the Assyrians and incorporated into their empire.

626 In Babylon, General Nabopolassar seizes power, gains independence from the Assyrians, and lays the foundation for the rise of the Neo-Babylonian Empire.

625 King Cyaxares II comes to power in the Median Empire in Iran.

614/612 The Medes and the Babylonians conquer Assur and Nineveh, dealing the Neo-Assyrian Empire a death blow. Its territory is divided up among the victors.

609 With the defeat of King Assuruballits II in the battle against the Babylonians in northern Syria, the Neo-Assyrian Empire collapses once and for all.

605 Nebuchadnezzar II follows as king of Babylon. Under his rule lasting until 562, the Neo-Babylonian Empire experiences a cultural flowering through extensive building activity, including the "Tower of Babel."

600 Sparta rises in the 6th century to become one of the leading Greek poleis and emerges around 560 as leader of the newly founded Peloponnesian League.

600 The Etruscans are able to extend their dominion over almost all of Italy in the 6th century B.C. and probably also provide Rome with its last kings. The mightiest of the Etrurian city-states join together in a loose federation of twelve city-states.

597 During the reign of King Zedekiah of Judah, the Babylonians capture Jerusalem for the first time and deport part of the population.

594 The process of democratization begins in Athens with the social and state reforms of the archon Solon.

587 The Neo-Babylonian king, Nebuchadnezzar II, captures Jerusalem, ransacks the city, and destroys the temple. Judah's upper class is deported to Mesopotamia into "Babylonian captivity."

560 Croesus becomes the new king of Lydia. He gains legendary wealth through the tribute payments of his vassal states.

560 Peisistratos comes to power in Athens and institutes a tyranny. He socially and economically consolidates the city-state.

559 Cyrus II, an Achaemenid, becomes king of Persia and with his conquests lays the foundation for the Persian Empire, the first real world empire in history.

550 The Persian king Cyrus II subjugates and annexes the kingdom of the related Median kings.

550 The Nabataeans, a northwestern Arabian ethnic tribe, migrate into present-day Jordan and build a kingdom there.

546 The Persian king Cyrus II defeats Croesus of Lydia at Sardis, giving the Persians hegemony over Anatolia and the Greek colonies on the west coast of Asia Minor.

540 In India, the rise of the Magadha Empire begins with King Bimbisara.

540 With their victory over the Greek Phocaeans at Alalia on Corsica, the Etruscans secure their dominance in the western Mediterranean region.

539 The Persian king, Cyrus II, captures Babylon and allows the Jews to return home, thus ending the "Babylonian exile."

529 The Persian king Cyrus II falls in the battle against the Massageteans.

522 Darius I ascends to the throne of Persia. During his reign, lasting until 486, the Achaemenid Persian Empire reaches its greatest extent.

512 A military campaign by Darius I against the Scythes is partially successful.

509 The Romans oust the last Etruscan king, Tarquinius Superbus. According to legend, the republic is introduced.

509 Rome and Carthage are thought to have concluded a treaty guaranteeing respect for each other's territory.

508/507 The reforms of Cleisthenes pave the way for democracy in Athens.

800 **Delphi**, with its famous **oracle**, becomes the most important shrine to Apollo and is considered by the Greeks to be the **center of the world**.

800 In the 8th century, the **Phoenicians develop** the bireme, a new **warship**.

800 The **rose** finds its way from **India to Greece**.

800/750 The **Greeks** develop their own **alphabet** based on the Phoenician alphabet.

750 The Greek poet **Homer** composes *The Iliad* and *The Odyssey*. This epic poetry is among the most influential in the Western World.

720 The Assyrian king Sargon II erects a **terraced palace** in Chorsabad.

692 **Glaucus of Chios** invents the **art of welding**.

800 In Europe, the **Celts** are thought to be the first **to develop steel**.

800 In **Greece**, new forms of house construction arise, such as **rectangular and oval houses**.

776 The **first Olympic Games** take place in Olympia. The athletic competions in honor of Zeus become one of the elements that help to form Greek identity.

750 The Assyrians start to decorate **clay vessels** with **kiln-fired art**.

714 The Sabaeans build the **Great Dam of Marib** in present-day Yemen.

700 **Hesiod**, the **first European poet** to be positively identified by name, composes didactic poetry in the formal style of Homer.

---

800 | **750** | **700**

---

800 **La Venta culture**: The civilization of the **Olmecs**, the **first empire in Central America**, expands from its center in La Venta in the present-day Mexican state of Tabasco.

800 The **Scythians**, a band of different **Indo-European horse-riding nomadic tribes**, leave their original homeland in southern Russia and penetrate into the south and west, displacing the **Cimmerians**, another horse people.

771 In **China**, the **Spring and Autumn Period**, named after the first Chinese state chronicles, begins under the **Eastern Zhu Dynasty**. The era is marked by innovations in agriculture and a differentiation of society and of ownership conditions.

746 **Tiglath-Pileser III** becomes the new king in Assyria. With his successful campaigns against his neighbors during his reign, he makes Assyria the unchallenged hegemonic power in the Near East before his death in 727.

714 The Assyrian king **Sargon II** is victorious over **Urartu** in present-day **East Anatolia** and the kingdom sinks into insignificance. After 600 B.C., the kingdom is subject to the Scythians.

700 In the 7th century, the Arabian **kingdom of Saba** experiences the zenith of its power under **Karib'il Watar I**.

800 The **Iron Age** begins in **Europe**. Mined iron ore is smelted in ovens and worked into tools and weapons. The period is also known as **"Hallstatt culture,"** named after an excavation site in Austria.

800 During the 8th century, the **kingdom of the Phrygians**, with their capital Gordion southwest of present-day Ankara, rises to dominance in **Asia Minor**. The Phrygians migrated across the Bosporus between 1200 and 800 B.C.

757 The **founding of Cumae** in Campania, Italy, is considered to be the **start of Greek colonization** of the Mediterranean and the region of the Black Sea.

740 The **Kushites** begin to expand their dominion from the central Nile (Sudan) north to Egypt. The rulers of Kush (Nubia) found the 25th dynasty in 712.

685 **Gyges** becomes king in the **kingdom of Lydia**.

750/700 The **Scythians** and **Cimmerians**, horse-riding peoples from the Black Sea region, penetrate well into Mesopotamia and Asia Minor.

738 **King Midas** is mentioned for the first time as **ruler of Phrygia**. Under his rule, the Phrygian Empire stretches over **large parts of Anatolia**. His fabulous wealth becomes a legend, according to which everything Midas touched turned to gold.

705 **Nineveh**, in present-day Iraq, is built up to be the imperial capital of **Assyria**, with at times as many as 17,000 inhabitants.

685 The kingdom is abolished in **Athens**. Head of the state are the **archons**, the chief magistrates.

700 The **rise of the Medes** to a major regional power in **northwestern Iran** begins.

675 The Assyrian king **Assurhaddon** begins with the reconstruction of **Babylon**.

735 **War** breaks out **between Sparta and Messenia**. It ends after 20 years with the subjugation of the Messenians.

700 **Etruscan seafarers** gradually gain control of the western Mediterranean during the 7th century and, in **alliance with Carthage**, become a **leading sea power**.

674–600 The **Cimmerians** conquer **Phrygia** and invade the kingdom of the Lydians.

733 **Syracuse**, the **most important Greek colony** in southern Italy, is founded.

753 According to the tradition of Roman historian Marcus Varro (died 27 A.D.), Romulus founds the **city of Rome** on Apr. 21. Part of the legend, known as **"the Rape of the Sabine Women,"** states that Sabine women are kidnapped in order to populate the city.

722 **Sargon II** overthrows the Assyrian king, **Shalmaneser V**, during the siege of Samaria and destroys the northern kingdom of Israel. The southern kingdom of Judah remains independent.

700 Supposedly on the initiation of the legendary **lawgiver Lycurgus**, Sparta is systemically transformed into a **military state** in the 7th century B.C.

HISTORICAL EVENTS

The Olmecs
During the first millennium B.C., the Olmecs developed Central America's first major civilization in the Mexican highlands, which influenced all later cultures down to the Mayas and Aztecs.

Around the turn of the first millennium B.C., the earliest advanced Mesoamerican civilization began to flourish in the subtropical coastal region of the present-day Mexican states of Tabasco and Veracruz. It emerged around **1600 B.C.** in the Mexican highlands and laid the foundation for the development of all subsequent cultures in Central America. The center of the Olmecs ("people from the rubber country"), as the people of the culture were later called by the Aztecs, was located after **800** in La Venta in Tabasco, which is why it is also known as the La Venta culture. Standing at the head of the hierarchically ordered tribal society were priests who led the religious and political life. Distinctive artifacts of the Olmec culture are earth-filled pyramids, including the 108-foot-high Great Pyramid, and the colossal stone heads reaching 11 feet in height, which presumably depict deities, outstanding personages, or cultural heroes. The Olmecs had their own system of writing and probably invented the 260-day calendar, later adopted by the Mayas. In addition, they are considered to be the inventors of chocolate. The word "cacao" supposedly derives from the Olmec language. The destruction of La Venta around 400 triggered the fall of their civilization.

The colossal stone heads of the Olmecs possibly depict deities.

"Ab urbe condita"
Between fact and fiction: The founding of the future world power, Rome, in the year 753 B.C. is shrouded in myths.

In the first century A.D., the Roman scholar Varro set the founding date of Rome precisely at **April 21, 753 B.C.** This day became the starting point of a calendar that was used until the early Middle Ages. According to the myth of the founding of Rome, the Trojan hero Aeneas fled from Asia Minor to Latium. His descendants, Romulus and Remus, conceived by a god, founded the city on the Tiber on seven hills. After the murder of his brother, Romulus became its first king and the city was named after him. As some archeologists argue, Rome was founded as a colony around 800 B.C. by the Etruscans, under whom the rise of the city began from **650**. Traditional myths state that the last Etruscan king, Tarquinus Superbus, was driven from the city in **509**, and a republic was then established. In fact, this occurred more likely around 475. The development of republican institutions headed by the senate continued over many years. In the third century B.C., Rome gained control of all of Italy—and later of the whole Mediterranean area.

According to legend, the abandoned twins, Romulus and Remus, were suckled by a she-wolf.

The theater in the Sicilian city of Syracuse was built around 475 B.C.

Greek Colonization
In the year 733 B.C., settlers from Corinth founded the city of Syracuse in Sicily, which developed into a center of Greek culture in the western Mediterranean.

From the 8th century B.C., overpopulation in the Greek city-states led to a shortage of land, growing poverty, and political conflicts. This resulted in a massive emigration movement. Ancient Greeks settled on the islands of the Mediterranean, along the coasts of Africa and southern Italy, in present-day Spain and France, and on the coasts of the Black Sea. The colonies were politically independent, but remained culturally tied to their mother cities. Particularly successful was the development of Magna Græcia, the colonies in Italy. The settlements there, however, had to defend against the increasing attacks of the Etruscans and Carthaginians. Dionysius I, who usurped total power in Syracuse in **405 B.C.** and spread his control over all of southern Italy, was one of the most significant Greek tyrants.

Phoenicia
The Phoenicians are said to be the first seafarers to have circumnavigated Africa in 600 B.C.

The Phoenician civilization developed along the coast of present-day Lebanon. Their name derives from the Greek word for the purple dye with which they traded. After the upheavals brought on by the migrations of the Sea Peoples that began in **1200 B.C.**, the Phoenician city-states—first Sidon, then Tyre—rose to become leading sea powers. In competition with the Greeks, the Phoenicians founded colonies and trading posts over the entire Mediterranean area, including Carthage in **814**. Their trading ties in the north reached to the British Isles. While Carthage at times dominated the whole western Mediterranean, the Phoenician mother cities fell under the control of the Assyrians, the Egyptians, the Babylonians, and the Persians, who all made use of the seafaring skills of the Phoenicians and allowed them autonomy in return. On command of Pharaoh Necho II, the Phoenicians completed the first circumnavigation of Africa around **600**. They

The Phoenicians were considered to be excellent and intrepid seafarers.

later comprised the greater part of the Persian fleet in battles against the Greeks. The most important achievement of the Phoenicians, however, was the invention of the alphabetic system of writing around **1300 B.C.**, from which our present alphabet evolved.

Babylonian Exile
The 50-year Babylonian exile strengthened the religious identity of the Jews.

After the death of King Solomon in **930 B.C.**, his kingdom broke up into two smaller states, Judah and Israel. These became pawns at the mercy of the warring major powers of the Near East. In the year **722** the Assyrians conquered Israel; in **587** the Babylonian king Nebuchadnezzar II destroyed Jerusalem and annexed Judah. A major part of the population, comprised mostly of the upper class, was deported to Babylon. The experience of the exile represents one of the most important caesurae of Jewish history. As a minority in a foreign and partially superior cultural environment, the deported Jews were forced to come to terms with their own traditions in order to maintain their faith and identity. Concentrating on the now-destroyed temple in Jerusalem, they replaced their cult offerings with prayer and the study of the Torah. After Cyrus the Great con-

With the return to Jerusalem, Babylonian exile ended after 50 years for many Jews.

quered Babylon in 539, the Jews were allowed to return to Jerusalem and rebuild their temple. A large and significant Jewish community, however, remained in Babylon.

Athens – "Cradle of Democracy"
The participation of all Athenian citizens in politics was achieved through a long process of reform.

A political system that involved every franchised citizen in the decision making concerning community matters gradually developed in the city-state of Athens. However, this affected only a small portion of the total population, less than 15 percent, since neither women nor foreigners (metics), let alone slaves, were considered to be full citizens. The franchised citizens, however, could gather together to reach political decisions based on the majority principle. The chief magistrate (archon) Solon was the first to break the power monopoly of the nobility through reforms in **594 B.C.** and to extend the right of political participation also to the lower classes. Cleisthenes' constitutional reforms of **507–08** finally made a radical break with the old system. All Athenian citizens were given equal voting rights and access to all political offices. Only the Areopagus, the high court of the nobility, at first retained its special status. Its authority was finally transferred to the popular organs in 462-61, where all future court decisions were made without respect to status. Under Pericles, democracy was finally achieved in **443**.

Against the opposition of the aristocracy, Solon implemented democratic reforms.

Etruscans
After their naval victory over the Greeks in 540 B.C., the Etruscans were the supreme power in the Italian Mediterranean area.

The origins of the Etrurian civilization, whose heartland was located in present-day Tuscany, is a matter of debate. Either they came from the eastern Mediterranean area to Italy during the time of the Sea People and the associated waves of migrations that began in **1200 B.C.** or they developed out of a local Villanova culture around **800**. What is certain, however, is that from **700** the Etruscans were successfully trading with the eastern Mediterranean world and had developed an advanced urban civilization. Heading their independent, loosely organized federation of city-states were priest-kings. The Etruscans began to steadily expand their sphere of power on the Italian mainland in **600**, provoking conflicts, primarily with the Greeks living in the south of Italy. Their victory at Alalia in **540** ensured the Etruscans the primacy of the sea for a short time. But with the incursions of the Celts from the north and the rise of Rome in the south, they increasingly found themselves on the defensive. With the fall of Veii in **396**, the decline and ultimate fall of the Etruscans began.

The Etruscans produced art objects like this bronze statue of an athlete.

The attacks of the Scythians were feared far and wide.

Scythians
Not even the massive military might of the Persians was able to defeat the Scythians.

This Indo-European horse people, Eurasian nomads in the steppes of present-day Ukraine, southern Russia, and Kazakhstan, began pushing to the west around **800 B.C.** The Scythians, as the Greeks called them, did not form a unified people but rather groups of different tribes led by kings or queens. The Greek myths about Amazons were probably based on experiences with the Scythians. Among them, women held eminent positions even in the military. The Scythians' art of warfare was feared; their bows were particularly considered to be super weapons. The fact that the agile, mounted warriors were able to vanquish armies with much larger numbers is proven in their victories over the Persians. Cyrus the Great lost his life in battle in **529** against the Scythians' relatives, the Massagetae, led by their queen, Tomyris. The Persian King Darius I failed in his campaign against the Scythians in **512**. It was not uncommon for Scythians to be hired as mercenaries or allies. Various finds from kurgans, the huge tumuli in which the Scythians buried their leaders, provide clues to the way of life of the horse people. Above all, the working of gold reached a high level.

480 The Greek philosopher **Heraclitus**, the first western **dialectician**, dies in Ephesus.

479 The philosopher **Confucius**, whose moral teachings later evolve to become a **national doctrine** in the West Asia region, especially in China, dies in the Chinese state of Lu.

450 **Herodotus** of Halicarnassus, "the Father of History," recites from his yet unfinished narrative, ***The Histories***, in Athens.

430 **Phidias**, the most important **sculptor** of Classic Antiquity, dies in Athens.

399 The **philosopher Socrates** is **sentenced to death in Athens**; he is accused of blasphemy and corrupting the youth.

370 **Hippocrates of Cos**, the most famous physician of antiquity and founder of **medicine as a science**, dies in Thessaly.

480 The Indian religious founder **Buddha**, properly **Siddhartha Gautama**, dies presumably on the northern Indian border to Tibet.

472 ***The Persians***, a tragedy by **Aeschylus**, is presented for the first time in Athens. It is considered to be the oldest surviving drama of the world.

447 Construction of the **Parthenon**, the temple to the patron goddess Athena, begins upon the **Acropolis in Athens**.

411 ***Lysistrata***, the best-known and most widely read comedy today of the Greek poet **Aristophanes**, has its premiere.

385 **Plato**, the father of **political theory** and proponent of **metaphysics**, founds his own school of philosophy, **The Academy**, in Athens.

334 In Priene, **Alexander the Great** dedicates a shrine to **Athena**, the patron goddess of Athens. It is considered today to be the epitome of Ionian temple construction.

500 ———————————————— **450** ———————————————— **400** ———————————————— **350**

495 **Alexander I** becomes king in **Macedonia**. During his reign, lasting until 450 B.C., he lays the foundation for the later rise of the empire.

477 The **Delian League** under the leadership of Athens pursues the goal of achieving **hegemony in the Aegean**.

450 **La Tène Culture:** The advanced civilization of the **Celts** expands out of Western and Central Europe.

415–413 An **Athenian fleet** commanded by Nicias sails **against Syracuse** and suffers a crushing **defeat**, triggering the fall of Athens as a powerful force in the Mediterranean world.

396 **Rome** conquers the largest Etruscan city, **Veii**, launching its **expansion in Italy**.

494 With the **destruction of Miletus**, the **Ionian uprising** of the Greeks against the Persians in Asia Minor that began in 500 B.C. is finally crushed.

465 **Artaxerxes I** succeeds his father, Xerxes I, as **the king of kings of Persia**.

449/48 The **Peace of Callias**, based on the status quo, ends the war between the **Persians** and the **Athenians**. Athens is the ruling power in the Mediterranean.

395 **Corinthian War:** Corinth, Athens, Thebes, and Argos, with the backing of Persia, form an **alliance against Sparta**.

490 The **Athenians** defeat a Persian army under the great king Darius I at **Marathon**.

461 **Athens** ends its anti-Persian alliance with Sparta and pursues an aggressive **policy of expansion**. In 460 the **First Peloponnesian War** breaks out between Sparta and Athens.

405 **Dionysius I** becomes **tyrant of Syracuse** and subsequently subjugates the Greek cities in Sicily.

387 The **King's Peace** (or the Peace of Antalcidas) is concluded between **Sparta** and **Persia**. The Greek cities in Asia Minor fall under Persian rule, while the rest are guaranteed autonomy.

362 Theban supremacy in Greece comes to an end with the death of **Epameinondas** in the **Battle of Mantineia** against a Spartan army.

486 **Xerxes I** succeeds his father, Darius, as Persian king and secures his reign by suppressing uprisings in **Egypt** and **Babylonia**.

446 The **First Peloponnesian War** between Athens and Sparta ends with a **peace treaty** to last for a period of 40 years.

405 The Spartan admiral **Lysander** inflicts a major defeat on the Attic fleet at the mouth of the river **Aigospotamoi**.

387 **Gauls**, who have been pushing into Italy since 390, take **Rome** and plunder the city, with the exception of the capitol.

360 **Pharaoh Teos** expands Egypt's reach of power to include **Palestine** and **Syria**.

454 The **Athenian fleet** is vanquished by **Persian forces** in the Nile Delta. As a result, Egypt once again falls under Persian rule.

443 **Pericles** is made chief strategist in **Athens**. With him, the **democratic and cultural development** of the city-state reaches its zenith.

404 **Artaxerxes II** becomes ruler over the **Persian Empire**. He is forced to accept the ultimate **loss of Egypt**.

378 To defend against Spartan imperialism, Athens founds the **Second Delian League**.

485 Under the tyrant Gelon, **Syracuse** begins its rise to becoming the most **important Greek colony in Sicily**.

450 In Rome, the **Law of the Twelve Tables** lays the foundation for **Roman civil rights**.

404 **Athens** is forced to capitulate after being **besieged by the Spartans**. Its walls are razed and it must surrender most of its fleet.

371 The Theban general **Epameinondas** defeats a Spartan army at Leuctra, making **Thebes** the leading power in Greece.

359 **Philip II** takes power in **Macedonia**, initiating the rise of his kingdom.

481 **Symmachy:** The Greek states form an alliance under the **leadership of Sparta**.

431 **Peloponnesian War:** With an invasion of Attica, Sparta launches the second "fratricidal war" against Athens for **supremacy in Greece**.

403 The **oligarchy** (The Thirty Tyrants) installed **in Athens** by **Sparta** is overthrown and **democracy reinstated**.

357–355 The cities of Chios, Rhodes, Cos, and Byzantion break away from the **Second Athenian Empire** and gain independence from Athens in the **Social War** or **War of the Allies**.

480 In the **sea battle of Salamis**, the **Greeks** led by Themistocles score a resounding **victory over the Persian fleet**.

421 Following negotiations led by Pericles, **Sparta** and **Athens** conclude the **Peace of Nicias**, which lasts only seven years.

400 As the new leading power in Greece, **Sparta** intervenes in Asia Minor and triggers a **war between Sparta and Persia** that lasts until 387.

367 In the **Republic of Rome**, the **Licinio-Sextian law** makes it possible for **Plebeians** to also become consul.

340–338 Through its victory in the **Latin War**, **Rome** gains supremacy over **Campania** and **Latium**.

Democracy and Autocracy

500–1 B.C.

The Greco-Roman civilization of the Mediterranean region is considered today as the foundation of Western culture. Greek literature, philosophy, and art, as well as Roman law and the Roman state organization, contributed to its rise. During the 5th century B.C., the structures of civic self-government first emerged in the Greek city-states, with democratic Athens taking the lead. The city-state was the intellectual and artistic heart of the Mediterranean region, even after it had long since lost its position of power to the Macedonians and Romans. In the wake of Alexander the Great's campaigns of conquest in Asia and Egypt, and later the emergence of the Diadochi Empire, Greek culture merged with influences from the Orient and became cosmopolitan-orientated Hellenism. Rome, which rose to become the hegemonic power in the Mediterranean in the 2nd century B.C., was also strongly influenced culturally by the Greeks.

Bronze sculpture from the Chinese Han dynasty

HISTORICAL FIGURES

Alexander the Great (356 B.C.–323 B.C.)
A brilliant general, choleric megalomaniac, and brutal tyrant: within just a few years, Alexander the Great created a world empire.

The son of King Philip II of Macedonia was educated by the philosopher Aristotle. In **336** B.C., Alexander took the throne and from then on led his troops from victory to victory in wars against the Persians. He marched through Asia Minor, where he triumphed over the Persians at the river Granicus and at Issus in **333**. In the following year, he went on to Egypt, where he was crowned pharaoh and founded Alexandria. The victory at Gaugamela in **330** marked the end of the Persian Empire. The king of Asia drove his troops on to India in 325, where he, however, was forced to turn back. Alexander died of a mysterious illness in Babylon in **323**. His empire quickly crumbled in the struggle for succession. What remained were the cities he founded and the spread of Greek culture.

Han Wudi (156 B.C.–87 B.C.)
The most important emperor of the Han dynasty stabilized China domestically and expanded his sphere of influence far into Central and Southeast Asia.

Han, who began his reign in 141 B.C., ended the power of the regional princes and laid the foundation for a centralized administration, whose principles were in use until the end of the imperial dynasties in the early 20th century. For the first time, specialized ministries were staffed with qualified officials. Wudi declared Confucianism to be the state philosophy in 135. Internal consolidation was followed by the expansion of the empire through war. In 119 he defeated the Xiongnu nomads of the north. In **111**, he conquered Vietnam, later Korea. Around 101 the Chinese penetrated far into Central Asia, securing access to trade on the Silk Road.

Cleopatra VII (69 B.C.–30 B.C.)
Her legendary beauty and arts of seduction made the last Ptolemaic queen of Egypt one of the most colorful figures in history.

Hardly any other female ruler has fired people's imagination more than Cleopatra VII. Through her personal relationships with Julius Caesar and Marc Antony, she significantly influenced politics in Rome. Driven out by her co-regent and brother-husband, Ptolemy XIII, she sought help in Rome from Caesar, who restored her to the Egyptian throne in **47** B.C. After his death, she started an affair with Marc Antony, the Roman ruler in the East, who considerably enlarged the queen's territory. In **31** they were both defeated at Actium by Octavian; Egypt was then occupied. Cleopatra is believed to have committed suicide by snakebite.

Augustus (63 B.C.–14 A.D.)
Domestic peace, growing prosperity, and a blossoming culture: the Roman Empire experienced its "golden age" under its first emperor.

Octavian, the grand nephew and main heir of Julius Caesar, had to share power with Marc Antony. When Antony allied himself with Ethiopian queen Cleopatra, Octavian decided to eliminate his rival. He scored a triumphant victory in the naval Battle of Actium in **31** and was now the uncontested ruler of the Roman Empire. In **27**, the Senate awarded him the honorific title of Augustus ("the revered one"). The new ruler considered himself to be "princeps," the first of citizens, and officially adhered to the republic. The principate of Augustus is regarded as the beginning of the Roman Empire. After long years of civil war, it experienced a period of stability and prosperity (pax augusta), lasting until Augustus's death in **14** A.D.

166 **Eumenes II of Pergamon** has the **Pergamon Altar** constructed to honor Zeus.

160 In Rome, the satirist **Gaius Lucilius** establishes **satire** in the form and meaning it has retained to this day with his humorous and critical observations of society.

150 The Greek astronomer, mathematician, and geographer **Hipparchos** compiles the first **star catalog**.

150 **Cato the Elder** writes *De agri cultura*, a farming manual, depicting rural life in the Roman Republic.

146 The Greek historian **Polybius** begins his work on *The Histories*, a monumental work of the history of Rome from 264 to 146.

104 The expansion of the **Chinese Empire** into Central Asia results in intensive trade and cultural contact with the **Mediterranean world** by way of the **Silk Road**.

100 The **runic script** emerges in **Germania** around the turn of the century.

59 **Julius Caesar** introduces the **Acta diurna**, daily Roman official notices engraved in tablets, an early form of **newspaper**.

46 The **Julian calendar** is introduced in the **Roman Empire** at Caesar's command.

43 **Marcus Tullius Cicero**, the Roman statesman, orator, writer, and philosopher, dies on Dec. 7 in Formia.

29 The Roman poet **Vergil** begins work on the *Aenaeis*, a national epic.

8 **Horace**, one of the leading poets of the **Augustinian period**, dies on Nov. 27.

---

150   100   50   1

154–151 **Celtic tribes** on the Iberian Peninsula penetrate into **Roman territory** and force the local governor, Marcellus, to a compromise.

149 The **Third Punic War:** A violation of the peace agreements gives **Rome** the excuse to declare war on **Carthage** again.

146 After a revolt, the Roman consul **Lucius Mummius** has **Corinth destroyed**.

146 **Roman troops** commanded by Scipio (Aemilianus) the Younger level Carthage. The **province of Africa** is established on its territory.

136–132 The first major **slave revolts** against their Roman masters take place in **Sicily**.

133 In his testament, **Attalus III of Pergamon** names Rome as the heir to his kingdom. Four years later, the **province of Asia** is established there.

133–121 The attempt by the plebeian tribune **Tiberius Gracchus** to institute radical **land reform** in favor of the impoverished classes leads to a serious **constitutional crisis** and civil war-like turmoil.

113 The **Cimbri** and the **Teutons**, Germanic tribes from northern Europe, score military victories against the Romans and plunder the country. The Roman general **Gaius Marius** is finally able to eliminate the "Germanic threat" for good with a victory at Vercellae in 101.

> *"Furthermore, I think Carthage must be destroyed."*
>
> A repeated saying of Cato the Elder (234–149 B.C.) before the Roman Senate

111 Under **Emperor Han Wudi**, **China** expands to the south and subjugates present-day **Vietnam**. Two years later, **Korea** also becomes a Chinese vassal state.

111 **Jugurthine War:** Rome battles the North African king **Jugurtha of Numidia**. The conflict ends with a Roman victory in 105.

89 After the end of the **Social War**, which broke out in 91, Rome grants **Roman citizenship to all inhabitants of Italy**, legally and politically unifying the country for the first time.

73–71 In Italy, an **army of slaves** led by **Spartacus** sparks a **revolt**; the insurrection can only be be crushed at **great military expense**.

51 In fierce battles, **Julius Caesar** is able to conquer all of **Gaul** with his troops as far as the Rhine. **Prince Vercingetorix is executed in Rome** in 46.

64/63 The **Romans** conquer the territory of the **Seleucid Empire**; Pontus and Syria are made Roman provinces. The territory conquered by the Romans now stretches across the **entire Mediterranean world**.

63 **Catiline conspiracy:** Consul **Cicero** uncovers plans for a coup d'etat by his rival, Catilina.

60/59 **Pompeius, Crassus**, and **Julius Caesar** form the First Triumvirate, virtually suspending the republican constitution.

88 Mithridates VI of Pontus occupies **Asia Minor** and **Greece**. The resulting **First Mithridatic War** ends in 85; Mithridates is forced to surrender his captured territory.

82 **Sulla** has himself appointed **dictator** by the Roman Senate, thus ending the **civil war** that broke out in **Rome** in 88. He voluntarily relinquishes all offices in 79.

53 The **Parthians** defeat the Roman troops commanded by Consul Crassus at the **Battle of Carrhae**. Crassus is killed shortly thereafter.

52 The last major uprising of the **Celtic Gauls** under **Prince Vercingetorix** takes place in present-day France.

49 **Julius Caesar** crosses the **Rubicon**, the river forming Italy's northern border, with his troops. A state of emergency is declared in Rome and a **new civil war** begins.

47 Upon the instigation of her lover, Caesar, **Cleopatra VII** becomes the sole ruler of **Egypt**.

46 After defeating his rivals, **Caesar** elevates himself to **dictator** for life in Rome.

44 On the **Ides of March** (March 15), Julius Caesar is stabbed to death by conspirators.

42 In the two engagements of the **Battle of Philippi**, Caesar's two successors, **Marc Antony** and **Octavian**, defeat the murders of Caesar, Brutus, and Gaius Longinus.

37 **Herod the Great** captures Jerusalem and is installed as Roman **vassal king of Judea**.

31 Octavian's fleet is victorious over the combined forces of **Marc Antony** and **Cleopatra** in the naval **Battle of Actium**. **Octavian** emerges the sole ruler of Rome.

30 Octavian occupies Alexandria. The Ptolemaic dynasty ends with **Cleopatra's suicide**, and **Egypt** is made a **Roman province**.

27 The Senate awards Octavian the honorific title **"Augustus,"** effectively the beginning of the Roman Empire.

12 **Roman troops** march into the heartland of the **Germanic peoples** as far as the Elbe river and **compel some of the tribes to pay tribute**.

6 **Jesus of Nazareth** is born around this date.

325 Euclid writes *Elements*, the best-known textbook of Greek mathematics.

322 Aristotle, student of Plato, teacher of Alexander the Great, and arguably **one of the most influential philosophers of all time**, dies on Euboea.

312 Construction begins on the **first Roman aqueduct** for supplying water, the **Aqua Appia**, and the **Via Appia**, which later becomes the main supply road linking Rome and Capua.

300 **Zeno of Citium** founds the **Stoic school of philosophy** in Athens.

299 The Greek architect Sostratus of Cnidus builds the **Lighthouse of Alexandria** on the former island of **Pharos**.

288 **Ptolemy II Philadelphus** builds the world famous **Library of Alexandria**. It makes the city the center of Hellenistic scholarship.

264 The **first gladiatorial combats** take place in **Rome**, which later become an integral part of mass entertainment in Rome.

250 In the Indian **Maurya Empire**, Ashoka convenes a Buddhist council, thus creating the conditions for the **propagation of Buddhism** throughout India.

213 To eradicate feudalistic traditions in China, Emperor **Qin Shi Huangdi** has all **books confiscated and burned**, including those of Confucius.

212 **Archimedes**, one of the most significant mathematicians and physicists of Antiquity, dies in Syracuse.

200 **Shintoism** is practiced in prehistoric **Japan**. To this day, this **nature-based religion**, along with Buddhism, is the religion that culturally shapes Japan.

300 | **250** | **200**

336 **Philip II of Macedonia** is murdered; his son, the future **Alexander the Great**, is made king.

332 **Alexander the Great** conquers **Egypt** and a year later founds the most important city named after him, **Alexandria**.

330 Following another victory by Alexander the Great at Gaugamela, the **Persian Empire collapses** for good. Alexander declares himself **"King of Asia."**

323 The **Seleucid Dynasty** emerges out of the collapsed empire of **Alexander the Great** who has died on June 13 in Babylon.

322 The **Maurya empire** emerges in **northern India** and rapidly expands.

305 **Ptolemy I**, one of Alexander the Great's generals, officially assumes rule over **Egypt**, thus founding the **Ptolemaic dynasty**.

287 The **Lex Hortensia** ends the class wars in **Rome**. All resolutions passed by plebeians are made binding on all citizens, giving **plebeians equal status with the patricians**.

281 The **Wars of the Diadochi** end with the victory of **Seleucus I** over Lysimachus at the **Battle of Corupedium**.

279 **Pyrrhic victory: Pyrrhus**, king of the Molossians in Epirus, invades lower Italy and, with **heavy loses**, defeats a Roman army.

277 **Antigonus II Gonatas** firmly establishes the **Antigonid dynasty in Macedonia**, which lasts until 168.

270 **Ashoka** becomes ruler of the **Maurya Empire** and by 230 b.c. has conquered almost the entire **Indian subcontinent**.

264 Due to a conflict of interest in **Sicily**, the **First Punic War** breaks out between **Rome** and **Carthage**.

263 After his victory over the Seleucids at Sardes, Eumenes I establishes the independent **kingdom of Pergamon** in Asia Minor.

216 In the **Battle at Cannae** on the Apulian plain, **Hannibal's mounted army**, despite having less men, inflicts the **worst defeat on the Romans** to date.

215 **Philip V** of Macedonia seeks to expand into Italy in alliance with Carthage and triggers the **First Macedonian War**.

212 The Roman army commanded by **Marcellus** is able to capture **Syracuse**, which is made into a **Roman provincial capital**.

209 **Roman armies** successfully attack **Carthaginian bases in Spain**.

206 Emperor Gaodi founds the **Han Dynasty**, which rules China—with interruptions—for 400 years.

205 The **First Macedonian War** ends with the **Peace of Phoenice**, which secures the status quo and allows Macedonia to retain its rule over Greece.

202 The victory of the Roman general **Scipio Africanus the Elder** at Zama in North Africa decides the **Second Punic War** in favor of **Rome**.

201 Rome imposes harsh peace terms on **Carthage**. Its territory is reduced to Africa, and Rome becomes the hegemonic power in the western Mediterranean.

200 **Germanic settlements** gradually expand from Europe's north down into the region of the **Rhine** and **Danube**.

197 **Rome** divides the coastal region of the **Iberian Peninsula** into two provinces.

197 The **Second Macedonian War** that broke out three years earlier is decided in Rome's favor by the victory at **Kynoskephalai**. Macedonia loses control over Greece.

188 The Armenian satrap (governor) **Artaxias** separates from the **Seleucid Empire** and founds the **Kingdom of Armenia**.

184 The **Maurya Empire** in India crumbles after the death of King Brhadrathas.

168/67 At the **Battle of Pydna**, the Macedonian king Perseus is defeated by the Romans. **Macedonia** is made a **Roman province**.

163 Following the **Maccabean Revolt** (since 167), the **Jews** force a break with the **Seleucid Empire** and found a minor state in Judea.

247–238 In Persia, the **Parni tribe** under **Arsaces I** breaks with the Seleucid Empire. The **Parthian Empire** under the Arsacid dynasty is created, which remains in power until 224 a.d.

241 The **Roman fleet** defeats the Carthaginians in the **Battle of the Aegates Islands**. Sicily falls to Rome, with the exception of the Kingdom of Syracuse. Rome has now established undisputed hegemony over Italy.

221 King **Zheng of Qin** unites all the various parts of China for the first time and establishes an **emperorship in China**.

218 The **Carthaginian general Hannibal** marches his army from Spain, across the **Alps**, and invades northern Italy. The **Second Punic War** has begun.

333 After victories at Abydos and Gordion, **Alexander the Great** decidedly defeats the Persian king **Darius III** at Issus.

HISTORICAL EVENTS

The Persian Wars
The first successful defense against a Persian army at Marathon strengthened the Greeks' self-confidence for the following encounters.

The Greek cities in Asia Minor rose up in revolt against Persian rule in 500 B.C. The uprising was the beginning of a long conflict between the Persians and the Greeks, which finally ended with the destruction of the Achaemenid Empire by Alexander the Great in **330**. After Darius I had crushed the rebellion in **494**, he wanted to launch the subjugation of Greece with a punitive action against Athens. An alliance between Athens and Sparta led by the Athenian Miltiades, however, was able to defeat a much larger army at Marathon in **490**. The messenger, who rushed from there to Athens and collapsed dead after making his report of the victory, is considered to be an invention of Roman historians. Hereafter, Athens armed its fleets under the statesman Themistocles. The defeat in the naval Battle of Salamis in **480** and at Plataiai in 479 forced the Persian king Xerxes I to retreat and reinforced Greek awareness of their cultural identity.

In the Battle of Salamis in September 480 B.C., the Greeks, commanded by the Athenian Themistocles, inflicted a painful defeat on the Persian king Xerxes.

The Peloponnesian War
The victory in 404 B.C. over Athens in the decades-long fratricidal war made Sparta the leading power in Hellas.

Following the Persian wars, Athens was the hegemonic power in Greece. With the help of the Delian League founded in **477** B.C., the city-state controlled the eastern Mediterranean and suppressed the other members of the naval alliance. Sparta alone, on the Peloponnesian Peninsula, defied the Athenian claim to power. In **461** and again in **431**, open warfare broke out between Sparta and Athens and their respective allies. The self-indulgent Athenian politics hindered lasting peace agreements. Sparta was only able to defeat the Athenian fleet in **405** in an alliance with the Persians. After a siege of their city, the Athenians were forced to capitulate in **404**. For a short time, Sparta held supreme power, but the city-states eventually weakened each other. In the end, Greece came under Macedonian control in **359**.

Greek sculpture of a fallen warrior

The Celts
The attack by the Celtic Gauls in the year 387 B.C. was a traumatic experience for the Romans.

Around **450 B.C.**, the Celts began spreading out in western and central Europe. From their heartland in present-day western France and southern Germany, Celtic tribes penetrated into Greece, where they plundered Delphi in 279. A short time later they were given a permanent settlement area in Galatia in central Anatolia. Other Celtic groups pushed into Italy, overcame a Roman army on the river Allia, and occupied the city of Rome in **387**, with the exception of the capitol. They could only be forced to withdraw after being paid a ransom. Romans and Greeks describe the Celts as "underdeveloped barbarians"—unjustly. Even if the Celts knew no form of writing, they still had developed a sophisticated civilization. They resided in permanent villages and lived from trade, farming, and animal husbandry. Particularly metalworking and the mining of ores, for which the Celts had set up large mines, attained a high level. At the head of a strictly hierarchically ordered society stood first kings and later select noble families. The Celts, however, did not de-

Under the leadership of Brennus, Celtic tribes conquered and sacked the city of Rome.

velop a unified state. Their foes took advantage of the enmity among the various tribes. By **51 B.C.**, the Celtic Gauls had been subdued by Julius Caesar; in Britannia there was one last uprising against the Romans in **61 A.D.**

Maurya Empire
Ashoka subjugated almost the entire Indian subcontinent. Then the ruler turned to Buddhism and tried to bring peace and prosperity to his subjects.

Starting in the region of Magadha in present-day Bihar, Chandragupta Maurya drove the successors of Alexander the Great out of the Indus Valley in **322** B.C., laying the foundation for the rise of the Maurya Empire. Starting in **270**, the third Maurya ruler, Ashoka, expanded the empire over almost the entire Indian subcontinent. Ashoka is considered the most important ruler of India in Antiquity not only because of his immense territorial gains but also because he was a prominent promoter of Buddhism. Ashoka turned to the teachings of Buddha after he had become acquainted with the brutality of war during his military campaigns. This experience made him reject further conquests on principle, and he regarded peace and tolerance as supreme virtues. He also called upon his subjects to be nonviolent. Ashoka strove to establish a type of welfare state and is the first documented proponent of such a concept. Apparently his contemporaries greatly objected. At any rate, reports of corresponding institutional reforms have not survived.

The Great Stupa at Sanchi built by Ashoka

The Chinese Empire

In 221 B.C., Qin Shi Huang became the first emperor of a unified China and thus founded a tradition that lasted for over 2,000 years.

The Chinese area of influence expanded dramatically through campaigns of conquest in the time of the Zhou Dynasty around **771 B.C.** The rulers of the Zhou divided the newly gained land among allied clan leaders, who increasingly ruled autonomously. During the Warring States Period from 481 to 221 B.C., seven of them contended for power. In the end, the centrally administered, West Chinese state of Qin prevailed. King Zheng of Qin founded a unified Chinese state in **221** and called himself "Shi Huangdi," the "First Emperor." A tightly organized central administration replaced the old feudal system. Within a few years the script and currency became standardized, comprehensive state infrastructure measures were introduced, and the building of the Great Wall of China was begun. While he was still alive, Zheng built a massive tomb with thousands of terra-cotta statues. By 206, only four years after Zheng's death, his family had already been ousted by the Han dynasty.

Life-size statues in the tomb of the first Chinese emperor discovered in 1974

The Punic Wars

Rome was facing its downfall in 218 B.C. after the Carthaginian general Hannibal's successful march across the Alps.

In the 3rd century B.C., the North African trading empire of the Carthaginians, called "Poeni" by the Romans, was Rome's main rival in the western Mediterranean. In the First Punic War from **264** to **241**, Rome had won extensive control of Sicily and Sardinia. The Carthaginian statesman and general Hannibal, however, did not want to bow down to the harsh conditions of peace. His plan was to win over the Roman allies and with their help defeat the Romans in their own backyard. Starting out in Carthaginian-occupied Spain in **218**, he traveled in a forced march with 60,000 soldiers and riders, as well as 37 war elephants, across the Alps into northern Italy. Hannibal defeated the Romans in a series of battles; at Cannae alone in **216** he destroyed eight legions. Yet he was still unable to dissolve the system of Roman alliances. The turning point came with Rome's successful counteroffensive that began in **209**. The Romans landed in North Africa, and Hannibal was forced to return to his homeland. He had to submit to a crushing defeat at Zama in **202**. In 183, he committed suicide while in exile in Asia Minor. A third war beginning in **149** led to the ultimate fall of Carthage. In **146** the Romans leveled the city and made slaves of the population.

Hannibal's war elephants in a skirmish between Carthaginians and Romans

The Spartacus Revolt

The Thracian gladiator Spartacus led the greatest slave revolt in the Roman Empire from 73 to 71 B.C.

As in all ancient societies, the economy in the Roman Empire was essentially dependent upon slave labor. Slaves did not form a homogenous group. They could perform heavy labor in the fields or be respected physicians working in the households of the Patricians. With the expansion of the empire, the number of prisoners of war who were sold into slavery increased. As their situation was becoming increasingly precarious, they began rebelling repeatedly after **136 B.C.** The most prominent slave uprising broke out in **73**. Spartacus, an escaped gladiator, amassed an army of almost 60,000 slaves and scored numerous military victories on his march to the north. In **71**

Gladiators fighting in the arena

Spartacus was defeated at Tarent and fell in battle. The surviving slaves were crucified along the Via Appia as a warning to others.

Some sixty people were involved in the assassination of Caesar in 44 B.C.

The Era of Caesar

On the Ides of March, 44 B.C., the Roman statesman and general Gaius Julius Caesar was murdered—shortly after being appointed dictator for life.

Social tension and partisan clashes between the Patricians and Plebeians in Rome from **133** to **121 B.C.** provoked a severe crisis in the republican institutions. Political careers were primarily determined by military success. By **31**, the empire was practically in a constant state of civil war that was only interrupted when Sulla took control of Rome in 82. In this political jungle, Caesar fought his way to the top of the state in just a few years. He was part of the "First Triumvirate" instituted in **60/59**, along with Pompeius and Crassus, and became governor in southern France, where he strengthened his power base by conquering all of Gaul in fierce battles by **51**. He had rid himself of all rivals by **46** and during his autocratic rule implemented progressive reforms like the introduction of the Julian calendar. In **44** Caesar fell victim to a conspiracy in which his pro-republican stepson Brutus was involved. Caesar had a significant lasting effect on history. He was a role model for his nephew Octavian, who later became emperor; also the titles "Zar" and "Kaiser" were derived from his name.

17 Banished in 8 A.D., the noted Roman poet **Ovid** (*Metamorphoses, The Loves*) dies in exile at Tomis on the Black Sea.

27 The wooden **amphitheater** in the town of **Fidenae** collapses. An ensuing **fire** causes the death of some 20,000 people.

40 The so-called **illusionism style** in Pompeian wall painting, characterized by its rich ornamentation, becomes popular.

44 The **geographer Pomponius Mela** writes the earliest work of geography in Latin literature, *De chorographia libri tres*.

70 **Mark the Evangelist** describes for the first time the **life and work of Jesus of Nazareth**. His work is later followed by the gospels of the evangelists Matthew, Luke, and John.

79 The cities of **Pompeii** and **Herculaneum** are totally destroyed by the eruption of **Mt. Vesuvius**. Nearly the entire population dies.

80 In **Rome**, Emperor Titus dedicates the Flavian Amphitheater, better known as the **Coliseum**. It accommodates around 60,000 spectators.

105 Cai Lun, an imperial court official in **China**, discovers a method of **producing paper**.

118 At Emperor Hadrian's command, the **construction of the Pantheon** begins in **Rome**. Its dome remains the largest in the world up to the modern age.

140 The Greek scholar **Ptolemy** writes the *Almagest*, the standard work of **mathematical astronomy**. The treatise supports the **geocentric model of the universe** that was not refuted until over 1,300 years later.

1 — **50** — **100** — **150**

6 **Judea** is placed directly under **Roman administration** and integrated into the Roman province of Syria.

9 **Arminius**, a chieftain of the **Germanic Cherusci**, wipes out three legions of Roman Governor Varus in the **Battle of the Teutoburg Forest**.

9 In **China**, **Wang Mang** becomes emperor and establishes the **Xin dynasty**, which only lasts until 23.

14 The Roman **Emperor Augustus** dies Aug. 19 in Nola near Naples. His stepson **Tiberius** becomes his successor.

14 The Roman general **Germanicus** begins his campaigns in **Germanic territory** that last until 16 but remain without resounding success.

19 **Goths** invade the territory of the **Marcomanni** and topple the first Germanic kingdom under King Maroboduus.

25 **Liu Xiu** founds the eastern Han dynasty in **China**.

28 A **revolt** against Roman rule and taxation arises in **Frisia**, Germania. The Frisian rebels are brutally defeated by the Roman army.

30 According to the Bible, **Jesus of Nazareth** is sentenced to death by the Roman governor, Pontius Pilate, in Jerusalem. A new religion emerges with his followers believing he was the Jewish Moshiac (messiah).

37 **Caligula** follows Tiberius as **Roman emperor**. His four-year rule is marked by despotism, megalomania, and brutality. He is murdered in 41 and his uncle Claudius succeeds him.

43 The Roman Emperor Claudius conquers **southern Britannia** and turns it into a **Roman province**.

"Let them hate so long as they fear."

Caligula, Roman Emperor, 37–41

46 After Rhoemetalces III is murdered by his wife, **Thracia** is incorporated into the **Roman Empire**.

46/47 The **Christian apostle Paul** begins his **missionary travels** in the eastern Mediterranean.

54 The **Roman Emperor Claudius is poisoned** by his wife on Oct. 13. The reign of his successor, **Nero**, becomes increasingly despotic after 59.

61 **Queen Boudicca** leads the **Celts** in Britannia in a **revolt** against the Roman occupiers. The uprising is crushed.

64 **Rome** is almost completely **destroyed by fire** on July 18–19. Emperor Nero accuses the Christians and initiates the **first persecution of the Christians**.

68/69 During the **Year of the Four Emperors**, four military leaders are declared emperor by their troops. In the end, **Flavius Vespasian** prevails.

70 **Titus** ends the **Jewish War** by conquering Jerusalem and destroying the Jewish Temple.

73 In Judea, the fortress of **Masada** on the Dead Sea falls. It is the **last bastion of Jewish resistance** to Roman rule. The besieged Jews commit **mass suicide**.

73 The **Chinese Han empire** starts its **expansion into Central Asia** and conquers Turkistan in 89.

85 The Romans erect a **border defense line** between the Rhine and the Danube. The **Limes** is meant to protect Roman Germania against invasion.

100 The north Indian empire of **Kushan** experiences a cultural and territorial blossoming around the turn of the century. Its most important ruler is the Buddhist **Kanishka I**, probably until c. 120.

96 The election of **Nerva** as Roman emperor ushers in the era of the **adoptive emperors**. Dynastic succession is abolished.

98 Nerva's co-regent, **Trajan**, follows his adopted father as Roman emperor. He begins an aggressive policy of expansion on the eastern borders of the empire.

106 **Trajan** conquers the **Dacians** in present-day Romania and the **Nabataeans** in present-day Jordan. Their territories are made **Roman provinces**.

117 With the **conquests of Armenia, Assyria, and Mesopotamia** by Trajan, the Roman Empire reaches its greatest extent for a short time.

117 **Hadrian's coronation** ushers in the **golden age of the Roman Empire**. He visits almost all of the provinces, follows a **defensive foreign policy**, and continues the building of Rome into a global city.

130 During a visit to Jerusalem, Emperor Hadrian decides to rebuild the city under the name **Aelia Capitolina**.

132 Once again, a **revolt** against Roman occupation breaks out in Judea, this time led by **Simon Bar Kochba**.

135 The Romans crush the **Bar Kochba revolt**. Jerusalem is made a **Roman provincial city** and Judea is again integrated into the Province of Syria.

144 **Unrest** flares up in **Mauritania**. Roman troops settle the rebellions by 150.

150 The **Champa kingdom** emerges on the territory of present-day **Vietnam**.

150 The **Nok civilization** blossoms in **West Africa**. Terra-cotta figures and utensils give evidence of a high state of cultural development in this region.

Beginning of the Christian Era

1–500 A.D.

At the beginning of the Christian era, the Roman Empire was at the zenith of its cultural and political power. From their magnificently built capital of Rome, the emperors reigned over a blossoming empire that stretched from a major portion of Britannia to the coasts of the entire Mediterranean, all the way to the territory of the Black Sea. The Romans' ability to integrate foreign cultures, rituals of power, and new religions like emerging Christianity reached its political and economic limits by the middle of the third century. Despite stubborn resistance, the Latin West of the Roman Empire finally collapsed in 476 under the pressure of invading Germanic tribes and Huns. "New Rome" was formed in the Greek East around Constantinople, the capital of Byzantium. The Christian-dominated Byzantine Empire began to experience a golden age. The Roman imperial concept also lived on in the West and was once again revived in the Early Middle Ages with the imperial coronation of Charlemagne in 800.

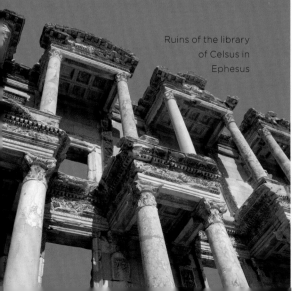

Ruins of the library of Celsus in Ephesus

HISTORICAL FIGURES

Paul (died c. 64 A.D.)
With his missionary travels, the Apostle of Jesus laid the foundation for the spread of Christianity.

Paul, a Jew from Tarsus in Cilicia, was originally a tent maker. At an early age, he was sent to Jerusalem to receive his education at a rabbinical school. As an orthodox Pharisee, Paul participated in the persecution of Christians. After Jesus had appeared to him in a dream, he became an ardent champion of Christianity. At the council of Apostles in 48–49 in Jerusalem, Paul convinced the followers of Jesus to accept non-Jews into their ranks, opening the new faith to the broad masses. On his missionary journeys through Asia Minor and Greece from **46–47**, he founded many Christian congregations. At the end of the 50s, he was arrested in Jerusalem and transferred to Rome. The exact manner of his death in 64 remains unknown.

Diocletian (c. 240 – c. 316 A.D.)
With a sweeping reorganization of the power structure, Emperor Diocletian brought on the final phase of the Roman Empire.

Diocletian ended the crisis of the third century that had begun in **235** and restored Rome's power for a short time. The soldier of humble beginnings was made emperor by the Roman army in 284. To address the empire's political instability and provide a greater control of the provinces, he instituted a tetrarchy in **293**, dividing imperial power among four rulers: two Augusti ("emperors") appointed two subordinate Caesars ("junior emperors"). In conflicts of interest, Diocletian as "senior emperor" had the final word. He also strove to revive ancient Roman beliefs and initiated the last great Christian persecutions in 303. After his abdication in 305, power struggles quickly destroyed the tetrarchic system and divided the Roman world.

Attila (c. 395–453 A.D.)
With his campaigns of conquest, the legendary king of the Huns brought fear and terror to the Roman world.

"The Scourge of God," as Christians later called Attila, became king of the Huns in **434**. The Huns were nomadic horsemen who penetrated into Europe from the steppes of Asia in the late 4th century and controlled a territory stretching from the Baltic Sea to present-day Ukraine. From **447** on, Attila was able to extort increased tribute from the Eastern Romans through his campaigns waged against them. Despite being defeated in **451** by the Roman general Aëtius in the Battle of the Catalaunian Plains in Gaul, he invaded Italy a year later. Pope Leo Diocletian I, however, dissuaded him from sacking Rome. Attila died in 453 under mysterious circumstances, whereupon the Hunnic Empire quickly collapsed.

Theodoric the Great (451/56–526 A.D.)
In a time of turmoil, the king of the Ostrogoths provided Italy with a period of peace lasting almost 30 years.

Theodoric was raised at the imperial court in Constantinople until he succeeded his father as king of the Ostrogoths in 471. In 488, his sovereign, the Eastern Roman emperor, tasked him with liberating Italy from the rule of the Germanic king Odoacer. After many battles, Theodoric killed Odoacer in **493**. As new sovereign of Italy, Theodoric repressed the influence of the Eastern Roman Empire through a clever policy of marriage and alliance. From Ravenna, he autonomously ruled an empire that stretched all the way from the Danube to Sicily. Domestically, Theodoric sought a balance between the Roman and Germanic cultures. He filled high offices with capable Romans. The military, however, was reserved for the Ostrogoths.

306 Diocletian's thermal baths are completed. As the largest building in **Rome**, it provides room for 3,000 bathers.

315 Arch of Constantine: Commissioned by the Senate, a **triumphal arch** is built in Rome honoring Emperor Constantine.

361 Martin of Tours founds the **first Christian monastery** in the Western world in Ligugé.

369 The Arian bishop **Ulfilas (Wulfila) translates the Bible** into Gothic for missionary purposes. In the process, he develops the first Germanic written language.

383 Jerome finishes a Latin translation of the Bible; his *Vulgata* becomes generally accepted by the 8th–9th century. The practice of **translating the Bible** is not taken up again until the Reformation.

426 Augustine, one of the most significant church fathers of Western Christianity, completes his theological history, *City of God*.

450 Teotihuacán in Central Mexico reaches its cultural zenith and influences a major part of Mesoamerica.

477 King Kassapa I of Ceylon moves into his marble **palace** surrounded by gardens on a rock overlooking his capital, Sigiriya. The ruins, decorated with wall paintings, are a world cultural heritage site today.

500 Originating in **China**, the knowledge of **bell making** reaches Europe.

500 Chaturanga is invented in **India**. It is the earliest known predecessor of the modern chess game as it is known today.

---

350   **400**   **450**   **500**

---

330 The **Ethiopian kingdom of Axum** reaches the zenith of its power under **King Ezana**. He introduces Coptic Christianity as the state religion.

350 The **Franks** expand their area of settlement far into the **northwest of present-day France**.

351 Roman Emperor **Constantius II** defeats the Frankish usurper Magnus Magnentius at Mursa and becomes the **sole ruler** in the empire until 361.

361 After the death of Constantius II, **Julian Apostata** ("the Apostate") is declared Roman emperor. During his short reign, Christianity is suppressed and the **ancient belief in the Roman gods is reanimated**.

363 Roman Emperor **Jovian** concludes a thirty-year peace pact with the Persian King **Shapur II** and by doing so accepts **considerable losses of territory** in the East.

365 **Imperial power** in the Roman Empire is once again divided. **Valentinian I** rules in the West and his brother, **Valens**, is made co-emperor in the East.

370 Scots and Saxons invading Britannia are successfully **repulsed by the Romans**.

375 Huns coming from China invade Eastern Europe and displace the **Goths** living in the Balkans, initiating the **Migration Period**.

378 The Visigoths defeat the armies of the Eastern Roman Emperor Valens at the **Battle of Adrianople**. They push further into the Balkans.

379 After the death of Valens, **Theodosius I** is declared co-emperor of the Eastern Roman Empire.

382 **Theodosius I** ends the dispute with the **Visigoths** and allows them to settle in the Roman Empire (Thracia) as allies. They are assured general autonomy in exchange for military service.

391 **Theodosius I** bans **heathen cults** to **reinforce Christianity** and establish it as state religion.

395 After the death of Emperor Theodosius I, **the Roman Empire splits in two**. His son Honorius becomes emperor of the **Western Roman Empire**, and his son Arcadius rules in the **Eastern Roman Empire of Constantinople**.

401 **Visigoths** penetrate into northern Italy from out of the Balkans and lay siege to Milan.

402 The highest-ranking general of the Western Roman Empire, **Stilicho**, defeats the Visigoths at Pollentia and relocates the capital to **Ravenna**.

406 The Romans withdraw from the empire's borders in Germania and Britannia. As a result, **Vandals**, **Burgundians**, **Suevi**, and other Germanic tribes advance unimpeded into the Roman Empire.

410 Visigoths led by **King Alaric I** take Rome on Aug. 24 and plunder the city for three days.

413 The **Burgundians** are given territory on the Rhine by Western Roman Emperor Honorius and found their first kingdom under King Gundahar.

418 The **Visigoth King Wallia** founds the **Tolosanian kingdom** in southwestern Gaul with Toulouse as its capital. It separates from Rome in 430.

425 Theodosius II names **Valentinian III** emperor of the Western Roman Empire. His power is dependent upon his highest military commander, **Flavius Aëtius**.

429 The **Vandals** cross the strait of Gibraltar to **North Africa** and found a kingdom independent of Rome under King Geiseric.

434 Attila becomes **king of the Huns**. From 445 he reigns as sole ruler.

436 Aided by the Huns, the Western Roman general **Aëtius** crushes the **Burgundian kingdom** on the Rhine, but allows the Burgundians to settle south of Lake Geneva in 443.

440 On Sept. 29, **Leo I** is made bishop of Rome. He establishes the **papal primacy** over the church.

449 The Huns led by King **Attila** invade **Dacia** and **Greece** and exact huge tribute payments from the Romans.

450 The Germanic tribes of the **Angles**, **Saxons**, and **Jutes** cross over to **Britannia** and begin colonization.

451 The **Council of Chalcedon** condemns monophysitic teachings as heresy. Nevertheless, the concept of the **absolute divinity of Christ** survives in many oriental churches.

451 In the **Battle of the Catalaunian Plains**, the Franks, Visigoths, and other Germanic tribes allied with the Romans under Aëtius defeat the **Huns** and force them to retreat.

454 In southeastern Europe the **Gepid King Ardaric** successfully rises up against **Hun sovereignity** and founds his own kingdom in the Carpathian Basin.

455 After the murder of Emperor Valentinian III, the **Western Roman Empire begins to crumble**. The Vandals under King Geiseric take **Rome** without a fight and plunder the city for two weeks.

476 With the **disposition of Emperor Romulus Augustulus** and the elevation of the Germanic military leader **Odoacer** to king in Italy, the **Western Roman Empire** is extinguished.

486 The **Merovingian Clovis I** defeats Syagrius, the last Roman governor in Gaul at Soissons, thus founding the **Frankish kingdom**.

493 The Ostrogoth king, **Theodoric the Great**, personally kills King Odoacer in Ravenna and founds the **Ostrogothic kingdom** in Italy.

498 After a victory over the Alemanni, **Clovis I** converts to Catholicism in Reims in 498 and establishes France's centuries-long close relationship with the **Roman Catholic church**.

160 The use of **gold** coins as **currency** declines in Rome.

166 A **plague epidemic** brought from the Parthian Empire leads to a massive **decimation of the Roman population**.

171/72 Aurelius's *Meditations*, reflections and aphorisms on life and governance, show the **Roman emperor** to be a significant **proponent of Stoicism**.

220 The art of **Feng Shui** reaches its zenith at the end of the Han dynasty.

224 **Zoroastrianism** gains strength under the Sassanids in the **Neo-Persian Empire**.

230 **Tertullian**, author and "father of Latin Christianity," dies in North Africa.

250 The **mathematician Diophantus of Alexandria**, the "father of algebra," writes his *Arithmetica*, the most important work on Algebra in Antiquity.

270 The **Greek philosopher Plotinus**, the founder of **Neoplatonism**, dies in Campania.

270 To protect **Rome**, Emperor Aurelian builds a nearly 12 mile-long **city wall** that still exists today.

274 In **Rome**, the **sun god cult** is promoted by the state.

277 **Mani**, the founder of **Manichaeism**, an influential religious movement of late Antiquity, dies in Persia.

300 Up until the 4th century, **Christians** in the Roman Empire bury their dead in a system of underground tombs known as **catacombs**.

300 **Vatsyayana Mallanaga** completes the *Kamasutra* in India. The manual of love becomes popular reading in Europe after about 1900.

200 — 250 — 300

161 The **"philosopher on the throne," Marcus Aurelius**, comes to power in Rome.

161 The Parthian invasion of Roman-occupied Armenia triggers a four-year **Roman-Parthian war** in the eastern Mediterranean. In the peace settlement of 166, Mesopotamia falls to Rome again.

166 **Rome** sends an **ambassador to China** for the first time to promote foreign trade.

174 The **Marcomanni**, who invaded the Roman Empire from out of Bohemia in 166–67, **are repulsed after heavy fighting**.

177 **Commodus** is given the title **Augustus**, thus ending the system of **adoptive emperors**.

180 After fending off a further **attack by the Marcomanni** in 177, Roman forces occupy **Bohemia** and **Moravia**.

180 After the death of Marcus Aurelius on March 17, his biological son, **Commodus**, is made the **new Roman emperor**. His reign becomes despotic after 183.

184 The religious revolutionary movement of the **"Yellow Turbans"** precipitates the **fall of the Han dynasty in China**.

193 The assassination of the Roman Emperor **Commodus** in 192 is followed by a struggle for the throne between four military leaders. **Septimus Severus** emerges as successor in April and implements far-reaching administrative and military reforms.

200 The heretofore warring **Germanic tribes** begin to join together into major tribes such as the **Alamanni** and the **Franks**.

200 **Funan** in southern Cambodia develops into a trading center between East and West. For 300 years Funan is the **largest and most prosperous state in Southeast Asia**.

200 The first embryonic **Mayan states** develop in the tropical forests of Central America. A royal dynasty becomes established in Tikal (Guatemala); **large cities** and monumental **temple complexes** arise.

208 Renewed fighting between **Romans** and **Caledonians** flares up in **Britannia**.

211 **Caracalla**, son of Septimius Severus, becomes the **sole ruler of Rome** and institutes a **regime of terror**. In the **Constitutio Antoniniana**, he bestows full Roman **citizenship** on all free men in the empire.

216 **Mani** is born in present-day Iran. A devout Zoroastrian, he becomes the prophet and founder of **Manichaeism**.

224 **Ardashir I** of the **Sassanid dynasty** overthrows the last Parthian king, Artabanos IV, and founds a new **Persian empire** on the territory of present-day Iran and Iraq.

235 Following the assassination of Severus Alexander, the era of the **"Barracks emperors"** begins. By 284, 22 emperors have been elevated by the army to rule the **Roman Empire**.

241 **Shapur I** assumes power in the **Sassanid empire**. He pursues an aggressive foreign policy against Rome.

249 The **first general persecution of Christians in the Roman Empire** occurs under Emperor Decius.

259 After a victory over the Franks in **Gaul**, the usurper **Postumus** declares a Roman **"Gallic Empire."**

260 In a battle between the armies of the Roman Empire and Sassanid forces at **Edessa**, **Roman Emperor Valerian is captured by the Persians**, and his entire army is crushed.

265 **China** is briefly reunited under the Western **Jin dynasty** before breaking apart again under the Eastern Jin dynasty in 316.

274 **Aurelian** restores the **unity of the Roman Empire** after he crushes the rebel empire of **Queen Zenobia** in Palmyra (Syria) and the rebel "Gallic Empire" of Tetricus in Gaul in 272–73.

293 To avoid further usurpations and manage the many challenges, **Emperor Diocletian** institutes the **tetrarchy** in the Roman Empire: one emperor in the West, one in the East, each with a subordinate emperor, called a Caesar.

300 The **kingdom of Ghana** emerges in West Africa.

300 **Armenia** under King Tiridates III becomes the first state to make **Christianity** its **state religion**.

313 Roman Emperor **Constanine** and co-Emperor Licinius order the **Edit of Milan** proclaiming religious **freedom in the empire**.

320 **Chandragupta I** founds the **Gupta empire**, which subjugates almost all of northern India by 350.

325 **Arianism** is discarded as a religious belief at the **Council of Nicaea**.

312 On Oct. 28, **Constantine I** defeats Maxentius, his rival in the West, in the **Battle of the Milvian Bridge** outside Rome and becomes the sole ruler of the Roman Empire.

HISTORICAL EVENTS

The Battle of the Teutoburg Forest, in which Germanic tribes annihilated three Roman legions, inspired nationalistic thought in the newly founded German Empire of the 19th century.

Battle of the Teutoburg Forest
The disastrous defeat at the hands of the Germanic Prince Arminius ended Roman plans of expansion.

Ever since the attack by the Cimbri and Teutons in **113 B.C.**, Germanic tribes had been repeatedly threatening the borders of the Roman Empire. The Germanic tribes continued to be a danger even after Caesar had occupied Gaul in **51 B.C.** and the empire's boundary had been advanced to the Rhine and Danube. By the beginning of the Christian era, the Romans were able to control the territory between the Baltic Sea, the Rhine, and the Elbe. When governor Varus tried to impose Roman law in Germania, there was a revolt. In a battle against the Germanic prince Arminius in **9 A.D.**, the Romans lost 15,000 soldiers. After the punitive expeditions that started in **14** had failed, Emperor Tiberius abandoned his plans of conquest. After **85**, the Romans erected the Limes, a defensive bulwark between the Rhine and the Danube. Nonetheless, there was lively contact across the border, and Roman influence fundamentally changed the societies of the Germanic peoples.

"Imperial Madness"
After a huge fire in the city of Rome in 64 A.D., the first major persecution of Christians took place under the despotic rule of the eccentric Roman emperor Nero.

His possession of unlimited power induced Roman emperor Nero to self-indulgence and megalomanic acts. From **54** on, his reign was marked by monumental building projects and unbridled passions, especially for singing. The emperor went "on tour" for a whole year to perform in public. He killed his rivals and critics—including his mother and his teacher, Seneca. When Rome almost burned to the ground in **64**, he accused the Christians of starting the fire and had them persecuted. Rebelling provincial governors finally drove him to suicide in 68. "What an artist the world loses in me" are said to have been his last words.

Nero's death sentence for a gladiator

Jewish–Roman Wars
After revolting against Roman rule, the Jews were driven out of the "Holy Land."

When in the first half of the first century A.D. religious repression and financial burdens brought on by the Roman occupation in Judea steadily increased, radical nationalistic religious forces gathered strength in the Jewish population. The struggle for an independent theocratical state appeared more urgent than ever before. Finally, in 66, an open rebellion was triggered when the Roman governor confiscated a part of the temple treasure in Jerusalem. By 67 Jewish fighters had been able to bring a major portion of Palestine under their control, but Rome recognized the threat and mobilized its military machinery. Bit by bit, territory was retaken. After heavy fighting, Jerusalem was won back in **70** as well. The fall of Masada in **73**, the last Jewish fortress, marked the final defeat of the revolt. Judea was then completely integrated into the Roman Empire. After a renewed insurrection in **132–135**, the Jews of Jerusalem were forbidden to practice their religion and were not even allowed to enter the city. The Jewish people were scattered into the Diaspora.

The later Roman Emperor Titus had the temple in Jerusalem destroyed in 70 A.D.

Sassanid Empire
The Sassanids founded a new Persian empire in 224 A.D. and became one of Rome's most powerful adversaries in the East.

The god Ahura Mazda hands over the insignia of power to Sassanid King Ardashir I.

Since the dawn of the 3rd century, the Parthian Empire had been in a process of internal dissolution. Beginning in 220, the Sassanid Ardashir steadily built up his power base in the ancient Persian homeland of Persis. He overthrew the last Parthian ruler in **224** and eventually established the dynasty of the Sassanids that reigned until **651**. It was based more on ancient Persian than on Parthian tradition, promoting the spread of the Zoroastrian faith, which was virtually given the status of a state religion. The once-broad autonomy of the provinces was abandoned in favor of a concentration of power in the imperial court. In terms of foreign affairs, the Sassanids saw themselves as heirs to the Achaemenid Empire and pursued an aggressive policy of expansion against the Roman-occupied territories in the East. In **260**, the Roman Emperor Valerian even fell into Persian captivity. Until 298, the advance of the Sassanids was not stopped in Armenia, which turned into a bone of contention between the Romans and the Persians. The conflict with the Persians became a constant in Roman and later Byzantine foreign involvements. Their mutual weakening of each other contributed considerably to the success of Arab expansion that began in **636**.

The Battle of the Milvian Bridge

The triumph of Constantine the Great over his rivals in the West marked the beginning of the triumphant march of Christianity in the Roman Empire.

After the tetrarchic system, introduced by Emperor Diocletian in **293 A.D.**, collapsed after 306, a number of pretenders were fighting over the imperial throne, particularly in the West. In a decisive battle between Constantine and his rival Maxentius at the Milvian Bridge outside the gates of Rome, Constantine emerged as the victor. Now the sole ruler of the Western Empire, he ascribed his success to the Christian god. Immediately before his victory, the sign of a cross is said to have appeared to him in a prophetic dream and a voice proclaimed, "In this sign, you will conquer." Constantine's triumph was the beginning of a golden age for the Christians. An edict of tolerance in **313** granted religious freedom. Constantine, who became the sole ruler of the Roman Empire in 324, integrated the followers of the new religion into the state, issued a pro-Christian legislation, and massively promoted the building of Christian churches. Constantinople (Byzantium), the city named after the emperor, was made the new capital in the East and became the heart of the imperial Roman Christian idea. In **391**, Christianity was officially declared state religion in the Roman Empire, and all heathen cults were banned.

Roman Emperor Constantine I paved the way for the Christianization of the empire.

The Kingdom of Axum

Africa's first Christian kingdom was in full bloom in the 4th century under the rule of King Ezana.

The kingdom of Axum was founded as early as 300 B.C. by southern Arabian immigrants. Named after its capital, Axum was located in the north of present-day Ethiopia and stretched to the shores of the Red Sea. Due to its favorable location, it became a hub of trade between Asia, Africa, and Europe around 250 A.D. bringing about a steady increase in wealth and power. This development reached its zenith under King Ezana. Around **330**, Ezana introduced Coptic Christianity as state religion, bringing Axum politically and culturally closer to Egypt and, above all, closer to Byzantium. The kingdom also reached its greatest extent during this period. To the west, Meroë, the capital of Nubia in present-day Sudan, was probably destroyed, and Yemen was conquered in the 6th century. With the spread of Islam that began in the 7th century, the kingdom of Axum became increasingly isolated, losing its political significance.

Massive stelae in Axum are reminders of a glorious past.

Migration Period

The appearance of the Huns in Eastern Europe in 375 A.D. triggered a series of migrations that lasted for centuries and gave the continent a new face.

The Migration Period was set in motion by Hunnic expansion that displaced the Goths from their Black Sea homeland. For over two hundred years, people were moving across the continent, joining together in tribes, founding kingdoms, and waging wars. The Visigoths plundered Rome in **410** and in **418** founded a kingdom in the south of France. The Vandals moved to Spain and in **429** entered North Africa, where they built a kingdom. The Angles, Saxons, and Jutes began their conquest of Britannia in **450**. The Lombards were the last to settle in Italy in **568**. Roman and Germanic traditions blended in the states that merged in the Western Roman Empire, laying the cornerstone for the culture of the Middle Ages.

Fight between Romans and Ostrogoths

Romulus Augustulus, the last Western Roman emperor, submits to the German Odoacer.

The Empire Splits Apart

The unity of the Roman Empire came to an end in 395 A.D. The empire in the West collapsed in 476, while the empire in the East, or the Byzantine Empire, held on until 1453.

After Diocletian's reform of the Roman Empire in **293**, the administration of the provinces became more and more decentralized. While Rome increasingly lost its significance as capital, Constantinople became established as the new seat of power after 330. When Germanic tribes began penetrating into imperial territory in **378** and settled there after **382** under the nominal sovereignty of the emperor, the disintegration of the empire's unity was inevitable. Theodosius I was the last emperor who ruled over the whole empire. After his death in **395**, however, the empire was divided into an eastern and a western part. While the Eastern Roman Empire became stable in the 5th century, the Western Roman Empire gradually collapsed due to internal power struggles and the continuing invasion and settlement of Germanic tribes. Finally, in **476**, the Germanic military leader Odoacer deposed Romulus Augustulus. From then on, there was only one Roman emperor—in Constantinople.

525 At the request of the pope, the monk **Dionysius Exiguus** formulates a **new system of dating** based on the assumed **birth year of Jesus**. It remains in force in the Christian world until the Gregorian calendar reform of 1582.

534 The codification of Roman law is completed under **Emperor Justinian I**. The **Codex Iustinianus** is the foundation of jurisprudence in modern Europe.

537 **Hagia Sophia:** The church of "Holy Wisdom" is completed in Constantinople. It is the most important surviving example of **early Byzantine architecture.**

550 Emperor Justinian I establishes the Greek Orthodox Saint Catherine's Monastery on **Mt. Sinai**, which still stands today.

555 Knowledge of **silk production** reaches Europe from China by way of Persia.

562 **Procopios of Caesarea**, one of the **most noted historians of Late Antiquity**, dies in Constantinople.

570 The **Christian philosopher and natural scientist, John Philoponus**, presumably dies in Alexandria.

600 **Lamaism**, a special form of Buddhism, takes root in **Tibet**.

620 The production of **porcelain** begins in **China** during the Tang dynasty.

636 **Isidore of Seville**, one of the most important **encyclopedists** of his day, dies. His comprehensive collection of the knowledge of Antiquity significantly influences education in the Middle Ages.

650 From China across Korea to Japan, **Buddhism** spreads all over **East Asia** in the 7th century.

651 Caliph Othman has the **Qur'an**, the holy scriptures of Islam, compiled from surviving oral and written narratives.

---

500 — **550** — **600** — **650**

---

507 The **Visigoths** are decisively defeated by Clovis I in the **Battle of Vouillé** and withdraw to Spain, where they establish a new kingdom with **Toledo** as its capital.

511 After the death of **Clovis I**, the **kingdom of the Franks** is divided among his four sons.

526 The **Ostrogothic kingdom** collapses after Theodoric the Great dies.

527 **Justinian I** is made Eastern Roman emperor on Aug. 1. Together with his wife, Theodora, he seeks to **restore the Roman Empire.**

529 **Benedict of Nursia** founds the first monastery of the Benedictine order named after him on **Monte Cassino** in Italy. His ground-breaking "Rule" for monks becomes influential in Western monasticism.

531 Aided by the **Saxons**, who control large parts of northwestern Germany, the **Merovingian Franks** conquer the **Thuringian kingdom.**

533 The **Byzantine general Belisar** attacks the **Vandal kingdom** in North Africa.

*"Ora et labora et lege —
Pray and work and read."*
Basic rule of the Benedictine monks

534 In the **Battle of Autun**, the Franks under King Clovis I conquer the **Burgundian kingdom.**

540 **Gothic War:** Under the leadership of **Belisar**, the Byzantines conquer Ravenna, the capital of the **Ostrogothic kingdom** in Italy.

540 The **Sassanid king Khosrau I** forms an alliance with the Goths and destroys **Antioch on the Orontes.**

552 **Byzantine armed forces** led by General **Narses** definitely crush the Italian **Ostrogothic kingdom.**

554 Byzantine forces conquer the Mediterranean provinces of the Spanish kingdom of the **Visigoth.**

561 After the death of **Chlothars I**, the Frankish kingdom of the **Merovingians** is divided among his sons into the kingdoms of Neustria, Austrasia, and Burgundy.

568 The **Lombards** under **King Alboin** invade northern Italy and establish a kingdom there with its capital at **Pavia.**

570 **Muhammad**, the founder of Islam, is born in **Mecca.**

572 Following the murder of **King Alboin**, the **kingdom of the Lombards** breaks up into several duchies.

581 General Yang Jian unifies **China**. As Emperor Wendi, he founds the **Sui dynasty**, which is already replaced by the Tang in 618.

584 To reinforce **Byzantine power** in the West, Emperor Maurice I establishes semi-autonomous provinces called exarchates in Ravenna and Carthage.

589 At the **Councils of Toledo**, the Visigoth king Reccared converts from Arianism to **orthodox Catholicism**, which is declared the state religion.

590 On Sept. 3, **Gregory I the Great** becomes the **first monk to be elected pope**. He promotes proselytizing, increases papal possessions, and establishes **Roman papal primacy.**

590 **Agilulf** is designated the **new king of the Lombards** by the Lombardian dukes. He abandons Arianism and draws closer to Catholicism. By 615 he has restored unity in the kingdom.

603 The **Sassanids** in Persia under **King Khosrau II** attack the **Byzantine Empire**. The war lasts until 628–29 and permanently weakens both empires.

610 **Heraclius** becomes **Byzantine emperor**. During his reign lasting until 641, marked by wars against Persia and the Arabs, **Greek** permanently replaces Latin as the **official language.**

618 Gaozu founds the **Tang dynasty**, under which China enjoys a political and cultural flowering until 906.

622 **Hijra: Muhammad** travels with his followers from Mecca to Medina, where he builds up an **Islamic polity**. This year marks the beginning of the **Islamic calendar.**

628 After the **Byzantines defeat the Sassanids** in the **Battle of Nineveh** in 627, Syria, Palestine, and Egypt fall to Byzantium again for a short time. Jerusalem is also won back in 629.

630 **Muhammad** returns to **Mecca**. The city, with the **Kaaba**, becomes the **religious and political heart of Islam.**

632 After the death of **Muhammad**, his senior companion, **Abu Bakr**, is designated the **first Caliph** ("successor") and leader of the faithful. The spread of Islam through **Arab expansion** begins under Abu Bakr and the second caliph, Omar I (from 634).

636 The **Muslims** are victorious over the **Byzantines** in the **Battle of Yarmouk** and conquer Syria. By 640, the Arabs have taken Jerusalem and Ktesiphon (Iraq), the capital of the **Sassanids in Persia.**

646 **Taika Reform:** Japan is reshaped using **China** as a model.

651 After the assassination of the Sassanid ruler, **Yazdegerd III**, all of Iran comes under the control of Muslim Arabs.

656 **Caliph Uthman** is assassinated. In the resulting battles, **Ali Ibn Abi Talib** is victor in the **Battle of the Camel** but is unable to maintain a lasting hold on the caliphate.

661 On Jan. 24, **Caliph Ali Ibn Abi Talib** is murdered. **Muawiyah I** seizes power and founds the **Sunni Umayyad dynasty** in the new capital of **Damascus.**

668 The **kingdom of Silla** conquers the other two kingdoms on the Korean Peninsula and creates a **Korean state.**

680 The **Bulgars** under **Khan Asparuch** found the **first Bulgarian empire** on the lower Danube.

Christianity and Islam

500–1050

The Migration Period, the fall of the Western Roman Empire, and the triumphant march of Christianity mark the end of Late Antiquity and the beginning of the Early Middle Ages. Above all, the Merovingian and Carolingian kingdoms of the Franks, which at times spanned across western and central Europe all the way to Italy and present-day Hungary, influenced the further development of the Christian West. It was a time when secular and religious leaders entered into close relationships, reaching a zenith in the imperial coronation of Charlemagne by the pope in Rome. The church also had a lasting influence on the formation of states in the British Isles, Scandinavia, and Eastern Europe. In parallel to this, the youngest of the world religions, Islam, emerged in the 7th century. The expansion of Muslim Arabs, reaching as far as the Iberian Peninsula and southern Italy, transformed the Mediterranean region forever. Only with great effort was the Byzantine Empire able to maintain its independence and its ancient cultural traditions.

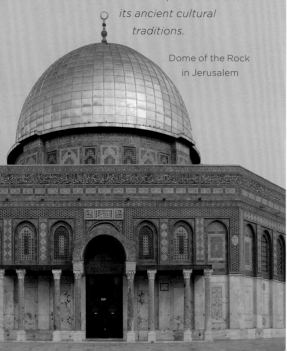

Dome of the Rock
in Jerusalem

HISTORICAL FIGURES

Justinian I (482–565)
The emperor and his wife had a decisive influence on the further development of the Byzantine Empire.

The Eastern Roman Empire reached its first peak after **527** under Justinian I. Many territories of the former Imperium Romanum could be reconquered through wars against the Vandals in North Africa in **533** and the Ostrogoths in Italy between **540** and **552**, even if the territorial gains were short lived. In the East, military campaigns and high tribute payments secured the borders to the Persian Sassanids. The imperial couple sought to settle the religious disputes within Christianity. In Constantinople, Justinian rebuilt the Hagia Sophia, the epitome of Byzantine architecture, by **537**. His most important achievement, however, was in the area of jurisprudence. By **534**, the Codex Iustinianus, a compendium of Roman law, was issued—a cornerstone of legal history that has influenced Western lawmaking to this day.

Muhammad (c. 570–632)
The Arab merchant who is believed to be the "Messenger of God" became the founder of Islam.

Muhammad grew up an orphan, married a wealthy merchant woman in 595, and came in contact with monotheistic teachings while on trading missions. According to legend, the Archangel Gabriel tasked him with converting mankind to Islam, the unconditional devotion to Allah, "the one and only God." "Divine instructions" were recorded in the Qur'an already during his lifetime. In **622,** he moved from the polytheistic city of Mecca to Medina, won many followers, and became the leader of an early Islamic polity. Muhammad conquered Mecca in **630** and made the Kaaba into the central shrine of the new religion. After his death in **632**, his successors, the caliphs, spread Islam beyond Arabia and created a world empire.

Wu Zetian (625–705)
Through her intelligent rule, the empress created the foundation for China's period of prosperity under the Tang dynasty.

History draws an overly negative picture of Wu Zetian, even though the intrigue and murder that gained her power were part of everyday political life at the time. At the age of 12, the merchant's daughter was brought as a concubine to the court of the ruling Tang dynasty that had been in power since **618**. She later married Emperor Gaozong and soon became involved in the affairs of state. In **690**, she deposed her son and mounted the dragon throne as the "Wise and Holy Emperor." She centralized the administration, enlarged the new capital of Luoyang, and proclaimed Buddhism to be state religion. Wu Zetian became ill in 703 and was removed from office by her son. Her descendents in the Tang dynasty remained in power until 906.

Charlemagne (c. 742–804)
The first Western emperor of the Middle Ages is regarded as the "Father of Europe" and founder of the Christian Western World.

Charlemagne was already called "the Great" by his contemporaries. After being crowned king of the Franks in 768, he began to expand his territory. In **772**, he launched a campaign against the Saxons, whom he forcibly converted to Christianity. He conquered the Lombard kingdom in **774**, and in **788** he imposed Frankish sovereignty over Bavaria. To secure his borders, he created a buffer zone of provinces, as in Spain in **801**. Crowned emperor by the pope in Rome in **800**, Charlemagne entered the tradition of the (Western) Roman emperors and established the idea of supreme power. Domestically, he promoted the sciences, standardized the alphabet and coinage, and had magnificent buildings erected. In **843**, Charlemagne's empire was divided among his heirs, creating the nucleus of present-day France and Germany.

868 The scholar, **Muhammad ibn Jabir al-Harrani al-Battani**, considered to be one of the most influential astronomers and mathematicians of the Islamic world, is born in present-day Turkey.

887 The **crossbow** is developed into a military weapon in Europe.

903 The Japanese scholar, **Sugawara no Michizane**, later honored as the **patron saint of Japanese art and science, dies**.

900 **Wind turbines** are used to generate energy in **Persia**.

925 The physician **Al-Razi**, author of an influential **encyclopedia of pharmacology**, dies in Rey, Persia.

942 **Saadia Gaon**, the father of **Jewish religious philosophy**, dies in Babylonia at Sura.

963 The **Monastery of Great Lavra**, the first monastery built on the "Holy Mountain," Mount Athos, is constructed in Greece. It later becomes a religious center of **Christian Orthodoxy**.

976 **Arabic numbers** are used for the first time in a European document.

977 The poet **Firdausi** begins writing his work, *Shahnameh*, the **national epic of Persia**, in Tus.

1000 In Italy, the **fork** is introduced as an **eating utensil** around 1000.

1015 **Bishop Bernward's Doors** are installed in the west wing of the **Hildesheim cathedral**. The set of two cast bronze doors, richly decorated with Biblical pictures, is considered to be the high point of **Ottonian art**.

1025 With his work, *Micrologus de musica*, the Italian music theorist **Guido of Arezzo** establishes the **4-line staff system of musical notation** used to this day.

---

900 — 950 — 1000 — 1050

---

862 **Swedish Vikings** (Varangians) found the Rurik dynasty in the north of **Russia** and establish themselves in **Novgorod**.

866 Sailing up the Thames Estuary, **Danish Vikings** begin conquering portions of the **British Isles**.

871 **Alfred the Great** is crowned king of Wessex; in 878 he retaliates against the Danes; in 886 he occupies London, unites the **Anglo-Saxon kingdoms**, and creates the basis for the formation of the **Kingdom of England**.

872 **Harald Fairhair** defeats an **army of minor Norwegian kings** around this date and imposes his sole **sovereignty**.

874 **Norwegian Vikings** begin settling **Iceland**. The island had been discovered some 14 years earlier.

882 Kievan Rus': **Oleg of Novgorod** unites the territories of the northern and southern Varangian princes, thus founding the **first Russian empire**, with Kiev as its capital.

890 **King Yasovarman I** makes **Angkor** the capital of the emerging Cambodian **Khmer Empire**.

900 The **Toltecs** begin their rise in the central highlands of **Mexico**. Their influence is felt all the way to the Yucatán peninsula.

909 **William I**, Duke of Aquitaine, establishes a monastery in **Cluny**, which becomes the starting point for the Europe-wide **Cluniac reform movement**.

911 The **Carolingians in East Francia die out** with the death of Louis the Child. **Conrad I** is chosen as the new king.

911 In the **Treaty of Saint Clair-sur-Epte**, Charles III the Simple of West Francia allows **Rollo**, leader of the Norman Vikings, to settle in **Normandy**. The later duchy becomes a tightly structured vassal state.

913 The **Christian kingdom of Léon** emerges in northwestern Spain, whose rulers style themselves emperors, in accordance with their claim of hegemony.

913 **Khan Simeon the Great** has himself crowned **emperor** of the **first Bulgarian empire**.

919 The Saxon duke **Henry I** is elevated to king in East Francia. He founds the **Ottonian dynasty** (until 1024), under whom the later **German Empire** finally splits from West Francia.

929 **Abd-ar-Rahman III** subjugates all of al-Andalus and founds the **Caliphate of Córdoba**. Under the Umayyads, the south of the Iberian Peninsula experiences a cultural flowering lasting until 1031.

934 **King Rudolph II** merges Upper and Lower Burgundy to form the **Kingdom of Burgundy**.

935 General **Wang Gon** reunites **Korea** and promotes the practice of **Buddhism**.

950 The **Toltec empire** reaches its high point, with Tula having a population of up to 60,000 people.

955 **King Otto I of East Francia** wins a crushing victory over the Hungarians in the **Battle of Lechfeld** at Augsburg, putting an end to their invasions into his kingdom.

959 **England** is united under **King Edgar**.

962 On Feb. 2, **King Otto I** is crowned **Roman emperor** by the pope in Rome. The resulting link established between the Germanic Eastern Francia and the **office of supreme emperor** continues to exist until 1806.

960 Duke **Mieszko I** unites the **Polish tribes** under his rule and converts to **Christianity** six years later.

960 **China** is reunited under **Emperor Taizu of Song** after decades of disunity. **Kaifeng** is the capital of the Song dynasty, who rule until 1280.

969 The **Shi'ite Fatimids** conquer **Egypt** and make the newly-founded palace city of **Cairo** the center of their empire.

976 **Basil II** ascends to the imperial throne in Byzantium. The **Byzantine Empire** reaches its greatest extent during his reign.

982 **Vikings** discover the island of **Greenland** and later colonize it under the leadership of **Eric the Red**.

987 The **reign of the Carolingians in West Francia ends** with the death of King Louis V. **Hugh Capet**, the first of the **Capetian dynasty**, ascends to the throne of France.

988 The Russian grand prince **Vladimir Sviatoslavich the Great** is baptized according to Orthodox rites in the capital of Kiev. This ushers in the **Christianization** of Russia.

1001 **Mahmud of Ghazni** begins his **raiding expeditions into India**, plundering wealth, and establishing Islamic mosques and shrines.

1009 The first **Dai Viet kingdom** under the **Li dynasty** is constituted in Annam. It is a precursor of **present-day Vietnam**.

1018 **Knut the Great** becomes **king in Denmark**. He is able to establish a **Danish empire** for a short while that even includes England.

1024 The first issuance of government-sponsored **paper money** occurs in China.

1029 **Sancho III of Navarre** unites wide areas of Christian **Spain**. The kingdoms of **Navarre**, **Aragón**, and **Castile** are created in 1035.

1031 The **Caliphate of Córdoba** in Arab **Spain** splinters into over twenty individual states.

1033 The **kingdom of Burgundy** is merged into the **Holy Roman Empire**.

1042 **Edward the Confessor** is made **king of England**. He is the last Anglo-Saxon ruler from the royal house of Wessex.

1044 The first **Burmese Empire** is founded under **King Anoratha** with its capital in Pagan.

674 The Byzantines use "Greek fire," a type of flame thrower, for the first time while defending Constantinople.

692 The **Dome of the Rock** is completed in Jerusalem under Abd al-Malik. It is the first important **Islamic sacred structure** outside Arabia.

735 The **Venerable Bede**, the Anglo-Saxon theologian, dies in an English monastery in Jarrow.

742 The **Chinese poet Li Bai** begins his work at the imperial court in **Xi'an**.

750 **John of Damascus**, considered to be the "last of the **Church Fathers**," dies on Dec. 4 in Palestine.

760 The temple monument of **Borobudur** on Java, one of the **central pilgrimage shrines of Buddhism** in Southeast Asia, is constructed.

770 The first public **apothecary** is opened in **Baghdad**.

784 Construction begins on the **Mezquita in Córdoba**. It remains to this day the **third largest mosque in the world**.

800 **Charlemagne** begins work on the **Palatine Chapel** in **Aachen**.

800 The *Book of Kells*, a masterpiece of illumination, is produced in Ireland.

850 **Gunpowder** is used in the manufacture of fireworks in **China** in the 9th century.

863 The Byzantine missionaries, **Cyril** and **Methodius**, translate the Bible. In the process, they devise their own Slavic script, the **Cyrillic alphabet**, used as the official alphabet in the Orthodox churches in Eastern Europe up into the 20th century.

868 The **world's first book** is printed in **China**.

700 — 750 — 800 — 850

680 In the **Battle of Karbala**, the Umayyads are victorious over Ali's son, Hussein, whose Shia factionists break away from the **Sunni** to become **Shi'ites**.

690 **Wu Zetian** is the first and only woman to ascend to the **throne of China**.

700 The **Zapotec civilization** in Mexico is in its prime. At the same time, the highly developed Native American **Mississippi culture** is spreading in present-day USA.

705 **Walid I** becomes the new caliph of the **Umayyad Empire**. Arab expansion during his reign reaches the Indian subcontinent in 711.

710 **Heijo-kyo**, present-day Nara, is made the imperial residence of the **Japanese court**.

711 **Arab forces** led by **General Tariq** cross over from Africa to Spain and destroy the **Visigoth kingdom of Toledo**. Except for the Christian kingdom of Asturia, the entire **Iberian Peninsula** falls under Muslim rule within a few years.

712 **Liutprand** becomes **king of the Lombards** in Italy. The country blossoms for a last time under his rule.

722 Pope Gregory II sends **Boniface**, an Anglo-Saxon **Benedictine monk**, on an **apostolic mission to the Germanic people**.

726 A heated **theological dispute** over the legitimacy of the **veneration of icons** breaks out in the **Byzantine Empire**. It is not settled in favor of icon veneration until 843.

732 A Frankish army under **Majordomo Charles Martel** is victorious over the Arabs in the seven-day Battle of **Tours and Poiters**, putting an end to their advance into Europe.

750 The **Umayyad dynasty** is overthrown in Damascus. **Abul Abbas** founds the **Abbasid Caliphate** that survives until 1258.

751 **Pippin III the Younger** is anointed **king of the Franks**. This is also the official beginning of the papal supported **Carolingian rule** over the Frankish kingdom.

756 After his victory over the **Lombards**, the Frankish ruler **Pippin III** grants the city of Rome and other territories in central Italy to the pope, which form the basis of the **Papal States**.

756 The **Umayyads** establish an emirate on the **Iberian Peninsula** with **Córdoba** as its capital. It becomes the most important cultural center of western Islam.

772 The Frankish king **Charlemagne** begins his campaigns to **subjugate and Christianize the Saxons**. After bloody battles, the annexation of the Duchy of Saxony is finally realized in 804.

774 **Charlemagne** conquers the **kingdom of the Lombards** and assumes the title "King of the Franks and Lombards."

786 **Caliph Harun al-Rashid**'s accession to power ushers in a period of cultural flowering in the Abbasid Empire. **Baghdad**, capital since 762, becomes the center of Arab scholarship.

788 The **Duchy of Bavaria** is the last dukedom on Frankish territory to be subjugated by **Charlemagne**.

793 The raid by **Scandinavian seafarers** at the **Abbey of Lindisfarne**, off the northeast coast of England, is the start of the **Age of the Vikings**.

794 **Heian**, present-day Kyoto, is made the new capital city of **Japan**. This marks the beginning of the **Heian period**.

800 The Frankish king, **Charlemagne**, is crowned **Emperor of Rome** by Pope Leo III on Dec. 25, re-establishing the ancient tradition of a supreme ruler in the West, in competition with Byzantium.

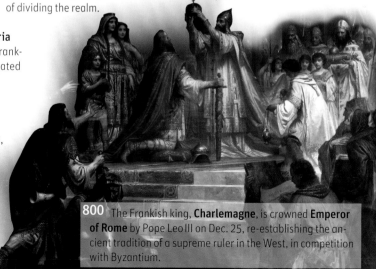

801 **Charlemagne** creates the **Marca Hispanica** as a defensive barrier against the Arabs on the Iberian Peninsula. **Barcelona** is made their capital in 803.

811 In the **Battle of Pliska**, a Byzantine army under **Emperor Nikephoros I** is forced to suffer a crushing defeat at the hands of the **Bulgars under Khan Krum**.

814 **Louis the Pious** follows Charlemagne as king of the Franks. In 817, with his **Ordinatio imperii**, an imperial decree on orderly succession, he attempts to break with the principle of dividing the realm.

829 King **Egbert von Wessex** is able to temporarily unite the small Anglo-Saxon kingdoms on the British Isles into a royal federation.

831 After four years of battle, the **Arabs take Sicily**.

840 After the death of Louis the Pious, a **fratricidal war** breaks out between his sons, Lothair, Louis, and Charles, **for supremacy in the Frankish Empire**.

843 The **Frankish Empire** is divided into three parts in the **Treaty of Verdun**: Lothair receives the central, Charles the Bald the western, and Louis the German the eastern part of the empire.

843 **Kenneth Mac Alpin** establishes the **first Scottish kingdom**.

850 The classic **Maya civilization** goes into decline on the Mexican peninsula of **Yucatán**.

858 Following the death of **Emperor Montoku** in Japan, the **Fujiwara**, a clan of regents, assumes virtual rulership of **Japan** for over 200 years.

HISTORICAL EVENTS

Catholic Kingdom of the Franks
King Clovis converted to the Catholic faith in 498, and thus founded a powerful tradition in the first empire of the European early Middle Ages.

Originally confined to a small area south of the Rhine estuary, the Frankish house of Merovingians under Clovis I had achieved a dominant position of power in Western Europe by 482. In **486**, he routed Syagrius, the last Roman governor of Gaul. By his death in 511, he had expanded the territories under his control all the way to the Pyrenees. Unlike other Germanic kings, Clovis did not accept Arian Christianity. He was baptized a Catholic, assumedly in **498** after his victory over the Alemanni in Reims. This act was of immense political and cultural significance. The common faith reinforced the indigenous Gallo-Roman Catholics' identification with their new Frankish lords, which abetted the expulsion of the Arian Visigoths to Spain in **507**. Moreover, Clovis's baptism created the basis for a close relationship between the Frankish kingdom and the church in Rome. In the coming years, this became a decisive pillar of support for the rule of the Merovingians and the Carolingians who followed them. Thus, Catholicism also spread along with the expansion of the Frankish kingdom in Europe.

Clovis I, king of the Franks, being baptized by Bishop Remigius of Reims

Scenes from the life of the regent, Prince Umayado, who prepared the Taika Reform

Taika Reform
The introduction in 646 of feudal structures based on the Chinese system reinforced imperial power in Japan.

Up until the 7th century, Japan was comprised of virtually autonomous principalities, which were only held together by the divinely legitimized emperor (tenno). In 646, Emperor Kotoku was the first to issue laws making Japan a unified state, based on the political structure of the Chinese Tang dynasty. The whole country became the property of the emperor and was allocated back to the princes as fiefdoms. The peasants were placed under the emperor as well. Japan was divided into 66 provinces and furnished with a central administration. The aristocracy gained privileged access to state offices. Japan's culture was progressively influenced by Chinese practices, and both Buddhism and Confucianism took root in Japan.

Islamic Fratricidal War
The Battle of Karbala in 680 sealed the schism of Muslims into Sunni and Shi'ites.

The Prophet Muhammad had left no heirs when he died in **632**. This was the cause of violent disputes among the Arab tribes over the position of rightful successor ("caliph") of the prophet, who would have command over the growing Islamic society as religious and political leader. During the reign of the fourth caliph, Ali, between 656 and 661, the first groups split off. While the Shi'ites (Shi'at Ali, Ali's party) saw in Muhammad's cousin and son-in-law the only legitimate successor, Muawiyah, the governor of Syria in Damascus and of the house of the Umayyads, refused his allegiance. In several battles, he established his claim to power. Following the assassination of Ali in **661**, he was recognized by most Muslims and established the hereditary caliphate of the Umayyad dynasty in Damascus (until **750**). He thus established the Sunni denomination in Islam, which is based on the tradition of the first caliphs and is followed by a clear majority in most Islamic countries to the present day. Under Ali's son, Hussein, the

In the Battle of Karbala, troops of the Umayyad caliphate defeated rebelling Shi'ites.

Shi'ites for the last time openly rose up against the Umayyads, but were defeated at Karbala in present-day Iraq in **680**. To this day, the Shi'ites commemorate the bloody defeat with processions of flagellants.

The Viking Age
The attack on Lindisfarne abbey in 793 marked the beginning of the Viking Age and their raids throughout Europe, striking terror to the hearts of the population well into the 11th century.

Heavily armed, the Vikings stormed out of their longships in **793** and pillaged the abbey on the island of Lindisfarne off the North Sea coast of England. They plundered and killed everything they could get their hands on and then disappeared as quickly as they had come. The pillaging of Lindisfarne was but the prelude to further attacks along the same pattern. Sailing out of their homelands in Scandinavia, the seafarers began terrorizing the coasts of Western Europe in the 9th century, reaching far inland along the river ways. Danish Vikings, for example, besieged Paris for almost a year in 885. The raids weakened the power of the Carolingians since the Frankish kings were unable to effectively protect their citizens. With their excellent ships, the Vikings even reached areas of North Africa and the Mediterranean. Later, the Norsemen also settled down permanently and established feudal states, for example, in Normandy (**911**), in southern Italy, and in present-day Russia. They also colonized the islands of Iceland and Greenland (**982**). Around 1000, they even reached North America.

The Vikings reached the furthest corners of Europe with their dragon boats.

Kievan Rus'
Scandinavian Vikings established the first empire on Russian soil in Kiev in the mid-9th century.

Since the 8th century, Scandinavian Vikings called Varangians had been penetrating deeply into the Slav populated territories of present-day Russia and the Ukraine and establishing settlements. Rurik, the legendary Varangian prince, assumed power in the trading capital of Novgorod in **862** and founded the first Russian dynasty, which reigned until **1598**. His successor, Oleg the Wise, expanded his territory to the south. In **882**, he conquered Kiev, which became the capital of an extensive empire (Kievan Rus'). Through trading privileges and dynastic marriages in the 10th century, the culture of Kievan Rus' increasingly came under the influence of the Byzantines. In **988**, Vladimir I accepted the rites of Orthodox Christianity and forced his subjects to be baptized as well. During the following centuries, Christian

Novgorod in northwestern Russia was the first center of the Varangians' domain.

faith spread throughout the later Russian Empire. After the conquest of Constantinople by the Ottoman Turks in **1453**, Russia became the center of Orthodox Christianity.

The temple complex of Angkor Wat attests to the great importance of the Khmer Empire.

Khmer Empire
The city of Angkor in present-day Cambodia became the center of the emerging Khmer Empire in 890.

Strongly influenced by Indian culture, the Khmer spread over the territory between India and China during the first centuries A.D. By the 7th century they had formed small, competing kingdoms, which Jayavarman II united into a larger kingdom in 802. He erected his new capital on Mt. Mahendra and proclaimed himself the god-king. Around **890** his son, Yashovarman I, founded Angkor, the city that became the cultural and political center of the growing Khmer Empire. The city was the site of innumerable magnificent buildings, artificial lakes, water management systems, and, by **1153,** of the world-famous temple complex of Angkor Wat. In the meantime, the Khmer had become the dominant power in Southeast Asia and controlled large areas of present-day Cambodia and parts of Laos, Thailand, and Vietnam. In the 14th century, the Thais began invading Khmer territory and finally, in **1431,** they conquered Angkor, which was subsequently abandoned.

The advanced civilization of the Maya left behind many temples for posterity.

The Fall of the Maya
The cause of the decline and fall of the highly developed civilization of the Classic Maya between 850 and 900 has yet to be explained beyond doubt.

The temple ruins that to this day tower up above the rain forests in Tikal and Palenque in the Mexican-Guatemalan border regions testify to the highly developed culture of the Maya civilization. The Maya had reached their greatest territorial expansion by **200**, but suddenly fell into decline around **850**. A unified Maya Empire probably never existed. It was rather subdivided into many independently ruled city-states that formed alliances or waged war against one another. Each city-state was ruled by a priest-prince, who conducted religious sacrificial ceremonies for the numerous deities. The Maya developed a hieroglyphic writing system and used an extremely complex calendar—the entries, however, end abruptly in 909. There has been much conjecture about the reasons for their sudden disappearance. Did the Maya flee their cities because of war, revolts or epidemics? A majority of researchers today assume that overpopulation and a period of extreme drought due to climate change caused the disintegration of the Maya urban civilization.

The Battle of Lechfeld
The victory over the Hungarians in 955 internally strengthened the kingdom of East Francia and paved the way for King Otto I the Great to take the title of emperor.

At the close of the 9th century, the Hungarians (Magyars) under Grand Prince Árpád made their way into the Carpathian basin, the area they still inhabit today. Operating from there, this equestrian people regularly staged raids into the territory of East Francia, present-day Germany. An army amassed by King Henry I was able to initially defeat the Hungarians in 933 but was unable to permanently eliminate their threat. A decisive victory was first achieved by his son, Otto I, with combatants from Bavaria, Franconia, Swabia, Saxony, and Bohemia, on **Aug. 10, 955**, at Lechfeld near Augsburg. In the aftermath, the Hungarians settled down and became increasingly receptive to Christianity. The victory reinforced Otto's authority over the German princes. He was also able to enforce his rule in Italy, where he was elected king in **951**. Finally, in **962**, the Pope in Rome crowned him emperor, establishing the link between the German kingdom in the Holy Roman Empire and the office of emperor that persisted until **1806**.

The Battle against the Hungarians fortified the unity of East Francia.

1051 The **first Russian Orthodox monastery**, the Kiev Pechersk Lavra (cave monastery), is founded.

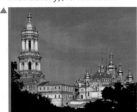

1055 The **Church of the Holy Sepulchre**, the holiest Christian site in the world, is rebuilt in Jerusalem.

1066 The Persian grand vizier, Nizam al-Mulk, founds the **Madrasa** in **Baghdad**, an **Islamic school of higher learning** that becomes a model for other institutions in the Islamic cultural world.

1074 In Valencia, in Muslim Spain, **paper is produced for the first time in Europe**.

1078 In **London** the construction of the **White Tower** for the protection of the city begins.

1080 **Anselm of Canterbury** tries to prove the existence of God in his *Proslogion*. Owing to this, he is referred to as the **founder of scholasticism.**

1094 After an extensive renovation period, **St. Mark's Basilica** in **Venice** is reconsecrated.

1087 **Constantinus Africanus**, physician and **translator** of important medical works from Arabic into Latin, dies.

1100 Originating in **southern France** around 1100, **minne lyrics** spread throughout the courts of Europe.

1100 The process of **Christianization** is completed in **Sweden**.

1095 The **Islamic mystic** and noted **philosopher of religion**, Abu Hamed Mohammad al-Ghazzali, writes his most important work, *Revival of Religious Sciences*.

1050 **1075** **1100**

1054 **The Great Schism:** The Pope in Rome and the Patriarch of Constantinople excommunicate each other, thus sealing the **schism between the Latin and the Greek Orthodox churches.**

1054 After the death of **Yaroslav I**, the central authority over the Kievan Rus' Empire crumbles.

1055 The **Seljuks**, led by Tughril Beg, take **Baghdad**; the Abbasid caliphs recognize the new balance of power.

1056 **Henry IV**, a Salian, is made **King of the Romans (King of the Germans)**, and in 1084 is crowned emperor.

1059 The **Pope invests the Norman Duke Robert Guiscard** with territories in southern Italy to secure him as an ally against the Arabs. By 1091, **all of Sicily is in Norman hands.**

1059 Pope Nicholas II issues a decree which declares that the **election of the Pope** is solely to be decided **by a college of cardinals**.

1061 The **Almoravid ruler Yusuf ibn Tashfin** takes power in **Morocco**, and subsequently expands his empire into Spain and Algeria. In 1062, he founds his new capital in Marrakech.

1063 The **new Seljuk sultan, Alp Arslan**, steadily expands his rule across **Persia and Central Asia**.

1066 **William the Conqueror**, Duke of Normandy, lands in **England** and, on Oct. 14, defeats the Anglo-Saxon King Harold II at the **Battle of Hastings**. By 1071, William has subjugated the Anglo-Saxons.

1068 In **China**, Wang Anshi, chancellor of the Song dynasty, introduces **administrative reforms** to create a more effective tax system.

1071 The **Seljuks**, under Sultan Alp Arslan, defeat and capture the Byzantine emperor, Romanos IV Diogenes, on Aug. 19 in the **Battle of Manzikert**. The Seljuqs occupy **Asia Minor**, where the **sultanate of Konya** is established.

1072 Faced by the overwhelming power of the English, the Scottish king, **Malcolm III**, recognizes the **sovereignty of King William I of England**.

1073 The dedicated "church reformer," **Gregory VII**, is **elected pope** on Apr. 22 in Rome.

1075 In his **Dicatatus Papae**, **Pope Gregory VII** formulates his **claim to universal sovereignty**.

1076 The **Seljuks capture Damascus**. The beleaguered Byzantines turn to Western Europe for help.

1077 **Walk to Canossa:** On Jan. 28, the excommunicated German king, **Henry IV**, prostrates himself before **Gregory VII** in Canossa. The **Investiture Controversy**, however, continues.

1079 King Henry IV invests **Frederick I von Staufen** with the **duchy of Swabia**.

1079 The childless **Matilda of Tuscany** bequeaths all her allodial properties in Upper and Lower Italy (Mathildian lands) to the pope.

1081 On Apr. 4, **Alexios I Komnenos** becomes **emperor of Byzantium**. Through alliances with West European powers, he is able to stabilize his empire **against the Seljuks.**

1084 The Norman duke, **Robert Guiscard**, ally of Pope Gregory VII, **captures** German-controlled **Rome** and plunders the city.

1085 **Reconquista:** King Alfonso VI of Castile **conquers Muslim Toledo**. The Spanish Muslims call upon the North African **Almoravids** for help, who, however, are not able to hold back the advance of the Christian armies in the long term.

1086 In **England**, William I orders the compilation of the **Domesday Book**. It is a detailed inventory of possessions in the entire kingdom and serves as the basis of a **centralized administrative system.**

1094 The **knight and Spanish national hero of the Reconquista**, Rodrigo Díaz de Vivar, known as **"El Cid,"** conquers Valencia and establishes his own realm.

"God wills it!"
Justification for the First Crusade, Council of Clermont, 1095

1095 At a synod in Clermont-Ferrand, on Nov. 27, **Pope Urban II** calls for the **First Crusade to free Jerusalem.**

1096 The **"People's Crusade,"** led by Peter the Hermit, is wiped out by the Seljuks.

1098 In the Near East, the **Crusaders** capture **Antioch** and **found a principality.**

1098 **Cîteaux Abbey** is founded in Burgundy as part of a reform movement of the Benedictine **Trappist or Cistercian Order**, which spreads across all of Europe.

1099 On July 15, the **Crusaders**, under the command of Godfrey of Bouillon, capture Jerusalem and kill more than 70,000 Muslims and Jews. Jerusalem is made the capital of a Christian kingdom.

1100 **Henry I**, son of William the Conqueror, mounts the **English throne**. Until 1135, he tries to reach a **compromise** with the Anglo-Saxons.

1100 The Native American **Anasazi culture**, from which the **Pueblo** culture evolves, reaches its peak in the **southwest of North America.**

1102 The **Pacta Conventa** confirms the **personal union of Croatia with Hungary**. It exists for more than 800 years.

1103 In the **imperial Land Peace of Mainz**, Henry IV formally places the **German Jews under his protection**.

1108 **Louis VI** succeeds to the **French throne** and **solidifies the king's power** against the aristocracy.

1119 For the protection of Christian pilgrims, Hugh of Payens founds the **Order of the Knights Templar** in **Jerusalem**. They conduct plundering raids on Muslims in the Holy Land.

Popes and Emperors

1050–1250

In the High Middle Ages, the relationship between the secular and the religious was very ambivalent. This became evident in the Investiture Controversy between the popes and emperors in the Holy Roman Empire. Other rulers, like the kings of England, were also confronted with a confident and self-assured clergy. At the same time, the Church offered the ruling monarchs the ideological legitimation for their fight against Muslims, alleged heretics, and heathens, even though their countless crusades were mainly motivated by political and economic interests. The combining of religion and war was most evident in the chivalric orders that emerged in the Holy Land and on the Iberian Peninsula. The mendicant orders that were founded at the same time sought to take the opposite path by deliberately renouncing worldly possessions. The numerous reform movements in the Church were a reflection of the people's intense involvement with questions of faith and the role of the Church and other institutions.

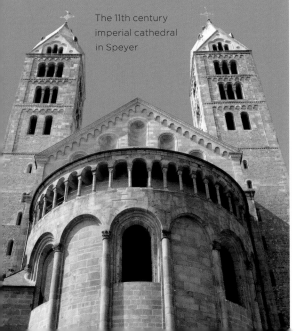

The 11th century imperial cathedral in Speyer

HISTORICAL FIGURES

William the Conqueror (1027–1087)   The illegitimate son of a Norman duke became the first Norman king of England.

After the death of his father Robert I in 1035, William became Duke of Normandy. Due to his illegitimate birth, he was forced to prove himself in countless battles against other pretenders. His actual goal, however, was the crown of England held by Edward the Confessor. When Harold II took the throne after Edward's death, William landed an invasion force of French and Norman knights on the southern coast of England. In the Battle of Hastings on **Oct. 14, 1066**, he defeated the Anglo-Saxons and on Christmas Day he was crowned king in Westminster. William immediately introduced a new feudal system in England and reserved key clerical and state positions to fellow Normans. In this way, he laid the foundation for a lasting centrally administered monarchy in England.

Genghis Khan (1155–1227)   The leader of the Mongols created the largest contiguous empire in human history.

There are only a few reliable accounts about the Mongol Prince Temujin. Some of his contemporaries report of his brutality, others praise his fatherly nature. It is certain that he united various Mongolian tribes, gave them a uniform law, and defeated the reigning Tartars. In **1206**, he took the title of Genghis Khan ("oceanic ruler"). He subjugated almost all of Asia with his mounted army. After his conquest of Beijing in **1215,** he invaded Korea. He occupied large parts of Turkistan and defeated Russian princes at Kalka in 1223. When Genghis Khan died in **1227**, his empire stretched from the Sea of China to Eastern Europe.

Innocent III (1160–1216)   Feared inquisitor, skilled in the politics of power, and church reformer: Under Innocent III's pontificate, the papacy was at the pinnacle of its secular power.

When Innocent III was elected pope in **1198**, he sought to strengthen the papal claim to universal sovereignty. While still a student he had claimed that the pope "is lesser than God, but greater than man." In the struggle for succession after the death of Emperor Henry VI in 1198, Innocent was able to augment the influence of the papacy and effect the imperial coronation of Otto IV in 1209. In addition, he further expanded the papal domain. Innocent fought perceived heretics, but also tried to assimilate religious movements by promoting mendicant orders like the Franciscans in **1209**. The high point of his pontificate was the Council of the Lateran in **1215**, which was the largest church congress of the Middle Ages.

Frederick II (1194–1250)   His contemporaries knew the Hohenstaufen king simply as Stupor Mundi—"the wonder of the world"—due to his outstanding education.

His claim to universal sovereignty caused Frederick II to repeatedly come into conflict with the German princes and the popes, although Innocent III had been central in elevating him to the throne. He led a crusade under his imperial power and crowned himself king of Jerusalem in **1229**. However, when Frederick, who was also king of Sicily, wanted to extend his rule over all of Italy, he made bitter enemies of the popes and was forced to grant broad privileges to the German princes in **1232**. Frederick's education was legendary. He spoke several languages, was in contact with Arab scholars, and occupied himself with mathematics and philosophy. His treatise on falconry is considered a masterwork of natural science. After his death in **1250**, the Hohenstaufen empire fell apart.

1180 The **step pyramid of Kukulcán** in the Mayan city of **Chichén Itzá** is completed.

1180 The English theologian **John of Salisbury** dies on Oct.25 in Chartres. His major work, *Policraticus*, is considered to be an influential theory of the state of the Middle Ages.

1185 In England, the first **windmills** with the sail-cross rotating on a vertical plane are built.

1200 The future German national epic, *The Song of the Nibelungs*, is written.

1204 The **Jewish philosopher Moses Maimonides** dies in Cairo on Dec.13. His work, *Guide for the Perplexed*, has a major effect on not only Jewish but also Arab and Christian religious thought.

1225 **Eike von Repkow** compiles the *Sachsenspiegel*, the first law book in the German Empire.

1209 **Nizami**, the greatest Persian literary figure and writer of classic epic poetry of his time, **dies in Azerbaijan**.

1230 The *Carmina Burana*, a collection of **songs and lyrics of Medieval Goliard poetry** in Latin, is compiled around this time.

1248 Construction begins on a **Gothic cathedral in Cologne**, which, after many interruptions, is finally completed in the year 1880, still following the original plans.

1230 **Walther von der Vogelweide**, the most famous German **poet of the Middle Ages**, dies in Würzburg.

1200 | **1225** | **1250**

1187 The **Ayyubid sultan Saladin** defeats the Crusaders at the **Battle of Hattin** and captures the **kingdom of Jerusalem** on Oct. 6.

1189 **Philip II**, king of France, and **Henry II**, king of England, call for a third crusade. On the way to the Near East, **Emperor Frederick I Barbarossa drowns** in eastern Anatolia on June 10, 1190.

1192 In **Japan, Minamoto no Yoritomo** assumes the title of a **shogun** (military dictator). A feudal military aristocracy evolves that is characteristic of the country well into the 19th century.

1196 Hohenstaufen emperor **Henry VI** fails in his attempt to introduce an **hereditary monarchy** in the Holy Roman Empire due to the **opposition of the princes**.

1198 **Lothar of Segni** is elected **Pope Innocent III** in Rome. He appeals for a fourth crusade.

1198 After the death of Emperor Henry VI, both the **Hohenstaufen Philip of Swabia** and the Welf **Otto IV** are elected king of the Romans.

1200 In present-day Peru, the **Incas** found **Cuzco** and use it as a base in building their empire.

1204 King **Philip II of France** confiscates the **holdings of the English kings in France**, thus enlarging his own power-base.

1206 **Qutb-ud-din Aibak**, a general and former soldier slave from Turkistan, founds the **Delhi Sultanate** in **North India**.

1206 Prince Temujin unites the **Mongolian tribes** and takes the title of **"Genghis Khan."**

1209 In the **south of France**, at the command of **Pope Innocent III**, a twenty-year crusade begins against the religious community of the **Albigenses** (Cathars), who are regarded as heretics.

1209 Pope Innocent III recognizes the community of **Franciscans** organizing around **Francis of Assisi**. The order, officially confirmed in 1223, develops into the most important **mendicant order**.

1212 During the course of the **Reconquista**, a Christian alliance defeats the Almohads in the **Battle of Las Navas de Tolosa**, permanently weakening the position of the Muslims in southern Spain.

1204 Contingents of the **Fourth Crusade** led by **Venetians** conquer the **Byzantine capital Constantinople** on Apr. 13. Baldwin of Flanders is the first ruler of the **Latin Empire of Constantinople**.

1214 The French king **Philip II** triumphs over the English king **John Lackland** on July 27 at **Bouvines** in Flanders.

1212 The **Hohenstaufen Frederick II, king of Sicily**, is elected **German king of the Romans** in Mainz.

1215 King **John Lackland** is forced to grant certain liberties to the English aristocracy in the **Magna Carta**. It becomes the first step leading to the rule of constitutional law in the English-speaking world.

1215 The **Mongols** under **Genghis Khan** capture **Beijing** and subjugate broad areas of Asia within a few years.

1220 On Nov. 22, **Frederick II** is crowned **emperor** in **Rome**. He is mainly concerned with the expansion of his kingdom in **Sicily**.

1225 After the **Almohads** have been **driven from Spain** and the loss of Córdoba in 1236 and Seville in 1248, only Granada still remains in Muslim hands.

1226 In the **Golden Bull of Rimini**, Emperor Frederick II confirms the **Teutonic Knights'** sovereignty over the Culmer Land. The expansion of the order into Eastern Europe begins with the **conversion of heathen Prussia** in 1230.

1227 After the death of **Genghis Khan**, the **Mongol world empire** is divided among his followers.

1229 During the **Fifth Crusade, Emperor Frederick II** captures **Jerusalem** without any battles and **crowns himself king** on March 18.

1232 In the **Statutum in favorem principum**, Emperor Frederick II confirms the **rights and privileges of the German imperial princes**. He had already issued a similar law favoring the clergy in 1220.

1235 In the kingdom of the Nasrid sultans of **Granada**, the culture of the Spanish Muslims (Moors) experiences a final flowering lasting until 1492.

1240 The **Mongols** led by **Batu Khan** conquer the Russian capital of **Kiev**. Russia is ruled by Mongols up into the 15th century.

1250 The **Inca** settle near **Cuzco** and later make it the capital of their empire.

1250 **Frederick II**, the **last great emperor of the Middle Ages**, dies on Dec. 13. He is succeeded by his son, Conrad IV, **but the power of the Hohenstaufen begins to crumble**.

1106 The rebuilding of the **Imperial Cathedral** in **Speyer** is completed. The burial place of the Salians is the largest surviving **Romanesque church** in the world.

1110 The *Song of Roland*, the oldest **French national epic**, is written.

1141 The Benedictine abbess and Christian mystic, **Hildegard of Bingen**, known for her holistic and natural views of healing, begins writing her first work.

1142 The controversial **philosopher of early scholastic, Peter Abelard**, dies on Apr. 21 in the priory of St. Marcel, in Burgundy.

1143 The English scholar, **Robert of Ketton**, completes the **first Latin translation of the Qu'ran** on the suggestion of the Abbot of Cluny.

1147 **Conrad III** is the first to use the term **"Austria"** in an official document. Austria was previously referred to as **Marcha Orientalis** or **Bavarian Eastern March**.

1153 Construction of the great **Hindu temple of Angkor Wat** in present-day Cambodia, the largest structure of its day, is completed.

1154 Commissioned by Norman King Roger II of Sicily, the **Arab geographer Al-Idrisi** inscribes an **atlas** of the known world on a massive solid **silver disc**.

1157 The Italian theologian **Peter Lombard** finishes writing his *Four Books of Sentences*, which becomes one of the **most important textbooks** of Christian dogma.

1158 The **University of Bologna** is the first to be granted **research autonomy** by Emperor Barbarossa.

1163 Construction on the gothic cathedral of **Notre Dame** begins in **Paris**. It is consecrated in 1345.

1173 On Aug. 9, construction begins on the Cathedral of Pisa, whose bell tower now leans to the south. The **Leaning Tower of Pisa** is a World Heritage site today.

1125 — 1150 — 1175

1122 On Sept. 23, the **Concordat of Worms** settles the **Investiture Controversy** between the king and the pope in the Holy Roman Empire.

1125 The **Jurchen people** in the **northeast of China**, who later adopt the name Manchu, found the **Jin dynasty** that rules until 1234.

1125 The German imperial dynasty of the **Salians** ends with the death of **Henry V**.

1127 The **Jurchens capture Kaifeng**, the capital of the northern Song dynasty, who have ruled since 960. The **southern Song dynasty** reigns over southern **China** from out of Hangzhou until 1279.

1130 The Norman **Roger II**, Duke of Sicily, **assumes the title of king** with the consent of Antipope Anacletus II and practically controls all of southern Italy.

1133 **Lothair III of Supplinburg is crowned king of the Holy Roman Empire**. In 1134, he invests Albert of Ballenstedt, called Albert the Bear, with the North March (Brandenburg), launching **German colonization to the East**.

1135 **The Anarchy**: The death of Henry I ignites an almost 20-year-long civil war between Henry's daughter, **Mathilda**, and his nephew **Stephen of Blois**, who is able to secure the **English crown**.

1137 **Louis VII** becomes **king of France**. He is married to **Eleanor of Aquitaine**; however, she divorces him in 1152.

1137 Count **Ramon Berenguer IV** unites the county of **Barcelona** (Catalonia) with the kingdom of **Aragón** through his marriage to the infant Petronella of Aragón.

1138 **Conrad III of Hohenstaufen is elected German king of the Romans** on March 7. His coronation triggers a feud between the **Hohenstaufen** and **Welf** families.

1138 Following the death of King Bolesław II, the **kingdom of Poland** crumbles into separate duchies by 1295.

1139 **Duke Alfonso I** proclaims himself prince of Portugal. In the course of the Reconquista, he battles against the Muslims and in 1147 captures **Lisbon**, later the capital.

1144 The **Seljuks** capture the **Crusader city of Edessa**, which ignites the **Second Crusade** in 1147. The Cistercian monk **Bernhard of Clairvaux** calls out for another crusade in Europe. It fails, however, outside Damascus in 1149.

1150 In the mid-11th century, **Novgorod**, an independent **city republic** since 1136, rises to become **Russia's most important trading center**.

1152 On March 9, the Hohenstaufen **Frederick I Barbarossa** is elected **German king of the Romans**. He plans to strengthen his position of power in Germany and Italy.

1154 On Dec. 19, **Henry II Plantagenet** becomes **king of England**. Through his wife, **Eleanor of Aquitaine**, he controls not only Anjou and Normandy, but also wide areas of southwestern France.

1156 To settle the **conflict between the Hohenstaufens and Welfs**, Frederick I Barbarossa transfers the duchy of Bavaria to his cousin, **Henry the Lion**, Duke of Saxony. Earlier, Frederick had separated **Austria** from ducal Bavaria as an **independent duchy in the Privilegium Minus**.

1157 **Valdemar I the Great of Denmark** is elected new king. He turns the country into a **leading power in the Baltic Sea region**.

1157 On June 11, **Albert the Bear** finally subdues the **Slavic tribes** in the Margraviate of Brandenburg. He launches a scheduled **colonization of German settlers**.

1158 At the **Diet of Roncaglia** near Piacenza, on Nov. 11–26, **Emperor Frederick I Barbarossa** attempts to establish his **sovereignty over Italy**.

1163 **Abd al-Mu'min**, the first **Almohad** ruler, dies. He had displaced the Almoravid dynasty in **North Africa** and **Spain**.

1164 **King Henry II of England** restricts the influence of the Church in politics with the **Constitution of Clarendon**. Two years later, he also reinforces his power over the aristocracy.

1167 On Dec. 1, several **northern Italian cities** unite in the **Lombard League** to counter Frederick I Barbarossa's imperial influence over Italy.

1171 **Sultan Saladin** establishes the rule of the **Kurdish Ayyubid dynasty** in **Egypt**. By 1175, he has also conquered **Syria**.

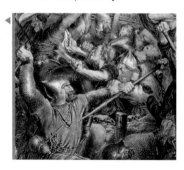

1175 The **Toltec Empire** that has spread across most of Mexico **comes to an end**.

1175 **King Henry II of England** gains nominal sovereignty of **Ireland**.

1176 **Emperor Frederick I Barbarossa** is defeated by the Lombard League in the **Battle of Legnano** and must reconcile with Pope Alexander III.

1176 The Byzantine army of **Emperor Manuel I Komnenos** suffers a devastating defeat at Myriokephalon at the hands of the Seljuks.

1180 **Stefan Nemanja** declares **independence from Byzantium** and founds his own **Serbian kingdom**.

1180 **Emperor Frederick I Barbarossa** strips **Welf Henry the Lion** of his lands. Bavaria is given to the **Wittelsbachs**, Westphalia to the archbishop of Cologne, and the eastern part of Saxony to the **Ascanians**.

1181 **Jayavarman VII** becomes ruler over the **Khmer Empire of Angkor**, which, by 1218, reaches the pinnacle of its power under his reign.

1183 **Emperor Frederick I Barbarossa** and the **Lombard League** sign the **Peace of Constance**. The northern Italian cities may decide who is to be their local ruler themselves.

1185 In the **Battle of Dan-no-ura**, a major sea battle, the **Minamoto clan** scores a decisive victory over the rival Taira family, thus ending the **Gempei War** for sovereignty over **Japan**.

1185 The Bulgarian princes **Ivan** and **Peter Asen** break away from Byzantium and found the **Second Bulgarian Empire**.

HISTORICAL EVENTS

The Battle of Manzikert

The devastating defeat at the hands of the Seljuk Turks in eastern Anatolia in 1071 forced the Byzantine Empire into retreat from Asia Minor and brought on its slow decline.

In the 11th century, the Seljuks pushed westward. In **1055**, they captured Baghdad and later advanced into the eastern borders of the Byzantine Empire. An attempt by Emperor Romanos IV Diogenes to eliminate the threat with a military campaign near the fortress of Manzikert ended in a fiasco in **1071**, when the emperor was taken captive. This opened the path for the Seljuks into inner Anatolia, where they established the Sultanate of the Rum Seljuks. In **1176**, the Byzantines were defeated again at Myriokephalon, which finally broke their power. They had to appeal to the West for help, thereby provoking the First Crusade.

A skirmish between Seljuk and Byzantine mounted troops

In the year 1111, Emperor Henry V takes Pope Paschal II and several cardinals captive.

Investiture Controversy

With Henry IV's legendary "Walk to Canossa" in 1077, the disagreement between the pope and the king over the right to appoint bishops in his empire reached its zenith.

Who has the final word in matters of faith in a Christian empire? The church or the monarch? The question of who holds ultimate authority over bishops in imperial lands flared up in the Holy Roman Empire resulting in the Investiture Controversy. Maintaining to be the highest figure in Christendom, Pope Gregory VII banned lay investiture in **1075**. When German King Henry IV, who had appointed a new bishop in Milan, defied Gregory's reforms, the pope excommunicated the king—a heretofore unheard of action. Henry had to yield. In **1077**, he crossed the snowy Alps and appeared in sackcloth and repentance before the pope at the castle of Canossa. Gregory was obligated to forgive, but this did not end the struggle. When the German princes elected an antiking, Henry appointed an antipope. The conflict dragged on for nearly fifty years, finally reaching a compromise in the Concordat of Worms in **1122**. According to this agreement, all bishops were elected solely by the clergy while the king was permitted to invest them with lay rights before their spiritual consecration.

"God wills it!" The Crusades

Incited by papal promises of salvation and prospects of a rich booty, Crusaders marched to the Near East to "liberate" the holy sites from the Muslims.

At the Council of Clermont on **Nov. 27, 1095**, Pope Urban II called upon all Christians to rescue the Holy Land from the Seljuk Turks. Supported by a large number of itinerant preachers, the idea of a crusade spread like wildfire. In "people's crusades," the rage of the incited mobs was also directed against the Jews, especially in the Rhineland. An army of German and French knights eventually conquered Jerusalem on **July 15, 1099**, and massacred the Muslim and Jewish population. Several crusader states were set up in the Near East with the kingdom of Jerusalem as the center. They were, however, constantly under threat from their Muslim neighbors, resulting in new crusades from Europe. Chivalric orders like the Knights Templar and the Knights Hospitaller were created in the Holy Land. The Christians were not able to prevail in the long run and were forced to abandon Acre, their last bastion in Palestine, on **June 17, 1291**. The notion of crusades lived on in Europe and was directed against religious movements such as the Albigensians in southern France in 1209 and from 1226 on against heathen Prussia.

The conquest of Jerusalem by the army of Christian Crusaders in the year 1099

The Angevin Empire

After the marriage of the heir to the English throne, Henry II Plantagenet, to Eleanor of Aquitaine in 1152, large areas of France came under English rule.

When the French King Louis VII separated from his first wife Eleanor in 1152, he certainly did not expect the pleasure-loving duchess of Aquitaine to marry his rival, Henry Plantagenet, the very same year. As Count of Anjou and Duke of Normandy, Henry not only had large holdings in France, but was heir to the English crown as well. Through his marriage with Eleanor of Aquitaine, he controlled the entire north and west of France. In **1154**, he finally mounted the English throne as Henry II. The Angevin Empire, named after Anjou, now stretched from the borders of Scotland to the Pyrenees, while the power of the French kings was concentrated in the royal demesne around Paris. The conflict with the English kings now dominated French politics. King Philip II of France was able to drive back the English in **1204** and **1214** so far that only Gascony in the southwest of France remained in English hands. The Angevin Empire was history, but it was not until the Hundred Years' War beginning in **1337/39** that the conflict with the English was permanently decided after costly battles in favor of the French kings.

Louis VII has his marriage with Eleanor annulled at the Council of Beaugency.

Hohenstaufen versus Welf

Hohenstaufen versus Welf The power struggle in the Holy Roman Empire between Emperor Frederick I Barbarossa and Duke Henry the Lion climaxed in 1180 in a spectacular trial.

Frederick I Barbarossa of the House of Hohenstaufen, who had been elected German King of the Romans in **1152**, wanted to restore the glory of the Holy Roman Empire. In order to do so, he sought to establish control over Italy, resulting in an ongoing dispute with northern Italian cities and the papacy. The German princes, however, also objected to a strong ruler. Frederick's most powerful rival was the duke of Saxony, Henry the Lion. To accommodate the Welfs, Frederick transferred the Duchy of Bavaria to him in **1156**. When Henry began to exercise nearly imperial powers, primarily in northern Germany, and refused to take part in the Italian campaign of **1176**, Frederick took drastic measures. He had Henry stripped of all his ducal territories by an imperial court in **1180**. When Frederick died on a crusade in 1190, the conflict between the Welfs and the Hohenstaufens flared up again and culminated in the election of two kings in **1198**. In the end, neither the Hohenstaufens nor their successors were able to build up a strong central authority in the Holy Roman Empire. Unlike England and France, the empire remained an elective monarchy with increasingly powerless emperors.

Henry the Lion is forced to submit to his cousin Emperor Frederick I Barbarossa in 1181.

"Reconquista"

"Reconquista" With their triumph in the Battle of Las Navas de Tolosa in 1212, the Christian rulers won a decisive victory over the Spanish Muslims.

In **711**, Muslim Arabs seized and occupied the entire Iberian Peninsula, with the exception of several border regions in the north where Christian princes defended their independence. With the fall of the Caliphate of Córdoba in **1031**, however, Christian rulers, especially the kings of Castile, began driving the Muslims (Moors) further southward. In **1085**, the Castilians occupied Toledo, the old and new center of Christian Spain. The Battle of Navas de Tolosa in **1212** in southern Spain was a turning point in the Reconquista (reconquest). In one of the greatest battles of the Middle Ages, some 90,000 Muslims lost their lives. The victory of the allied Christian kings against the Almohads opened up the way to Andalusia, the heartland of Moorish rule. By 1250, the Christians were able to capture Córdoba, Seville, and the Algarve in Portugal. Only the Nasrids, who had been ruling in Granada since **1235**, were able to withstand the onslaught of the superior Christian forces until **1492**.

A standard believed to have thaumaturgical powers accompanied the Christian soldiers.

Magna Carta

Magna Carta The Great Charter of 1215 is considered a milestone on the path to parliamentary democracy.

Continuing failures in foreign matters and an increasing tax burden brought the English King John Lackland into grave disrepute with his Anglo-Saxon barons. They wrung broad concessions from the king that were recorded in the Magna Carta in **1215**. The majority of the 63 articles deal with feudal law, setting limits to royal intervention; added to that were general protective rights restricting the powers of the crown. The original version even provided for direct challenges to the king's authority, but many clauses were repealed by the 19th century. However, the charter was the initial step towards British parliamentary democracy. To this day, the Magna Carta is considered the cornerstone of English constitutional law.

Pressure from revolting English barons forced King John to grant political civil rights to the English aristocracy in the Magna Carta.

A caravan of pilgrims on their way to Mecca

The Mali Empire

The Mali Empire Under Kankan Musa, the West African empire reached the zenith of its power. The lavish pilgrimage of its Muslim ruler to Mecca testifies to the immense wealth of the country.

In the first half of the 13th century, the Mali Empire in West Africa became a regional hegemonic power and eventually controlled the territory between the Atlantic coast in the west and present-day Nigeria in the east. Through its trade in salt and gold, Mali acquired fabulous wealth. Under the influence of the Almoravids, who had been ruling in Morocco since **1061**, the Malinke people converted to Islam. In the first half of the 14th century, under King Mansa Musa I, Mali developed into a center of Islamic scholarship. Famous universities and Qu'ran schools sprang up in the capital of Timbuktu and other places. When Musa set off on a pilgrimage to Mecca in **1324**, he was accompanied by 12,000 slaves and 800 ladies-in-waiting for his wives. He gave away so much gold while traveling that the price of gold plummeted worldwide. The Egyptian currency was ruined for decades. It was not until **1400** that the Songhai Empire took over the position of hegemony in West Africa from the Malinke.

1250 Public baths—a place for socializing as well as medical and hygiene purposes—reach the height of their popularity in **Europe**.

1252 An almost 52-foot-high statue of **Buddha** is erected in **Kamakura**, the **imperial seat of Japan**.

1267 English scholar **Roger Bacon**, pioneer of experimental empiricism and inventor of the magnifying glass, writes his major work, *Opus maius*.

1274 **Thomas Aquinas**, the most prominent exponent of medieval philosophy (**scholastic**), dies on March 7. He tried to reconcile **Christian faith** with the ancient **philosophy of Aristotle**.

1275 The **first mechanical clocks** (wheel clocks) are used in English monasteries.

1280 In Byzantine, the physician **Nicholas Myrepsos** writes the *Dynameron*, the most comprehensive **pharmacopoeia** of the Middle Ages.

1284 The first gold ducats are minted in **Venice**.

1295 The trader **Marco Polo** returns home to Venice after staying at the Chinese imperial court for 20 years. His **travel reports** from Asia shape the **image of China in Europe** for a long time.

1316 In Bologna, the physician **Mondino dei Luzzi** writes the first systematic **textbook on anatomy**.

1320 The extension of the **Grand Canal** as a trading link between North and South **China** is completed.

1250 | 1275 | 1300

1250 The **Mamluks**, former slave soldiers, form a new dynasty in **Egypt** under their leader Aybak. The dynasty remains in power until 1517.

1250 The **Sixth Crusade** to liberate Jerusalem ends in a catastrophe. **King Louis IX** of France is taken captive in Egypt.

1254 **Conrad IV**, the **last of the Hohenstaufen** rulers, dies. There is no generally recognized king in the Holy Roman Empire until 1273.

1256 **Mongols** under Hulagu Khan subjugate **Iran** and found an **Ilkhanate** there that lasts until 1335.

1258 With their destruction of **Baghdad**, the **Mongols** end the almost 500-year rule of the Abbasid caliphs.

1259 In the **Treaty of Paris**, Henry III of England renounces a large part of his claim to ownership of land in France but retains Gascony.

1261 After the peaceful occupation of Constantinople, **Michael VIII Palaiologos** forms the **Palaiologan dynasty** that rules the late Byzantine Empire until 1453.

1262 **Norway** secures **control of Iceland** with a treaty, also of Greenland in 1264.

1265 The **Second Baron's War** in England is crushed. However, a great **council of barons**, a form of parliament, is allowed to convene.

1268 **Charles of Anjou** defeats Conradin, the last legitimate scion of the imperial dynasty of the Hohenstaufens, in the **Battle of Tagliacozzo** and becomes king of Sicily. He has the 16-year-old Conradin executed.

1270 On the **Seventh Crusade, Louis IX of France** dies on Aug. 25 outside Tunis. This ends the last major crusade in the Near East.

1270 **Yekuno Amlak** becomes **emperor of Ethiopia**. He considers himself the **refounder of the Solomonic dynasty**.

1273 **Rudolf I of Habsburg** is elected the **new German King of the Romans**.

1278 On Aug., 26 German king **Rudolf I** defeats **Ottokar II** of Bohemia in the Battle of Marchfeld.

1280 **Lübeck** takes a leading role in the **Hanseatic League** around 1280. The activities of the league of cities increasingly serve to achieve political ends.

1282 **King Rudolf I** invests his sons with Austria and Styria, and thus lays the territorial foundation of the **House of Habsburg**.

1279 **Kublai Khan** conquers southern China, and so unites all of China under the rule of the **Mongolian Yuan dynasty**; his capital is present-day Beijing.

1281 The **Mongols** fail in their second attempt **to conquer Japan** after 1274. Their invasion fleet is destroyed by massive storms (kamikaze).

1282 Sicilian Vespers: With the support of the Byzantines and Aragonese, the Sicilians drive out Charles of Anjou, and **Sicily falls to the House of Aragón**. Charles remains ruler of only the Kingdom of Naples.

1283 After heavy fighting, the **Order of the Teutonic Knights** completes the **conquest of Prussia** and christianizes the land.

1284 In the struggle for **supremacy in the Mediterranean** between the Italian city-states, **Genoa** wins over **Pisa** in the **Battle of Meloria**.

1285 On Jan. 6, **Philip IV the Fair** is made **King of France**.

1291 The **collapse of the Ilkhanate in Persia begins** and culminates with the death of Ilkhan Ghazan in 1304.

1291 The cantons of Uri, Schwyz, and Unterwalden band together on Aug. 1 in an "eternal alliance." The **Rütli Oath** is considered the founding act of the Swiss Confederacy.

1295 For the first time, the **"model parliament"** convened by King Edward I, includes representatives of **English cities** besides clergy and nobility.

1299 Turkish military leader **Osman I** assumes the title of sultan and, with his campaigns of conquest against the Byzantines, forges the **Ottoman Empire** in the northwest of Asia Minor.

1301 The dynasty of the Arpads ends with the **death of King Andrew III of Hungary**.

1302 The rebelling **cities of Flanders** are victorious over an army of French knights on July 11 in the **Battle of the Golden Spurs** at Courtrai.

1302 **Boniface VIII** proclaims absolute **papal authority** over secular rulers in his **Unam Sanctam**. He is subsequently taken prisoner in 1303 by the order of the French king.

1306 The **Vietnamese Dai Viet Empire** puts pressure on the Khmer, steadily reducing their territory.

1308 **Henry VII of Luxemburg** is elected **German King of the Romans**. Four years later, he also receives the **emperor's crown**.

1309 Driven out of the Near East, the **Knights Hospitaller** gain control of the island of Rhodes.

1250-1450

The Late Middle Ages was a time of change. The emerging regions of Flanders and northern Italy, where the economic strength of the cities dominated, forged the basis for many new developments like Humanism, the Renaissance, and early capitalist economies. The policies of the European rulers were still shaped by dynastic thought, even though their mounting financial needs increasingly forced them to set up modern administrative systems. Significant changes also took place in religious life. Many people sought a new approach to religion, mostly due to the traumatic experience of the plague epidemic since 1348. At the same time, the secularization of the late medieval Church provoked massive criticism, which led to the era of Reformation. With the fall of the Mongols, the rise of the Ottoman and Russian empires on Europe's borders began to loom. Mongol rule was also shaken off in China, where the Ming dynasty founded a new imperial realm.

Karlštejn Castle near Prague; its construction was begun by Charles IV in 1348.

HISTORICAL FIGURES

Philip IV the Fair (1268–1314)   Philip laid the groundwork for a modern monarchy in France by ruthlessly increasing his power relative to the aristocracy and clergy.

Philip IV imposed centrally administrated royal justice and higher taxes for the privileged classes to finance his costly war against England and Flanders. When Pope Boniface VIII refused the taxation of the French Church, Philip had him kidnapped in 1305 and in **1309** appointed a crony as Pope Clement V in Avignon.

The papacy remained under French control for decades. The King had the powerful Teutonic Knights eliminated by **1312** and confiscated their wealth. He sought support from the bourgeoisie to an unprecedented extent, and in 1302 convened the Estates-General for the first time.

Timur the Lame (1336–1405)   At the close of the 14th century, the Mongol Prince, known as Tamerlane, combined Islamic and Mongolian traditions in a vast empire, which soon began to decay after his death.

In the tradition of Genghis Khan, Timur created a new Mongol Empire in Central Asia in the 14th century. Called "the Lame" because of an injury in his right leg, he began expeditions of conquest in **1370**, leading to his seizure of Baghdad in **1393** and Damascus in 1401. He inflicted devastating defeats on the Golden Horde in southern Russia and in 1399 expanded his territories to the East across Afghanistan to India. His cruelty was legendary. He had human heads stacked up in pyramids and had people walled in alive. As patron of the arts, he built magnificent mosques and madrasas in Samarkand and turned the city into a cultural center. He died while invading China in 1405—allegedly in an alcoholic stupor.

Margaret I (1353–1412)   The most prominent woman regent in Scandinavian history combined the monarchies of Denmark, Norway, and Sweden in a personal union in 1389.

When King Valdemar IV Atterdag of Denmark died in 1376, his daughter Margaret took over the affairs of state. After the death of her husband, King Haakon VI of Norway, she also became regent there and founded the Danish-Norwegian personal union that endured until 1814. She gained the crown of Sweden by defeating King Albert of Mecklenburg in 1389. In order to realize her goal of a grand Scandinavian Empire, she united Denmark, Norway, and Sweden in the "Kalmar Union" in **1397** that lasted until 1523. Except for a common crown and foreign policy, the nations remained largely independent.

Joan of Arc (1412–1431)   The simple farmer's daughter from Lorraine turned the tide against England in the Hundred Years' War in favor of France and is honored to this day as one of the Patron saints of France.

Joan of Arc grew up in a time of crisis. The English had been devastating the north of France and were pressing in on the crowned prince, Charles VII. Convinced she was chosen by God to save France, Joan was allowed to lead an army dressed as a man. On **May 8, 1429**, the young girl was able to drive the English out of Orléans and bring about the decisive turning point in the Hundred Years' War. After the victory in Patay, Charles VII was crowned king on **July 17.** However, he abandoned the celebrated folk heroine. Joan was delivered to the English by the Burgundians, placed on trial for heresy, and burned at the stake as a witch on **May 30, 1431.** The Church rescinded the verdict in 1456 and declared her a saint in 1920.

1380 English theologian and church reformer **John Wycliffe** condemns the Pope's claim to political power in a paper, making him a theoretical **forerunner of the Reformation**.

1387 **Geoffrey Chaucer** begins work on his *Canterbury Tales* in Middle English vernacular.

1397 With the **founding of a bank in Florence,** Giovanni di Bicci de' Medici lays the cornerstone of the rise of the **Medici** to one of the richest and most politically powerful families in Italy of the 15th and 16th centuries.

1404 The **Bibi-Khanym Mosque,** the largest mosque of its time in the Asiatic region, is completed.

1405 Chinese imperial eunuch and admiral **Zheng He** leads his first of seven **expeditions** in the Indian Ocean for the **Ming Dynasty**. The enormous treasure junks travel as far as the Horn of Africa.

1418 On the initiative of **Henry the Navigator,** the Portuguese begin with the **systematic exploration of Africa's west coast**.

1425 Italian sculptor **Lorenzo Ghiberti** begins to design the "Gates of Paradise," bronze doors for the Florence Baptistery.

1437 Spanish early **humanist** Iñigo López de Mendoza publishes the **first poetry in the Spanish language**.

1438 **Jacopo della Quercia**, Italian Early Renaissance sculptor, dies in Sienna on Oct 20.

1441 The **Portuguese** are the first Europeans to begin **slave trade in West Africa**.

1400 — **1425** — **1450**

1381 The **War of Chioggia** between the trading powers of **Genoa** and **Venice** for hegemony in the Mediterranean ends after three years with a compromise.

1385 The marriage of the **Grand Prince of Lithuania Władysław Jagiełło** with **Queen Jadwiga of Poland** founds the personal union of Poland and Lithuania (until 1572).

1386 The **Swiss** are victorious over the Habsburgs at **Sempach**. The Habsburgs are forced to relinquish their ancestral homeland and recognize the de facto **independence of the Confederacy**.

1389 Ottoman Turks defeat a Christian coalition led by the Serbian Prince Lazar in the **Battle of Kosovo. The Balkans come under Ottoman rule**.

1392 **Korean General Yi** founds the dynasty of the same name, which rules over **Joseon** (Korea) until 1910. The empire with its capital in Seoul is culturally and politically linked with China.

1393 Mongol Khan Timur Lenk captures **Baghdad** and totally destroys the city. Two years later, he also defeats the **Golden Horde**.

1397 **Kalmar Union:** Denmark, Norway, and Sweden are joined in a personal union. Until her death in 1412, **Margaret I** is the de facto regent of the three kingdoms.

1400 The **Songhai Empire** replaces Mali as the **supreme power** in West Africa and becomes one of the largest political entities in African history.

1401 **Klaus Störtebeker** and **Godecke Michels**, the leaders of the **"Victual Brothers,"** are **executed in Hamburg**. The pirates had been a threat to the Hanseatic League in the North and Baltic Seas since the mid-1350s.

1402 **Timur Lenk** annihilates the Ottoman army at Ankara. Sultan Bayezid I is taken prisoner.

1410 In the **greatest knights battle of the Middle Ages**, a Polish-Lithuanian army defeats the Teutonic Knights in the **Battle of Grunwald**. The **Polish-Lithuanian Union** becomes the leading power in Eastern Europe.

"The pope is a bishop... and no more."

Bohemian reformer Jan Hus, 1415

1415 The Bohemian church reformer **Jan Hus is burned at the stake** at the **Council of Constance** as a heretic. As a result, the Hussites in **Bohemia**, who follow some of his teachings, rise up against the rule of the Luxemburgs.

1415 English **King Henry V is triumphant at Agincourt** over the French army. After the Fall of Paris in 1418 and the flight of the king, France stands shortly before a devastating defeat.

1417 On Nov. 11 at the **Council of Constance**, a new Pope agreeable to all is elected, **Martin V**, thus ending the **Western or Papal Schism**.

1428 The **Aztec Empire** in **Mexico** ermerges as the dominant force in Central America.

1429 On May 8, **Joan of Arc**, "The Maid of Orléans," **forces the English to withdraw** from the city. This turning point in the Hundred Years' War enables the crowning of **Charles VII** on July 17 in Reims.

1431 **The Thai capture and sack Angkor**, the capital of the Khmer Empire. The Khmer relocate their capital to Phnom Penh in 1434.

1433 On May 31, **Sigismund**, the German King of the Romans, is crowned emperor.

1434 **Cosimo de' Medici** establishes the rule of his family in the **Republic of Florence**.

1435 The **Treaty of Vordingborg** ends the war between Denmark and the Hanseatic League and confirms the **trading privileges of the Hanseatic League**.

1435 In the **Treaty of Arras**, King Charles VII of France reaches an accord with **Burgundy**. The Hundred Years' War, however, continues until 1453.

1436 The ratification of the **Compact of Iglau** ends the **Hussite Wars** raging for 16 years in Bohemia.

1438 In Peru, **Pachacuti Inca Yupanqui** establishes the **Inca dynasty** as a major power in South America.

1431 Following her capture the previous year, French folk hero, **Joan of Arc**, is condemned as a heretic and **burned at the stake** on May 30.

L. PATROIS

1321 Shortly before his death, the Italian poet **Dante Alighieri** finishes one of the most influential works in world literature, *The Divine Comedy*.

1325 **Tenochtitlan is founded** by the Mexica people. It becomes the capital of the Aztec civilization.

1326 The first reference to **firearms** occurs in Europe.

1330 The first outbreak of the **bubonic plague** hits **China** and spreads to Europe through trade.

1334 Italian painter and pioneer of the Italian Renaissance **Giotto di Bondone** is chosen architect of the cathedral in Florence.

1348 At the suggestion of King Charles IV, the **first university in the Holy Roman Empire** is founded in **Prague**, the new royal residence.

1348 The **plague** rages in Europe until 1351.

1352 The **first carillon** with moving figures in Europe is installed in the **Strasbourg Cathedral**.

1363 The pope's physician, **Guy de Chauliac**, compiles a surgical compendium that remains authoritative for three centuries.

1368 Finishing work begins on the **Great Wall of China**, bringing it to its present form.

1374 The prominent Italian **poet** and **humanist Petrarch** (Francesco Petrarca) dies in Arquà.

1374 Gao Qi, the most noted **poet of the Ming period**, dies in China.

1325 | **1350** | **1375**

1309 Babylonian Captivity of the Papacy: Due to the unstable conditions in Rome, **Pope Clement V moves his residence to Avignon** in southern France.

1309 The **Majapahit Empire** under King Jayakatwang in **East Java** begins its expansion over all of **Indonesia**.

1312 Initiated by French King Philip IV, the **Order of the Knights Templar** is disbanded and eradicated. It is accused of heresy and financial corruption.

1312 **Mansa Musa** begins rule in **Mali** at the height of its empire. Following an extravagant pilgrimage to Mecca in 1324, he helps spread Islam throughout Mali.

1319 The royal **House of Sverre dies out in Norway**. The country is ruled by Swedish or Danish kings in personal union until 1905.

1320 **Władysław the Short** is crowned **King of Poland** in Kraków. The country is again united after almost 200 years.

1324 **Kankan Musa, the King of Mali** in West Africa, undertakes a pilgrimage (hajj) to Mecca.

1328 The **House of Valois** gains the French throne in the person of **Philip VI**. Edward III of England, the nephew of Philip's predecessor, **lays claim to the throne of France** as well.

1328 The Prince of Moscow, **Ivan I Kalita** ("Moneybag"), is named **Grand Prince of Russia** by the Mongol Khagan.

1332 Lucerne joins the **Swiss Confederation**; by 1353, Zurich and Bern have followed suit.

1335 In the Congress of Visegrád, **Casimir III the Great** relinquishes his claims to Silesia and in return is recognized by King John of Bohemia as **King of Poland**.

1336 The **Hindu Empire of Vijayanagar** emerges in the south of India and impedes the further expansion of Islam on the subcontinent.

1337/39 With his claim to the French throne, **Edward III of England** launches the **Hundred Years' War**, which lasts until 1453. One of the first attacks by the English is against Cambrai in 1339.

1338 The **Ashikaga Family** comes to **power in Japan** in a civil war and supplies the country's **Shoguns** (hereditary military dictators) up until 1573.

1341 A Portuguese expedition explores the **Canary Islands** and, at the beginning of the 15th century, the Azores and Madeira as well.

1346 **Stephen Uroš IV Dušan of Serbia** assumes the title, **"Tsar of the Serbs and Greeks."** The Serbian Empire is at the pinnacle of its power.

1346 On July 11, **Charles IV of the House of Luxembourg** is elected **German King of the Romans**. By 1347, he has prevailed over his rival.

1346 On Aug. 26, an **English army devastates Philip VI's larger army of knights** at Crécy.

1347 **Cola di Rienzi**, Tribune of the Roman people, establishes a republic in **Rome**.

1350 Tibet declares **independence from the Mongols** and is able to maintain it until 1724.

1351 **Ramthibodi I** founds the **Kingdom of Ayutthaya** in present-day Thailand.

1350 Polynesians found the **Maori** culture in New Zealand.

1351 Moroccan **Ibn Battuta** visits the **Mali Empire**. His account of the Swahili city of **Mogadishu** offers insight into mercantile and social customs of the area.

1355 **King Haakon VI Magnusson** assumes power in **Norway**.

1356 **Emperor Charles IV** fixes in writing for the first time the rules for electing the **"King of the Romans"** in the **Golden Bull** issued on Jan. 10.

1356 An English army defeats the French in the **Battle of Poitiers**. The French **King John II of Valois** is **taken captive**.

1361 Following the conquest of Gotland by Denmark, the **Hanseatic League** suffers losses and therefore wages war between 1367 and 1370.

1363 King John II of France invests his brother, **Philip II the Bold**, with the **Duchy of Burgundy**. He launches the country's rise to a leading power in Europe.

1368 The rebel movement of the **Red Turbans** drive the **Mongols** out of China. Emperor Hung Wu begins the reign of the domestic Ming dynasty, which rules until 1644.

1370 **Timur Lenk** (the Lame) declares himself **Amir (Kahn) of the Mongols** in Samarkand.

1375 The **Songhai Empire** in West Africa, controlled by **Mali** until now, gains its independence.

1377 **Pope Gregory XI** leaves Avignon and **returns to Rome**. The Vatican becomes the papal residence.

1378 The **Western Schism:** After the papal election of the Italian Urban VI in Rome, a **French Antipope**, Clement VII, is elected in Avignon.

1380 The **victory of the Grand Prince of Moscow, Dmitry Donskoy**, over the Mongols of the Golden Horde in the Battle of Kulikovo on Sept. 8 precipitates the **end of Mongol rule over Russia**.

1370 The **Treaty of Stralsund** of May 24 ends the war between the **Hanseatic League** and Denmark. The Hanseatic League secures its **hegemony in the Baltic Sea**.

HISTORICAL EVENTS

Kamikaze: The sea battle for Japan

The "divine wind," in Japanese Kamikaze, saved the Japanese in 1274 and 1281 from having their island conquered by the Mongols.

No one seemed able in the 13th century to halt the advance of the Mongols in Asia. By **1280**, they had secured control over China, where they founded the Yuan dynasty. Korea had already been annexed, an ideal bridgehead to launch an invasion of Japan and gain control of all of Asia. When, in 1274, almost 35,000 Mongol soldiers under Kublai Khan crossed over to Japan with the help of a Korean fleet, the ponderous Japanese Samurai warriors were soon on the defensive. However, an unexpected typhoon destroyed almost a third of the invasion fleet, forcing the Mongols to retreat. A second attempt to invade also failed in **1281** because of storm winds. The Japanese subsequently spoke of Kamikaze, god or divine winds, which protected their country from foreign attacks. It was not until **1945**, at the end of the Second World War, that the USA became the first foreign power to succeed in occupying Japan.

Even the suicide attacks of Japanese combat pilots, also called Kamikaze, were no longer able to prevent Japan's defeat.

As if by a miracle, heavy storms thwart the attacks of the Mongols on Japan.

The Birth of the Swiss Confederacy (1291)

The legend of the history of Switzerland begins with the confederation of three cantons on Rütli meadow.

On the night of **Aug. 1, 1291**, representatives of the three "original cantons" of Uri, Schwyz, and Unterwalden swore an oath of mutual support above Lake Lucerne. The scene is undoubtedly the result of subsequent national glorification, but the confederation of the three cantons is supported by historical evidence and builds the nucleus of modern Switzerland. With the joining of Lucerne (1332) and later Zurich and Bern, the confederacy of the "Acht Alten Orte" (eight old places) was formed. It was able to successfully withstand sovereignty claims by the Habsburgs in 1386, who finally were forced to recognize the Confederacy's independence. Switzerland was also officially granted its independence from the empire in the Peace of Westphalia in 1648.

The mythological portrayal of the Rütli Oath shows representatives of the three original cantons, Uri, Schwyz, and Unterwalden.

The Battle of Crécy (Hundred Years' War)

The first major battle of the Hundred Years' War ended in the year 1346 with the demise of the army of French knights.

The issue of the rightful claim to the throne of France culminated in **1339** in a war between England and France that lasted almost 100 years. After a first victory in a naval battle at Sluys, English King Edward III landed his army in Normandy. The first major battle took place on **Aug. 26, 1346**, near Crécy. Despite larger numbers, the French units suffered a momentous defeat. The use of the longbow had a devastating effect on the army of ponderous knights. So many Frenchmen died in the hail of English arrows that French morale suffered for a long time. As a result, the English were able to penetrate deep into the interior of France.

The English gained their first important victory in the Battle of Crécy.

They captured Calais on the coast, which they turned into their strategic base of operations. Despite their defeat in 1453, the English maintained their occupation of Calais until 1558.

The population of Europe was helpless in face of the impact of the plague.

Black Death

The plague raging in Europe between 1348 and 1351 resulted in widespread deaths that depopulated whole areas of the continent.

The "Great Mortality" hit the harbor city of Genoa in January **1348**. The bacteria that had people dying in agony within a few days after infection had come by merchant ships from Asia to Europe. Since the plague was highly infectious, it spread like wildfire over almost the entire continent—only a few areas, like Bohemia and Poland, were spared. Whole cities like Venice were placed under quarantine. About a third of the population at the time fell victim to a quick succession of waves of further epidemics lasting into the 15th century. The impact was devastating to all areas of life. Trade almost came to a complete standstill, the land became desolate, and the population, even the aristocracy, became impoverished. Christian lay movements of flagellants, who sought God's grace by scourging themselves, became enormously popular. Others believed the Jews were to blame. Pogroms were organized in many places, bringing death to additional thousands.

The Golden Bull

In what is arguably the most significant law of the Holy Roman Empire, the royal election procedure was legally set down in 1356.

In order to end the ongoing power struggles for the title of king and prevent a double election in the future, King Charles IV pushed through an imperial decree that, for the first time, constitutionally regulated the election of the king and the position of the imperial princes during a gathering of nobles called Court Days in Nuremberg and Metz in **1356**. Seven prince-electors were signified as royal electors, among them the Margrave of Brandenburg, the Duke of Saxony, and the Archbishops of Mainz, Cologne, and Trier. A simple majority was all that was needed for the election; the approval of the Pope was not necessary. The prince-electors were forbidden to enter alliances other than "land peace"; in return they were granted broad privileges such as tax sovereignty and jurisdiction in their own land. The territories of the prince-electors were declared indivisible. All in all, the Golden Bull strengthened their position of power, thus preventing the development of the empire into a (as perceived today) modern, centrally controlled state.

King Wenzel had 1,400 ornate copies of the Golden Bull made.

The Western or Papal Schism

The political divide in the Catholic Church that lasted from 1378 to 1417 weakened the moral authority of the papacy.

The Curia's return to Rome from exile in Avignon forced by Pope Gregory XI in **1377** exacerbated the political power struggle for the highest spiritual office in Christianity. The election of the Archbishop of Bari as Pope Urban VI in **1378** was not recognized by the French cardinals. In the same year in Avignon, they elected the Frenchman Clemens VII as their "God's representative." Both popes received support from different European countries. This only served to make the Church, now divided into two powerful camps, a pawn of foreign interests. The internal attempt to overcome the schism by convening a council in 1409 initially failed—instead a third pope was elected. It was not until the Council of Constance chaired by the King of the Holy Roman Empire, Sigismund, in 1417 that the schism was finally ended with the election of Martin V, who was recognized as pope by all sides.

The papal palace in Avignon, symbol of the unbridled politicization of the Church in the Middle Ages

The Battle of Kosovo

The Christian coalition led by Serbian Prince Lazar suffered a later, often mystical, defeat on Nightingale's Field at the hands of the Ottoman Turks in 1389.

After breaking away from Byzantium after 1180, the Serbs were able to expand in the Balkans through successful campaigns. Since Stephen Uroš IV Dušan had taken the title "Tsar of the Greeks and Serbs" in 1346 and had founded a state church, the Serbs had been in competition with Byzantium for the role of leader of Christian Orthodoxy in the southeastern European region. The Ottoman conquests, beginning in 1371 and supported in part by Constantinople, however, quickly brought on the collapse of the Serbian Empire.

The devastating defeat on **June 15, 1389**, in the Battle at Nightingale's Field in present-day Kosovo became imprinted in the collective memory of the Serbs. The Balkans was open territory to the Ottoman Turks. Serbia itself became an Ottoman vassal state. To this day, Christian nationalistic forces in Serbia justify the claim to Kosovo with the "heroic sacrifice" of **1389**. The myths began forming directly after the defeat. Part of this is also the fact that the leader of the Serbian army, Prince Lazar, has been canonized by the Serbian Church.

The elite troops of the Janissary played an essential role in the victories of the Ottoman Turks.

Hanseatic League

At the height of its power at the turn of the 15th century, the Hanseatic League was forced to defend against massive attacks by pirates.

The Hanseatic League began developing in the 13th century from regional alliances of Low German foreign traders into a transnational league of cities with political clout that controlled trade in the entire Baltic region and far beyond. From its regional centers in London and Bruges in the west, to the emerging imperial city of Lübeck and all the way to Novgorod, the main base in the east, the trading empire of the Hanseatic League spanned over almost all of northern Europe. With trading boycotts and successful wars against Denmark, the Hanseatic League was able to defend their interests in the 14th century even against individual nations. Raids by the "Victual Brothers" operating from their bases on the Baltic island of Gotland and the East Frisian Islands, however, became a greater problem at the end of the 14th century. They brought the Baltic trade almost to a halt. In **1401**, their leader, the legendary pirate Klaus Störtebeker was captured and executed. Yet, piracy outlived the Hanseatic League, which rapidly lost importance in face of the increasing nationalization of trade policies.

A seal of the city of Stralsund, exceeding thirty feet in size, from the year 1329

New Horizons

1455 The German **Johannes Gutenberg** develops the technology of **printing** with movable type, laying the groundwork for the first media revolution. In 1455, the *Gutenberg Bible* is printed.

1459 Venetian monk **Frà Mauro** publishes an innovative **world map**.

1466 Italian **sculptor Donatello**, who became famous mainly for his bronze statues, dies on Dec. 13 in Florence.

1467 **Ulrich Han** prints Italy's first book with **wood engravings** in Rome.

1469 **Thomas Malory** writes a novel about the legendary King Arthur, which is first published posthumously in 1485 with the title *Le Morte d'Arthur*.

1476 **Regiomontanus**, one of the most significant **mathematicians** since Antiquity, dies on July 6 in Rome.

1473 Under commission of Pope Sixtus IV, **Giovanni de' Dolci** begins constructing the **Sistine Chapel** in Rome.

1478 The **Inquisition** is placed under state control in present-day Spain and systematically used to persecute **"heretics,"** Jews, and Muslims.

1482/84 **Portuguese** explorer Diogo Cão becomes the first European to explore the **Congo**.

1450   **1460**   **1470**   **1480**

1450 In the mid-15th century, almost simultaneously with the fall of the Mayas, the **Aztecs** form on their island capital Tenochtitlán in present-day Mexico, their **Triple Alliance** of city-states with the Tepanecs from Tlacopan and the Acolhua from Texcoco.

1452 The last German King of the Romans, **Frederick III**, is crowned emperor by Pope Nicholas V in Rome.

1453 **Austria** is officially elevated to an **archduchy** on Jan. 6.

1453 **Sultan Mehmed II** conquers **Constantinople** (Istanbul) on May 29, putting an **end** to the **Byzantine Empire**. Mehmed II makes the city the capital of the **Ottoman Empire.**

1454 **Milan** and **Venice** make peace with the **Treaty of Lodi** on April 9. In a loose alliance with Naples, Florence, and the Papal States, they are able to maintain peace in Italy until 1494.

1455 The **Battle of St. Albans** marks the outbreak of open hostilities, called **The Wars of the Roses**, in the **struggle for the English crown**. It is named after the coat of arms of the two warring branches of the House of Plantagenet, in power since 1154: **the Houses of Lancaster** (red rose) and **York** (white rose). The war finally ends in 1485.

1457 The **Teutonic Knights** lose Marienburg to the Polish King **Casimir IV Jagiellon**. **Königsberg** later becomes the new seat of the order.

1458 On March 2, **George of Podbrady** is made the next **King of Bohemia.**

1459/63 After the annexation of Serbia and Bosnia, the **Ottoman Empire** is the **dominant power in the Balkans.**

1460 Danish King Christian I is chosen Duke of **Schleswig and Holstein**. The region remains under **Danish rule** until 1864.

1460 Portuguese Prince **Henry the Navigator** dies on Nov. 13. The seagoing expeditions along Africa's coast initiated by him launched **Portugal's rise as a sea power.**

1461 With the **Empire of Trebizond**, founded in 1204 in present-day northeastern Turkey, the **Ottoman Turks** conquer the last remnant of Byzantine imperial tradition.

1461 **Louis XI** becomes **King of France.**

1462 **Ivan III Vasilyevich** is made **Grand Prince of Moscow**. He considers himself heir to Byzantium and also custodian of Orthodoxy and by 1505 has united the Russian territories under his rule.

1463 The Holy Roman Emperor **Frederick III** recognizes **Mathias I. Corvinus** as **King of Hungary**. He later captures parts of Bohemia.

1464 **Sunni Ali** becomes king of the **Songhay Empire**. He sets out to conquer his neighbors and bring the trading centers of Timbuktu and Jenne under his control.

1467 The **Ashikaga Shogunate**, the central power in **Japan**, crumbles. A civil war ensues among the local rulers (Daimyo).

1468 The West African **Songhai Empire** captures **Timbutku.**

1469 **Isabella I of Castile** and **Ferdinand II of Aragón** marry on Oct. 19. The marriage of the two heirs apparent of both Spanish kingdoms lays the cornerstone of future **Spanish unity.**

1470 Around 1470 the **Incas** conquer the **Chimú Empire** on the Peruvian coast and extend their territory southward to present-day Chile and northward to Columbia.

1471 In **England**, **Edward IV** of the House of York ends the monarchy of the House of Lancaster. **Henry VI is murdered** on May 21.

1474 Charles the Bold of Burgundy and Emperor Frederick III arrange the **marriage** of their two children, **Mary of Burgundy** and **Maximilian of Austria**. The Habsburgs gain the **Netherlands** through this marriage in 1477.

1474 **Perpetual Accord:** The **Habsburgs relinquish their Swiss territory** on March 30. Burgundy is the common enemy of both treaty partners.

1475 The **Khan of the Crimean Tatars** submits to the Ottoman Sultan.

1477 **Charles the Bold** falls on Jan. 5 in the **Battle of Nancy** against an allied army of Swiss and Lorraine. This marks the beginning of the **decline of the Burgundian interim realm**. A struggle of succession breaks out between the Duchy and France.

1479 In the **Treaty of Alcáçovas**, **Portugal and Castile** lay their quarrels aside and come to an agreement over their **areas of interest in the Atlantic**. The Portuguese receive a maritime monopoly in the African region—with the exception of the Canaries.

1479 After 16 years of war, **Venice** must concede territories in **Albania** and **Greece** to the **Ottoman Turks**. Later, however, the republic gains the island of **Cyprus**, which remains Venetian until 1571.

1480 Grand Prince of Moscow **Ivan III** stops paying tribute to the **Golden Horde**. This ends centuries of subservience to the Mongol princes.

1482 The **Portuguese** found the **Fort São Jorge da Mina** in present-day Ghana, which later becomes a central hub for the **transatlantic slave trade.**

1485 On Aug. 22, **Henry Tudor** defeats the English King Richard III in the **Battle of Bosworth Field** and mounts the throne as Henry VII, putting an end to the Wars of the Roses.

1486 The Habsburg **Maximilian I** is chosen **German King of the Romans** on Apr. 9.

1487/88 The Portuguese explorer **Bartolomeu Diaz** is the first European to sail around the southern tip of Africa and to discover the **Cape of Good Hope.**

1450–1560

The 15th century was a time of new horizons, particularly since mid-century, when the long-smoldering thirst for intellectual and religious renewal and disentanglement from traditional constructs and paradigms of thought began to be openly expressed. The Reformation movement successfully questioned the authority of the Catholic Church, fragmenting Western Christianity into different denominations. There was a rediscovery of the ideals of Antiquity in art, literature, and architecture. Italian princely dynasties like the Medici of Florence played a major role as patrons in contributing to the blossoming of Humanism and the Renaissance. Many critical scientists increasingly distanced themselves from the Christian interpretation of the world. Its high point was reached in a new social and scientific curiosity that significantly increased European knowledge of the world within just a few years and made it possible for Europeans to colonize foreign continents.

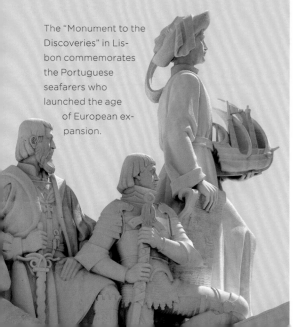

The "Monument to the Discoveries" in Lisbon commemorates the Portuguese seafarers who launched the age of European expansion.

HISTORICAL FIGURES

Lorenzo I de' Medici, the Magnificent (1449–1492)

The prototype of a Renaissance prince, he led the Republic of Florence to an economic, political, and cultural flowering.

Lorenzo was a member of the Medici Family, who came to wealth and influence through trade and banking and had controlled the city-state of Florence since **1434**. After a humanistic education, he succeeded his father as head of the republic in 1469. Through his balance-of-power policies, he secured peace in Italy and solidified the position of his home state. In the tradition of his family, he was a patron of scholars and artists like Michelangelo and Botticelli. His efforts as a poet also conformed to the ideal image of a Renaissance ruler. Until his death in 1492, Lorenzo had made Florence into one of Europe's leading cultural metropolises.

Henry VIII (1491–1547)
A tyrant, who used up women: The Tudor king and founder of the Anglican Church is one of the most colorful figures in English history.

England changed fundamentally after Henry VIII became king in **1509**. Henry, a Catholic, attempted a divorce from Catherine of Aragon because he lacked a male heir and was infatuated with his wife's maid of honor, Anne Boleyn. When Pope Clement VII refused, Henry broke with Rome. In **1534**, he made himself the official head of the English Church with the Acts of Supremacy. He subsequently had monasteries disbanded and Church property nationalized. Opponents to his policies were liquidated, and thousands of Catholics and Reformists were murdered. His papal excommunication hardly impressed him. Henry married another five times after his first marriage—and had two of his wives executed.

Suleiman I (c. 1494–1566)
The Ottoman Empire under his reign was politically and culturally at its prime and became a recognized major European power.

The son of Selim I became Sultan in 1520 and successfully continued his father's campaigns of conquest, which had already doubled the size of the Ottoman Empire. He conquered Belgrade in 1521, defeated the Hungarians in **1526**, and in 1529 stood for the first time at the gates of Vienna. The much proclaimed "Turkish threat" terrified Europe. Suleiman I also extended his empire to the east with the capture of Baghdad in **1534**. His greatest accomplishment, however, was in his efforts of internal consolidation, primarily through administrative, legal, and tax reforms, which earned him the name "the Lawgiver."

Ivan IV, the Terrible (1530–1584)
The first to be crowned Tsar, he brutally subjugated Russia and ruthlessly expanded his authority and his territories far into the east.

When Ivan IV Vasilyevich succeeded his father at the age of three, there was a struggle for the crown among the Russian hereditary nobility, the Boyars. On **Jan. 16, 1547**, he was crowned the "Tsar of all the Russias" and made a great effort to consolidate his power. He centralized the administration, introduced a new legal code, and unified church rituals and regulations, but also broke the power of the Boyars with all available means. His policies began showing signs of paranoia in 1560. With open terror, he proceeded against his enemies and even killed his own son in a fit of rage in 1581. At his death in 1584, Ivan left behind an enlarged but shattered empire. His dynasty ended in **1598** during the "Time of Troubles."

1527 Europe's **first Protestant university** is founded in **Marburg** on the instructions of Philip I, Landgrave of Hesse.

1528 Geman painter, printmaker, and art theorist **Albrecht Dürer**, who became famous for his woodcuts, among other things, dies on Apr. 6 in Nuremberg.

1539 **Guru Nanak Dev**, the founder of the Hindu **Sikh movement**, dies in India.

1541 Shortly before his death, **Michelangelo** completes the *Last Judgment*, marking the end of his work in the **Sistine Chapel**.

1543 The Flemish personal physician of Charles V, **Andreas Vesalius**, authors a medical textbook, which becomes the **foundation of modern anatomy**.

1543 Astronomer **Nicolaus Copernicus** dies . His **heliocentric model** of the universe not only revolutionizes astronomy, but also how the world is viewed in general.

1551 **South America's first university** is founded in **Lima**.

1545 The discovery of silver in **Potosí** in present-day Bolivia launches a **silver boom** in Europe as well.

1554 Jesuit **Manuel de Nobrega** founds the city of **São Paulo** in Brazil on Jan. 25.

1559 In Rome, **Pope Paul IV** issues an **index of banned books**. This is continued on into the 20th century.

1530 | **1540** | **1550** | **1560**

1521 The Spanish conquistador **Hernán Cortés** destroys the **Aztec Empire** in Mexico.

1523 **Gustav I. Vasa** frees Sweden from Danish rule and founds a **Swedish monarchy**. As king, he introduces the **Reformation** into Sweden.

1526 On Aug. 29, the **Ottoman Sultan Suleiman I** defeats the **Hungarians** at **Mohács** and annexes broad areas of the country. In 1529, the Ottoman Turks lay siege to **Vienna**.

1536 The radical reformer **John Calvin** tries to implement his teachings in Geneva, which he is only able to do after 1541. The Calvinist reform movement spreads out of Geneva and is most successful in the Netherlands and France.

1552 **Matteo Ricci** is born in Macerata, Italy. In 1582, he founds a **Jesuit mission in China**. Matteo's mastery of Chinese impresses the imperial court, which serves to open doors for the Jesuits in China.

1557 **Khan Abd Allah II** conquers **Buchara** and makes the city the center of a short-lived **Usbekian Empire**.

1527 **Sacco di Roma:** On May 6, thousands of Spanish Habsburg troops **capture** Rome and sack **the city**.

1538 The **Truce of Nizza** of June 18 ends a third Italian war between **France** and the **Habsburgs**.

1553 On July 19, **Mary I** ascends to the throne of **England** and launches a violent **recatholicization** of the country.

1524 **Peasants' War:** Influenced by the ideas of the Reformation, peasants in many parts of the empire rise up against **servitude** and the increase in their taxes. They receive support from the theologian **Thomas Müntzer**. By 1525, the uprising has been brutally suppressed, and Müntzer tortured and executed.

1540 The **Jesuit Order**, founded in 1534 by **Ignatius von Loyola**, is officially recognized by the Pope. It is meant to advance the spread of the **Catholic faith**.

1542 After **Bartolomé de Las Casas** reports of the **mistreatment of the native inhabitants** of the New World, Emperor Charles V enacts **"new laws"** for their protection. But they are largely ignored.

1555 On Sept. 25, the **Peace of Augsburg** ends the religious war in the empire. The **Lutheran faith** is recognized as a religion, and the princes are free to choose a mandatory religion for their subjects.

1558 After the death of Mary I, **Elizabeth I** is crowned the next **Queen of England** on Nov. 17. Under her rule, the country experiences a cultural and political flowering.

1525 On Feb. 24, **Emperor Charles V** defeats **Francis I of France at Pavia**, ending the **First Italian War** in favor of the Habsburgs.

1533 The Spaniard **Francisco Pizarro** conquers the core of the **Inca Empire** in present-day Peru and, bit by bit, subdues all the other Inca territories.

1543 The Portuguese reach **Japan** for the first time.

1545 On Dec. 13, the Catholic Church opens the **Council of Trent** that launches **a counter reformation** (Catholic Reformation).

1525 The Grand Master of the Teutonic Knights, **Margrave Albert of Brandenburg**, secularizes the order's state and on Apr. 8 introduces the **Reformation** into the newly created **Duchy of Prussia**.

1534 English King **Henry VIII**, excommunicated in 1533 by the Pope because of his divorce, separates the English Church from Rome and declares himself **head of the Anglican Church**.

1546 The **Schmalkaldic War** breaks out in the Holy Roman Empire between Charles V and the Schmalkaldic League of German Protestant princes, which is dissolved in 1547.

1547 Grand Prince of Moscow **Ivan IV**, called **the Terrible**, has himself **crowned the first Russian Tsar**.

1556 **Akbar the Great**, the most important **Mughal ruler** of India, ascends to the throne.

1559 On Apr. 3, the **Peace of Cateau-Cambrésis** finally ends the **conflict over Italy** between France and the Habsburgs, in favor of the **Spaniards**.

1526 On Apr. 21, the **Mughal Prince Babur** is victorious over Ibrahim Lodi, Sultan of Delhi, in the **First Battle of Panipat** and founds the **Mughal Empire in India**.

1534 French explorer **Jacques Cartier** discovers **Newfoundland** and claims the territory for France.

1536 **King Christian III** enforces the **Reformation** in **Denmark** and **Norway.**

1549 The Jesuit **Francisco de Xavier** is given permission by **Japanese** princes to **proselyte Christianity** in the country.

1552 **Princes' Uprising: Maurice of Saxony**, in alliance with France, leads an **uprising of Protestant Princes** against Emperor Charles V.

1556 **Emperor Charles V** abdicates on Jan. 16 or Sept. 12. His son, **Philip II**, inherits Spain and the Netherlands, among other things, while Charles's brother, **Ferdinand I**, succeeds as **Holy Roman Emperor**.

1485 Construction of the **stone wall** around the **Kremlin** in **Moscow** begins.

1486 Philosopher **Giovanni Pico della Mirandola** presents a modern, humanist view of man in his *Oration on the Dignity of Man*.

1487 The Dominican and Inquisitor **Heinrich Kramer** publishes *The Hammer of Witches*, which offers a theoretical basis for the **witch hunts** in the following centuries.

1492 The poet and scholar **Jami** dies on Nov. 9. He is the last representative of classic **Persian literature**.

1494 The Humanist **Sebastian Brant** publishes his *Ship of Fools* in Basel. The **moral satire** is read throughout all of Europe.

1501 **Michelangelo** begins work on his monumental statue of *David*.

1503/06 **Leonardo da Vinci** completes the *Mona Lisa*, arguably the most famous work of art in history.

1506 **Alfonso I**, a Christian convert supported by the Portuguese, assumes the throne of the **Kongo Empire**.

1510 Dutch scholar and proponent of European Humanism, **Erasmus of Rotterdam**, publishes his satire *The Praise of Folly*.

1513 In his book, *The Prince*, Italian philosopher and politician **Niccolò Machiavelli** elevates **reason of state** to the highest principle of political action.

1516 Dutch painter **Hieronymus Bosch** dies.

1516 The later English Lord Chancellor **Thomas More** introduces the word **"Utopia"** into the universal language in his *Utopia*, a satire critical of the times.

1519 Portuguese explorer **Ferdinand Magellan** sets out to **circumnavigate the world**.

1490   **1500**   **1510**   **1520**

1489 **Sikandar Lodi** becomes **Sultan of Delhi** and by 1517 has expanded his territories beyond the north of India.

1491 In the **Peace of Pressburg**, Habsburg King Maximilian I recognizes the sovereignty of Vladislaus II over **Hungary** and **Bohemia**, but secures the hereditary right to the territories.

1492 **Alexander VI Borgia** becomes the new **pope**. During his tenure, lasting until 1503, **moral decline** and **corruption** in the Vatican reach their lowest point.

1492 On Oct. 12, the Genoese navigator **Christopher Columbus** lands on an island in the Bahamas and unknowingly discovers a new continent: **America**.

1492 The last Muslim bastion on the Iberian Peninsula falls with the Spanish **conquest of Granada** on Jan. 2. The **Reconquista** is completed.

1493 **Askia the Great** becomes ruler of the **Songhai Empire** in West Africa that reaches the pinnacle of its power by 1529.

1494 In the **Treaty of Tordesillas** on June 7, newly discovered lands and trade routes are divided along a specified line of demarcation between the two leading sea powers, **Castile** and **Portugal**.

1493 With the coming to power of **Huayna Cápac**, a golden age begins for the **Inca Empire** in South America.

1498 On May 22, the Portuguese **Vasco da Gama** becomes the first European to reach India by sea and lands in **Calicut**.

1499 The imperial war against the Swiss ends on Sept. 22 with the **Treaty of Basel**. Switzerland is de facto no longer part of the Empire.

1500 Portuguese explorer **Pedro Álvares Cabral** discovers, probably by chance, **Brazil** and claims it for the Portuguese crown.

1502 **Moctezuma II** becomes ruler of **Tenochtitlan**. His reign is brought to an end with the conquest of Mexico by the Spanish starting in 1519.

1503 **"Casa de Contratación de Indias"** is founded in **Seville**. It has a state mandate to organize all overseas trading.

1504 **Ferdinand II of Aragón**, ruler in Spain, has the **Kingdom of Naples** occupied despite resistance from the French; a large section of **Navarre** is also annexed in 1512.

1505 The nobility in **Poland** forces the crown to accept the transference of all **legislative power** to them.

1508 German King of the Romans, **Maximilian I**, takes the title of an **"Elected Emperor."**

1509 **Henry VIII** Tudor mounts the throne of **England** on Apr. 21.

1510 Portuguese navigator **Afonso de Albuquerque** conquers **Goa** on the west coast of India and builds it into a central base for **Portuguese expansion**.

1511 **Cuba** is taken into permanent possession by the Spanish.

1512 **Selim I** is the **new Ottoman Sultan**. By 1520 he has conquered **Syria** and **Egypt**, as well as the holy sites in Arabia, and takes on the title of Caliph in 1517.

1513 The **victory of the Swiss at Novara** on June 6 forces the French led by **Louis XII** to retreat from Italy.

1514 In the **Battle of Chaldiran**, the **Ottomans** defeat the **Safavids**. Their two empires are in conflict for the next two centuries.

1515 After being soundly **defeated** by the French **at Marignano** on Nov. 13–14, the Swiss decide to make **Switzerland "eternally neutral."**

1517 The German monk **Martin Luther** publishes his **95 Theses** in Wittenberg criticizing the Pope's **selling of indulgences**. The authority of the Catholic Church in the empire is shaken to its core.

"Here I stand; I cannot do otherwise."

Martin Luther in Worms, 1521

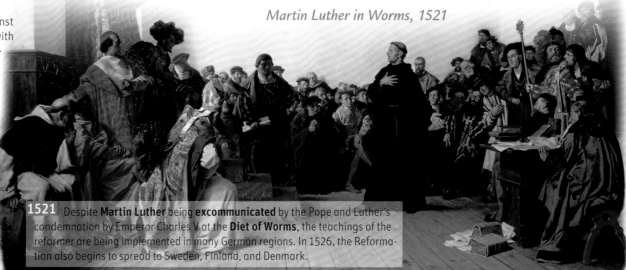

1521 Despite **Martin Luther** being **excommunicated** by the Pope and Luther's condemnation by Emperor Charles V at the **Diet of Worms**, the teachings of the reformer are being implemented in many German regions. In 1526, the Reformation also begins to spread to Sweden, Finland, and Denmark.

HISTORICAL EVENTS

Fall of Constantinople 1453   After having survived for over a thousand years, the conquest of Constantinople by the Ottoman Turks on May 29, 1453, put an end to the Byzantine Empire.

By the mid-15th century, large areas of the once mighty Byzantine Empire had been captured by the Ottoman Turks so that it had been reduced to a small area surrounding its capital of Constantinople. In April 1453, Ottoman Sultan Mehmed II began his massive assault on the former center of Christianity. Despite being outnumbered—7,000 defenders faced as many as 10,000 attackers—the troops under the last Byzantine emperor, Constantine XI Palaiologos, offered bitter resistance for seven weeks. On **May 29, 1453**, the Ottoman Turks were finally able to breach the walls of the city. Byzantium, which had upheld the Roman imperial tradition in the East, had finally become history. Constantinople, now referred to as Istanbul, became the new capital of the Ottoman Empire. Numerous churches became mosques, and first in line was Hagia Sophia. But, as the hub of a world empire, the city once again experienced a renaissance.

The Byzantines were forced to bow to the might of the Ottoman Empire.

The Discovery of America   On Oct. 12, 1492, Genoese explorer Christopher Columbus landed on an island in the Bahamas and discovered for the Europeans, without knowing it, the New World.

Intensive cosmographic research had convinced Columbus that he had found the way to East India by sea. When he was soliciting support for his voyage of discovery in 1486, he promised the Spanish ruling couple massive amounts of gold and silk. It worked, and he was given the necessary money, plus the privilege of becoming viceroy of all the territories he took possession of for Spain. On Aug. 3, 1492, Columbus set sail and, on **Oct. 12, 1492**, reached an island in the Bahamas that he named San Salvador. He called the natives "Indians." His lust for gold led him further to Cuba and Haiti, and, by 1504, he had also discovered Puerto Rico and Jamaica. This was the start of European colonization and exploitation of the continent of America, which had been unknown to the rest of the world until then. In **1494** Spain and Portugal divided the New World amongst themselves with a papal mandate to Christianize it. Columbus died convinced he had reached India, but had lost all claims due to alleged abuse of authority.

When Columbus landed on San Salvador, he was convinced he had arrived in India.

Persia under the Safavids   The founder of the Persian Safavid dynasty, Shah Ismail I, introduced the unique Shia path of national development into what is present-day Iran.

Since the mid-15th century, the Safaviyya Sufi order had been gaining strength within the territory of Iran, which was splintered into many locally ruled territories. In **1502**, the leader of the order, Ismail I, rose to become the Shah of Persia. He laid the territorial and cultural foundation for the Safavid dynasty, which ruled until **1722**. By 1510, Ismail I had subjugated all of Iran, driven out the Uzbeks, and conquered Iraq. But he was defeated by the Ottoman Turks in 1514. From his imperial residence in Tabriz, he began to build up a centralized national administration and made Shia Islam the state religion.

Ismail's son, Tahmasp I, receiving the Indian Mughal Emperor Humayun at his court

The German Reformer and former Augustine monk, Martin Luther, delivering a sermon

The Reformation   Martin Luther's open criticism of the Pope selling indulgences in 1517 triggered the Reformation, during the course of which the Holy Roman Empire was split both politically and religiously.

Abuses within the Church, plus the increasing secular interests of the Pope and bishops, had already provoked the formation of various religious reform movements in the 15th century. The reform movement initiated at the beginning of the 16th century by the German Martin Luther had, within a few years, finally destroyed the exclusive authority of the Catholic Church in Western Christianity. In **1517**, Luther posted his 95 Theses for reforming the Church in Wittenberg, resulting in a break with Rome three years later and in a break with Emperor Charles V in Worms in **1521**. The support that Luther received from powerful territorial princes transformed the movement into a revolutionary dynamic of its own. Although the social unrest in the Empire ignited by the events had been brought to its knees by **1524**, all attempts by Emperor Charles V to restore church unity failed. More and more princes were instituting state churches in line with Luther's teachings. On **Sept. 25, 1555**, the Emperor was forced to recognize Protestantism in the "Peace of Augsburg" and grant the territorial lords their free choice of confessions. In the meantime, the reform movement, which had spread in Europe, had split. The Protestants in France and the Netherlands followed the teachings of the Geneva reformer John Calvin.

The Aztecs present gifts to the Spanish Conquistador Cortés upon his arrival in Mexico.

Colonization of Central America
The subjugation of the Aztecs begun by Hernán Cortés in 1519 was the starting point for establishing a Spanish colonial empire on the American mainland.

When the Spanish Conquistador Hernán Cortés reached Mexico in 1519, the Aztec Empire was both culturally and politically at its prime. The Aztec ruler, Moctezuma II, reigned over 38 subservient city-states, and his royal residence, Tenochtitlán, was considered the most magnificent city in all of Central America. The king cordially received Cortés, who was seen as a deity whose arrival had been prophesied. Cortés, however, had Moctezuma taken prisoner, destroyed the religious ritual sites, and conquered Tenochtitlán in heavy and costly fighting on **Aug. 13, 1521**, with the aid of native Totonac and Tlaxcala. Cortés was appointed governor of New Spain and the last Aztec ruler, Cuauhtémoc, was executed in 1525. Piece by piece, the Europeans subjugated the whole continent.

Battle of Pavia
The failed invasion of Italy in 1525 was France's first attempt to free itself from the embrace of the Habsburgs.

At the beginning of the 16th century, the Habsburgs had been able to enlarge their territories through cleverly arranged dynastic marriages. When Charles V, who already controlled the Netherlands, also inherited Spain in 1516, France found itself surrounded by Habsburg territory. The battles between France and the Habsburgs were repeatedly waged in Italy. There, King Francis I was taken captive by the Spanish near Pavia in **1525**, but it was not until **1559** that France recognized Habsburg hegemony over Italy. After the Thirty Years' War in **1648** and the War of the Spanish Succession in **1713-14**, the tide finally turned. In coalition with different partners, France reduced Habsburg's influence. Confronted with the growing power of Britain and Prussia, France and the Habsburgs joined together in an alliance for the first time in 1756 in the run-up to the Seven Years' War.

Spanish soldiers swarm into the French camp during the Battle of Pavia.

Council of Trent – Counter-Reformation
The Catholic Church reacted to the success of the Reformation with the reform resolutions of Trent and increased proselyting and propaganda.

Among the resolutions reached at the Council of Trent between **1545** and **1563** were those banning the accumulation of multiple offices and the sale of indulgences. At the same time, the Church's theological profile was more sharply defined to differentiate it from Protestant teachings. The plan was to strike out in a propaganda counteroffensive with well-educated clergy. The "Society of Jesus" had already been acting along these lines since **1540**. The Jesuits established priest seminaries and took over universities. The Pope reorganized the Roman inquisition and compiled an index of banned publications. Finally, the Catholic princes rededicated themselves to recatholization and thus increased tension among the confessions.

Representatives of the Catholic Church convene in the cathedral of the city of Trent.

Inca Empire
At the beginning of the 16th century, the ancient American civilizations were in full bloom. Inner unrest facilitated the Spanish conquest that began in 1532.

The Incas, whose ruler was worshiped as the "Son of the Sun," make an offering to the sun.

In **1438**, the Incas began building up the largest empire in ancient America from their base in Peru. During the reign of Huayna Cápacs, which began in **1493**, the Inca Empire spanned the Pacific coast of South America from present-day southern Columbia to the north of Chile. The rulers governed the empire with the aid of a well-conceived, strictly hierarchically organized state administration. All subjects of the ruler had to serve him in their specified fields. The infrastructure and communications system were highly developed. Farming was communally organized. But when Cápacs died in 1527, a five-year fratricidal war broke out that paralyzed the empire. The Spanish Conquistador Francisco Pizarro took advantage of the Incas' weakness and, by **1533**, had subjugated the huge empire. The highly advanced civilization crumbled within a few years due to wars and diseases.

1566 **Nostradamus**, who gained world fame through his **prophecies** written in verse, dies in Salon-de-Provence, France, on July 2.

1569 Spanish **missionary Fray Bernardino de Sahagún** finishes his work *Historia general de las cosas de Nueva España*, considered to this day to be the most important source on **Aztec life**.

1574 **Selimiye Mosque** in Edirne, a prime example of Ottoman architecture, is opened on Nov. 27, after five years of construction.

1576 French **philosopher Jean Bodin** introduces the concept of absolute sovereignty in his work *Six Livres de la République*.

1576 The **plague** rages in the city-state of **Venice**.

1580 A **stud farm** is founded in the present-day Slovakian city of Lipica, which later breeds the famous **Lipizzans**.

1580 French humanist and free-thinker **Michel de Montaigne** publishes the first volume of his *Essays*, inventing the essay literary form.

1582 **Pope Gregory XIII** announces a **calendar reform**, which is initially adopted only in various Catholic countries.

1563 At the instigation of **King Philip II of Spain**, construction begins on Apr. 23 of the monastery and royal palace of **El Escorial**, the largest Renaissance complex in the world.

1560 | **1570** | **1580** | **1590**

1560 Systematic **witch hunts** begin in Europe that only gradually subside in the mid-17th century.

1560 Instigated by Scottish reformer **John Knox**, the **Treaty of Edinburgh** provides for the **removal of all French troops from Scotland**, ending the alliance between Scotland and France that had existed since 1295.

1561 Spanish **King Philip II** makes **Madrid** the new capital of his realm.

1562 French Regent **Catherine de' Medici** guarantees Huguenots unlimited **religious freedom** in the Edict of Saint-Germain-en-Laye.

1562 The **massacre** of Protestants in Wassy by Catholic **Francis Duke of Guise** ignites the Huguenot wars that last a total of 36 years.

1563 The **Council of Trent**, convened to reform the Catholic Church, concludes on Dec. 4.

1563 The **Northern Seven Years' War** between **Sweden** and **Denmark** breaks out, which ends in 1570 without any territorial change.

1565 The **Knights Hospitaller** successfully defend the island of **Malta** against an Ottoman attack.

1566 **Beeldenstorm** or **Iconoclastic Fury in Flanders:** Protestants attack Catholic churches in the Netherlands, igniting an uprising against Spanish sovereignty. King Philip II begins its brutal suppression in 1567.

1569 **Union of Lublin:** The personal union between **Poland** and **Lithuania**, which has existed since 1385, becomes a real union on July 1. The noble class reserves the right to choose the king.

1570 **Ottoman troops** capture **Cyprus** and hold the island totally under their rule.

1571 On Oct. 7, an alliance of Spanish and Venetian ships defeats an Ottoman fleet off the Greek coast in the **Battle of Lepanto**. Spain becomes the leading sea power in the western Mediterranean.

1571 After **conquering the Philippines** between 1565 and 1570, the Spanish colonial masters found its later capital, **Manila**.

1572 **St. Bartholomew's Day massacre:** On Aug, 24, thousands of Huguenots are killed in a massacre by fanatic Catholics in France.

1572 At the age of ten, **Wanli** becomes the new **emperor of China**. He lives in the Forbidden City in Beijing and chooses to conduct business through eunuch intermediaries, leading to corruption and the weakening of the **Ming state**.

1573 Warlord **Oda Nobunaga** overthrows the last Ashikaga Shogun. He ends the **Warring States Period** and attempts to **reunite Japan**.

1574 **Henry III** is made the **new king of France**.

1576 On Oct. 12, Habsburg **Rudolf II** is **chosen Holy Roman Emperor**. He introduces the pompous Spanish court ceremonial.

1578 **King Sebastian of Portugal** and his invasion army are crushingly defeated in Morocco at **al Qsar al Kabir**; the king falls.

1579 On Jan. 6, the southern Catholic provinces in the **Netherlands** join together in the **Union of Arras** in support of the Spanish governor general; the Calvinist northern provinces establish the **Union of Utrecht** on Jan. 23.

1580 On Jan. 30, **King Philip II of Spain** violently takes the Portuguese throne and unites both countries in a personal union.

1581 The **Protestant Netherlands** secede from Spain and found the **Republic of the Seven United Provinces** under Stadtholder **William I of Orange**.

1581 On behalf of the merchant family **Stroganov, Jermak, the leader of the Cossacks**, begins his conquest of the Mongol khanate in **Siberia**.

1582 After years of unsuccessful invasion attempts, Russian **Tsar Ivan IV (the Terrible)** reaches a peace accord with **Poland-Lithuania** on Jan. 15 near Pskov.

1582 After Oda Nobunga dies, **Prince Toyotomi Hideyoshi** assumes power in **Japan**. Five years later he bans Christianity.

1583 Commissioned by Queen Elizabeth I, **General Sir Humphrey Gilbert** occupies Newfoundland, launching the **English colonization of North America**.

1586 Indian Mughal Emperor **Akbar the Great** conquers **Kashmir**.

1587 After being imprisoned for 19 years, **Scottish Queen Mary Stuart is executed** on Feb. 8 at the command of English Queen Elizabeth I.

1588 The **Spanish Armada is destroyed** by an English fleet in the English Channel during July and August.

The Time of the Religious Wars
1560–1650

After the Reformation and the subsequent Catholic Counter-Revolution, Europe was aflame with confessional conflicts between Protestants and Catholics. The Huguenot Wars in France, the war for independence in the Netherlands, the Spanish-English antagonism, and, finally, the Thirty Years' War show to what extent religion had been politically instrumentalized. In the Thirty Years' War, the Holy Roman Empire became a military staging arena for foreign armies, who left the country in ruins and the population reduced almost by half. The political interests of the conflicting parties became increasingly apparent. In the end, the war brought the downfall of the Habsburgs from their dominating position in Europe. France and Sweden, with their strongly centralized governments, emerged as the new major powers, while England and the Netherlands built up their positions as trading nations.

A soldier from the time of the Thirty Years' War (painting by Diego Velázquez, dated 1635)

HISTORICAL FIGURES

Akbar I (1542–1605) The Muslim Grand Mughal expanded his rule far beyond India and sought tolerance for the Hindu faith.

The Indian Mughal Empire created by Babur in **1526** was on the verge of disintegration when Akbar came to power in **1556**. By 1580, however, he had been able to win back lost territory in northern India and expand further south. He sought to bring unity to the internally heterogeneous nation. In order to overcome religious tension through toler-ance he abolished the Jizya, a tax paid by non-believers. A melding of Muslim and Hindu traditions can especially be seen in the arts. Akbar's imperial residence of Fatehpur Sikri belongs to the World Cultural Heritage. The Mughal ruler left behind secure borders and an efficient administration for his successors.

Tokugawa Ieyasu (1542–1616) After ten years of fighting, the warlord was able to bring about Japan's unification in 1603 and lay the foundation for the 250-year rule of his family.

After the fall of the Ashigkaga Shogunate in **1467**, Japan splintered into many regionally ruled dominions. Ieyasu allied with the warlord Oda Nobunga in 1560 and, after his death, with the military leader Toyotomi Hideyoshi in **1582**. Hideyoshi had brought the country under his control by 1590, but it was Ieyasu who eliminated the last rival. For doing so, he was appointed hereditary shogun in **1603** by the Japanese emperor. Under Ieyasu's rule, Japan began to isolate itself from foreign influences. He prohibited local princes from trading with Europeans and in **1614** banned Christian proselyting. The Tokugawa family ruled over Japan until 1868.

Cardinal Richelieu (1585–1642) King Louis XIII's chief minister created the basis for an absolutist monarchy and France's rise to hegemonial power on the European continent under Louis XIV.

Richelieu, the scion of landed gentry, was bishop in the Vendée before he was brought to the royal court, where he began his meteoric career. In 1616, he became Maria de' Medici's secretary of state. In **1624**, he was made Louis XIII's chief minister and during the next 18 years strengthened the power of the French state both domestically and abroad. He deprived the aristocracy and the Huguenots of their political privileges and built up a bureaucracy loyal to the king. The creation of the Académie française in 1635 made it possible for the state to control literature and language. In order to weaken the Spanish Habsburgs' hegemony in Europe, Richelieu supported the Protestant warring parties in the Thirty Years' War. This way he was able to prolong the war that brought France large territorial gains in 1648.

Gustav II Adolf of Sweden (1594–1632) Under the rule of Gustav II, Sweden's most famous monarch, the country rose for a brief time to become the leading power in northern Europe.

The reign of Gustav II Adolf fundamentally changed Sweden. By modernizing education, the administration, and the military, he was able to build up one of the most powerful armies in Europe and thus pursue an aggressive policy of expansion. In wars against Russia, Poland, and Denmark, Gustav II Adolf seized large parts of the Baltic. In the Thirty Years' War, he sided with the German Protestant princes. After a victory against the imperial army at Breitenbach in **1631**, he invaded Bavaria but was killed in the Battle of Lützen on **Nov. 16, 1632**. Due to his achievements, however, Sweden would rise to become a major power by 1648.

1626 120 years after it was built, **St. Peter's Basilica** in **Rome** is solemnly consecrated on Nov. 18 by Pope Urban VIII.

1626 **Francis Bacon**, founder of **empiricism** and father of **modern natural science**, dies in London.

1637 French philosopher and mathematician **René Descartes** publishes his paper *Discours de la méthode* and so establishes **rationalism** ("I think, therefore I am").

1638 **Torture** is abolished in **England**.

1639 Italian **philosopher** and **poet Tommaso Campanella**, author of the utopian *City of the Sun*, dies on May 21 in Paris.

1642 Italian **astronomer** and **mathematician Galileo Galilei** dies on Jan. 8 in Florence. He is considered to be the symbol of the struggle for a scientific view of the world.

1642 The **Dalai Lama** merges **political and religious power** of **Tibet** in his capital city, Lhasa.

1642 Dutch Baroque artist **Rembrandt van Rijn** completes his painting *The Night Watch*.

1643 Mathematician **Blaise Pascal** develops a **calculating machine**.

1648 After 17 years of construction, the **Taj Mahal** in Agra is finished. It represents the zenith of Indian **Mughal architecture**.

1630 **1640** **1650**

1628 On June 7, **King Charles I** formally agrees to the **"Petitions of Rights"** of the English Parliament but calls no more parliaments until 1640.

1629 The **Massachusetts Bay Company** is granted a royal charter. A year later, a group of Puritans under John Winthrop begins to settle North America.

1632 **Swedish King Gustav II Adolf** falls on Nov. 16 in the **Battle of Lützen**. His under-age daughter, **Christina**, succeeds him.

1632 In **Poland-Lithuania**, **Władysław IV Vasa** is chosen king and grand prince.

1640 **Frederick William I, the Great Elector**, comes to power and by 1688 has created the foundation for the **rise of Brandenburg-Prussia**.

1636 The **Japanese government bans foreign travel for its citizens**. The harbor of Nagasaki remains the only trading post open to Europeans from 1639 to 1835.

1641 The **Dutch capture** the important Portuguese **trading post of Malacca** in present-day Malaysia.

1626 **Dutch merchants** purchase the peninsula of Manhattan in North America and found **New Amsterdam**. Under English rule, it is renamed **New York** in 1664.

1627 The **Korean Choson Empire** falls under **Manchu domination**.

1628 Imperial forces led by **Wallenstein** drive the Danes out of northern Germany.

1631 The **imperial troops** under Tilly capture the Protestant city of **Magdeburg**. There is plundering, rape, and murder; some 20,000 inhabitants lose their lives. The atrocities shock Europe. "To magdeburgize" becomes a synonym for the **terrors of the Thirty Years' War**.

1633 On June 22, astronomer **Galileo Galilei** renounces his **"mistake"** that the earth circles around the sun.

1634 On Feb. 25, **Wallenstein is murdered** by imperial officers in Eger for alleged high treason.

1635 The **last phase** of the **Thirty Years' War** begins on Sept. 18 with Emperor Ferdinand II's **declaration of war on France**.

1637 On July 18, **English colonists massacre** the **Pequot tribe** during the violent takeover of their land in North America.

1639 The **Treaty of Zuhab** ends the war that broke out in 1623 between the **Ottoman Empire** and **Persia**.

1640 **Portugal** is able to free itself of **Spanish rule** through an uprising. The Duke of Braganza is made the **new king**, John IV.

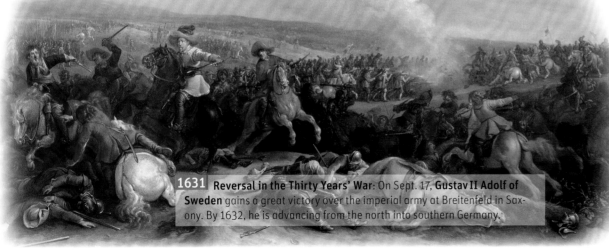

1642 After a failed arrest of opposition members of Parliament, a **civil war between the Crown and Parliament** begins in **England** on Jan. 10.

1642 After the **death of Richelieu** on Dec. 4, **Cardinal Jules Mazarin** is made France's chief minister and continues under the new king, the underaged Louis XIV, in 1643.

1644 The native **Ming dynasty** ends in **China**. The monarchy is taken over by the **Manchurian Qing dynasty** (until 1912).

1645 The **Treaty of Brömsebro** ends the **Torstenson War** between Denmark and Sweden in favor of Sweden.

1648 The **Peace of Westphalia** of Oct. 24 between the Holy Roman Empire, Sweden, and France **ends the Thirty Years' War**.

1649 In England, a "Rump Parliament" arranges for the execution of **Charles I** on Jan. 30. **England is proclaimed a republic** under the leadership of Oliver Cromwell.

1631 **Reversal in the Thirty Years' War**: On Sept. 17, **Gustav II Adolf of Sweden** gains a great victory over the imperial army at Breitenfeld in Saxony. By 1632, he is advancing from the north into southern Germany.

1595 Dutch spectacle maker **Sacharias Jansen** and his father, Johannes, invent the first true **compound microscope**.

1595 Michelangelo Merisi, known as **Caravaggio**, the founder of Roman Baroque painting, creates *Bacchus*.

1597 **William Shakespeare**, one of the most significant playwrights in literary history, publishes his romantic tragedy *Romeo and Juliet*.

1599 Flemish Baroque artist **Peter Paul Rubens** paints *Leda and the Swan*.

1600 Italian natural philosopher **Giordano Bruno** is executed in Rome as a heretic on Feb, 17 because of his thesis on the **infinity of the universe**.

1605 Spanish poet **Miguel de Cervantes** publishes his first volume of *Don Quixote*.

1608 **Johannes Lippershey**, Dutch watchmaker, invents the **telescope**.

1614 Christian proselyting is banned in Japan. It is extended to a total ban on Christianity in 1637–38.

1614 **El Greco**, the most important Spanish painter of **Mannerism**, dies in Toledo on Apr. 7.

1619 German astronomer **Johannes Kepler**, founder of "celestial physics" (modern astrophysics), publishes his major work, *Harmonices mundi*.

1625 *De jure belli ac pacis* by Dutch scholar **Hugo Grotius** is published in Paris. It lays the foundation for **modern international law**.

1600 · **1610** · **1620**

1591 **Moroccan Sultan Ahmad al-Mansur** conquers the **Songhai Empire**, and thus obliterates the last West African empire.

1593 **Irish Catholic resistance** to English rule remains unsuccessful.

1598 Persian **Shah Abbas I** makes **Isfahan** his new capital. By 1629 he has expanded his Safavid empire through wars against the Ottomans.

1598 **Tsar Feodor I** dies on Jan. 17, the last of the **Rurik dynasty** that has ruled Russia since the 9th century. A **"Time of Troubles"** ensues (Smuta).

1603 The Japanese emperor appoints **Tokugawa Ieyasu** hereditary **shogun** (military regent). Under his rule, **Japan** experiences a **golden age**. His family remains in power until 1868.

1604 French navigator and diplomat **Samuel de Champlain** founds **Port Royal**, the first permanent French settlement in present-day Canada **(Nova Scotia)**.

1610 **Henry IV of France** is murdered by a fanatical Catholic on May 14. His son succeeds him as King Louis XIII.

1611 **Gustav II Adolf Vasa** mounts the royal throne of **Sweden** on Oct. 30.

1617 In December, the Spanish establish the provinces of **Rio de la Plata**, present-day Argentina, and **Guairá**, present-day Paraguay in South America.

1620 Imperial troops led by General Tilly defeat the Bohemian army of Elector Frederick V in the **Battle of White Mountain** on Nov. 8. The uprising in Bohemia is ended and a massive recatholization is launched.

"Paris is well worth a Mass."

Henry IV, converting to Catholicism in 1593

1596 King **Sigismund III Vasa** makes **Warsaw** the new capital of **Poland-Lithuania**.

1598 On Feb. 27, **Henry of Navarre**, who converted to Catholicism in 1593, is **crowned King Henry IV of France** in Reims, ending the years-long confessional conflict in France.

1598 On May 2, the **Peace of Vervins** ends the war between **Spain** and **France** that broke out in 1595.

1598 On May 13, **Henry IV** signs the **Edict of Nantes**. In principle, **French Huguenots** are placed on equal footing with Catholics.

1599 English merchants found the **East India Company**. It will become the executor of English or British colonial policy.

1602 The **Dutch East India Company** is founded in the **Netherlands**. It financially outstrips all of its rivals and makes an essential contribution to the buildup of the Dutch colonial empire in Southeast Asia.

1603 After the **death of Elizabeth I** on Mar. 24, **James VI of Scotland** also becomes **king of England**. Both countries are now under personal union.

1606 The **Peace of Zsitvatorok** ends the "Long War" (since 1593) between the **Habsburgs** and **Ottomans**; the territorial status quo remains unchanged.

1607 Settlers found **Jamestown** in **Virginia**, the first permanent **English settlement** in North America.

1608 **Samuel de Champlain** founds **Québec** in present-day **Canada**, which becomes the center of French colonial possessions in the New World.

1612 **England** captures the **Bermuda Islands** off the coast of America.

1613 The **Treaty of Knäred** secures territorial gains for **Denmark** in the war that broke out with Sweden in 1611.

1613 The **Time of Troubles** ends on July 11 with the coronation of **Michail I Romanov** as the new Russian tsar. The **Romanov dynasty** rules Russia until 1917.

1609 The **War of the Jülich Succession** breaks out in the **Holy Roman Empire** between Brandenburg and Palatinate-Neuburg. It ends in 1614.

1617 On March 9, Russia cedes its Baltic territories to Sweden in the **Treaty of Stolbovo**.

1617 The Habsburg **Ferdinand II** becomes **king of Bohemia** and launches a violent **recatholization**.

1618 **Defenestration of Prague:** On May 23, in the course of the Bohemian Revolt against the Habsburgs, two Catholic lord regents are thrown out of a window of Prague Castle; the **Thirty Years' War** begins.

1620 On Dec. 25, the **Pilgrim Fathers**, Protestant dissidents from England, onboard the *Mayflower*, land in Massachusetts. They found the Plymouth Colony, the nucleus of New England.

1623 Dutch entrepreneurs build **New Amsterdam**, later renamed New York.

1624 **Nzinga a Mbande** becomes queen of the **Ndongo Kingdom** in southwestern Africa. She leads a forty-year resistance against Portuguese forces for Angola.

1625 In May, **Danish King Christian IV** intervenes in the war in Germany on the side of the Protestants. This leads to the beginning of the **second phase of the Thirty Years' War**. In April, the noted General Wallenstein had been put in command of Emperor Ferdinand II's armies.

HISTORICAL EVENTS

Witch Hunts
"Root out the devil": Witch hunts that had been flaring up repeatedly in Christian Europe since the 14th century reached their high point in the 17th century.

A witch being burned at the stake on the marketplace of the Isle of Guernsey in England, c. 1560

Up into the age of Enlightenment, when critical thinking gradually took a foothold, people firmly believed in the existence of witches and warlocks. In response to the Church Inquisition, the superstitious belief that witches and warlocks were slaves of the devil and had conspired against Christianity began to emerge in the 13th century. By the 15th century, mass persecutions of alleged female witches and their male counterparts, warlocks, were taking place, for the most part in France, but after 1560 increasingly in German territories as well. The witch hunts reached their peak during the Thirty Years' War. In witch trials, the suspects were forced to confess under torture and, as a rule, burned alive at the stake afterward to purify them. The Church, however, was not the initiator but rather the public—with the consent or toleration of the authorities. Hundreds of thousands of people, mostly women, lost their lives this way. The last legal execution of a witch occurred in 1782.

Union of Lublin
In 1569, the Polish–Lithuanian Commonwealth was founded, but it was in effect an oligarchy of the nobility.

Poland and Lithuania had been ruled in personal union by monarchs of the House of Jagiellon since **1385**. The rise of Russia under Ivan IV had placed Lithuania in a dangerous position. In order to strengthen his position against his eastern neighbors, Polish King Sigismund II Augustus sought a real union with Lithuania. After lengthy negotiations, the Polish and Lithuanian aristocracies agreed to a single state union on **July 1, 1569** in Lublin, which existed until the partition of Poland in **1792** and **1795**. A common parliament (Sejm) chose a king. In addition, a common currency and foreign policy was agreed upon. However, two separate armies and administrations continued to exist. When the last of the Jagiellons died in 1572, the country was turned into an oligarchy. The noble class secured the right to elect the king and to resist the monarch. This weakened the position of the king, and Poland-Lithuania became a pawn of its neighboring major powers.

St. Bartholomew's Day massacre
The massacre of Huguenots in Paris on the night of Aug. 24, 1572, intensified the religious war that had broken out in France.

The murder of Brious, a Protestant governor, on St. Bartholomew's Night

In the mid-16th century, the Protestant Reformed Church gained a growing following in France, particularly among the French aristocracy. The Catholics felt threatened by the Huguenots, as most Calvinist Protestants were derisively called—perhaps a French corruption of the German word for "confederate." A civil war broke out in France in **1562**, which the regent, Catherine de' Medici, was unable to contain. In order to win over the Huguenots, she agreed to the marriage of her daughter to the Protestant Henry III of Navarre. But on the night of **Aug. 24, 1572**, followers of the Catholic dukes of Guise, with Catherine's knowledge, killed Huguenot leader Gaspard de Coligny and massacred thousands of Huguenots who had gathered in Paris for the wedding. The killing continued in the Province for days. The Huguenots now closed ranks. Soon France was divided into two enemy camps. It was not until Henry of Navarre, who inherited the French crown and converted, restored peace in 1598 with the Edict of Nantes by making the Huguenots equal to the Catholics.

The Dutch Revolt
After a long struggle, the United Netherlands broke free of their Spanish sovereigns in 1581.

Burghers, organized in defense guilds, supported the Netherlands' fight for independence.

Religion was central to the start of the Netherlands' fight for freedom. Since 1540, Calvinism had been spreading rapidly in the Netherlands, which led to violent acts of protest against the reign of the Spanish Catholics in **1566**. When Philip II of Spain showed no willingness to compromise and had the Duke of Alba march into the Netherlands in 1567, open rebellion ensued. Despite acts of massive retaliation, the resistance movement led by William of Orange gained strength—also through the influx of Calvinist refugees from the Holy Roman Empire. In **1579**, the northern provinces of Holland, Zeeland, Utrecht, Guelders, Overijssel, Friesland, and Groningen formed the States-General. As the Republic of the Seven United Provinces they seceded from Spain in **1581**. However, the attacks of the provinces loyal to Spain in the south of present-day Belgium continued until 1609. The independence of the Netherlands was only officially recognized in 1648.

The Destruction of the Spanish Armada

The spectacular defeat of the mighty Spanish fleet in 1588 off the coast of England precipitated the fall of Spain as the Catholic hegemonic power in Europe.

In **1556**, Philip II inherited a world empire from his father, Charles V, with overseas possessions, the Netherlands, and Italy. The deeply religious king envisioned himself as the spearhead of the Counter-Reformation in Europe. Elizabeth I of England, on the other hand, was a Protestant, supported the Calvinists in France and in the Netherlands, and had had Catholic Maria Stuart executed in **1587**. She also supported the attacks of the English buccaneers on Spanish ships. A counterattack by Spain ended in a fiasco in **1588**. The Spanish war fleet, the Armada, set sail in April to invade England with some 130 ships. The English executed a crushing surprise attack on Aug. 8 in the English Channel. In addition, severe storms lashed the fleet, and the Spanish were forced to retreat. Spain's mastery of the seas was broken and England's rise to become the leading sea power had begun.

In 1588, the English fleet destroyed Spain's invincible Armada in a battle in the English Channel.

Defenestration of Prague

After two lord regents of the Catholic emperor had been thrown out of a window of Prague Castle, the long, smoldering dispute between the confessions in the Holy Roman Empire escalated into a conflagration.

Catholic and Protestant imperial estates formed coalitions against each other in the Holy Roman Empire in 1608–09, further escalating the tension between the two confessions. A regional conflict over allocation of power between the reformed nobility in Bohemia and the ruling Catholic Habsburgs in **1618** was the final straw. On May 23, Bohemian nobles forced their way into Prague Castle and threw two imperial lord regents out of a window. Emperor Ferdinand II was deposed as king of Bohemia and Calvinist Frederick V, Elector Palatine, was elected new king. After a number of victories by the imperial troops, the at times brutal recatholization began, not only in Bohemia. In **1625**, foreign powers began intervening in the conflict, which increasingly lost its confessional character and degenerated into an open battle between the royal houses of Eu-

Bohemian nobles throw two imperial lord regents out of a window of Prague Castle.

rope for supremacy on the continent. The threat of a Habsburg hegemony prompted Catholic France to enter the war on the side of Protestant Sweden.

The Pilgrim Fathers

God's own country: The landing of the English religious refugees on the *Mayflower* on Nov. 21, 1620, in North America became part of the folklore of America's founding.

They were not the first English settlers in North America, but they were the first to establish a permanent settlement. The 100 Pilgrim Fathers from central England set sail in September **1620** aboard the *Mayflower* and three months later went ashore at Cape Cod in North America. The new arrivals were Puritans, a separatist group persecuted by the English state church. To them, America seemed like the Promised Land, where they could live a life according to their own convictions. The settlers founded the Plymouth Colony as a formative nucleus of New England and provided themselves with the first American constitution. Next, New Hampshire, Connecticut, Rhode Island, and Massachusetts were founded. After 1630, more Puritans arrived and settled in large numbers along the North American coastline. Meanwhile, the British government had begun promoting overseas settlements by granting land ownerships. In 1664, the Dutch colony of New Amsterdam was taken over by the English. After the duke of York, later King James II, had been granted the city, it was renamed New York.

The *Mayflower* brought the Puritan culture to America in the 17th century.

The Münster oath of peace sealed the end of the Thirty Years' War.

Peace of Westphalia

With the end of the Thirty Years' War, the sovereignty and religious freedom of the imperial estates were recognized. The actual winners were, however, France and Sweden.

When in 1648, after 30 years of war, the guns finally fell silent in the Holy Roman Empire, the population had been decimated by half through massacres, pillaging, starvation, and disease. With the peace treaty of **1648** signed in the Westphalian cities of Münster and Osnabrück, the Habsburg emperor lost more of his authority in the empire. The imperial estates had their free choice of confessions confirmed and their legislative powers and governmental sovereignty further strengthened over the emperor. In addition, they were granted freedom in forming alliances as long as these were not directed against the emperor. Catholics, Lutherans, and Calvinists were given equal standing. France was awarded territories in Alsace, and Sweden territories in North Germany on the North Sea and Baltic Sea. France and Sweden were thus able to reinforce their positions as major powers at the expense of the empire.

1651 *Leviathan*, written by **Thomas Hobbes**, is published in England. It is the first modern theory of state. Its centerpiece is the **"social contract"** between citizens and the state.

1652 **George Fox**, a shoemaker and itinerate preacher, founds the religious **Society of Friends (Quakers)** in England.

1658 Dutch biologist **Jan Swammerdam** discovers **red blood cells** for the first time through a microscope and describes them.

1661 **Louis XIV** begins construction of the **Palace of Versailles**, which will serve as royal residence from 1677.

1666 French Minister of Finance **Jean-Baptiste Colbert** founds the **Académie Royale des Sciènces** in Paris.

1669 **Rembrandt van Rijn**, the renowned Dutch Baroque painter, **dies** on Oct. 4 in Amsterdam.

1670 **Colonial trade** results in the spread of **tobacco, chocolate, and coffee** across the European mainland.

1677 Dutch philosopher **Baruch Spinoza**, one of the most noted **rationalists** and **Biblical critics** of his time, dies in Den Haag on Feb. 21.

1673 The comedy *The Imaginary Invalid* by French playwright **Molière** has its premiere performance in Paris on Feb. 10.

1682 The comet later named **Halley's Comet** after Edmund Halley is visible in the sky. In 1705, Halley correctly predicts its return in 1758.

1687 English mathematician **Isaac Newton** formulates the **law of gravity** in his work *Mathematical Principles of Natural Philosophy*, revolutionizing celestial mechanics.

1650 **1660** **1670** **1680** **1690**

1652 Dutchman **Jan van Riebeeck** founds the settlement of **Cape Town** in South Africa on April 6.

1653 After dissolving the Rump parliament, **Oliver Cromwell** assumes the title of **Lord Protector** of England, Scotland, and Ireland on Dec. 16 and establishes a dictatorial style of government.

1654 The **Treaty of Westminster** ends the **First Anglo-Dutch War** on April 5 in favor of England.

1655 The **Little Northern War** for supremacy in Eastern Europe begins with **King Charles X Gustav of Sweden's** invasion of Poland.

1658 On July 18, the king of Hungary and Bohemia, **Leopold I**, is chosen **emperor** of the Holy Roman Empire.

1658 **Aurangzeb** becomes **ruler of the Indian Mughal Empire** and brings it to the height of its power.

1659 On Nov. 7, **France** and **Spain** conclude the **Treaty of the Pyrenees**. France replaces Spain as the strongest power in Europe.

1660 The **Treaty of Oliva** ends the **Little Northern War** with a compromise.

1660 The **monarchy is reintroduced** in England on May 29. New king is Charles II.

"L'État c'est moi"

Maxim of Absolutism, attributed to Louis XIV, 1661

1661 On July 1, the **Treaty of Cardis** ends the **Russo–Swedish War** that broke out in 1656. Russia must withdraw from territories on the Baltic Sea.

1662 **Kangxi** becomes emperor of the **Manchu Empire**. During his reign, China sees a flowering in both domestic and foreign policies.

1663 The **Imperial Diet**, an assembly representing the imperial estates, becomes firmly anchored in the Holy Roman Empire.

1665 In the **Lex Regia**, the absolute power of the king is made law in Denmark.

1666 **Moulay ar-Raschid** takes over the rule of virtually all of **Morocco** and founds the **Alaouite dynasty** that remains in power to this day.

1667 **France** attacks the **Spanish Netherlands** on May 24, starting the **War of Devolution**.

1669 The once powerful **Hanseatic League** holds its last formal assembly in Lübeck.

1670 The West African **Bambara tribe** captures Timbuktu, destroying the last remnants of the Mali Empire.

1672 In March, **France**, in alliance with England and several German princes, begins a **war of conquest against the Netherlands**.

1675 The army of Frederick William, Elector of Brandenburg, drives back invading Swedish troops in the **Battle of Fehrbellin** and goes on to conquer Swedish Pomerania.

1675/76 In New England, **King Philip's War** breaks out between the English colonists and several Native American tribes.

1679 In **England** on July 12, King Charles II approves the **law of habeas corpus of 1628**, which protects citizens from arbitrary arrest, and therefore represents an important step in the development toward a nation under the rule of law.

1661 **King Louis XIV** begins his reign in **France** on March 10, 1661, and rules as a virtually **absolute monarch** until his death in 1715.

1681 English King **Charles II** permits the founding of a **Quaker colony** under **William Penn** in Pennsylvania in North America.

1683 In the **Battle of Vienna** (Kahlenberg), a **German-Polish army** defeats the **Ottomans**, led by Grand Vizier Kara Mustafa Pasha. The victory ends the two-month siege of Vienna.

1685 **Louis XIV of France** limits confessional freedom with the **Edict of Nantes** on Oct. 18. The result is a **mass exodus of Protestant Huguenots**, primarily to Brandenburg and the Netherlands.

1688 The **War of the Palatine Succession** (the Nine Years' War) is ignited when invading French troops cross the Rhine.

1678/79 The **Treaties of Nijwegen** secure for France a major part of the territory it captured in the German Empire, while the Netherlands have their possessions returned.

1689 The **Glorious Revolution**: William III of Orange's coronation on Feb. 16 establishes a **constitutional monarchy in England**.

1689 **Tsar Peter I the Great** takes power in Russia on Sept. 12.

Absolutism and Enlightenment

1650–1770

After the devastating era of religious wars, many rulers struggled to expand their territories. Assuming a leading role in European politics and culture, France served as a model of absolute monarchy. Claiming the "divine right of kings," sovereigns reduced the authority and influence of the nobility and the Church and modernized the military, their educational systems and administrations. Inspired by the Enlightenment, criticism of social conditions grew, above all, among the educated bourgeoisie. As "servants of the state," some rulers also felt committed to reason. In England a constitutional monarchy was established. In foreign affairs, the British sought to create a balance of power, while steadily building up their own position as a major sea and trading power. Although the empires of the Ottomans, Safavids, Mughals, and Manchu were still in their prime, the colonial supremacy of the Europeans was already beginning to loom on the horizon.

The Baroque gardens of Versailles, residence of the French kings

HISTORICAL FIGURES

Louis XIV (1638–1715)
The French Sun King is considered to be the embodiment of Absolutism. His style of ruling and the pompous way he held court in Versailles was imitated by rulers all over Europe.

The civil unrest known as Fronde, that occurred between 1648 and 1653, was a formative experience for the young Louis. When he came of age in **1661**, he sought an autocratic rule. He centralized the government, gave Minister Colbert a free hand in trade and finances, and bound the once assertive nobility to his court. In **1685**, Louis restricted the freedom of religion. His royal residence in Versailles became the paragon of Baroque splendor. By trying to secure supremacy over his neighbors in several wars of aggression (**1667, 1672, 1688, 1701**), the king kept Europe in turmoil for nearly half a century. His death in **1715** marked the end of an era. He had enlarged France, but his wars and his opulent court ruined the country.

Peter I, the Great (1672–1725)
The tsar made Russia into a modern state and a leading European power.

Russia gained an impetuous reformer when Peter I became absolute monarch in **1689**. While traveling incognito throughout Europe as a young man, he had developed an idea of progressive work techniques and even labored as a carpenter. Back in Russia, he used western Europe as a model and, within two decades, modernized the backward, largely isolated agrarian country. Peter established an efficient bureaucracy, had factories and transport routes built, and brought the church under his control. A new army and navy proved themselves in the Great Northern War (1700–1721) against Sweden and ensured Russia's rise as a major power in the Baltics. By founding St. Petersburg in **1703**, the tsar built a monument to himself.

Nadir Shah (1688–1747)
The founder of the Afsharid dynasty expanded Persia's territories all the way to India.

The son of impoverished Turkmen peasants possessed military skills that made him a legend during his lifetime. He was compared to Alexander the Great because of his extensive military campaigns. Named a general in 1719 by Safavid Shah Tahmasp II, Nadir Khan freed Persia of Afghan, Ottoman, and Russian occupation within 17 years. In **1736**, Nadir Khan declared himself shah. Two years later he marched into Afghanistan, and in **1739** advanced as far as Delhi in India. There he seized the Peacock Throne, which became a symbol of the Persian monarchy. His wars of conquest, however, ruined the country. Domestically, the Shah's rule became increasingly brutal until he was finally murdered by his own officers in **1747**.

Maria Theresa (1717–1780)
The only woman at the head of the House of Habsburg insured the succession of her family.

Although Maria Theresa's right to succession was granted by edict in **1713**, when her father, Emperor Charles VI, died in **1740**, she was forced to defend her claim to the throne in several wars. She lost Silesia to her main adversary, Frederick II, King of Prussia, in **1742–45**, and unsuccessfully tried to regain the territory in the Seven Years' War (**1756–63**). However, Maria Theresa was able to defend her family's position of power. She obtained the imperial crown for her husband, Francis Stephan, in **1745**, and gained additional territories such as East Galicia in **1772**. The empress reinforced the central power of the state and modernized the army and state finances. A pious Catholic, she was skeptical of the Enlightenment but, urged by her son, Joseph II, she introduced relevant reforms in education and the judiciary.

1732 The **Ladoga Canal** is completed in Russia. It is one of the largest hydroengineering facilities of its time, linking the Baltic and the Caspian Seas.

1733 Commissioned by the **Saint Petersburg Academy of Sciences**, an international team of scientists begins the exploration of **Siberia** and the **Artic**.

1741 Scottish philosopher **David Hume** publishes *Essays Moral and Political*.

1742 **Messias**, an oratorio by the German-British Baroque composer **George Frederick Handel** celebrates its premiere on April 13 in Dublin.

1748 **Charles Baron de Montesquieu**, a French philosopher of the Enlightenment, ▶ publishes his treatise on political theory, *The Spirit of the Laws*.

1750 **Johann Sebastian Bach**, one of the most famous German Baroque composers, dies in Leipzig.

1751 The French philosophers **Denis Diderot** and **Jean le Rond d'Alembert** publish the first volume of their *Encyclopédie*. A large number of like-minded philosophers contribute to the important compendium of knowledge by 1772.

1755 Tens of thousands of people die in a devastating **earthquake in Lisbon**.

1762 **Jean-Jacques Rousseau** publishes *Of The Social Contract*. Its ideas of human equality help inspire political reforms in Europe.

1764/65 Originally from America, the **potato** becomes established as a food staple in the **Holy Roman Empire**, and is especially popular in the **Prussian territories**.

1740 — **1750** — **1760** — **1770**

1735 Frederick August II, Elector of Saxony, is recognized as August III, **king of Poland**, in the Prepeace of Vienna.

1736 After driving out the Afghans, **Nadir Khan** makes himself the new **Shah of Persia**.

1739 In Great Britain, the **Wesley Brothers** found the **Methodist religious revival movement**, which finds great popularity, primarily in the English colonies of North America.

1739 After military failures, Austria loses part of its Balkan territories to the Ottoman Empire in the **Treaty of Belgrade**.

1739 **Nadir Shah** invades India and **captures Delhi**, bringing the Indian Mughal Empire to the brink of collapse.

1740 After the death of Emperor Charles VI, his daughter, **Maria Theresa**, is **not recognized as successor** by Bavaria, Prussia, France, and others. The invasion by Prussian king Frederick II into Silesia ignites the **War of the Austrian Succession**.

1740 **Balaji Bajirao** becomes ruler of the Hindu **Empire of Maratha** in India. It becomes the strongest power on the subcontinent.

1741 After a year of struggle for the throne, **Elizabeth Petrovna**, daughter of Peter the Great, is declared **empress of Russia** on Nov. 25.

1742 In the **Treaty of Berlin** of July 28, **Prussia** gains a major part of **Silesia** from Austria.

1743 After a military defeat in 1741, **Sweden must relinquish the eastern part of Finland to Russia**.

1745 After the death of Wittelsbach emperor Charles VII, Maria Theresa's husband, Francis Stephen, Duke of Lorraine, is crowned **Francis I, Emperor of the Holy Roman Empire**.

1745 The **Treaty of Dresden**, signed on Dec. 25, ends the **Second Silesian War** between Prussia and Austria in favor of Prussia.

1747 **Ahmed Shah Durrani** is declared **emir** in Kandahar, thus founding the **Durrani (Afghan) Empire**.

1747 On July 19, **Nadir Shah** is murdered by soldiers in Persia.

1748 On Oct. 18, the **Treaty of Aachen** ends the **War of the Austrian Succession**. **Maria Theresa** is recognized as ruler of **Austria**.

1750 Spain and Portugal come to an agreement over **Brazil** in the **Treaty of Madrid**.

1750 The **Ethiopian Empire** begins to **disintegrate into territorial principalities**.

1751 China conquers Tibet and makes the country into a protectorate.

1752 **King Alaungpaya** establishes a rapidly expanding kingdom in **Burma** with Yangon as capital.

1754 French and Indian War: With the support of warring Native American tribes, the British and the French begin a fight for supremacy in North America. Later, the conflict also spreads to India.

1755 An **uprising** against the **rule of Genoa** begins on the Mediterranean island of Corsica.

1756 The **attack on Saxony** on Aug. 29 by **Frederick II**, King of Prussia, provokes the **Seven Years' War**. Prussia and Austria fight in Europe; France and Great Britain in the New World.

1757 **Closed Door Policy:** **China** closes its harbors to European ships.

1756/57 Under **Emperor Qianlong**, China reaches its maximum size with the conquering of the Tarim Basin.

1757 In **India**, British troops under General Robert Clive defeat the Nawabs of Bengal, allies of France, marking the beginning of massive British expansion on the Indian subcontinent.

1759 **Portugal expels the Jesuits**, thus beginning the fight of "enlightened" governments against the order.

1762 Russian **Tsar Peter III**, crowned on Jan. 5, **leaves the anti-Prussia coalition** in the Seven Years' War and concludes a separate peace with Prussia.

1762 On June 28, Tsar Peter III is overthrown in Russia by his German wife. Her reign as **Empress Catherine II the Great** marks a golden age in Russian history.

1763 On Feb. 15, **Austria** and **Prussia** conclude the **Treaty of Hubertusburg** on the basis of the territorial status quo of 1756. Silesia is recognized as a Prussian possession.

1763 The **Treaty of Paris** of Feb. 10 **ends the Seven Years' War** between Great Britain, France, and Spain. All French colonial holdings in North America fall to Great Britain, which also gains colonial dominance in India.

1765 On Aug. 18, **Joseph II** is made the **new Austrian emperor**, but stays under the influence of his mother, Maria Theresa, until her death in 1780.

1767 **Burmese forces** conquer and destroy **Ayuthaya**, the capital of the Thai Empire.

1690 English philosopher **John Locke** publishes *Two Treatises of Government*, the first theory on the **separation of powers**.

1690 Based on his steam digester, French inventor **Denis Papin** builds a model of the first **piston steam engine**.

1695 French **fabulist Jean de La Fontaine** dies in Paris on April 13.

1700 Antonio Stradivari constructs a **violin** named after himself.

1701 On Oct. 9, a collegiate school is founded in Connecticut, which later becomes **Yale University**.

1710 St. Paul's Cathedral, rebuilt by Christopher Wren, is consecrated in **London** after 35 years of construction.

1707 German polymath **Gottfried Wilhelm Leibniz** attempts to prove the existence of God based on the suffering and evil in the world in his work *Essais de théodicée*.

1714 German physicist and inventor of measuring instruments **Daniel Gabriel Fahrenheit** introduces **mercury** as a thermoscopic liquid.

1719 The adventure novel *Robinson Crusoe* by **Daniel Defoe** is published in Great Britain.

1722 On April 5, Dutch explorer **Jacob Roggeveen discovers Easter Island** in the South Pacific, which becomes world famous for its Moai, colossal stone statues.

1723 Italian architect **Francesco de Sanctis** begins construction in Rome of the **Spanish Steps**, the largest monumental stairway of its day.

1729 **Johann Sebastian Bach** premieres his *St. Matthew Passion* on April 15 in Leipzig.

1700 — 1710 — 1720 — 1730

1692 **William III of Orange's** fleet beats back a **French invasion of England** at La Hague.

1695 **Pre-censorship of printed material** is abolished in **England**.

1696 **China** annexes **Mongolia**.

1697 The last fortress held by the **Maya**, Tayasal, in present-day Guatemala, falls to **Spain**.

1697 The Elector of Saxony, **August the Strong**, is elected **king of Poland** June 27.

1697 The **Treaty of Rijswijk** ends the **War of the Palatine Succession**. Except for Alsace and Strasbourg, France must relinquish all territories captured on German soil, but in return is given the western part of the Caribbean island of Haiti.

1699 The **Treaty of Karlowitz** seals the Ottoman Empire's defeat at the hands of Austria in the 15-year-long **Great Turkish War**. Austria gains Hungary and territories in the western Balkans and becomes a major power in Europe.

1700 **Habsburg rule over Spain** comes to an end with the death of **Charles II**.

1700 The invasion of Saxon-Polish troops into the Swedish Baltic in February marks the beginning of the **Great Northern War for supremacy in the Baltic**. Saxe-Poland-Lithuania fight together with Russia against Sweden in the conflict that lasts until 1721.

1701 On Jan. 18, the **elector of Brandenburg, Frederick III** crowns himself **King Frederick I of Prussia** in Königsberg.

1701 The twelve-year-long **War of the Spanish Succession** begins. The Holy Roman Empire, England, and the Netherlands form a **"Grand Alliance"** against France's claim to the Spanish throne.

1703 Russian **Tsar Peter I the Great** founds the city of **St. Petersburg**. It is made the new Russian capital in 1713.

1707 **England** and **Scotland** form a real union, the **United Kingdom of Great Britain**.

1708 Under the **military rule of Prince Agaja**, the West African kingdom of **Dahomey** expands to the Atlantic coast. Slave trade with the Europeans is the main economic activity.

1709 After the **Grand Alliance's victory** at **Malplaquet, France** is on the verge of collapse.

1710 **Russia occupies** vast areas of the **Swedish Baltic** in the Great Northern War.

1711 On Oct. 12, **Charles VI**, who had laid claim to the Spanish throne, is made **emperor** of the **Holy Roman Empire**.

1713/14 The **Treaties of Utrecht** and **Rastatt** end the War of the Spanish Succession. The Bourbon **Philip V** is recognized as **king of Spain**. Through territorial gains and trading privileges, Great Britain becomes the leading colonial power.

1713 On Jan. 25, **Frederick William I** is crowned new **king of Prussia** and turns the land into a tightly organized **military state**.

1713 On April 19, Emperor Charles VI issues the **"Pragmatic Sanction."** The edict forbids the partition of the Habsburg dominions and provides for succession by females.

1714 **Queen Anne's death** on Aug. 1 ends the reign of the Stuarts; new king of Great Britain is **George I of Hanover**.

1718 In the **Treaty Passarowitz**, the Ottoman Empire relinquishes parts of the Balkans to Austria.

1718 On Dec. 11, **Swedish king Charles XII** falls during the siege of **Frederikshald**. His sister, Ulrika Eleonora, becomes queen.

1720 **Victor Amadeus II, Duke of Savoy**, turns over Sicily, which he had received in 1713, to Austria and is given the **kingdom of Sardinia** in return.

1720 **Brazil** gains the status of a **Portuguese Viceroyalty**.

1721 The **Treaty of Nystad** of Sept. 10 ends the Great Northern War. **Russia** becomes the **hegemonic power in the Baltic region**.

1721 Russian **Tsar Peter the Great** assumes the title **"Emperor of all the Russias."**

1722 In Persia, the **Afghans** overthrow the **Safavid dynasty** that has ruled since 1502.

1724 In **China**, the **religious freedom** granted in 1692 is rescinded and Christianity banned.

1725 In West Africa, the **Fulbe people** form an Islamic theocratic state.

1730 An **uprising of the Janissary** in the Ottoman Empire **forces Sultan Ahmed III to abdicate**. It takes his successor, **Mahmud I**, years to suppress the revolt.

1730 In **Great Britain**, King George II confirms **Sir Robert Walpole** as **"prime minister"** of his government, thus institutionalizing the office of prime minister.

1731 Great Britain, the Netherlands, and Prussia recognize the **"Pragmatic Sanction"** of Emperor Charles VI.

1733 After the death of **August the Strong**, a dispute flares up among the major powers over the Polish succession. The conflict culminates in the **War of the Polish Succession**, which lasts until 1735.

1734 Russian and Saxon troops conquer **Poland** and force **King Stanisław I Leszczynski** into exile in France.

1735 **Muhammad ibn Sa'ud** founds the **Sa'ud dynasty**, grounded in the Islamic teachings of al-Wahhab, on the Arabian Peninsula.

HISTORICAL EVENTS

Manchu Dynasty in China
The Manchu Qing dynasty became established in China after 1644. Its first ruler stabilized the country and built it into a major power in Asia.

In alliance with the Mongolians, the Tungusic tribes of Manchuria had been steadily expanding their territory southward since the late 16th century. In **1644**, they seized Beijing and overthrew the Ming dynasty that had been in power for almost 300 years. The new Manchu rulers were nevertheless not able to eliminate all rebel groups and gain broad acceptance before 1681. This was the start of a long period of cultural and political flourishing and prosperity in China, also due to the prudent politics of the Manchu emperors, Kangxi and Yongzheng. In order to secure their monarchy, they sought compromise with the ethnic groups in the realm. The power of the emperor was further strengthened under Yongzheng by centralizing the finance system and bureaucracy and setting up an intelligence service. China reached its maximum size under the Manchu. By 1689, Kangxi had secured the borders with Russia. He conquered Mongolia in 1696, and declared Tibet a protectorate in **1751**.

A relief army ends the months-long siege of Vienna. John III Sobieski of Poland storms into the tent of the Ottoman Grand Vizier Kara Mustafa in the Battle of Vienna at Kahlenberg Mountain.

Turks outside Vienna 1683
After the failed siege of Vienna in 1683, the Ottoman Empire was forced into the defensive, while Austria rose to become a leading power in Southeast Europe.

During the 16th century, the Ottoman Empire had steadily extended its territory further into Central Europe, inciting a deep-seated fear of Turks in Christians of all denominations. In **1683**, the ambitious Grand Vizier Kara Mustafa Pasha once again attempted a breakthrough to the West and encircled Vienna with his army on July 14. The imperial city was able to be saved in the last minute. A coalition army led by Polish King John III Sobieski was victorious on Sept. 12 in the Battle of Vienna and routed the Ottomans. Austrian General Prince Eugene of Savoy and other military commanders subsequently drove the Ottomans further back. In **1699**, all of Hungary and Croatia fell to Austria. In **1718**, parts of Serbia and Wallachia were conquered. Russia's drive for expansion was now also felt by the Ottomans. The gradual decline of their empire had begun.

The Great Elector of Brandenburg-Prussia welcomes the Huguenots who had fled France.

Edict of Potsdam
The mass acceptance of Huguenots into Prussia by the Great Elector, Frederick William, starting in 1685, was an important step in Prussia's rise to a major European power.

When Frederick William came to power in Brandenburg in 1640, his lands were in ruins. The Thirty Years' War had depopulated whole regions. Broad parts were occupied by Swedish troops and the finances devastated. In order to modernize the country, the Great Elector centralized the administration and enlarged the state's territory after his victory over Sweden at Fehrbellin in **1675**. The Edict of Potsdam of **1685**, inviting Huguenots to settle in Brandenburg-Prussia, proved to be very profitable as well. Among the 20,000 immigrants were many craftsmen and scholars who were crucial for the recovery of the country. By 1688, Frederick William was able to make his country a force to be reckoned with in Europe's political power games. His son Frederick I, king of Prussia from **1701** to **1713**, created an army that allowed Frederick II the Great to wage his wars of conquest from **1740**.

Glorious Revolution
The establishment of a parliament-controlled monarchy in England in 1689 ended a decades-long conflict over the distribution of power between king and parliament.

The English Parliament had had political influence since the 14th century, but in the 17th century the Stuart kings repeatedly tried to curtail it. Religious issues additionally exacerbated the conflict. After the execution of Charles I in **1649**, a republic was proclaimed that, however, fell into disrepute after **1653** through the dictatorial rule of the radical Protestant Oliver Cromwell. The restoration of the monarchy in **1660** was widely hailed. When King James II, a Catholic, began seeking ties with absolutist France in 1685, Parliament offered the crown to the Protestant Wilhelm of Orange. The ruler of the Netherlands landed in England in 1688, forced James to flee, and ascended to the throne as William III on Feb. 13, **1689**. The Bill of Rights, which has been considered England's basic law since then, guarantees Parliament all of the ancient privileges. At the height of European Absolutism, England established Constitutionalism with the Glorious Revolution.

William III of Orange arrives in England.

Enlightenment
One of the most important developments in European intellectual history reached its height in the mid-18th century and triggered the emergence of the modern era.

In the course of the 17th century, the European intellectual world liberated itself from the pervasive restrictions imposed by the Church and emphasized the role of reason. The validity of traditions and the justification of authority were put into question by philosophers like Jean-Jacques Rousseau. In his *Social Contract* of **1762**, he developed a utopia based on an analysis of human nature. According to Rousseau, the state represents the "general will" of the citizens that aims at the common good. Due to its implicit radical criticism, the work was immediately banned in France. Propagators of Enlightenment like Rousseau and later Kant had a lasting influence on intellectual thinking. In Prussia and Sweden, for example, monarchs felt subsequently more bound to the state than to God. The Enlightenment paved the way for the democratic revolutions at the end of the 18th century.

Montesquieu, Diderot, d'Alembert, and others, reading from the works of Voltaire in Paris

War of the Spanish Succession
In 1701, a war began between the major European powers over the line of succession for the Spanish crown.

Charles II, the last Habsburg king of Spain, died in 1700. Louis XIV of France declared his grandson, Philip of Anjou, king of Spain and thereby provoked an alliance between England, Austria, and the Holy Roman Empire. In order to ensure a balance of power in Europe, the so-called "Grand Alliance" of **1701** declared war on France. French troops were put on the defense, especially after their defeat at Malplaquet in **1709**. When Archduke Charles of Austria, who had been declared Spanish counterking, was crowned Holy Roman emperor in **1711**, the British withdrew from the war for fear of a Habsburg dominance of power. The peace treaties of **1713–14** were satisfying for all parties involved. Philip V was recognized as king of Spain; Austria gained Spanish possessions in the Netherlands and Italy; Great Britain won Gibraltar as well as part of the French colonial territories in North America.

Battle between the Dutch, Austrians, and French at Denain on July 24, 1712

Human Merchandise
The transatlantic slave trade reached its height in the 18th century.

The European colonization of the Americas in the 17th century fostered a continuing need for cheap labor to mine, harvest, and process raw materials in the New World. Since the Native American population had been decimated to some extent by epidemics, famine, and warfare, and often proved unsuitable for labor on the newly founded plantations, attention was turned to abducting people from Africa. Slave trade ultimately became an integral part of the lucrative transatlantic triangular trade. Traders exchanged goods from Europe for slaves on the coast of West Africa, brought them to America and in return received colonial products like sugar, coffee, cotton, and tobacco for sale in Europe. Between 1450 to 1850 millions of Africans were taken to the Americas. Many of them died during the voyage on board the slave ships. In Great Britain, which was the leading colonial power in the 18th century, opposition to slavery increased markedly after

Brutal punishment of black slaves

1750, but it was not until the early 19th century that the European states banned slavery. In the USA, the issue of slave ownership led to the outbreak of the Civil War in **1861**.

Seven Years' War / French and Indian War
Great Britain emerged strengthened in its position as the world's leading colonial power out of the first conflict among major European powers spanning all of the continents.

In the course of the colonial war in America, the British landed in Cuba and besieged Havana in 1762.

Maria Theresa of Austria refused to accept the loss of Silesia to Prussia and in **1756** sought aid from France and Russia. When King Frederick II of Prussia, who was allied with Great Britain, preempted an attack by his opponents, he unleashed the Seven Years' War. Prussia could only be saved from a crushing defeat when Russia, under the new Tsar Peter III, withrew into neutrality in **1762**. In the course of the conflict, the British increasingly focused on the war overseas. Hostilities with France had first errupted in **1754** over colonial possessions in North America and India. In 1761, Spain entered the war, which eventually involved the whole world. In the end, France was so weakend by the conflict in Europe that Great Britain was able to seize almost all of her overseas colonies. The peace accords of **1763** preserved the status quo in Europe but sealed the decline of France and laid the foundation for the rise of the British Empire in the 19th century.

1770 French inventor **Nicholas Cugnot** constructs a **steam-powered cart** considered to be the world's first self-propelled mechanical vehicle.

1771 On Feb. 16, **French astronomer Charles Messier** is the first to completely and reliably **catalog** all the **celestial bodies** known at the time.

1774 English theologian, chemist, and physicist **Joseph Priestley** discovers **oxygen**.

1776 British economist and moral philosopher **Adam Smith** establishes liberal economics with his major work *The Wealth of Nations*.

1778 **Voltaire**, religious critic and **Enlightenment philosopher** known throughout Europe, dies in Paris on May 30.

1779 German writer **Gotthold Ephraim Lessing** publishes his famous plea for tolerance, the play *Nathan the Wise*.

1781 German Enlightenment philosopher **Immanuel Kant** publishes his *Critique of Pure Reason*.

1782 **Serfdom** is abolished in Austria.

1783 French chemist **Antoine Laurent de Lavoisier** discovers that contact with **oxygen** is responsible for all **combustion processes**.

1770 — **1775** — **1780** — **1785**

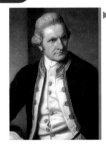

1770 **James Cook** reaches the **east coast of Australia** and claims the continent for Great Britain.

1770 On March 5, five Bostonians are killed in a **clash between colonists and British soldiers** in **Boston**, Massachusetts, known as the Incident on King Street.

1772 In the **First Partition of Poland** on Aug. 5, **Prussia**, **Austria**, and **Russia** divide major parts of Poland amongst themselves.

1772 On Aug. 19, **Swedish King Gustav III** eliminates the domineering nobility and establishes an absolute monarchy.

1773 **Boston Tea Party:** Bostonians destroy cargoes of English East India Company tea to protest against British tax policies on Dec. 16.

1773 In response to pressure largely from Latin countries, **Pope Clement XIV dissolves** the **Jesuit Order** on July 21.

1773 **Great Britain** places the national **East India Company** under government control, effectively limiting it to trade. Warren Hastings is made the first governor-general of British East India.

1774 **Louis XVI** becomes **king of France** on May 10.

1774 To ensure the loyalty of the predominantly Catholic French inhabitants of the Province of Quebec in North America, the **British government grants Quebec full religious freedom and its own legislative council**.

1774 In the **Treaty of Küçük Kaynarca** of July 21, the Ottoman Empire is forced to cede large areas of its border territories to Russia. The Crimea gains independence for a brief time.

1775 The **13 colonies** in North America begin their **struggle for independence** against British colonial power on April 19.

1776 On Jan. 2, **Emperor Joseph II** bans the **use of torture** in Austria.

1777 The outnumbered and ill-equipped **Continental Army** defeats the British forces on Oct. 17 in the **Battle of Saratoga**.

1778 The **USA** concludes a **Treaty of Amity and Commerce** with **France** on Feb. 6, whereupon Great Britain declares war on the French.

1779 A **civil war** breaks out in **Persia** after the death of its ruler, **Karim Khan Zand**.

1776 The autonomous **Spanish Viceroyalty** of the **Rio de la Plata**, with Buenos Aires as its capital, is created in South America.

1778 A **war** breaks out between **Prussia** and **Austria** on July 5 over the open **succession in Bavaria**. It ends one year later with a compromise.

1778 On his last voyage, **James Cook** discovers the **Hawaiian Islands**. He is killed there by the natives a year later.

1780 With the death of Maria Theresa on Nov. 29, **Emperor Joseph II** becomes the sole ruler in the Habsburg hereditary lands. Domestically, he pursues a course of enlightened reform.

1780 **Russia** reacts to the naval fighting between the **French** and the **British** with a declaration of "armed neutrality" at sea on March 11.

1781 **French Finance Minister Jacques Necker** is dismissed on Sept. 19 after the new state budget is made public.

1781 In the fall, French-American forces achieve a decisive victory over the British army under General Cornwallis in the **Siege of Yorktown**.

1782 On April 6, **General Rama I** becomes the new **king of Thailand**, founding the **Chakri dynasty** that rules to this day, and resides in the new capital of Bangkok.

1783 In the **Treaty of Paris** of Sept. 3, Great Britain recognizes the **independence of the USA**.

1776 The **USA**, which at first constituted a loose federation of 13 colonies , is created in Philadelphia with the **Declaration of Independence**.

The Era of Revolutions

1770–1815

The core ideas of the Enlightenment became the foundation of the American declaration of independence in 1776. In France, social discontent and harsh criticism of the monarchy's claim to absolute power resulted in the French Revolution in 1789. With cries of "Liberté! Égalité! Fraternité!," the revolutionaries were echoing the Enlightenment's aspirations to political emancipation. However, external pressure twisted the revolution into a murderous reign of terror. Napoleon Bonaparte was the first to be able to end the chaos. When the European powers waged war against revolutionary France, Napoleon became determined to spread the ideas of the Revolution by increasing French dominance all over Europe.

The symbol of the French revolution on a military drum of the period

HISTORICAL FIGURES

The Qianlong Emperor (1711–1799)   Imperial China experienced its last great period of power and prosperity under the Qianlong Emperor. He was the longest reigning ruler in the history of the country.

Qianlong—"heavenly prosperity"—was both the motto of the government and the name of the emperor of the Manchu dynasty that ruled over China from 1736–1795. During his reign, the state territory was extended considerably into Central Asia, reaching its greatest extent in China's history. In addition, Burma to the south was made a tributary state in 1788. The economy, and particularly the arts, experienced a major upswing during his reign. The emperor himself was an enthusiastic calligrapher and poet and had palaces and imperial residences lavishly expanded, especially in Beijing.

George Washington (1732–1799)   In the United States of America, the first U.S. president is considered to be the "Father of the Country."

The son of wealthy plantation owners was a member of Virginia's upper class and held important positions as politician and military leader. In 1774–75, Washington was chosen a delegate to the Continental Congress to organize resistance to British colonial power. With French support, the commander in chief of the American revolutionary army forced the British army to capitulate at Yorktown in **1781** and ultimately recognize the independence of the USA. In **1789** Washington was unanimously elected the first president of the USA. As president of the Constitutional Convention in Philadelphia, he also played a decisive role in the drafting of the American constitution.

Maximilien de Robespierre (1758–1794)   The radical proponent of the Enlightenment was a towering figure of the French Revolution. During his Reign of Terror, enemies of the republic were ruthlessly eliminated.

From the very start in **1789**, Robespierre was an active participant in the French Revolution. He soon became a leading figure in the Jacobin Club that sought to create a republic based on Rousseau's ideas of equality. Robespierre, known as "The Incorruptible" because of his rigid morals, was involved in the destruction of the Girondists and the execution of Louis XVI in **1792–93**. In order to establish a "republic of virtue," he made the Committee of Public Safety into a powerful instrument of terror and had thousands of alleged counter-revolutionaries executed. Robespierre was overthrown on **July 27, 1794** and guillotined the next day.

Napoleon Bonaparte (1769–1821)   Dictator, conqueror, and enforcer of the French Revolution: The rise of the brilliant military strategist and unscrupulous, power-greedy politician to become Europe's most powerful man is doubtlessly unprecedented in history.

After the Corsican Napoleon Bonaparte attended military school, he began his meteoric career in the French revolutionary army. His marriage to Joséphine de Beauharnais in 1796 assured him access to politically influential circles. In a coup d'état in 1799, Bonaparte placed himself at the head of the state and ruled dictatorially thereafter. In **1804** he assumed the title of emperor. At the same time, he institutionalized basic civil rights in his Code Civil. Soon vast parts of Europe were under French control, but his defeat in Russia in **1812** triggered the wars of liberation that ultimately ended in the occupation of Paris in 1814. The Battle of Waterloo in **1815** sealed Napoleon's fate. He died in exile in 1821 on St. Helena in the Atlantic.

1804 In **France**, the **Code Civil** goes into effect on March 21, putting into law the liberal achievements of the French Revolution and exerting a great influence on legislation in all of Europe.

1808 The most important writer of German Classicism, **Johann Wolfgang von Goethe**, publishes the first part of his tragedy *Faust*.

1807–1810 Living in exile in Germany, **French writer Madame de Staël** writes her most noted work *De l'Allemagne* (*On the Germans*), shaping the image of Germany as "the land of poets and thinkers."

1813 British writer **Jane Austen** publishes the novel *Pride and Prejudice*.

1801 Spanish painter **Francisco de Goya** paints *The Nude Maja*, unleashing a public scandal.

1809 The **Frederick William University** (Humboldt University) is founded in **Berlin** on Oct. 16.

1812 The first volume of *Children's and Household Tales* by the **Brothers Grimm** is published on Dec. 20.

1814 **Pope Pius VII** restores the **Jesuit Order**.

1805 · **1810** · **1815**

1800 On Jan. 18, Napoleon founds the **Banque de France**.

1801 On March 4, **Thomas Jefferson** is sworn in as the third president of the USA.

1801 Great Britain and Ireland join together to form the **United Kingdom of Great Britain and Ireland** on Jan. 1.

1803 The **Helvetic Republic** is dissolved by the **Act of Mediation**.

1809 In the **Treaty of Fredrikshamn** on Sept. 17, Sweden is forced to accept the annexation of Finland by Russia. Prior to this, the Swedish parliament had toppled Gustav IV Adolf and replaced him with his uncle, Charles XIII.

1810 On July 27, a British-Portuguese army led by Field Marshall Arthur Wellesley, who later becomes the **Duke of Wellington**, puts an end to Napoleon's **attempted occupation of Portugal**.

1801 On March 24, **Alexander I** becomes Emperor of Russia; during his reign until 1825, Russia becomes a decisive factor in concert with the major European powers.

1803 **British forces capture the city of Delhi** and by 1818 have control of the entire the Maratha Empire.

1805 In the **Battle of Trafalgar** on Oct. 21, the British fleet under Admiral Nelson affirms its mastery of the seas over France.

1811 On Feb. 5, **King George III's eldest son** takes over the reins of government as **prince regent for his mentally ill father**. He succeeds him as George IV in 1820.

1805 On May 25, **Napoleon** crowns himself **King of Italy** in Milan.

1808 On Nov. 15, **Mahmut II** becomes **Sultan of the Ottoman Empire**.

1812 The **French** are driven **out of Madrid** on March 18.

1801 In the **Treaty of Lunéville** of Feb. 9, Austria and the Holy Roman Empire are forced to recognize the Rhine as the border to France and, in doing so, Napoleon's conquests.

1804 **Napoleon Bonaparte crowns himself Napoleon I, Emperor of the French**, on Dec. 2.

1805 Napoleon's victory over Austria and Russia on Dec. 2 in the **Battle of Austerlitz** secures France's supremacy on the European continent.

1812 **Napoleon's Russian campaign** that began in June results in a military disaster. The decimated Grande Armée is forced to retreat with the onset of winter.

1803 On April 30, the **USA purchases** the **Louisiana territory** west of the Mississippi from France for 28 million dollars.

1806 The **Confederation of the Rhine** is formed on July 12. Under the protectorate of Napoleon I, **16 German states** join together, putting an end, after more than 1,000 years, to the Holy Roman Empire of the German Nation.

1813 In the **Battle of the Nations** at **Leipzig** from Oct. 16 to 19, the **largest battle to date in history**, the coalition consisting of Russia, Prussia, Austria, and Sweden inflict a decisive defeat on Napoleon, who is forced to retreat out of Germany.

1804 The Serbs rise up under the peasant leader **Kara Djorde Petrovic** against Ottoman rule and by 1813 have wrested wide-ranging **autonomy for Serbia**.

1804 In the north of present-day Nigeria, the radical Muslim leader **Usman dan Fodio** conquers the Hausa Kingdoms and sets up the **Caliphate of Sokoto**.

1807 In the **Treaties of Tilsit** on July 7–9, Prussia loses almost half of its state territory. Russia and France reapportion Eastern Europe according to their interests.

1814 The allies occupy Paris on March 31; **Napoleon is forced to abdicate** and withdraw to Elba.

1815 On March 1, Napoleon returns back from Elba to France; the **"Hundred Days of Napoleon"** begin.

1804 After a successful uprising against their French colonial masters, **Haiti declares independence** on Jan. 1. For the first time, **a slave population has gained its freedom**.

1806 In the **twin battles of Jena and Auerstedt** on Oct. 14, Napoleon inflicts defeat on Frederick William III of Prussia.

1807 **Great Britain** and the **USA pass an act for the abolition of the slave trade,** which is, however, hardly enforced.

1808 **Napoleon's occupation of Spain** in April and the imposed installation of his brother, Joseph Bonaparte, as king incite violent resistance by the Spanish population and result in a years-long guerilla war.

1815 In the **Battle of Waterloo** on June 18, Napoleon, who had reassumed power, is defeated once and for all by a British-Prussian coalition. Napoleon is banned to the island of St. Helena, where he dies in 1821.

1789 French cleric and publicist **Emmanuel Joseph Sieyès** becomes the leading spokesman of the third estate in the National Assembly through his pamphlet *What is the Third Estate?*

1790 Irish philosopher Edmund **Burke** publishes his critical *Reflections on the Revolution of France*, making him the pioneering theorist of emerging conservatism.

1791 On Dec. 5, a few weeks before the premiere performance of *The Magic Flute*, the Austrian composer **Wolfgang Amadeus Mozart** dies in Vienna.

1793 **Universal compulsory military service** for all men between 18 and 25 is introduced in **France** on March 28.

1791 Prussian architect **Carl Gotthard Langhans** completes construction of the **Brandenburg Gate** in Berlin.

1794 The **Ecolé Politechnique** is founded in France. It becomes the model for all technical universities in Europe.

1795 German philosopher **Immanuel Kant** publishes his essay *Perpetual Peace*.

1796 British physician **Edward Jenner** successfully carries out a **smallpox vaccination** for the first time on May 14.

1795–1797 Scottish explorer **Mungo Park** becomes the first European to penetrate into the interior of **Africa** on his expedition in the **Niger and Senegal territories**.

1800 On April 24, the **Library of Congress** is founded in **Washington D.C.** To this day, it is one of the largest libraries in the world.

1790 | **1795** | **1800**

1786 When **Frederick II** dies on Aug. 17, his nephew, **Frederick William II**, becomes **king of Prussia**.

1787 The **constitution of the USA**, which provides for a federation of states, is ratified in **Philadelphia** on Sept. 17.

1788 On Jan. 16, the British found the **first penal colony in Sydney**, launching the European colonization of Australia.

1789 The U.S. Congress passes the **Bill of Rights** as an amendment to the constitution on Sept. 25, establishing basic human and civil rights.

1789 On April 7, **Selim III** becomes the **new Sultan of the Ottoman Empire**. He introduces comprehensive modernization, particularly in the military.

1789 **George Washington** is unanimously elected the **first President of the USA** on April 6.

1789 **Tennis Court Oath**: During the assembly of the Estates-General in Versailles, the **Third Estate**, the bourgeois and wage-laborers, begin calling themselves the French National Assembly.

1790 The **Treaty of Värälä** of Aug. 14 ends the two-year **Russo-Swedish War** without any territorial changes.

1790 The French National Assembly abolishes the **privileges of the aristocracy. The clergy are made civil servants.**

1789 After abolishing the feudal system, the French National Assembly ratifies the **Declaration of Human Rights** on Aug. 26.

1789 On July 14, a mob storms the **Bastille**, the Paris city prison. The **French Revolution** has begun.

1792 After the **murder of Gustav III** on March 29, his son, Gustav IV Adolf, ascends to the throne of Sweden.

1790 In preparation for their **anti-French coalition**, Austria and Prussia set aside their differences on July 27 in the **Reichenbach Convention**.

1791 On Sept. 14, King Louis XVI accepts a liberal constitution. For a short time **France** is a **constitutional monarchy**.

1791 **Europe's first modern written constitution** is ratified in **Poland** on May 3.

1791 The **Canada Act** of June 10 divides Quebec Province into a British Upper Canada and a French Lower Canada.

1791 On Aug. 27, Prussia and Austria declare their solidarity with the French monarchy in the **Declaration of Pillnitz**.

1792 The **War of the First Coalition** of the allies Austria and Prussia against revolutionary France begins on April 20.

1792 After the storming of the French King's residence on Aug. 10, the **French National Assembly proclaims King Louis XVI deposed and the country a republic**.

1793 On Jan. 21, former French **King Louis XVI is executed on the guillotine**. His wife, Marie Antoinette, follows him to the guillotine on Oct. 16.

1794 As **Shah of Persia, Agha Muhammad Khan Qajar** founds the **Qajar dynasty** that rules over the country until 1925.

"Men are born and remain free and equal in rights."

Article 1 of the Human Rights of August 26, 1789

1794 The **execution of Maximilien Robespierre** on July 28 ends his months-long regime of terror.

1796 The French, under the command of the popular **General Napoleon Bonaparte**, begin a successful campaign against the Austrians on April 10 and establish several satellite states in Italy.

1798 In the **Battle of the Pyramids** on July 21, Napoleon defeats the Egyptian army. By the summer of 1799, the French have occupied Egypt.

1795 On Jan. 19, French-occupied United Netherlands is proclaimed the **Batavian Republic**.

1795 On April 15, Austria, Prussia, and Russia further divide Poland amongst themselves in the **Third Partition of Poland**.

1795 Chinese Emperor **Qianlong** abdicates on Feb. 7 after a reign of almost 60 years. Under his reign, China had experienced an unprecedented boom.

1795 A liberal democratic, five-man executive body, the **Directory**, is instituted in **France** on Oct. 31 and a new constitution is ratified.

1797 In the **Treaty of Campo Formio** of Oct. 17, Austria is forced to recognize France's conquests, ending the War of the First Coalition.

1798 With the help of French occupation forces, Swiss liberals set up the **Helvetic Republic**.

1799 Russia, Austria, and Naples join Great Britain in a **coalition against France** and manage to roll back Napoleon's control in Italy for a short time from April to July.

HISTORICAL EVENTS

Boston Tea Party
The revolt of American colonists against the tax policies of the British colonial government in 1773 was an important step on the path toward American independence.

Boston citizens dressed as Indians during the Boston Tea Party in 1773.

The imposition of import taxes by the English parliament in 1767 met with violent resistance in the North American colonies. They were supposed to pay but had no say in how the monies were spent. With cries of "No taxation without representation," boycotts took place against British products, leading to the first bloody clash between British soldiers and American colonists in the so-called Boston Massacre on **March 5, 1770**. After that, Britain rescinded all import taxes—except the one on tea. In an act of defiance, about fifty colonists disguised as Indians boarded British ships moored at Boston harbor on **Dec. 16, 1773**, and heaved a cargo of tea by the East India Company into the ocean. English parliament swiftly asserted its authority by closing Boston harbor and dissolving colonial parliament in Massachusetts. This further inflamed anti-British sentiment and pushed most colonies to the brink of revolution.

American War of Independence
After eight years of intermittent fighting, the North American colonies were able to gain their independence from the British motherland.

When the 13 colonies declared their independence on **July 4, 1776**, the initial skirmishes between American militias and British troops turned into a full-scale war. George Washington was commissioned by the Continental Congress to lead the American army that claimed its first victory over the British northern army at Saratoga on **Oct. 17, 1777**. The crucial turning point came in **1778**, when France, joined by Spain and Holland, entered the war on the side of the rebels. A combined American and French army forced the surrender of the British troops in the Battle of Yorktown on **Oct. 19, 1781**. In 1783, Great Britain had to recognize the United States by signing the Treaty of Paris that officially ended the American Revolution. The colonies joined in a loose federation on Nov. 15, 1777, but it was not until **1787** that the constitution was adopted.

A scene from the War of Independence: Washington crossing the Delaware with his troops.

Infuriated Parisians storm the Bastille, which for them was the symbol of royal tyranny.

The Storming of the Bastille
The storming of the state prison in Paris on July 14, 1789 is celebrated to this day as the glorious beginning of the French Revolution.

Periodic economic crises in absolutist France since the early 1780s, as well as the inability of the monarchy to bring about reform, led to growing frustration within the French population. In the summer of 1789, long-simmering tensions boiled over. On **June 17, 1789**, the Third Estate declared itself a National Assembly and drew up a constitution. When the king assembled troops around Paris and dismissed the popular finance minister Necker on July 11, people were outraged. On **July 14, 1789**, a frenzied mob stormed the Bastille, a prison-fortress in Paris. The revolution could no longer be halted. Peasants all over the country armed themselves and pillaged the chateaux of the rural aristocracy. Many nobles fled to escape the turmoil and joined the opponents of the revolution. On **Aug. 26, 1789**, the Assembly adopted the Declaration of the Rights of Man. The Ancien Régime had collapsed.

Women in the French Revolution
Women's hopes of equal rights were not fulfilled.

Women were part of the revolution from the start, including the storming of the Bastille and the battles of the revolutionary wars. The protest march of thousands of Parisian market women to Versailles on Aug. 5, **1789**, forced Louis XVI to return to the capital. Women like Théroigne de Méricourt and Madame Roland saw the revolution as a chance to promote their own agendas. Women's clubs in support of equal rights sprang up all over France. The male revolutionaries, however, continued to deny women a political voice. In an act of protest, writer Olympe de Gouges published a declaration in 1791, demanding civil equality for women.

Execution of Louis XVI

The beheading of Louis XVI provoked unrest at home and outrage abroad. Internally, the revolution subsequently degenerated into terror.

On **Sept. 3, 1791**, King Louis XVI swore an oath to the constitution, which substantially reduced his power and turned France into a constitutional monarchy. An attempt by the royal family to flee Paris had been foiled, which gave the supporters of the republic a further boost. After the victory of the Revolutionary army over the Austrian-Prussian coalition on **Sept. 20, 1792**, the rage over the king's hostile attitude toward the Revolution was uncontainable. The monarchy was abolished on **Sept. 21, 1792**, and Louis XVI was placed under arrest. As "Citizen Capet," the king was sentenced to death by the convention and guillotined on **Jan. 21, 1793**. The ensuing emergency situation led to the dictatorship of the radical Jacobins that began in 1793, and to the mass liquidation of political opponents.

The execution of Louis XVI on Jan. 21, 1793 on the Place de la Concorde in Paris.

Prussian Reforms

Beginning in 1807, fundamental reforms were introduced in Prussia to modernize the state and society.

Prussia's catastrophic defeat at the hands of Napoleon's forces in **1806** revealed the backwardness of the corporative agrarian state. Far-reaching reforms were carried out under the leadership of the ministers Stein and Hardenberg. They sought to modernize both the Prussian society and state, making them more efficient without impinging on the monarchic principle. On the national level, the administration was centralized beginning in 1807 and the army reorganized according to the performance principle. In 1808, self-administration was introduced at the municipal level. On the social level, hereditary serfdom of peasants was abolished in 1807, and in 1812 Jews gained social equality. To educate the citizens in line with the new state goals, extensive reforms in schooling and education were introduced, such as the founding of the Frederick William University in Berlin in **1809**.

Statue of the scholar Wilhelm von Humboldt in front of the university he helped to found.

In the three-day "Battle of Nations" at Leipzig in Oct. 1813, the Russians, Prussians, Austrians, and Swedes defeated Napoleon's forces that were only aided by Polish and Saxon troops.

Napoleonic Wars

From 1799 on, Napoleon's armies rushed relentlessly from one victory to the next. It was not until the disastrous Russian campaign of 1812 that his empire began to falter.

From **1792**, revolutionary France engaged in a series of "coalition wars" and established a new order in Europe. In **1805** Napoleon put Italy and, in **1808**, Spain under his control. After the defeat of Austria in the Battle of Austerlitz in **1805** and of Prussia in the twin battles of Jena and Auerstädt in **1806**, only Great Britain was left to oppose the rampant imperialism of the French emperor. When Russia entered into trade relations with Great Britain against Napoleon's will, the French invaded Russia in **June of 1812**, but suffered massive losses. The almost total disintegration of the Grande Armée strengthened resistance in the occupied countries and launched the wars of liberation. In the "Battle of Nations" at Leipzig from **Oct. 16–19, 1813**, a coalition consisting of Prussia, Austria, Sweden, and Russia defeated Napoleon, who was forced to withdraw to French soil.

Battle of Waterloo

Napoleon's defeat in June 1815 achieved proverbial status and marked the end of the emperor's final bid for power.

After the Allies had marched into Paris, Napoleon was forced to abdicate on **April 6, 1814** and sent into exile on the island of Elba. During the Congress of Vienna, however, he was able to make a spectacular return to Paris on **March 1, 1815**, and once again assume power ("Hundred Days of Napoleon"). French soldiers and volunteers flocked in droves to join the emperor. In reaction, Great Britain and Prussia mobilized a large contingent of troops under the command of the Duke of Wellington and Field Marshal von Blücher. The deciding battle took place near the Belgian village of Waterloo on **June 18, 1815**, in which Napoleon's army, after initial victories, suffered a crushing defeat. On June 22, Napoleon abdicated (again) and was banished by the British to the island of St. Helena in the South Atlantic. The first French Empire was now history.

Napoleon was defeated by Britain and Prussia at Waterloo in present-day Belgium.

1815 Karl Friedrich Schinkel is appointed surveyor of the Prussian Building Commission in Berlin. In the following years, his neoclassical buildings make him the most noted architect in Prussia.

1817 German inventor **Karl Drais** develops a wooden "running machine" with two wheels and a handlebar, a **forerunner of the bicycle**.

1819 The **steamboat revolutionizes maritime traffic**. In March, the *Savannah*, a paddle steamer, crosses the Atlantic for the first time in 26 days.

1821 English **physicist and chemist Michael Faraday** develops the basic principle of the **electric motor**.

1822 English mathematician **Charles Babbage** constructs the model of **a mechanical computer**.

1824 Beethoven's 9th Symphony premieres in Vienna on May 7.

1825 The world's **first railroad line is opened** between the English towns of Stockton and Darlington.

1825 Louis Braille invents a **raised dot system of reading and writing for the blind**. Three years later, he also develops music notation.

1815

1820

1825

1815 On June 8, the individual **41 German states** join together to form the **German Confederation**. Its highest council is the Bundestag (Federal Assembly) seated in Frankfurt on Main.

1815 The European powers sign the **Final Act of the Congress of Vienna** on June 9. Prussia, Great Britain, Austria, and Russia work for a lasting peace in Europe.

1815 Russia, Austria, and Prussia agree upon a **"Holy Alliance"** on Sept. 26 to safeguard conservative state and social order.

1816–1828 **Zulu King Shaka's campaigns of conquest** cause the collapse of the political and social order in South Africa.

1817 **Ninko** is crowned the **120th emperor of Japan**.

1817 At the **Wartburg Festival** German student fraternities gather at Wartburg Castle on Oct. 18–19 to demonstrate for national unity and liberal freedoms.

1818 At the **Conference of Aix-la-Chapelle** (today's Aachen) France is reinstated as an equal member in the circle of major European powers (Holy Alliance) on Nov. 21.

1818–1844 Sweden and Norway experience economic prosperity and a cultural bloom under **King Charles XIV John (Bernadotte)**.

1819 The British establish a **trading post in Singapore** on Jan. 29. The port city quickly becomes an important trading hub between Asia and Europe.

1819 On Feb. 15, Venezuela and Colombia join together to form the **independent state of Gran Colombia**.

1819 The so-called **Hep-Hep riots, pogroms against Jews**, take place in many cities in Europe.

1819 Carlsbad Decrees: Instigated by Metternich, on Sept. 20 the German confederate states agree upon **defensive measures against national-liberal aspirations**, such as increased press censorship and a central investigating commission against "revolutionary plots and demagogical associations."

1820 At the **Congress of Troppau**, Austria, Russia, and Prussia decide to militarily support any European country in danger of being overthrown.

1820 To maintain a **balance between slave states and free states**, the U.S. Congress stipulates in the **Missouri Compromise** that territories north of parallel 36°30' north are to be slave-free.

1820 Bowing to pressure from the people, King Ferdinand VII of **Spain** accepts a **liberal constitution**.

1821 At the **Congress of Laibach** (Jan. to May), the conservative powers in Europe decide to intervene militarily in the kingdom of the Two Sicilies to suppress an uprising.

1821 The eight-year **struggle for Greek independence** begins on March 25 with an armed uprising against Ottoman rule.

1821 A **constitutional monarchy** is established in **Portugal**.

1822 Brazil declares **independence from Portuguese rule** on Sept. 7.

1822 **Freed American slaves** settle in West Africa, laying the foundation for the state of **Liberia** that is proclaimed in 1847.

1823 **U.S. President James Monroe** formulates his **Monroe Doctrine** in a foreign policy statement on Dec 2. According to the president, the USA will not interfere in European affairs if the Europeans respect the autonomy of the American nation.

1823 During the so-called "Spanish Expedition" a **French army of intervention** commissioned by the Holy Alliance drives out the revolutionary government in Madrid and reinstates the **absolute monarchy** under Ferdinand VII in **Spain**.

1824 On Sept. 16, **Charles X** ascends to the French throne and establishes an extreme reactionary regime.

1824 On Oct. 4, **Mexico** becomes a **republic** with a federal constitution.

1825–1828 **Argentina** and **Brazil** wage war over the territory of present-day Uruguay.

1825 **John Quincy Adams** becomes president of the USA.

1825 **Bolivia** in South America is declared an independent republic on Aug 6.

1825 **Nicholas I** becomes Tsar of Russia on Dec. 1. He crushes the **Decembrist Revolt** and tightens his absolutist system of government.

1826 The underaged **Maria II Gloria** is made **queen in Portugal**. The battle between the conservatives and liberals intensifies.

1827 In the **Battle of Navarino**, fought during the Greek War of Independence, a British-Russian-French fleet defeats the Ottoman-Egyptian fleet off the Greek coast on Oct. 20.

After the upheavals of the French Revolution and the Napoleonic Wars, the leading powers of Europe, along with the ruling class of nobility, began their quest to restore the pre-revolutionary social order. However, the Revolution's ideals of civil liberties and national self-determination had developed a dynamic of their own, not least of all in the Balkans and the overseas colonies. Fueled by economic concerns as well as the long suppressed demands of the middle class for democratic rights and liberties, several waves of revolutionary uprisings spread like wildfire all across Europe, culminating in the revolutions of 1848. Called the "Springtime of peoples" by contemporraries, these upheavals were rather short-lived. In the end, the old powers were able to prevail once more.

Petit bourgeois idyll in revolutionary times in a painting by Carl Spitzweg.

HISTORICAL FIGURES

Andrew Jackson (1767–1845)
During the presidency of Andrew Jackson, the United States moved toward party rule and the rise of mass democracy.

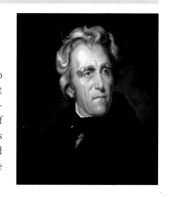

Jackson rose to be one of the leading political figures in the state of Tennessee when he was elected senator in 1797. The ambitious "self-made man" first gained national attention through his military "successes," especially for the ruthless displacement of Native Americans. His defense of New Orleans against the English in 1815 made him popular with the masses. In 1828, Jackson became the first president who did not benefit from the nation's east-coast elite. Supported by a coalition of farmers, laborers, and planters, he propagated the politics of the "common man" and filled government posts with his supporters. He continued the forced relocation of Native Americans dictated by the relentless westward expansion of the USA.

Mohammed Ali (1769–1849)
The Egyptian Pasha strengthened his country and founded a dynasty that ruled until 1953.

The son of Albanian parents distinguished himself in the fight against Napoleon's troops in 1799 in Egypt. In 1805, the Ottoman sultan appointed Ali governor. As such, he modernized the army, eliminated the Mamluk upper class, and made himself the undisputed ruler of Egypt. Following successful campaigns into Arabia, he gradually became a rival for Ottoman supremacy in the region. It took an intervention by the European powers in the "Oriental Crisis" to force Ali to retreat in **1840**. All the same, the Ottoman Turks had to recognize Ali as hereditary viceroy of Egypt, laying the foundation for the country's later independence.

Prince Klemens von Metternich (1773–1859)
As Austrian foreign minister, the scion of ancient Rhenish nobility pursued a policy of restoration that aimed at reestablishing the pre-revolutionary, traditional order in Europe.

After the French occupation of the Rhineland, Metternich went to Vienna in 1794, where his career in the Austrian civil service advanced rapidly. Foreign minister since 1809, he was crucially involved in coordinating the Wars of Liberation and became a leading figure at the Congress of Vienna in **1814–15**. He pursued a foreign policy of a balance of European powers under the supervision of a strong Austria. Domestically, he was intent on establishing the sole authority of the monarchy and hounded national and democratic movements. The revolution of **1848** forced Metternich, a symbol of the reactionary forces, into exile.

Simon Bolívar (1783–1830)
Known as the Liberator, Bolívar spearheaded the Latin American fight for independence from Spanish colonial rule.

Born into Venezuela's creole aristocracy, Bolívar was educated in Europe where he became an ardent admirer of the French Revolution. In 1807, he joined the Latin American freedom movement and quickly took over the political and military leadership. Within a few years, he carried the war for liberation to all countries of South America. On **Feb. 15, 1819**, Bolívar created Gran Colombia—an entity combining Venezuela, Colombia, and Ecuador, and in 1825, he founded the republic of Bolivia in Upper Peru. However, his dream of a confederation of all Latin American nations under his leadership crumbled, when Gran Colombia disintegrated in 1830.

1837 French painter **Louis Daguerre** invents the **first practical photographic process** (daguerreotype).

1838 In May, the first steamship from Europe arrives in New York, marking the beginning of **steamship traffic between the USA and Europe**.

1840 On May 1, the "Penny Black," the **world's first postage stamp**, is issued in Great Britain.

1841 German philosopher and atheist **Ludwig Feuerbach** publishes his treatise *The Essence of Christianity*.

1841 **Thomas Cook**, a Baptist preacher, organizes the first rail excursion in England, ushering in the age of organized **mass tourism**.

1842 American surgeon **Crawford Long** uses anesthesia for the first time during surgery, thus establishing the field of **anesthetics**.

1844 German-Jewish poet and literary critic **Heinrich Heine** publishes his satirical epic poem *Germany: A Winter's Tale*.

1844 On May 24, American inventor **Samuel Morse** sends the first **telegraph message** from Washington to Baltimore.

1847 The speech, **"Russia as it really is,"** makes Russian anarchist and revolutionary **Mikhail Bakunin** famous throughout Europe.

1848 On Feb. 21, **Karl Marx** and **Friedrich Engels** publish *The Communist Manifesto*.

1840 — 1845 — 1850

1837 On June 20, **Victoria becomes queen of Great Britain**, thus ending the personal union between the United Kingdom and Hanover that has existed since 1714.

1837 Ill-fated speculations precipitate the **first severe economic crisis in the USA**. Many banks become insolvent.

1838 In May, members of the radical **Chartists**, Great Britain's first working class movement, publish the **"People's Charter,"** demanding a reform of British society and the introduction of universal male suffrage.

1838–1839 Thousands of people die on the infamous **"Trail of Tears,"** the forced relocation of Native American tribes ordered by the U.S. government.

1838 The **British** set out from India to invade **Afghanistan**, provoking a four-year war, known as "Auckland's Folly."

1838 On Dec. 16, the **Boers** are victorious over an army of **Zulus** in the **Battle of Blood River**.

1839 The **Ottoman Empire** fails in its attempt to wrest Syria back from Egypt. The European powers intervene in the **"Oriental Crisis"** that lasts until 1841.

1840 On Feb. 6, the **Maori** sign the **Treaty of Waitangi**, agreeing to a colonization of New Zealand by the **British**.

1840 On July 15, Prussia, Austria, Great Britain, and Russia pledge to protect the **Ottoman Empire** in the "Oriental Crisis."

1840 British forces attack the Chinese city of Canton (Guangzhou) in July in response to the Chinese ban on opium imports, igniting the **First Opium War**.

1841 In the **London Straits Convention** of July 13, the major European powers agree to close the Turkish straits to all non-Ottoman warships in the event of war.

1842 The **Treaty of Nanking** marks the end of the **First Opium War** on Aug. 29. Great Britain gains Hong Kong as a colony and unrestricted access to five Chinese ports.

1842 The Boers found the **Orange Free State** between the Orange and Vaal rivers in southern Africa.

1843 The **British annex the Boer Natalia Republic** founded in 1839.

1844 The **eastern part of Haiti** declares itself independent on Feb. 27 to become the **Dominican Republic**.

1844 On March 8, **Oscar I** succeeds his father, Charles XIV John, as **king of Sweden and Norway**.

1844 Bowing to pressure from the people and the military, Otto I of Greece accepts a liberal constitution. **Greece becomes a constitutional monarchy**.

1844 A **weavers' revolt in Silesia** is brutally crushed.

1848 **February Revolution:** The **"Citizen King," Louis Philippe of France**, abdicates on Feb. 24. One day later, the Second Republic is proclaimed. In December, the future Napoleon III becomes president.

1845 On Dec. 29, **Texas**, which has been an independent republic since 1836, **joins the Union**.

1846 In a dispute over Texas, a two-year **war** breaks out between **Mexico** and the **USA**. Mexico is subsequently forced to cede a large part of its territory to the USA, including California.

1846 In the **Treaty of Oregon** of June 15, the USA and Great Britain agree on Parallel 54°40' north as the boundary between the USA and Canada.

1848 **Elizabeth Cady Stanton** organizes the **Seneca Falls Convention** for women's rights.

1846/1847 Extreme **grain and potato crop failures** result in a devastating famine across Europe, with Ireland being hit particularly hard.

1848 After French colonial **slavery** had been reestablished under Napoleon Bonaparte in 1802, it is **abolished** by decree of April 27 **in France**, its colonies, and overseas possessions.

1848 The various **democratic uprisings** beginning in March in a majority of the **German Confederate states** and other nations challenge the European status quo.

1848 In June, a **social revolutionary workers' insurrection** in Paris is brutally suppressed.

1848 As a result of the **uprising in Palermo**, a **constitution** for the Kingdom of the Two Sicilies is adopted on Jan. 12.

1849 The National Assembly, convening in St. Paul's Church in Frankfurt, passes **a democratic German imperial constitution**, but it is never put into effect.

1828 German chemist **Friedrich Wöhler** succeeds in synthesizing ammonium cyanate from urea, becoming a **pioneer in organic chemistry and biochemistry**.

1829 **Charles Fourier**, an important representative of early French socialism, publishes his main essay *The New Industrial and Social World*.

1829 George Stephenson's **locomotive**, the **Rocket**, attains a speed of 45 kilometers (28 miles) per hour.

1831 For the first time, almost all of Europe is ravaged by a **cholera epidemic**.

1832 German poet **Johann Wolfgang von Goethe** publishes the second part of his tragic play *Faust*.

1832 The first **horse-drawn streetcar** goes into operation in **New York**.

1833 The **writer Rahel Varnhagen**, whose drawing room has been a hive of critical conversation since 1820, dies in Berlin on March 7.

1834 The **Catholic inquisition** is abolished in Spain.

1834 The German writer **Georg Büchner** propagates the slogan **"Peace to the huts, war to the palaces,"** intending to stir up defiance against the authorities.

1835 Danish writer **Hans Christian Andersen** begins writing his *Fairy Tales for Adults*.

1836 **Samuel Colt** invents and produces the first **percussion cap revolver** in Texas.

1835 French jurist and political thinker **Alexis de Tocqueville** publishes *Democracy in America*, which has become one of the most influential texts in social science.

1837 The English novelist **Charles Dickens** publishes the socio-critical novel *Oliver Twist*.

1830 — 1835

1829 On Sept. 15, **Mexican President Vicente Guerrero signs a decree abolishing slavery** throughout the republic.

1829 The **Treaty of Adrianopel** on Sept. 14 seals the defeat of the Ottoman Empire in the war against Russia. Ottoman sovereignty experiences a deep crisis.

1830 On Feb. 3, the sovereignty of Greece is confirmed by Russia, Austria, and Great Britain in the **London Protocol**.

1830 **July Revolution:** An uprising in France from July 27–29 topples the reactionary regime of King Charles X. Louis Philippe of Orléans becomes king of the French and accepts a liberal constitution.

1830 On Nov. 18, **Belgium declares its independence from the Netherlands**. A year later, the new nation adopts a liberal constitution and chooses Leopold I of Saxe-Coburg and Gotha as king.

1831 In July, antimonarchist Giuseppe Mazzini forms a secret society in Marseille called **"Young Italy,"** which fights for the independence and unification of Italy.

1831 The **Canut revolts in Lyon**, an uprising of silk workers in France, are the first social uprisings of the ongoing Industrial Revolution.

1832/33 When South Carolina passes an **ordinance to nullify the tariffs of 1828 and 1832**, a dispute develops over the right of individual states to supersede federal laws within their borders.

1832 From May 27–30, 30,000 activists demonstrate during the **Hambach Festival** for **German unity** and recognition of democratic sovereignty.

1832 On June 4, for the first time in Great Britain since 1430, a **parliamentary reform** is passed. The number of people eligible to vote increases significantly.

1832 On Aug. 8, the National Assembly chooses **Otto von Wittelsbach of Bavaria** as **king of Greece**.

1831 A **revolt in the kingdom of Poland (Congress Poland)** is brutally suppressed in November by its ruling power in Russia.

1833 On Apr. 3, students in Frankfurt fail in their attempt to launch a **revolution in Germany** by **storming the Hauptwache**. Subsequently, persecution of liberal thinkers is intensified.

1833 **Mohammed Ali**, the viceroy of Egypt, **occupies Syria**, putting the strength of Ottoman sovereignty into question.

"Liberty Leading the People"
Eugène Delacroix, 1830

1833 By an act of the parliament of the United Kingdom, **slavery is abolished** throughout the **British Empire**.

1835 Francis I dies and his mentally retarded son, **Ferdinand I, becomes emperor of Austria** on March 2. Affairs of government are taken over by an advisory body led by Chancellor Klemens von Metternich.

1836 **Andrés de Santa Cruz,** dictator of Bolivia, achieves a political union with Peru by forming the **Peru-Bolivian Confederation**.

1835–1843 During the **"Great Trek"** the Boers migrate to the north of South Africa.

1830 Inspired by the French **July Revolution**, a wave of liberal democratic and nationalist uprisings sweeps across all of Europe. Most of them, however, fail.

HISTORICAL EVENTS

Congress of Vienna
After the defeat of Napoleon Bonaparte, the major European powers reached agreement at the largest peace conference of modern times.

Under the protection of Great Britain, Russia, Prussia, and Austria, the territorial adjustments of post-Napoleonic Europe were negotiated in Vienna from Sept. 18, 1814 until **June 9, 1815**. The objective was to reestablish the balance of power and restore and secure the traditional dynastic order domestically (Restoration Policy). As a result of the congress, Russia, Prussia, and Austria were able to substantially enlarge their territory. Great Britain remained the leading sea power, and France retained its status quo of **1792**. The Kingdom of the Netherlands was newly founded as a buffer to France, and the German Confederation was created to succeed the Holy Roman Empire. To mutually ensure their policy of restoration, Austria, Prussia, and Russia joined together to form the "Holy Alliance" on **Sept. 26, 1815**. All the other European monarchies later joined the alliance, except Great Britain, the Vatican, and the Ottoman Empire.

The "Citizen King" Louis Philippe arrives at the Hotel de Ville in Paris.

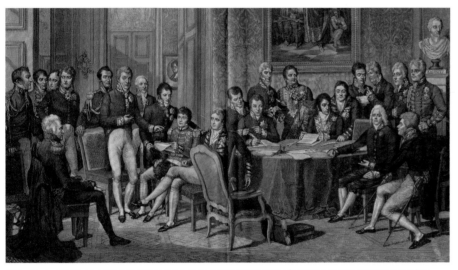
The representatives of the European powers at the Congress of Vienna; in the center, Austrian state chancellor, Prince Metternich, who wielded substantial influence on the negotiations.

Hambach Festival
The mass rally at Hambach Castle in 1832 was the first high point of the civil opposition movement in the German states.

From **May 27–30, 1832**, some 30,000 liberals and republicans from all parts of Germany gathered at Hambach Castle near Neustadt in the Palatinate to celebrate the ideals of the French July Revolution of **1830**. Among the participants of this first mass demonstration in the German states were men and women from all ranks who denounced the repressive measures of the Metternich system, such as the censorship of the press and the restriction of the right to association. The ringleaders of the Hambach Festival, such as the writer Ludwig Börne, demanded national unity, democracy, civil liberties and equality of all citizens before the law, and an alliance of European democracies. In reaction to the event, the German government intensified all its efforts to suppress the movement. The organizers of the rally were temporarily placed under arrest and the display of the black, red, and gold flag, the symbol of German unity and liberty, was forbidden.

July Revolution
An uprising in Paris in July 1830 toppled the Bourbon monarchy, leading to the rule of the bourgeoisie.

Charles X of France was dearly opposed to the notion of a constitutional monarchy that had been introduced in **1815**. When the king dissolved the deputy chamber after the election victory of the liberal opposition, a revolt broke out on July 26, 1830. The insurgents captured Paris in heavy street fighting between **July 27** and **29, 1830**, forcing Charles to abdicate and flee. The Parliament elected Louis Philippe of Orléans king of France on Aug. 7. The rights of the "Citizen King" were curbed in favor of both chambers of parliament.

The black-red-gold flag symbolizes the pursuit of liberty and unity.

Allegorical depiction of the Greek struggle for independence against the Ottoman Turks.

Greek Struggle for Independence
With outside help, the Greeks gained an independent nation state after eight years of war against the Ottoman Empire.

The first insurrections against Ottoman rule occurred on the Greek Peninsula in **March 1821**. With volunteers from all over Europe, Greek freedom fighters captured almost all of the Peloponnesus in 1822, but were subsequently driven back by Ottoman-Egyptian forces. The war took a deciding turn when the major European powers intervened on the side of the Greek rebels in **1827**. On **Oct. 20**, a British-Russian-French fleet defeated the Ottoman-Egyptian fleet in the Battle of Navarino. The Ottoman Empire was forced to acknowledge Greek autonomy in **1829–30**.

The Boers' Great Trek

The Boers' mass exodus out of the British Cape Colony between 1835 and 1843 led to major migrations in southern Africa, primarily through the displacement of the Black population.

The Boers, Dutch settlers in South Africa, resented British colonial rule, above all when the British banned slavery in their colonies in 1834. In **1835**, more than 10,000 Boers marched into the north of the present-day Republic of South Africa in the "Great Trek" to find new land. After the victory over the Zulu on **Dec. 16, 1838**, a group of Boers led by Andries Pretorius settled in the region of Natal and founded a republic, Natalia. Following the annexation of Natalia by the British in **1843**, the people of Natalia moved further northward and joined the settlers on the other side of the Vaal and Orange rivers in the two Boer republics of Transvaal and Orange Free State. Great Britain refused to recognize the two new nations at first. Later, the conflict between the Boers and the British escalated into the first and second Boer Wars.

A Boer family resting on the Great Trek.

Trail of Tears

The brutal dislocation of Native American tribes from their traditional homelands is one of the darkest chapters in American pioneer history.

In the early years, the USA was seeking compromise with America's original inhabitants. Faced with an exploding population and the growing belief that their nation had been chosen to occupy all of the North American continent, Americans began in the 1820s with the ruthless and unrelenting settlement of the American West. As part of Andrew Jackson's Indian policy, the U.S. Congress passed the Indian Removal Act in 1830 that allowed the forced relocation of Native American tribes to an inhospitable reservation in present-day Oklahoma. Thousands died from disease, malnutrition, and exposure en route to their destinations. In **1838–39**, after the forced march that became known as the Trail of Tears, only 13,000 of the 17,000 Cherokees who had started out arrived at their assigned reservation.

U.S. soldiers oversee the forced relocation of the Cherokee.

Street fighting in Frankfurt on Main in September 1848.

Revolution of 1848/49

Starting in France, popular uprisings erupted almost all over Europe in the year 1848 due to a variety of objectives. But after a few initial successes, the old monarchies managed to prevail again everywhere.

After an economic crisis, democratic forces in Paris pressured "Citizen King" Louis Philippe to abdicate in **February 1848**. The proclamation of a republic on **Feb. 25** served as the starting signal for other revolutionary movements in Europe. Beginning in **March 1848**, demonstrations and battles with the military took place in Berlin, Vienna, and many other capitals of the German Confederation. While the insurgents in Germany were primarily interested in a liberal constitution and national unity, the revolutionaries in the multi-ethnic Habsburg Empire wanted national autonomy.

The uprisings in Hungary, Bohemia, and in Russian Poland, however, had all been crushed by the military by 1849. Ever since the failed socialistic workers' revolt of **June 1848** in Paris, the conservatives had been forcing the revolutionaries into the defensive. The last insurrection of radical democrats in Germany was suppressed by July 1849. In France, the new president, Louis Napoléon, who later became Emperor Napoleon III, established a regime that increasingly restored ancient rights and privileges. The democratic movement in Europe had failed in every respect.

Oriental Crisis

The European powers issued a declaration at the Convention of London in 1840 stating that they would collectively protect the sovereignty of the Ottoman Empire.

The Ottoman Empire had experienced a period of political decline since the start of the 19th century. Despite internal reforms, the central government in Constantinople was increasingly losing its authority in its provinces. As a result, the Ottoman Empire was forced to accept Serbia's broad autonomy and Greece's independence in **1830**. When the Egyptian viceroy, Mohammed Ali, openly rose up against Ottoman rule, the major European powers began to intervene in the "Oriental Crisis" in **1839** on the side of the Ottoman sultan. On **July 15, 1840**, Great Britain and Russia, along with Prussia and Austria, pledged to stabilize the Ottoman Empire. France also committed itself to this promise on July 13, 1841. The treaty of London made more than clear that the Ottoman Empire, the "Sick man of Europe," had finally become the pawn of competing European powers.

1852 Harriet Beecher-Stowe, an opponent of slavery, publishes her novel *Uncle Tom's Cabin* on March 20.

1853 Giuseppe Verdi's opera *La Traviata* premieres in Paris on March 6.

1855 Scottish Africa explorer **David Livingston** discovers the **Victoria Falls** on Nov. 16 in East Africa.

1851 The **first World Exhibition** opens in London on May 1.

1856 **Henry Bessemer** builds a **blast furnace**, making it possible to produce steel cheaply and in larger quantities.

1859 Naturalist **Charles Darwin** publishes his work *On the Origin of Species*, laying the foundation for the modern theory of evolution.

1863 The **world's first subway** goes into operation in London on Jan 10.

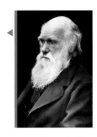

1863 On the initiation of Swiss merchant **Henri Dunant**, the **International Red Cross** is founded on Oct. 26 in Geneva to help the war wounded.

1865 British mountaineer **Edward Whymper** and his team climb the **Matterhorn** in Switzerland for the first time on July 14.

1850 — **1855** — **1860** — **1865**

1850 **La Reforma**, a reform movement, starts in **Mexico**, aiming to limit the power of the military and the Roman Catholic church in Mexican society.

1850 Sect leader Hong Xiuquan leads a rebellion against the ruling Manchu dynasty in China. Several million people have died by 1864 in the course of the **"Taiping Rebellion."**

1851 In a coup d'état **President Louis Napoléon** seizes total power in France on Dec. 2. A year later, as Napoleon III, he founds the **Second French Empire**.

1851 By a document known as the Sylvester Patent, Austrian **Emperor Franz Joseph I** repudiates the **Stadion Constitution of 1849** on Dec. 31 and restores **absolute monarchy**.

1852 Under Prime Minister **Camillo Benso, Count of Cavour**, the Kingdom of Piedmont-Sardinia becomes the motor of the **Italian unification movement**.

1852 Great Britain recognizes the **independence of the Boer republic Transvaal**.

1853 Russian troops march into Ottoman territory, triggering the **Crimean War** (until 1856).

1854 Opponents of slavery found the **Republican Party** in the USA on Feb. 28.

1854 In the **Convention of Kanagawa**, the USA coerces the opening of two Japanese ports for trade traffic, thus ending **Japan's** years-long policy of **isolation**.

1855 After conquering vast areas of **Ethiopia, Theodore II** is declared **emperor** on Feb. 11.

1855 **Alexander II becomes tsar of Russia** on March 2. By the end of his reign in 1881, he has implemented a series of domestic reforms, including the abolition of serfdom.

1856–1860 England and France exploit China's internal weaknesses during the **Second Opium War** to extract further concessions. In the end, China must allow the European powers and the USA free trade and the establishment of embassies.

1857 The **Mexican Constitution** of 1857 sets forth the ideals of **La Reforma** by curtailing priest and military prerogatives, guaranteeing universal male suffrage, and other civil liberties.

1857 A **stock market crash** in New York triggers an **economic crisis** in August that also seizes Europe.

1858 After **bloodily suppressing an Indian rebellion**, the British government formally takes over power in India on Nov. 1. The last Indian Grand Mughal is deposed.

1858–1861 When the liberal reformer **Benito Juárez** takes over the government in Mexico, a civil war erupts between the liberals and conservatives. The French subsequently install Austrian Archduke **Maximilian I** as emperor of Mexico in 1864. By 1867 Juárez has driven out the French and defeated the conservatives loyal to the emperor.

1859 In a punitive campaign against the Vietnamese, **French colonial forces capture Saigon** on Feb. 18. The city becomes the center of French Indochina, which also includes Laos and Cambodia.

1858 On Oct. 26, **William (I)** assumes **regency in Prussia** for his mentally retarded brother, Frederick William IV.

1859 The Kingdom of Sardinia-Piedmont, allied with the French, defeats the Austrians in the **Battle of Solferino** on June 24. This opens the way for the **national unification of Italy**.

1860 When **Abraham Lincoln** is elected president on Nov. 6, many southern states stand their ground in opposition to him. Within a few months, 11 states secede from the **Union** to protect their right to slavery and join together to form the **Confederacy**.

1861 In March, the king of Sardinia-Piedmont, **Victor Emanuel II**, is proclaimed the first **king of a united Italy**. The temporary capital of the newly created national state is Florence.

"All wheels stand still, when our strong arm wants it."
From the "Anthem of the General German Workingmen's Association" by Georg Herwegh, 1863

1862 On Oct. 13, King **William I** appoints the conservative Junker squire **Otto von Bismarck** minister president of Prussia.

1863 In the **Battle of Gettysburg** on July 3, the Union Army of the northern states gains a crucial victory over the southern Confederate States in the **American Civil War**.

1861 The **American Civil War** between the North and the South begins on Apr. 12 when soldiers of the Confederate Army fire on **Fort Sumter** in North Carolina.

1864 The **International Workingmen's Association** (the First International) is constituted under the leadership of **Karl Marx** in London on Sept. 28.

1864 Defeated by Prussia and Austria, **Denmark cedes Schleswig, Holstein,** and **Lauenburg** on Oct. 30 to the German Confederation.

1865 The thirteenth amendment to the U.S. constitution, **abolishing slavery** is finally ratified on Dec. 6.

Industrialization and Imperialism

1850–1900

In the second half the the 19th century, European imperialism cast a long shadow over the world. The European powers forcibly imposed colonial rule in China, India, and Africa, while Japan was restructuring itself in the European mold. In Europe, nationalistic interests became the focus of politics. The middle classes, whose influence on society was steadily growing, were the main beneficiaries of the rapid industrialization and the expanding trade with the colonies. In order to improve their living conditions, members of the newly emerging working class demanded a political voice as well. At the same time, hundreds of thousands of immigrants were seeking their fortune in the USA which, like Japan, moved up into the circle of leading nations at the close of the century.

New railroad lines opened up the expanses of the North American continent.

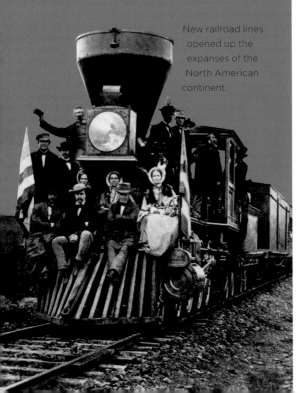

HISTORICAL FIGURES

Abraham Lincoln (1809–1865)
To this day, the 16th president of the USA is a symbol of the country's unity and democratic tradition.

Although Lincoln was not an abolitionist, he believed that slavery was a moral wrong and sought to prohibit its further extension to new territories. In 1856, he joined the newly-founded Republican Party and in **1860**, he was elected president of the USA by the votes of the Northern states. Soon, the slave states in the South seceded from the Union, triggering a four-year civil war in **1861**. Throughout the conflict, Lincoln remained committed to reconciliation with the South. On April 15, **1865**, he was assassinated by a sympathizer of the South.

Otto von Bismarck (1815–1898)
The scion of ancient Prussian nobility was the first chancellor and chief architect of the German Empire of 1871.

Bismarck, a South Elbian squire, became minister president of Prussia in **1862**. Domestically, he championed the interests of the throne against the liberal majority in parliament. Following military successes over Denmark in **1864**, Austria in **1866**, and France in **1870**, he sealed German unity under Prussian leadership in **1871**. As chancellor, he governed with shifting majorities and launched unsuccessful campaigns against Catholics and Social Democrats. Between 1883 and 1889, Bismarck passed progressive social welfare legislation that established health and old age insurance. In terms of foreign policy, he was dedicated to preserving the status quo. His system of alliances quickly disintegrated after his death in 1898.

Karl Marx (1818–1883)
The brilliant intellectual and founder of "Scientific Socialism" was the most influential pioneer of the international labor movement of the 19th century.

Marx gained his doctorate in Philosophy in 1841. After the failed uprisings of **1848**, he worked as publicist for the revolutionary overthrow of capitalism. In London, he founded the first workers' association (First International) in **1864**, but withdrew from practical politics in 1876 because of internal conflicts. Marx saw history as a succession of class wars and believed that workers were bound to free humanity from oppression and establish an egalitarian society. *Das Kapital*, Marx's major scientific work published in **1867**, is to this day considered an important work of political economics.

Queen Victoria (1819–1901)
For over 60 years, the monarch from the house of Hanover stood at the helm of Great Britain. The Victorian Age marked the high point of the British Empire.

Victoria followed her uncle, William IV, on the British throne in **1837**. In 1840, she married her cousin, Prince Albert of Saxe-Coburg and Gotha. A liberal thinker at first, she increasingly became more conservative under his influence. Her great interest in politics often brought her into conflict with her prime ministers, but she always respected the parliamentary form of government. Under her reign, Great Britain experienced a rapid economic upswing and a period of democratization. In foreign affairs, the British colonial empire grew steadily. In **1877**, Victoria assumed the title of "Empress of India." At the time of her death in **1901**, the British Empire, with possessions on every continent, was at the zenith of its power.

1886 German engineer **Karl Benz** constructs the world's first automobile in Mannheim.

1887 On July 6, American pharmacist **John Pemberton** has **Coca-Cola** syrup patented.

1888 The population of **London** is terrified by the serial killer **"Jack the Ripper."**

1889 The **Eiffel Tower** constructed by French engineer Gustave Eiffel for the **World Exhibition in Paris** is completed.

1891 Swedish writer **Selma Lagerlöf** publishes her first novel *Gösta Berling*.

1891 Work on the **Trans-Siberian railroad** begins in Russia.

1895 The **first motion pictures** are publicly shown in Berlin and Paris.

1895 German physicist **Wilhelm Conrad Röntgen** discovers **X-rays**, which are named after him in many languages.

1896 The **first Olympic Games of modern times** are opened in Athens on Apr. 6.

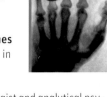

1899 The Viennese neurologist and analytical psychologist **Sigmund Freud** publishes his work *The Interpretation of Dreams* and founds **psychoanalysis**.

1885 — **1890** — **1895** — **1900**

1884 The **German Empire** gains **Southwest Africa** as its **first colony**.

1885 The **Berlin Conference** ends with the signing of the **Congo Act** on Feb. 26. The Congo is recognized as the private property of King Leopold II of Belgium.

1885 **France** assumes control over **Madagascar** on Dec. 17.

1886 After the **Third Anglo-Burmese War**, Burma is made part of British India on Jan. 1.

1887 Russia and Austria-Hungary agree upon Ferdinand I of Saxe-Coburg as Prince of Bulgaria and settle the **Bulgarian Crisis**, smoldering since 1886.

1887 The German Empire and Russia conclude a **Reinsurance Treaty** on June 18 in which both agree to observe neutrality in the event of war.

1887 France forms a federation of the protectorates of Annam, Tonkin, Cochinchina, and Cambodia, resulting in the **Indochinese Union**.

1890 The bloody massacre at **Wounded Knee** on Dec. 29 ends the "Indian" wars in the USA.

1891 In his encyclical, *Rerum Novarum*, Pope Leo XIII affirms the right of workers to protect their interests in unions.

1888 On May 13, **Brazil** becomes the **last Latin American nation to abolish slavery**.

1888 After ascending to the throne, **Emperor William II** pursues an aggressive foreign policy. He demands **"a place in the sun"** for the German Empire in the ongoing colonial race.

1889 The **Young Turks**, a nationalistic movement seeking to modernize the Ottoman Empire, takes shape in Constantinople.

1889 On Feb. 11, **Japan** becomes a **constitutional monarchy** modeled after Germany.

1889 On Nov. 15, **Emperor Pedro II of Brazil is overthrown** and a republic is proclaimed.

1893 Count Sergei Witte implements the **Witte System** in Russia aimed at removing unfavorable economic conditions.

1893 The **Independent Labour Party** is founded in **Great Britain** on Jan. 14, from which the **Labour Party** emerges in 1906.

1893 **Hawaii becomes a republic** with the support of the USA. Five years later, the islands are incorporated into the USA.

1894 The **Dreyfus Affair:** When French army officer Alfred Dreyfus, a Jew, is sentenced to life-imprisonment for alleged treason on Dec. 22, France becomes embroiled in a long-running political crisis. Amid rising anti-semitism, debates about Dreyfus, who is exonerated in 1906, divide French society.

1894 The **Natal Indian Congress** is founded in Natal, South Africa under the leadership of lawyer **Mahatma Gandhi**.

1895 After being defeated by Japan in the **First Sino-Japanese War**, China is forced to accept Korea's independence in the **Treaty of Shimonoseki** on Apr. 17.

1897 On Dec. 4, following the end of the Greco-Turkish War over **Crete**, the island gains broad **autonomy**.

1898 The German government launches a massive program to build up its fleet on 28 March, setting off an **Anglo-German arms race**.

1898 After losing the **Spanish-American War**, Spain cedes the Philippines and Puerto Rico, as well as control of Cuba to the USA. While the **USA** becomes a **colonial power**, Spain finally loses its status as a world power.

1898 After a long period of crisis, a phase of **economic prosperity** starts in **Europe**.

1896 **Great Britain** declares the West African **Ashanti Empire** (in modern-day Ghana) a protectorate.

1896 Journalist **Theodor Herzl** publishes his book, *The Jewish State*, in Vienna and founds Zionism.

1899 On March 21, France and Great Britain end the **Fashoda Crisis** and come to an agreement over their colonial interests in Central Africa and the Sudan.

1899 The **Tripartite Convention** divides the Samoan archipelago in the South Pacific between the USA and the German Empire.

1899 "Laws and customs of war on land" are adopted at the **First Hague Convention** on July 29, which include a binding regulation of the status of prisoners of war.

1867 The first volume of *Capital: Critique of Political Economy* by **Karl Marx** is published on Sept. 11. It is the cornerstone of Marxist theory.

1869 The German **Lothar Meyer** and his Russian colleague **Dmitri Ivanovich Mendeleev** independently compile similar versions of the **periodic table** of chemical elements.

1869 After ten years of construction in Egypt, the **Suez Canal** is dedicated on Nov. 17.

1870 **John D. Rockefeller** founds the **Standard Oil Company** in the USA on Jan. 10.

1874 For the first time, **30 impressionist painters** collectively exhibit their works in **Paris** on Apr. 15.

1875 On Aug. 24–25, the British **Matthew Webb** is the first **to swim the English Channel**.

1876 **Alexander Graham Bell** receives a patent in the USA on March 7 for the **invention of the telephone**.

1879 American inventor **Thomas Edison** introduces the modern **filament light bulb**.

1880 After 600 years of construction, the **Gothic cathedral in Cologne** is finally finished.

1882 German bacteriologist **Robert Koch** discovers the **tuberculosis pathogen**.

1882 The world's **first electricity generating plant** begins operation in **New York**.

1883 German philosopher **Friedrich Nietzsche** publishes the first part of his work *Thus Spoke Zarathustra*.

1870 | **1875** | **1880**

1865 The **American Civil War** ends with the surrender of the Southern Army on Apr. 9 and a victory for the North. A short time later, **President Abraham Lincoln is assassinated**. During Reconstruction, the southern states are reintegrated into the Union.

1867 On July 1, **Canada is constituted as a confederated dominion** and becomes a self-governing colony of the British Empire.

1874 **Egypt expands its territory** around southern Sudan all the way to the northern border of the Congo.

1880 As a result of its defeat in the **Second Anglo-Afghan War**, Afghanistan is forced to cede control of its foreign affairs to British India on Sept. 1.

1881 On March 26, **Prince Karl of Hohenzollern-Sigmaringen** becomes **king of Romania** as **Carol I**.

1868 After **Emperor Mutsuhito (Meiji) assumes power** on Jan. 3, a process of social and economic reforms begins in Japan. The Shogunate is abolished.

1875 With a narrow majority, the French National Assembly passes a constitutional law on the election of the president of the Republic on Jan. 30. **France is a republic again**.

1881 On May 12, **Tunisia** becomes a **protectorate of France**.

1866 In the **struggle for supremacy in Germany**, Prussia defeats Austria in the deciding **Battle of Königgrätz** on July 3. The German Confederation is subsequently dissolved.

1870 Prussia gains a decisive victory in the **Franco-German War** on Sept. 2 in the **Battle of Sedan**. French Emperor Napoleon III is taken captive; two days later the Third Republic is proclaimed in Paris.

1870 The Pope's reign over the Papal State ends on Sept. 20 after the **occupation of Rome** by Italian soldiers. Italian unification is completed.

1871 The social revolutionary **uprising of the Paris Commune** is brutally crushed by government forces between May 21 and May 28.

1876 On June 25, Native Americans led by **Chief Sitting Bull** defeat a regiment of the U.S. Cavalry in Montana in the **Battle of Little Bighorn**. In the end, the victory can only delay the subjugation of America's original inhabitants.

1876 An **uprising in Bulgaria** is brutally suppressed by the Ottoman Empire.

1877 On Jan. 1, British **Queen Victoria** officially assumes the title of **"Empress of India."**

1877 The **Russo-Turkish War:** The Russians declare war on the Ottoman Empire on Apr. 24. They are supported by the Serbs and Bulgarians.

1877 After a long struggle, the Japanese government is able to suppress a **revolt by traditional Samurai**.

1878 The European great powers implement a reorganization of the Balkans at the **Congress of Berlin** on June 13. The Ottoman Empire loses a major part of its possessions. **Rumania**, **Serbia**, and **Montenegro** become independent.

1878 On an anti-revolutionary platform the German Reichstag (Parliament) passes the so-called **Anti-Socialist Laws** on Oct. 18, banning Social-Democratic activities outside of the Reichstag.

1881 Violent **anti-Semitic pogroms** break out in Russia after the **assassination of Tsar Alexander II**. In the aftermath, many Jews immigrate to America or Palestine.

1882 With the **British occupation of Egypt** on July 11, the country becomes a protectorate of the British Empire. Nominally, Egypt remains part of the Ottoman Empire.

1883 **Health insurance for workers and employees** is introduced in the German Empire on June 15. This is the start of a comprehensive social insurance plan that will become a model for other European states.

1879–1883 A dispute between Chile and Bolivia over mineral-rich provinces in Peru and Bolivia results in the **War of the Pacific**.

1884 The U.S. Congress passes the **Organic Act**, providing **Alaska** with its first **civil government**.

1871 Prussian **King William I** is proclaimed first German Emperor on Jan. 18 in the Hall of Mirrors in the Palace of Versailles. **Otto von Bismarck** is made first chancellor of the **German Empire**, which emerged out of the unification of the North German Confederation with the four southern German states.

HISTORICAL EVENTS

The use of machines led to a rapid increase in productivity. Child labor was one of the negative aspects of industrialization: a young girl in a cotton mill.

The Industrial Revolution
Technical innovations and new work methods fundamentally changed society in many parts of the world in the 20th century.

Around 1900, the world was becoming totally transformed: Cars and trains created new options of spatial mobility; in factories, goods were produced by machines rather than by hand; and electric lights emancipated mankind from the natural rhythm of day and night. Starting in England, scientific developments and the introduction of broad economic freedom unleashed a powerful economic dynamic in many European countries and North America. Iron and steel became the symbols of the age. Rising productivity made successful entrepreneurs wealthy, such as the German steel king Alfred Krupp, and American oil magnate Rockefeller who was considered the richest man in the world at the time.

Crimean War
The first war between European powers since 1815 flared up over the Ottoman Empire.

Russia, who wanted control over the straits between the Black Sea and the Mediterranean, took advantage of the weakness of the Ottomans and occupied the Balkan principalities of Moldavia and Wallachia in July **1853**. Concerned about Russian expansion, France and Great Britain formed an alliance with the Ottoman Empire in 1854. The fall of the naval port of Sevastopol on the Crimean Peninsula sealed the Russians' defeat. The Treaty of Paris of **March 30, 1856**, forced Russia to withdraw completely from the Balkans and accept the demilitarization of the Black Sea.

The storming of the Russian fortress of Sevastopol by the French on Sept. 8, 1855

The Demise of Chinese Power
The Opium War, the so-called Unequal Treaties with foreign powers, and the Taiping Rebellion were the start of the demise of the Chinese Empire.

China increasingly became subject to European influence from the mid-19th century. Both Opium Wars (**1840–1842** and **1856–1860**) had severely damaged China's economy. After its humbling defeat at the hands of the British, the country was forced to allow the trade with opium. In addition, the Treaty of Tientsin forced the empire to cede territory and open numerous ports to international trade in 1858. Domestically, the Manchu dynasty also lost authority. The Taiping movement led by Hong Xiu-quan had risen up against the empire in 1850 and had established a kingdom in the south of the country with Nanjing as its capital. It took the aid of the British and the French in a costly civil war to finally crush the rebellion in 1864.

Britain's lucrative trade with opium led to major social problems for China.

The Northern States' victory in the Battle of Gettysburg in Pennsylvania on July 3, 1863

The American Civil War
The smoldering, unresolved issue of slavery escalated into a civil war between the individual states of the Union between 1861 and 1865.

The gulf between the industrialized North and the agrarian South, whose plantation economy was based on slavery, deepened in the course of the 19th century. The election of Abraham Lincoln as president in **1860** precipitated the secession of North Carolina and subsequently other states from the Union. In February 1861, they formed the Confederate States of America. A four-year civil war ensued after an attack by Southern militia on the Union's Fort Sumter on **12 April, 1861**. At first, the Confederate troops were successful against the Union army, but the North's victory at Gettysburg on **July 3, 1863**, was the turning point of the war. The South surrendered on **April 9, 1865** and reestablished national unity. As a result, slavery was completely banned in the USA. However, the national reconciliation policies failed to provide for a basic societal reform in the Southern States.

Social Issues
Exploitation, poverty, and worker's lack of rights gave substance to the labor movement in the industrialized nations in the second half of the 19th century.

The economic upswing of the 19th century also had a reverse side. The lower classes became dependent on the industrialists and lived in desolate economic conditions. After the failed revolutions of **1848**, an increasing number of workers' unions, associations, and political parties formed in the countries of the Industrial Revolution, fighting for political participation and a greater share in the economy. One of the dominating ideological forces in Europe was the socialist theory of Karl Marx that declared the working class to be the revolutionary agent of social change. In 1864, Marx founded the International Workingmen's Association in London. Workers and soldiers attempted to implement socialist principles within the framework of the Paris Commune in **1871**. A little later, the German workers' movement took a leading role in Europe. Despite all the repressive measures taken against it, the Social Democratic Party was to become the strongest force in the German Empire by 1912. However, with the growth of the workers' movement, the smoldering conflict between the supporters of a revolutionary overthrow and the proponents of political reform from within also came to the forefront.

Whitechapel—a typical slum in the London West End in the 1870s

Japan's Leap into Modern Times
Beginning in 1868, Japan was transformed under Emperor Mutsuhito from a feudalist state to a leading industrial nation and great imperial power in the Asiatic region.

The backwardness of the Tokugawa Shogunate was clearly revealed, when the USA forced Japan to open the country to the Western world in 1854. As a result, nationalistic forces pushed for a political restructuring of the country. With the overthrow of the last Shogun and the Emperor's coming to power on **Jan. 3, 1868**, a rapid process of western-style modernization began. Adopting the motto of the Meiji, "enlightened rule," Emperor Mutsuhito introduced far-reaching reforms. The traditional feudal structure was abolished, and the army and the legal and educational systems were modernized along Western lines. In addition, the infrastructure of the country was renewed and the industrialization of the economy pushed forward. On **Feb. 11, 1889**, the country was officially changed into a constitutional monarchy adhering to a religiously motivated emperor cult and a politically powerful military. Japan's victories over China in **1895** and Russia in **1904** and 1905 secured the country a dominant position in the Asiatic region.

Emperor Mutsuhito in his family circle

The national monument to the first Italian King in modern times, Victor Emmanuel II, in Rome

Latecomers Germany and Italy
Under military auspices, the Italians and Germans at long last found their own nation states in 1870–1871.

In **1852**, Camillo di Cavour, a champion of Italy's unification, became prime minister of the strong kingdom of Piedmont-Sardinia. Nearly all of the minor Italian states had linked themselves to Sardinia by 1860 after Cavour had wrested Lombardy from Austria in **1859** with the aid of the French. At the same time, the freedom fighter Garibaldi, with his "Expedition of the Thousand," first conquered Sicily and then Naples. Finally, Victor Emmanuel II was proclaimed king of Italy in **March 1861**. Meanwhile in Germany, Minister President Otto von Bismarck pushed German unification forward under the leadership of Prussia. After Austria had been eliminated in **1866** and France had been defeated in **1870**, King Wilhelm I of Prussia was proclaimed German Kaiser on **Jan. 18, 1871**. Italy also became a unified state in **1870** after the occupation of the Papal State.

The Race for Africa
At the Berlin Africa Conference in 1884–85, the great European powers came to a general understanding about the division of Africa into colonies.

Driven by a lust for power, a zealous sense of mission, and a huge demand for raw materials, the great powers of Europe jostled in the 1880s to acquire colonial territories in Africa. The exploration of the Congo basin begun by Henry M. Stanley in 1878 and the founding of the Congo Free State by Belgian King Leopold II in 1885 launched the expansion into the interior of Africa. To avoid war and come to an agreement over the division and "lawful" acquisition of African territory, the colonial powers met in a three-month conference in February **1885** in Berlin. And so began a ruthless race to gain territory without regard to existing structures, borders, or cultures, not to mention the interests of the native population. At the dawn of the 20th century, almost all of Africa was under the control of the Europeans.

Caricature of the Berlin Conference on the Congo, chaired by Otto von Bismarck

1900 German scientist **Max Planck** develops the **quantum theory** and revolutionizes physics.

1900 On July 2, Count **Ferdinand von Zeppelin** flies aboard the first **airship** named after him over Lake Constance.

1901 The first Noble Prizes, named after the Swedish inventor **Alfred Nobel**, are awarded in Stockholm for outstanding scientific and cultural achievements. The **Noble Prize** is considered to this day to be the world's most prestigious award.

1901 A team of British explorers, led by Royal Navy officer **Robert Falcon Scott**, embarks on the first official **expedition to the Antarctic.**

1901 On Dec. 12, Italian **Guglielmo Marconi** sends the first **wireless transmission** across the Atlantic, thus becoming the inventor of radio.

1902 On Sept. 1, Georges Méliès presents to an audience in Paris the world's **first fiction film, "A trip to the Moon."**

1903 On Dec. 17, the **Wright brothers** make the first controlled and powered flight in the USA.

1904/05 German sociologist and political economist **Max Weber** publishes his work *The Protestant Ethic and the Spirit of Capitalism.*

1906 On April 18, a strong earthquake in **San Francisco** destroys almost the whole city.

1900

1900 After the **assassination of Umberto I** on July 29, his son, **Victor Emmanuel III**, becomes the **next king of Italy.**

1901 The **Boxer Protocol** of Sept. 7 requires China to make massive **indemnity payments** to the Western powers and dispatch **"envoys of regret"** to their capitals.

1901 On Sept. 14, U.S. **President William McKinley is assassinated** by an anarchist. He is succeeded by his vice president, **Theodore Roosevelt.**

1902 On Jan. 7, the **Chinese imperial** court returns to the **"Forbidden City"** in Beijing after one year of exile in the wake of the Boxer Rebellion.

1900 **Boxer Rebellion:** A German diplomat is murdered in Beijing on June 20 by a member of the Boxers, a national opposition movement. This assassination triggers a military intervention by the Western powers that include Russia and the USA.

1900 Count **Bernhard von Bülow** becomes the new **chancellor** of the **German Empire** on Oct. 16.

1901 On Jan. 1, **Great Britain grants Australia home rule** as a dominion, the second after Canada. The newly created national state accepts the British Queen as its head of state.

1901 **Queen Victoria** dies on Jan. 22 and her son, **Edward VII**, becomes the new ruler of the British Empire.

1901 The **Socialist-Revolutionary Party** is founded in **Russia.**

1902 After officially gaining independence from Spain, **Tomás Estrada Palma** is made the **first president of the republic of Cuba** on May 20, but quickly falls under the influence of the USA.

1902 On July 12, **Arthur James Balfour** becomes the **new prime minister** in Great Britain.

1903 Following the murder of Alexander Obrenovic, **Peter Karadordevic** becomes the **new king of Serbia** on June 15.

1903 After the death of Leo XIII, **Pius X is elected pope** on Aug. 4. Until the end of his tenure in 1914, he fights against democratic tendencies in the Church and the state.

1903 During exile in London, the members of a **revolutionary cadre party** headed by **Lenin** split from the Socialist-Democratic Workers' Party of Russia, the Mensheviks ("minority") on July 30 and call themselves **Bolsheviks** ("majority").

1903 Aided by the USA, **Panama** gains **independence from Colombia** on Nov. 3 and in return grants the USA the right of sovereignty in the Panama Canal Zone.

1904 The **Russo-Japanese War** over control of Manchuria and Korea begins with a Japanese attack on the Russian Port Arthur naval base (Lüshunkou) on Feb. 9.

1904 On July 30, **France breaks off diplomatic relations with the Vatican.**

1904 The indigenous population of **German South-West Africa** (Namibia) take up arms against their colonial masters on Jan. 12. The **uprising of the Herero and the Nama** is brutally suppressed by 1907.

1905

1905 **St. Petersburg's Bloody Sunday:** After the violent dispersal of a peaceful demonstration on Jan. 22, unrest flares up all over Russia (in the so-called Russian Revolution of 1905).

1905 The visit by German Kaiser Wilhelm II to Tangiers on March 31 provokes the anger of France that is trying to establish a protectorate over Morocco at this time and ignites the **First Moroccan Crisis.**

1905 After a national referendum, **Norway** dissolves the personal union with Sweden on June 7. Prince Carl of Denmark is elected king as **Haakon VII** on Nov. 18.

1905 The **Treaty of Portsmouth**, signed at Kittery, Maine on Sept. 5, seals Russia's defeat in the war against Japan. Parts of Manchuria fall to Japan, and Japanese control of the nominally independent Korean Empire is confirmed.

1905 The **Sinn Féin party**, committed to independence from Great Britain, is founded in **Ireland** on Nov. 28.

1906 At the **International Conference of Algeciras** from Jan. 16 to April 7, France and the German Empire resolve their **conflict over Morocco** (First Moroccan Crisis) with a compromise.

1906 On April 23, **Tsar Nicholas II** issues the so called "Fundamental Laws," which create the first Russian constitution and assign legislative authority to the Duma.

1906 **Persia's first Madjilis or national assembly** convenes on Oct. 7 in Teheran.

1906 **Universal suffrage for males** is introduced in **Austria** on Dec. 1, while **census suffrage** continues to exist in **Hungary.**

The Collapse of the Old Order
1900–1920

In the Western world, the century began with great expectations. People had their hopes up that the enormous advances in technology and science would improve their lives in the long run. European powers tried to impose their notion of civilization on their colonies around the world. However, the arms race and unbridled nationalism led to the catastrophe of the First World War in 1914. At first, boundless enthusiasm for the war dominated everywhere, each side confident in its own strength. As the conflict dragged on, the reverse side of technical progress became evident in the senseless battles of attrition, submarine operations, and poison gas attacks. At the end of the war, social orders that had existed for centuries collapsed in many places. The peace accords that were meant to give Europe and the world a new face only laid the foundation for future conflicts.

Gasmasks to counter the new chemical weapons of the First World War

HISTORICAL FIGURES

Bertha von Suttner (1843–1914)   The Austrian pacifist became the first female Nobel Peace Prize laureate, a prize she inspired in 1905.

Countess Bertha Kinsky came from an impoverished aristocratic family. From 1873, she was the governess of the wealthy von Suttner family and married their youngest son, Arthur, in 1876. The couple moved to the Caucasus where she experienced the horrors of the Russo-Turkish War. Upon her return to Austria, she joined the pacifist movement. Her novel *Lay Down Your Arms!* was one of the most successful books published at the close of the 19th century and made Suttner a symbolic figure of the peace movement. To industrialist Alfred Nobel she suggested the creation of a prize for international understanding. In 1905, she was awarded the Nobel Peace Prize herself. Suttner died on June 21, **1914**, in Vienna.

Woodrow Wilson (1856–1921)   During the First World War, American President Wilson devised a plan for a peaceful post-war order.

Woodrow Wilson was an academic. It was not until 1910 that the professor of political economy entered politics. A supporter of the liberal progressive movement, he gained the Democratic nomination for president in 1912. On the domestic front, he pushed through antitrust legislation and introduced social reforms. In foreign policy, he pursued an interventionist policy toward Latin America, but justified America's entry into the First World War on **Apr. 6, 1917**, as a "crusade for democracy." The peace treaties of 1919–20 were based in large part on the guidelines Wilson had formulated in his Fourteen Points speech on **Jan. 8, 1918**. Wilson co-initiated the League of Nations in **1919**, but his own congress vetoed American participation in this organization. In 1921, he retired from politics due to failing health.

Kaiser Wilhelm II (1859–1941)   His swaggering Huns speech contributed in no small part to the isolation of the German Empire on the eve of the First World War.

Wilhelm II, German Kaiser since **1888**, sought political influence to promote the international status of the prospering German Empire. His political interference in social issues brought him in conflict with Chancellor Bismarck, whom Wilhelm forced to resign in 1890. His foreign policy included the pursuit of imperialistic goals and the support of the naval armament race against Great Britain. His belligerent "Huns speech" of 1900 or the "Daily Telegraph Affair" in 1908 caused the British and French to close ranks. The German Revolution in November **1918** forced Wilhelm to abdicate and to flee into exile to Holland, where he died in 1941.

Lenin (1870–1924)   The Russian socialist developed the concept of the revolutionary cadre party and led the Bolsheviks to power in 1917.

Vladimir Ilyich Uljanov grew up in an intellectual middle-class family. He joined the Russian revolutionary movement and immigrated in 1900 to Western Europe. Under the assumed name of Lenin, he rose to become one of the leading theorists of the radical Left. The Russian Social Democrats eventually splintered over his concept of a dictatorship of the proletariat. Following the overthrow of the tsar on March 15, 1917, Lenin returned to Russia. There, he initiated the seizure of power by the Bolsheviks on **Nov. 6-7, 1917**, and virtually became the new head of government.

1913 The **Woolworth Building**, the **tallest skyscraper in the world** until 1930, is dedicated in New York on April 14.

1913 On Nov. 13, the first part of **Marcel Proust's** monumental cycle of novels, *In Search of Lost Time* or *Remembrance of Things Past*, is published in France. It is one of the most influential literary works of the 20th century.

1914 The **Panama Canal**, which connects the Atlantic and the Pacific oceans, is completed. It remains under U.S. sovereignty until 1999.

1915 German physicist **Albert Einstein** formulates his **general theory of relativity**.

1915 The technically innovative film *The Birth of a Nation* by **American film director D.W. Griffith**, is a box-office smash. Despite being explicitly racist in content, it becomes the most successful film of the silent film era.

1917 The first **Pulitzer Prizes for outstanding journalistic achievement** are awarded in New York on June 4.

1918 **Spanish Flu:** An **influenza pandemic** claims at least 25 million victims worldwide by 1919–20.

1919 **Max Planck**, originator of the quantum theory, receives the Nobel Prize for physics.

1915 — **1920**

1914 A **French-British coalition** halts the German advance on Paris by Sept. 12 at the Marne. The Western front settles into **trench warfare**.

1915 **Japan** makes its **Twenty-One Demands** on **China**, aimed at securing temporary hegemony over China.

1915 The German Empire announces unrestricted **submarine warfare against Great Britain** on Feb 22.

1915 The **Lusitania**, a British passenger ship, is sunk by a German submarine on May 7. The **USA** condemns the sinking and threatens to **intervene in the war**.

1915 Germans use **lethal gas** for the first time in the **First Battle of Ypres** in Flanders on April 22.

"The lamps are going out all over Europe"
British Foreign Minister Edward Grey, August 14, 1914

1915 **Italy declares war on Austria-Hungary** on May 23 and later also on the Ottoman Empire.

1915–1917 Hundreds of thousands of **Christian Armenians** become **victims of expulsions and genocide** in the Ottoman Empire.

1916 German forces begin their attack on French positions near **Verdun** on Feb. 21. Despite the massive deployment of men and materials, the front lines hardly change.

1916 In the secret **Sykes-Picot Agreement** of May 16, the British and the French define how the Ottoman Empire will be divided after the war.

1917 A **liberal and socially progressive constitution** is adopted in **Mexico** on Feb. 5 under the presidency of Venustiano Carranza.

1917 **February Revolution:** Tsar Nicholas II is forced to abdicate on March 15 under pressure from insurgent workers and the military. **Russia becomes a republic for a short time**.

1916 In the **largest naval engagement of the war**, the **Battle of Jutland** (between the Danish and the Norwegian coasts), from May 31 to June 1, neither the German nor the British fleet are able to gain a decisive advantage.

1917 The **USA enters the First World War** on the side of the Triple Entente (Allies) on Apr. 6.

1917 **Balfour Declaration:** On Nov. 2, British Foreign Minister Balfour promises the **Jewish settlers** a **national homeland in Palestine**.

1917 **October Revolution: The radical Bolsheviks led by Lenin storm the Winter Palace** in Petrograd (St. Petersburg) in Russia on Nov. 6–7 and topple Kerenski's provisional bourgeois government.

1918 On Jan 8, U.S. President **Woodrow Wilson** announces his **"Fourteen Point Plan" as a basis for peace**. The centerpiece is each nation's right to self-determination.

1918 After the violent dispersal of the constituent National Assembly by the Bolsheviks on Jan. 19, the **Russian civil war** breaks out. The Red Army of the Bolsheviks, who demand that authority should be given to the Soviets, fights against the White Army of the anti-Bolsheviks.

1918 Russia and the Central Powers conclude peace on March 3 in the **Treaty of Brest-Litovsk**. This ends the war on the Eastern front.

1918 The defeat of the German forces in the **tank battle of Amiens** from Aug. 8–11 once and for all crushes the Central Powers' hope for victory in the war.

1918 **Austria-Hungary begins to disintegrate** into numerous individual states in October. On Nov. 11, Emperor Charles I refuses further involvement in government affairs.

1918 Under pressure from mutinying workers' and soldiers' councils, **German Kaiser Wilhelm II is forced to abdicate**. Social Democrat Philipp Scheidemann proclaims a republic on Nov. 9. In 1919, Friedrich Ebert is elected its first president.

1918 On Nov. 11, the Allies and Germany sign an **armistice agreement** in a railroad car outside Compiègne, France.

1919 To maintain world peace, the victorious Allies agree on April 29 to found the **League of Nations**, based in Geneva.

1919 On June 28, the **peace accord between the Allies and the German Empire** is signed in **Versailles**. Germany must accept territorial losses and is burdened with huge reparation payments. It is also compelled to yield control of its colonies.

1907 Pablo Picasso becomes a **pioneer of Cubism** with his painting *Les Demoiselles d'Avignon*.

1909 The cornerstone for the **first modern Jewish settlement in Palestine**, which is given the name **Tel Aviv**, is laid on April 11.

1909 On April 6, American Explorer **Robert Edwin Peary** claims to have been the first man to reach the **North Pole**.

1909 German chemists **Fritz Haber** and **Carl Bosch** develop a **method for synthesizing ammonia** and revolutionize the production of fertilizers.

1911 The Expressionist painters, **Wassily Kandinsky** and **Franz Marc**, form a **group of artists** in Munich called *The Blue Rider*.

1911 **Gustav Mahler**, Austrian conductor and **composer**, dies on May 18 in Vienna. His symphonies have a considerable influence on the development of music in the 20th century.

1911 British physicist **Ernest Rutherford** develops the groundbreaking **model of the atom** named after him.

1912 The *Titanic*, the largest passenger ship to date, collides with an iceberg on April 14 and drags some 1,500 people to their death.

1913 **Automobiles** are mass-produced for the first time on a moving **assembly line** in Henry Ford's factory.

1910

1906 **Arms Race:** The **largest ironclad battleship** to date, the "Dreadnought," is launched in Great Britain on Feb. 10.

1907 **Europe's first freely elected parliament** in which women also hold a political mandate convenes in the Grand Duchy of **Finland** on May 25.

1907 **Great Britain** and **Russia** agree upon their respective areas of control in Persia and Afghanistan on Aug. 31 in the **Anglo-Russian Convention**.

1907 **Great Britain** grants **New Zealand dominion status** on Sept. 26.

1908 The **Young Turks** force Ottoman Sultan Abdul Hamid II to reinstate the **liberal constitution** of 1876 on July 24. He is deposed in 1909 and a constitutional monarchy is instituted.

1908 On Oct. 5, **Austria occupies Bosnia and Herzegovina**, which provokes Serbian resistance.

1908 **Bulgaria** declares its **independence from the Ottoman Empire** on Oct. 5. Prince Ferdinand I assumes the title of tsar.

1908 The **Belgian state takes over the Free State of Congo** on Nov. 15, which had been the private property of King Leopold II until now.

1908 Only three years old, **Pu Yi** is crowned Xuantong, **emperor of China** on Dec. 2.

1909 Jewish settlers found the **first kibbutz** in **Palestine**.

1909 **Annexation Crisis:** After an ultimatum, **Serbia accepts Austria's annexation of Bosnia-Herzegovina** in March. Through the Treaty of Berlin (1878), a war in the Balkans is averted.

1910 On Jan 15, **France** combines its **colonies in Central Africa** into the general government of French Equatorial Africa.

1910 On May 31, the British combine the Cape Colony, Transvaal, and Orange in the **South African Union** that is granted home rule as a dominion.

1910 On Aug. 22, **Korea** is officially **annexed by Japan** and renamed Chosen.

1910 **Portugal** is proclaimed a **republic** on Oct. 5 following the expulsion of King Emmanuel II. The first president is Teófilo Braga.

1911 One of the last bastions of Absolutism in Europe falls with the introduction of a **constitution** in the **Principality of Monaco** on Jan. 8.

1911 An era of revolutionary social unrest begins on May 25 in **Mexico** with the overthrow of **dictator Porfirio Diáz**. The country's social conditions change fundamentally.

1911 **Italy declares war on the Ottoman Empire** on Sept. 29 and by 1912 gains present-day Libya and the Dodecanese with Rhodes.

1911 On Nov. 4, the German Empire recognizes France's claim to Morocco, thus ending the **Second Morocco Crisis**.

1912 **Raymond Poincaré** becomes French Prime Minister in January. The later president (1913–1920) introduces three-year military service.

1912 After months of insurrection, the last Chinese emperor, **Pu Yi**, is **forced to abdicate** on Feb. 12. China officially becomes a republic.

1912 On Nov. 28, **Albania** separates from the Ottoman Empire and **declares its independence**.

1913 After the murder of King George I by an anarchist, his son becomes **King Constantine I of Greece** on March 18.

1913 In the **Treaty of London** of May 30, the Ottoman Empire that had allied itself with the Serbs, Bulgarians, Greeks, and Montenegrins in the **First Balkan War**, is forced to recognize its defeat in 1912. It loses almost all of its European territories.

1913 The **Second Balkan War** between the victors of the First Balkan War over the division of Macedonia ends on Aug. 10 with the defeat of Bulgaria. Serbia becomes the dominant power in the Balkans.

1914 The **assassination of the Austrian heir apparent, Archduke Franz Ferdinand,** by the Serbian nationalist Gavrilo Princip, on June 28 in Sarajevo unleashes the **First World War**.

1914 After receiving unconditional support of the German Empire, **Austria-Hungary declares war on Serbia** on July 28.

1914 On Aug 1, **the German Empire declares war on Russia**, which supports Serbia.

1914 Following the unprovoked **German invasion of neutral Belgium**, France declares war on Germany and Austria-Hungary on Aug. 3; **Great Britain** follows suit on Aug. 4.

1914 On Aug. 23, **Japan** declares war on the German Empire and **occupies its Chinese-leased territory of Kiautschou**.

1914–1915 German and Austrian-Hungarian forces **repel the Russians out of East Prussia**.

HISTORICAL EVENTS

A group of Suffragettes protesting in London

Women's Suffrage
It was not until after the First World War that women's movements in many European countries were able to enforce their demands for equal voting rights.

Women's movements committed to gaining equal status for women in society had been spreading since the mid-19th century. The central demand for women's suffrage, that was granted for the first time in Finland in **1907**, unified the various political currents within this movement. The "Suffragettes" attracted great attention, especially in Great Britain, by making hunger strikes and the destruction of property their means of protest and defiance. On March 19, 1911, millions of women took to the streets on the first International Women's Day and marched for the right to vote—an event that was initiated by German socialist Clara Zetkin. As a result of the social and political upheavals, accelerated by the First World War, women became enfranchised in most of the industrial nations after 1918.

Republic of China
The revolution of 1911 put an end to imperial rule in China that had lasted for over two thousand years.

On **Feb. 12, 1912**, the last emperor of China, Pu Yi, was forced to abdicate. The authority of the Manchu dynasty had been in steady decline since European powers had crushed the Boxer Rebellion in **1900**. The liberal reforms introduced in 1905 came too late to prevent the growing popularity of the revolutionary movement led by Sun Yat-sen. After a military revolt, he became the first president of the Republic of China, but resigned in favor of Yuan Shikai. Until his death in 1916, Shikai tried in vain to restore the imperial dynasty under his name. The struggle over China's political system only ended with the Communist victory in **1949**.

Chinese having their pigtails, a sign of Manchurian rule, cut

"July Crisis" 1914: The immediate cause of the First World War
The assassination of the Austrian heir apparent ignited the First World War, which no country wanted but none could prevent.

The international crisis that led to the outbreak of the First World War began on **June 28, 1914**. The Archduke Franz Ferdinand, heir to the throne of Austria-Hungary, was assassinated by a Serbian nationalist in Sarajevo. Exactly one month later, Austria declared war on Serbia that would escalate into "the great seminal catastrophe of this century." However, the course for a war had been set much earlier, as a result of the ongoing arms race, aggressive nationalism, and growing tensions between the major European powers. The complex web of military alliances and treaties in Europe made war even more inevitable. Belated attempts, especially by Great Britain, to solve the crisis at the conference table ultimately failed.

The attack on Archduke Franz Ferdinand and his wife Sophie in Sarajevo

The Battle of Verdun, re-enacted by veterans for a documentary film in 1928

"The Hell of Verdun"
Like no other battle in the First World War, the Battle of Verdun symbolizes the brutality of mechanized war.

Shortly after the outbreak of the First World War, German troops marched into Belgium and northern France, aiming to capture Paris in a frontal assault. A successful counter-attack by the Allies on **Sept. 12, 1914**, however, stopped the German advance. The highly mechanized armies neutralized each other from then on. By war's end, the front lines had hardly moved. The "bloody war of atrition" reached its peak in the Battle of Verdun. On **Feb. 21, 1916**, German troops opened their offensive with heavy artillery fire, but encountered fierce French resistance. Soldiers on both sides were ready to dispute each inch of ground, even by using lethal gas. The battlefield soon looked like a crater landscape due to the permanent barrage of shells and the hail of bullets. By the end of the German offensive in the summer of 1916, each side had lost well over half a million soldiers. Hardly anyone had gained ground.

The War's Turning Point 1917

When the USA entered the First World War on the side of the Entente in 1917, the balance of power shifted to the disadvantage of Germany and its allies.

At the outbreak of the First World War, the USA was officially neutral, but took sides by providing Great Britain with weapons and economic assistance. The Americans were primarily interested in keeping the sea routes safe for commercial shipping. However, when on **May 7, 1915** the British passenger steamer *Lusitania* was torpedoed by a German submarine and sank with 139 Americans onboard, relations between the USA and Germany took a turn for the worse. The German decision to adopt unrestricted warfare in protest of a British naval blockade caused the USA to declare war on Germany on **April 6, 1917**. Compared to the Entente states, the Central Powers were at a hopeless disadvantage in terms of manpower and material resources. In June 1918, a final attempt by the Germans to win the war on the Western front before the arrival of American troops completely failed. The First World War had been decided.

Poster against the use of German submarines

The October Revolution

The Bolsheviks seized power in Russia and established the Soviet Union (USSR), the world's first Communist-ruled state.

Growing out of a mounting economic crisis and a general war fatigue, revolutionary upheavals emerged in Russia in 1917 that substantially influenced the course of history in the 20th century. After the overthrow of Tsar Nicholas II on **March 15, 1917**, known as the February Revolution, the provisional government of liberals and social democrats proved unable to solve the lingering social problems. This gave a powerful boost to the radical Bolsheviks, whose popular leader, Lenin, had secretly returned to Russia from his exile in Switzerland in April 1917. On **Nov. 7, 1917** (October Revolution), the Bolsheviks overthrew the government and seized power in Russia. In the same year, they arranged a truce with the Central Powers and domestically launched the Communist restructuring of Russian society. In a costly three-year civil war that began in **Jan. 1918**, the Communists were able to establish their control over the territories of the former Russian Empire. In 1922, the individual Soviet republics were unified to become a powerful Communist confederation—the USSR.

Lenin on a tank as leader of the Russian October Revolution

The Balfour Declaration

Great Britain's contradictory position on Jewish immigration into Palestine laid the groundwork for the Middle East conflict that erupted after 1945.

The spread of anti-Semitism in Europe at the turn of the century strengthened the Zionist movement that sought to create a Jewish state in Palestine. Zionist attempts to achieve a declaration of British support for their aims were recognized on **Nov. 2, 1917**, when British Foreign Minister Balfour, seeking Jewish support for the Allied war effort, promised a homeland to the Jews on the territory of the Ottoman Empire. The promise contradicted an earlier pledge by the British government to Arab nationalists to support the establishment of an Arab state in these same territories after the war. Yet secretly, Britain and France had agreed on **May 16, 1916** to divide up the Middle East and control it themselves. Further conflicts were bound to occur when Great Britain was allocated the mandate for Palestine in 1920.

British soldiers under General Allenby marching into Jerusalem on Dec. 9, 1917

The signatories to the peace accords in the Hall of Mirrors of the Palace of Versailles on June 28, 1919

Europe's New Order

The Peace Treaties of Versailles and St. Germain that were signed between 1919 and 1920 redrew the European map and shifted the balance of power worldwide.

The First World War had not only cost millions of lives, it had also cost a lot of money. Even victorious powers like Great Britain and France faced financial reckoning. The real winner was the USA, who finally entered the circle of the great powers. The principle of self-determination, formulated by American President Woodrow Wilson on **Jan. 8, 1918**, played a major role in the consolidation of post-war Europe. With the breakup of the multiethnic Austro-Hungarian Empire that began in **Oct. 1918**, Austria was forced to recognize the sovereignty of Hungary, Czechoslovakia, and Poland. The newly founded League of Nations allotted mandates to France and Great Britain to govern parts of the Ottoman Empire. According to the peace terms imposed by the Allies in **1919** and **1920**, at the peace conferences of Versailles and St. Germain, Germany had to give up its colonies and was forced to accept massive reparation payments. After the collapse of their monarchies, parliamentary democracies emerged in Germany and Austria in **Nov. 1918**.

1920 The first **commercial radio station** goes on air in **Pittsburgh**, Pennsylvania on Nov. 2.

1922 The novel *Ulysses* by **James Joyce** is published in Paris on Feb. 2.

1922 British archaeologist **Howard Carter** discovers the untouched **tomb of the Egyptian Pharaoh Tutankhamun** dating from the 14th century B.C. The find is a worldwide sensation.

1923 On March 3, the first issue of the American **news magazine** *Time* appears on the newsstands.

1924 Czech author **Franz Kafka**, who wrote in German, dies on June 3 in Austria. His work gains international acclaim after his death.

1924 French writer **André Breton** publishes *The Surrealist Manifesto*, which subsequently influences painters like **Dalí** and **Picasso**.

1926 American **Gertrude Ederle** becomes the first woman to swim the **English Channel** on Aug. 6.

1927 The film *Metropolis* by German-American director **Fritz Lang** celebrates its premiere in Berlin on Jan. 10. It is considered a milestone in cinematic history.

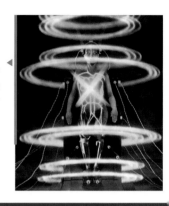

1920 ——— **1925**

1920 **Kapp Putsch:** An attempted putsch by right-wing officers in **Germany** on March 13 fails after a few days because of a concerted general strike by Germany's workers.

1920 The **Treaty of Trianon** of June 4 reduces Hungary's territory by two-thirds.

1920 The Allies officially conclude **peace with the Ottoman Empire** on Aug. 10 in **Sèvres**. Almost all of the empire is partitioned. Syria and Lebanon come under French control; Iraq, Jordan, and Palestine under British control. Greece and Italy control portions of present-day western Turkey.

1920 On Aug. 26, **women** are granted full **voting rights** in the USA. Women's suffrage was introduced in many European countries directly after the First World War.

1920 The **Russian civil war** ends with the defeat of the White Forces by the **Red Army** at the Crimea in November.

1921 After a military putsch, **Resa Pahlevi**, a military officer, establishes a dictatorial regime in **Persia** (Iran) on Feb. 21.

1921 At a congress meeting in Russia in March, **Lenin** announces a **"new economic policy,"** allowing for limited private enterprise.

1921 The **Peace of Riga** ends the Polish-Soviet War on March 18. Victorious Poland gains parts of Belarus and the Ukraine.

1921 On Dec. 6, **Great Britain grants Ireland its independence**. Northern Ireland, with its Protestant majority, remains a part of Great Britain.

1922 On Feb. 28, **Great Britain grants Egypt** limited **independence**. Sultan Fuad I assumes the title of king.

1922 The Central Committee of the Communist Party names **Josef Stalin** as **General Secretary** on April 3.

1922 In the **Treaty of Rapallo** of April 16, both the German Reich and Russia renounce all claims to reparation.

1922 On Oct. 31, Victor Emmanuel III appoints Fascist leader **Benito Mussolini** as Italian Prime Minister. The king bows to pressure from ten thousand Fascists who had marched on Rome.

1922 The declaration on the **founding of the Union of Socialist Soviet Republics** (USSR/Soviet Union) is signed at the First Congress of Soviets in Moscow on Dec. 30.

1923 Due to a default in reparation payments, **French and Belgian forces occupy the German Ruhr** on Jan. 11.

1923 The **Treaty Lausanne** of July 24 ends the Greco-Turkish War and awards the newly created Republic of Turkey all of Anatolia and parts of East Thrace.

1923 With the King of Spain's consent, General Miguel Primo de Rivera establishes a **military dictatorship** on Sept. 13.

1923 The **Turkish National Assembly** in Ankara proclaims a **republic** on Oct. 29 and chooses Mustafa Kemal Pascha, who was given the name **"Atatürk"** in 1934, as president.

1923 **Hitler Putsch:** An attempted putsch in Munich by the right radical **National Socialists** is crushed on Nov. 8–9.

1923 In an effort to stabilize the German currency, the **Rentenmark** is introduced on Nov. 20, ending hyperinflation.

1924 **Lenin**, leader of the Bolshevik Revolution in Russia, dies of a stroke near Moscow on Jan. 21.

1924 On March 3, the **Caliphate is constitutionally abolished in Turkey**. The last Caliph of the House of Ottoman leaves the country with his family.

1924 On March 25, a **republic** is proclaimed in **Greece**. Conditions in the country remain unsettled and, in 1935, Greece becomes a monarchy again.

1924 In order to stabilize the German economy, the **Dawes Plan** scales down the German reparation payments to 2.5 billion gold marks annually on April 9.

1924 **Mongolia** is proclaimed a **people's republic** on Nov. 26, becoming closely aligned to the Soviet Union.

1925 The monarchist and former General Field Marshal **Paul von Hindenburg** is elected the new **president of the German Reich** on April 28.

1925 On Oct. 31, **Resa Pahlevi** assumes the title of **Shah in Iran** and founds the Pahlevi dynasty that reigns until 1979. He attempts to modernize the country along Western lines and free it from British and Russian influence.

1925 In the **Treaties of Locarno** signed on Dec. 1, European nations agree upon a mutual guarantee of the borders between Germany, France, and Belgium.

1926 The **German Reich** joins the **League of Nations** on Sept. 9.

1926 On Nov. 18, the **Balfour Declaration** grants the **Dominions equal status to Great Britain** within the British Empire. This leads to the formation of the **British Commonwealth of Nations** on Dec. 11, 1931.

1926 **Hirohito** succeeds his father as **emperor of Japan** on Dec. 25.

Totalitarianism and Mass Culture

1920–1939

The seismic political and social upheavals in the wake of the First World War led to fundamental changes in society and culture. The new leading power, the USA, spurred the development of capitalist consumer societies through industrial mass production and modern forms of communication such as advertising, photography, motion pictures, and the radio. Almost everywhere in Europe, the old elites had lost their political power to mass democracies. The Soviet Union, the successor state of the Russian Empire, became the first Communist regime calling for a world revolution. The economic problems that culminated in a worldwide crisis in 1929 gave a further boost to left-wing and right-wing forces. Political violence was the order of the day in many places, culminating in civil wars in Spain and China. Since the 1930s, a new aggressive form of nationalism took hold in many places in Europe, particularly in Germany—in the form of Nazism.

Scene from the film *Modern Times* (1936), by and starring Charlie Chaplin

HISTORICAL FIGURES

Mohandas Karamchand "Mahatma" Gandhi (1869–1948)
The charismatic leader of the Indian independence movement remains a model and a symbolic figure of pacifism in the present-day world.

A lawyer and devote Indian Hindu, Gandhi had already been fighting against the discrimination of Indian minorities in the South African province of Natal before the First World War. There, he developed his strategy of non-violent resistance: non-compliance with colonial offices, boycotts of British products, and the promotion of one's own cultural tradition. With this program, Gandhi became the spiritual and political leader of the growing national independence movement in India in 1920. In **1930**, several hundred thousand people joined him in his peaceful protest march against the British salt monopoly. Great Britain finally granted India independence in **1947**. However, Gandhi was unable to prevent the outbreak of bloody clashes between Hindus and Muslims and the partitioning of India. He was killed by a fanatical Hindu in 1948.

Josef Stalin (1878–1953)
Through his unscrupulousness and organizational skills, the former novice priest from Georgia became the feared sole ruler of the Soviet Union.

Stalin, whose actual name was Iosif Dzhugashvili, was brought into the leading circle of the Bolsheviks at the behest of Lenin in 1912. He entered the new Soviet government after **1917**. From 1922, he deviously built up his personal power apparatus within the office of General Secretary. After Lenin died in **1924**, he was able to eliminate his rivals and create a personal dictatorship. The socialist restructuring of society that he initiated was accompanied by terror and mass deportation. Millions of people died in the course of the forced collectivization of 1928 and the "Great Purge" from **1934–1937**. Stalin was able to repel the German invasion of **1941** and establish satellite states in Eastern Europe after the war.

Mustaf Kemal Atatürk (1881–1938)
Atatürk—the "Father of all Turks"—created a modern, Western-style Turkish state.

During his military training, Mustafa Kemal was exposed to nationalistic ideas. Decorated as a military leader in the First World War, he successfully fought against an allied occupation of the Turkish homeland after the collapse of the Ottoman Empire and proclaimed a republic in **1923**. He ruled largely autocratically and shaped Turkey into a secular state. He abolished the Caliphate in **1924**, suspended Islam's status as a state religion and replaced Sharia law with Western jurisprudence. He also introduced the Latin alphabet and established equal status for women. Revered for his social reforms, he was given the name "Atatürk."

Adolf Hitler (1889–1945)
The failed landscape painter became Germany's dictator in 1933 and plunged the world into a murderous war.

He never graduated, had no training, and no permanent residence: nothing would have suggested Adolf Hitler's fatal career. Before he registered for military service in **1914**, he kept his head above water with odd jobs in his native country of Austria. Germany's defeat in the First World War drove him into politics. A racist with a contempt for democracy, he joined the radical right-wing National Socialist Workers' Party and, due to his oratory talents, quickly became its leader. With the help of the conservative state elite, Hitler was made chancellor in **1933**. Only a few months after seizing power, he had erected a totalitarian dictatorship. With the aim of providing the German people with "living space in the East," he attacked Poland in **1939** and unleashed the Second World War. In April 1945, he committed suicide in Berlin.

1931 The **Empire State Building** is opened in **New York** on May 1. It is the highest building in the world until 1972.

1935 The world's first complete **television program** is transmitted in Berlin on March 22. The USA follows suit six years later.

1936 *Modern Times*, a comedy film by British actor and filmmaker **Charlie Chaplin**, premieres in New York on Feb. 5. Chaplin's tramp figure has made him world famous.

1936 The American track athlete **Jesse Owens** wins four gold medals at the **Olympic Games in Berlin**, making him the most outstanding competitor of the sports event.

1938 German researchers **Otto Hahn** and **Fritz Strassmann** discover **nuclear fission** on Dec. 17 in Berlin.

1938 German engineer **Konrad Zuse** develops the first programmable calculator using binary numbers, earning Zuse the title of **"Father of the Computer."**

1939 The monumental film *Gone with the Wind* celebrates its premiere in New York on Dec. 15.

1935   **1939**

1934 The **Soviet Union** is accepted into the **League of Nations** on Sept. 18, and is thus officially recognized.

1934 The **"Long March"** led by Mao Zedong begins on Oct. 27 in the northwest of China with the construction of a military base.

1934 **Japan** withdraws from the **London Naval Conference** on Dec. 28 that provided for a limitation of armament.

1935 **Germany** declares itself no longer bound by the armament restrictions of the Versailles Treaty and introduces **universal compulsory military service** on March 16.

1935 **Comintern** (Communist International) speaks out for a popular front in cooperation with the Social Democrats and the labor and liberal camps to **fight against Fascism** on Aug. 20.

1935 Against the will of President Roosevelt, the **USA** pledges **strict neutrality** in the event of war on Aug. 31.

1935 The **Nuremberg Laws**, enacted in Germany on Sept. 15, make **anti-semitism** legal and official ideology.

1935 **Italian forces** invade **Ethiopia** on Oct. 3. Despite massive violent reprisals against the population, the Italians are driven out by 1941 with British help.

1936 Following the murder of a group of Jews in Jaffa, the **first serious clashes** occur in **Palestine** between Arabs and Jews on April 19. Since Hitler took power in Germany, over 30,000 Jews have fled to Palestine.

1936 On June 4, **Léon Blum** forms a government in **France** comprised of Social Democrats, Socialists, and Communists.

1936 A coup d'etat by Right-wing General **Francisco Franco** on July 18 leads to the outbreak of the **Spanish Civil War** between the Republicans and Nationalists. The intervention of foreign powers on both sides gives the conflict an international dimension.

1936 Great Britain grants **Egypt complete autonomy** on Aug. 26, but reserves access to the Suez Canal in the event of war.

1936 **Germany** and **Japan** sign an **Anti-Comintern Pact** on Nov. 25, which **Italy** also joins a year later.

1937 In the course of the Spanish Civil War, **German bombers** destroy the Basque town of **Guernica** on April 26.

1937 **Japan's invasion of China** begins on July 7 with an engagement at the **Marco Polo Bridge** near Beijing. Chinese Nationalists and Communists join forces in a defensive alliance of convenience.

1937 **Italy** withdraws from the **League of Nations** on Dec. 11.

1938 After German troops march into Austria, Adolf Hitler announces the **annexation** (Anschluss) of his homeland, **Austria**, into the German Reich on Heldenplatz ("Heroes' Square") in Vienna on March 13.

1938 Desperate to avoid war, France, Great Britain, and Italy are forced to accept the annexation of the German-settled **Sudeten territories** of Czechoslovakia by the German Reich in the **Munich Agreement** of Sept. 29.

1938 Mexico's President **Lazaro Cardenas** nationalizes the oil industry.

1939 The **German Reich** and the **Soviet Union** sign a **non-aggression pact** in Moscow on Aug. 23. In a secret appended protocol, they come to an agreement over the **partitioning of Poland** in the event of war.

1939 **German forces** occupy **Czechoslovakia** on March 15. One day later in Prague, Hitler proclaims the Protectorate of Bohemia and Morovia.

1939 On April 1, three days after General Franco's troops captured Madrid, the **Spanish Civil War** ends with a **victory for the Nationalists**. Franco rules as dictator over Spain until his death in 1975.

1939 On Aug. 25, **Great Britain** assures **Poland** of **military support** in the event of war.

1939 **Germany** invades **Poland** on Sept. 1 and sets off the **Second World War**.

1938 During the **Kristallnacht**, Nov. 9–10, SA-coordinated attacks against Jews take place throughout the whole of Germany. Synagogues are set on fire and residences are demolished. A total of 26,000 Jews are deported to concentration camps.

1927 American pilot **Charles Lindbergh** makes the first non-stop flight across the Atlantic on May 20–21.

1927 German theoretical-physicist **Werner Heisenberg** formulates his **uncertainty principle** and revolutionizes quantum mechanics.

1928 **Walt Disney** and artist Ub Iwerks jointly create the animated film and comic figure **Mickey Mouse**.

1928 Scottish bacteriologist **Alexander Fleming** accidentally discovers the antibiotic properties of **penicillin**.

1928 The *Threepenny Opera* by **Bertolt Brecht** with music by **Kurt Weill** has its premiere on Aug. 31 in Berlin. The stage musical becomes a worldwide hit.

1929 The anti-war novel *All Quiet on the Western Front* by German author **Erich Maria Remarque** is published on Jan. 29.

1930 The first **soccer world championship** is held in Uruguay. The competition that takes place every four years becomes the world's most important sports event next to the Olympics.

1930 German **boxer Max Schmeling** becomes the first non-American to gain the World's Heavy Weight title on June 12.

1930 The first volume of the novel *The Man Without Qualities* is published in November. The uncompleted work by Austrian **Robert Musil** is considered one of the most significant novels of the 20th century.

1930

1927 At the end of the year, **Josef Stalin** forces rivals like Leo Trotzki out of the Communist Party and subsequently establishes himself as **sole power in the Soviet Union**.

1928 **Briand-Kellog Pact:** On Aug. 27, the USA, Great Britain, Germany, and twelve other nations convene in Paris and pledge for the **renunciation of war as an instrument of national policy**.

1930 To protest the British salt monopoly, **Mahatma Gandhi**, leader of the Indian fight for independence, organizes a **demonstration march** to the **salt fields** on the coast on March 12 that launches the **Civil Disobedience Movement**.

1930 The **National Socialist Party**, led by **Adolf Hitler**, comes in as a surprising second in the German Reich's **national elections** on Sept. 14.

1931 **Spain** is declared a **republic** after King Alfonso XIII abdicates on April 14.

1931 Japanese forces occupy Chinese Manchuria on Sept. 18. Five months later, the **Japanese puppet state of Manchukuo** is established, but is not internationally recognized.

1933 On Jan. 30, **Adolf Hitler** is appointed **German Chancellor** by Hindenburg. Within a few months, he erects a National Socialist dictatorship.

1933 The **USA** begins its **Good Neighbor Policy** to improve relations with **Latin America.**

1933 The **first concentration camp** for opponents of the Nazi regime is constructed near Munich in **Dachau** on March 20. By 1939, some 60,000 racially, politically, or socially undesirable persons had been imprisoned and in part used as forced labor.

1927 **Sexual intercourse** outside of marriage **between Blacks and Whites** becomes a prosecutable offense in South Africa on Sept. 30.

1929 In the **Lateran Treaty** of Feb. 11, Italy recognizes the **sovereignty of the Vatican State**. In return, the Pope recognizes Rome as the capital of Italy.

1931 **Afghanistan** is changed under Shah Nadir Shah to a **constitutional monarchy** on Oct. 31.

1932 **António Salazar** becomes Prime Minister of Portugal on July 5. A year later he erects an **authoritarian corporative state** along Fascist lines.

1932 **Unemployment** resulting from the Great Depression reaches its height in all of Europe.

1933 **Day of Potsdam:** The inaugural celebrations of the new Reichstag held in Potsdam on March 21 herald the symbolically important alliance between the **Nazis** and the **elite Prussian military**.

1927 On Dec. 14, **Great Britain** formally recognizes **Iraq** as an independent sovereign state.

1929 Alexander I changes the name of the Kingdom of Serbs, Croats, and Slovenes to **Yugoslavia** on Oct. 3 and establishes a **personal dictatorship**.

> *"The only thing we have to fear is fear itself."*
>
> U.S. President Franklin D. Roosevelt, March 4, 1933

1933 At the seventh **Pan-American Conference** in Montevideo on Dec. 26, all American states subscribe to the **principle of non-intervention** in the internal and external affairs of other states.

1928 In February, the Kuomintang under **Chiang Kai-shek** form a **new national government** in Nanjing. Civil war-like battles ensue with the Communists.

1929 **Black Tuesday:** The market prices crash in the **New York Stock Exchange** on Oct. 25. The result is a **severe economic depression** in all industrialized nations of the world.

1930 **Carol II** becomes **king of Romania** on June 6. With the support of the Fascists, he erects an authoritarian regime.

1932 German reparation payments are suspended at the **Lausanne Conference** (June 16– July 9).

1933 **New Deal:** President Roosevelt announces a package of government **measures to overcome the Great Depression** in the USA.

1934 **Night of the Long Knives:** Members of the SA leadership and other opponents of Hitler are liquidated on June 30.

1928 A five-year plan targeting rapid industrialization is implemented on Oct. 1 in the **Soviet Union**. The **forced collectivization of agriculture** results in **famine** and the death of millions.

1930 General **Getúlio Vargas** takes over power in **Brazil** on Oct. 24 and rules from then on with dictatorial powers.

1932 **Abdul-Aziz ibn Saud**, who has conquered vast areas of the Arabian Peninsula, founds the **Kingdom of Saudi Arabia** on Sept. 23.

1932 **Franklin D. Roosevelt** is elected the 32nd president of the USA on Nov. 8.

1934–1939 Millions die as victims of **Stalin's "Great Purge"** through forced labor in **Gulag camps** or arbitrary murder.

HISTORICAL EVENTS

March on Rome
Benito Mussolini gained political power in Italy in October 1922 and created a new type of totalitarian dictatorship, the forerunner and in part the model for Fascist movements worldwide.

Italy paid a high prize for the small amount of territory it had gained in the First World War. A severe economic crisis ensued, out of which the nationalistic, anti-democratic right led by Benito Mussolini emerged stronger than ever before and developed into a violent mass movement. "Fascisti" from all parts of the country gathered in Rome on Oct. 27–30, 1922 to claim governmental power. King Victor Emmanuel III, bowing to the pressure of the masses, named Mussolini prime minister on **Oct. 31, 1922**. With the consent of the elite, Mussolini turned the country into a Fascist dictatorship. Political parties were eliminated, parliament was dissolved, and Mussolini's position of power strengthened by institutional means. The monarchy and the Church, however, remained largely untouched.

Mussolini (center) surrounded by followers in the March on Rome on Oct. 28, 1922

Worldwide Economic Crisis 1929–1932
The New York stock market crash of 1929 triggered a worldwide economic depression. The social crisis that swept many countries gave rise to radical political forces.

In the 1920s, the thriving economy in the USA led to a boom in stocks and investments. However, the prosperity of the post-war years crashed in **October 1929** with the collapse of the New York stock exchange. The plunge in prices resulted in a wave of bank closures and business bankruptcies. Due to the global network of economic flow, Europe also became locked in a profound depression. Unemployment soared. Mounting discontent among the masses strengthened the appeal of anti-democratic forces, e.g. in Germany. In the USA, President Roosevelt promised a "new deal," introducing a series of social reforms in **1933**.

Stockholders following the price movement of the New York Stock Market in October 1929

The Fight for China's Unity
The Chinese National Party led by Chiang Kai-shek was able to unite China in 1928, but was weakened in internal political conflicts with the Communists under Mao Zedong.

Since 1916, China had lacked a central government. The country was ruled by regional military leaders, particularly in the north. In order to unite China, Sun Yat-sen, the founder of the nationalist Kuomintang Party, decided to enter a tactical alliance with the Communists in 1923. Troops led by Chiang Kai-shek defeated the warlords in the north, and in **1928** a national government was established in Nanjing. To secure dictatorial power, Chiang Kai-shek launched the persecution of Communists led by Mao Zdedong and forced them to retreat to the north in **1934** (the "Long March"). With the Japanese invasion of China in **1937**, the Kuomintang and the Communists formed a new united front that, however, soon collapsed after the Japanese surrender in **1945**. The Communists were victorious in **1949**, and Chiang Kai-shek withdrew to Taiwan.

Chiang Kai-shek with his wife, Song Mei-ling, the sister-in-law of Sun Yat-sen, in 1927

The representatives of the British Empire at the conference in London in 1926

Statute of Westminster
Consisting of its former colonies, Great Britain formed a federation of equal and sovereign states: the British Commonwealth of Nations.

After Canada had gained Dominion status, Australia, New Zealand, the Union of South Africa, and Ireland also demanded home rule from Great Britain at the beginning of the 20th century. Following the First World War, the Dominions were given control of their foreign policy affairs. At a conference in London in **1926**, Great Britain granted them full autonomy. Through the Commonwealth of Nations, the Dominions and former colonies remained linked to their former motherland. The Statute of Westminster of 1931 gave the federation a legal basis. This "group of self-governing communities," as expressed by British Foreign Minister Arthur Balfour, consisted of "autonomous communities ... equal in status, though united by a common allegiance to the crown." Participation in the Commonwealth was voluntary for the member states. At present, there are 54 countries in the Commonwealth.

Soviet prisoners at work in a stone quarry.

The "Great Purges" in the Soviet Union
Josef Stalin's reign of terror in the Soviet Union reached its peak in the 1930s.

Between **1934** and **1939**, the Soviet dictator Stalin launched a campaign of terror to fight anti-Socialist elements. In the course of the "great purge," he eliminated all imagined and potential adversaries. The persecution indiscriminately reached into every corner of the party, state, industry, and cultural organizations. Millions of people were considered "vermin" or spies and deported to labor camps and penal colonies known as "gulags." Prominent party members were executed after public show trials. By 1938, a major part of the military leadership had also been eliminated. When the wave of terror had subsided in 1939, all central positions in the state had been filled with party apparatchiks loyal to Stalin.

Germany under the Swastika
After Hitler had seized power in 1933, the state and society were systematically reshaped to bring them in line with Nazi ideology.

Germany's democracy was turned into a dictatorship when Adolf Hitler came to power on **Jan. 30, 1933**. The new chancellor used the burning of the Reichstag building in Berlin on Feb. 27, 1933 as an excuse to override basic political rights and introduce emergency regulations. On March 24, 1933, all political parties, except the NSDAP (Nazi Party), had to transfer their full legislative powers to Hitler's government. By the end of the year, single party rule had been established and the NSDAP was the only party left in Germany. With the murder of the SA leadership on **June 30, 1934** (Night of the Long Knives), Hitler had also eliminated inner-party opposition. Following the death of President Hindenburg in August 1934, Hitler proclaimed himself "Fuehrer" of the German Reich and made the army pledge allegiance to him. The Nazis maintained their power by propaganda and coercion. Workers and the youth were forcibly collected in Nazi

At the "Day of Potsdam," Hitler shows deference to President Hindenburg.

organizations, and concentration camps were set up to deal with political enemies. In line with the racial ideology of the Nazis, the Jews were deprived of their property and civil rights and were forced to flee the country.

Spanish Civil War 1936–1939
The three-year civil war in Spain between conservative Nationalist and socialist Republican forces was a trial run for the Second World War.

The Spanish Republic, founded in **1931**, collapsed in the turmoil of warring factions. A right-wing military revolt led by General Franco against the elected leftist Popular Front government on **July 18, 1936** unleashed a brutally waged civil war that gained international significance when foreign powers entered the conflict. Italy and Germany supported the Nationalists, who had built up a counter-government in Burgos in the north of Spain. On **April 26, 1937**, the Basque town of Guernica was leveled by a bombing raid of the German Luftwaffe. Tens of thousands of volunteers from Europe and the USA formed into international brigades and fought on the side of the government which continually received arms supplies from the Soviet Union. The hostilities ended on **April 1, 1939** with a victory of the Nationalists. Their leader Franco ran the country as a Fascist military dictatorship until his death in 1975.

A union poster of the Unión General de Trabajadores dating from the civil war

The Munich Agreement
In the Sudetenland Crisis of 1938, France and Great Britain embraced, in vain, a policy of appeasement towards the German Reich.

Hitler faced hardly any objections when he declared that Germany would ignore the constraints imposed by the Treaty of Versailles. In violation of the accord, he rebuilt the German armed forces in **1935** and occupied the Rhineland in 1936. In **March 1938**, he invaded and annexed Austria. Later the same year, Hitler's demands became even more aggressive. He threatened to unleash a war unless the Sudetenland, a border area in Czechoslovakia containing a large ethnic German population, was ceded to Germany. France and Great Britain, eager to appease Hitler, gave in. At a conference in Munich on **Sept. 29, 1938**, they agreed to hand the Sudetenland over to the Reich. Only after the Germans had marched into Poland in **1939**, did the Western powers pursue a policy of confrontation.

Hitler and Chamberlain on the day of the signing of the Munich Agreement

1939 On Aug. 2, the love song **"Lili Marleen"** is recorded by German singer Lale Andersen. During the course of the war, it becomes the favorite song of not only the German but also of the Allied armed forces, especially in the version sung by **Marlene Dietrich**.

1939 On Sept. 17, Finnish track athlete **Taisto Mäki** becomes the first person to run **10,000 meters in under 30 minutes**.

1939 An **earthquake** destroys the city of **Erzincan** in eastern Turkey on Dec. 26, costing the lives of close to 30,000 people.

1939 The first **Batman comic** is published in the USA.

1940 The first McDonald's fast food restaurant is opened in San Bernardino, California, on May 15.

1940 The antisemitic Nazi propaganda film *Jud Süß* by Veit Harlan has its premiere on Sept. 5 at the Venice Film Festival.

1940 The first nylon stockings are sold in select American cities on May 15.

1940 Charlie Chaplin's film satire of Hitler, *The Great Dictator*, has its premiere in New York on Oct. 15.

1939

1940

1939 On the pretext of retaliation for an attack, German soldiers march into Polish state territory on Sept. 1. **The German invasion of Poland marks the start of the Second World War.**

1939 On Sep. 3, **Great Britain** and **France declare war on the German Reich** after its invasion of Poland.

1939 South African Prime Minister **Barry Hertzog** is forced to turn over his office to Jan Smuts on Sept. 5 because of his **refusal to declare war on Germany**.

1939 In accordance with the secret **Molotov-Ribbentrop Pact**, Soviet troops occupy eastern Poland on Sept. 17.

1939 After weeks of resistance, **Warsaw falls to German troops** on Sept. 27; the **Polish army surrenders** on Oct. 6.

1939 The mass murder of handicapped and sick persons is begun in October in the German Reich as part of **"Action T4,"** a euthanasia program.

1939 The **USA and 20 other American countries** declare their neutrality in the event of war on Oct. 2 at a **Pan-American Conference**.

1939 On Oct. 19, a **mutual aid pact** is signed in Ankara by the **British, French,** and **Turks**.

1939 On Oct. 25, the eastern part of German-occupied Poland is declared a **"General Government"** in which the population is subjected to a **German reign of terror**. The western portion was incorporated into the German Reich on Oct. 8.

1939 The **USA relaxes its policy of neutrality** on Nov. 3 and allows France and Great Britain to buy armaments.

1939 **Adolf Hitler** barely escapes an **attempted bomb assassination** in the Munich Bürgerbräukeller beer hall on Nov. 8.

1939 The **"Winter War"** between the **Soviet Union** and **Finland** begins on Nov. 30 with the Soviet invasion of Finland. The Soviets are met with stiff resistance.

1939 On Dec. 14, **the Soviet Union is expelled from the League of Nations** for invading Finland in November. Eager to furnish aid to Finland, the Western powers land in Norway.

1940 On Feb. 8, the **first Jewish ghetto** is set up by the Germans in **Łódz**, Poland.

1940 On March 12, the **Moscow Peace Treaty** is signed by **Finland** and the **Soviet Union**. It marks the end of the "Winter War." Finland retains its independence but must accept a considerable loss of territory.

1940 On Mar. 27, SS head Heinrich Himmler orders the **construction of the Auschwitz concentration camp** in present-day Poland.

1940 In order to secure Scandinavian ore deposits, **Germany launches an attack on Denmark and Norway** on April 9. Denmark surrenders and Norway capitulates on June 10.

"I have nothing to offer but blood, toil, tears and sweat."

Churchill on May 10, 1940, in a government statement to the House of Commons

1940 On May 10, an **all-party war cabinet** is formed in **Great Britain** under the leadership of the new Prime Minister **Winston Churchill**.

1940 On May 10, **German forces** occupy the **Netherlands, Luxemburg,** and **Belgium**.

1940 The **Netherlands capitulate** on May 15. Rotterdam had been destroyed by German air strikes the day before.

1940 **Operation Fall Rot**: On June 5, the **German offensive against France** begins. On June 14, Paris is occupied without resistance.

1940 On June 10, **Italy** declares war on **France** and **Great Britain**.

1940 On June 15, **Soviet troops occupy Lithuania** and two days later **Latvia** and **Estonia**. By July 1, the Romanian territories of Bessarabia and North Bukovina have been taken.

1940 On June 18, French **General de Gaulle** appeals from London to the French will to resist. With the support of British and American soldiers, he afterwards recruits for the **fight against German occupation**.

1940 On June 22, defeated **France** agrees to a truce with the German Reich. French **Marshal Pétain** establishes a German-friendly regime in **Vichy**, in the unoccupied section of France, on July 1.

1940 On Aug. 13, Hitler announces intensified **aerial attacks against Great Britain**. After heavy German losses, the planned invasion of England on Sept. 17 is postponed indefinitely.

1940 The **war in North Africa** begins on Sept. 13 with an Italian offensive out of Libya against the British in Egypt.

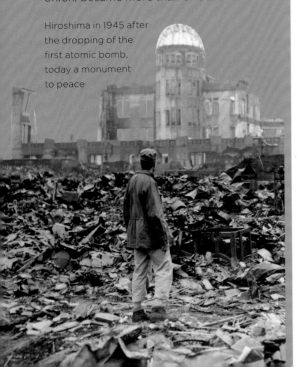

The Second World War
1939–1945

The war in Europe began when German troops marched into Poland in 1939. Almost the whole continent was forced under the tyranny of the German Nazis who committed incomprehensible crimes. Millions of people became victims of German racial fanaticism that resulted in the mass extermination of Jews. The Japanese followed a similar course of expansion and provoked America's entry into the war, making it truly a world war. Despite the clear superiority of the Allies, the German and Japanese troops fought ruthlessly to the bitter end. The German Reich surrendered in May 1945, while the Japanese only considered to quit the war after Americans had dropped a second atomic bomb on their country. Shortly after the war, the victors' alliance of convenience crumbled and the antagonisms between the two new super powers, the USA and the Soviet Union, became more than evident.

Hiroshima in 1945 after the dropping of the first atomic bomb, today a monument to peace

HISTORICAL FIGURES

Winston Churchill (1874–1965)   Through his unyielding strength, the British prime minister became the symbolic figure of the struggle against Nazi Germany.

Churchill's political career spanned the first six decades of the 20th century, but his finest hour came on **May 10, 1940**, when he was elected prime minister of Great Britain. He had held various offices in several governments since 1908. In the 1930s, he primarily devoted himself to journalistic writing and publishing. The Second World War brought the opponent of the British appeasement policy toward Hitler back in the limelight. As leader of an all-party government, Churchill organized both the national and international resistance against the German aggressor and in **1941** was instrumental in establishing a coalition between the British, Soviets, and Americans. In July 1945, he was forced out of office.

Hideki Tojo (1884–1948)   The omnipotent prime minister led Japan into the Second World War in 1941.

In the 1920s, Tojo, a graduate of the Imperial Military Academy, had already been entrusted with preparations for war. By 1940, he had also gained direct political power as minister of the army. Tojo made an alliance with Hitler and propagated the objective of an East Asian federation under Japanese leadership. Shortly after he assumed power as prime minister, he initiated the attack on the U.S. military base at Pearl Harbor on **Dec. 7, 1941** which marked Japan's entry into the Second World War. During the course of the war, he gained virtual dictatorial powers, but was forced to offer his resignation after military set-backs began in 1944. Tojo was sentenced to death by an international military tribunal in 1948.

Georgy Zhukov (1896–1974)   The Red Army Marshal led the Soviet Union to victory over Nazi Germany.

Trained as a shoemaker, Zhukov served as a cavalryman in the Red Army during the Russian Civil War. Due to his skills in military strategy, Zhukov's rise in the ranks was meteoric. Following the German invasion on **June 22, 1941**, Stalin repeatedly assigned him to critical sectors. As commander-in-chief, he beat back the Germans from Moscow and won the decisive battle of Stalingrad in **1942–43**. When his forces took Berlin in **May 1945**, Zhukov was at the height of his fame and practically the second most powerful man in the USSR. Stalin now regarded him as a threat and demoted him in rank. After Stalin's death in **1953**, the former war hero returned to favor and was appointed deputy minister of defense.

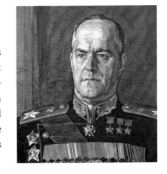

Heinrich Himmler (1900–1945)   The head of the SS built up a vast apparatus of terror both at home and abroad, making him the principle figure in the massive displacement of people and the death of millions.

Himmler adhered to a pseudo-scientific Germanic cult and dreamed of a Nordic master race that ruled the world. In 1929, Hitler appointed him Reichsführer of the SS and within a few years Himmler turned the small elite squad into the central military agency of suppression and control in Nazi Germany. He eventually became one of the most powerful men in the Reich as chief of the German police, Reich commissioner for the consolidation of German nationhood, minister of the interior, and commander of the replacement army. Without Hitler's consent, he tried to negotiate peace with the Western powers in April **1945**. When the war ended, Himmler went into hiding. After being discovered, he committed suicide.

1943 The stage play *The Good Person of Szechwan* by German dramatist **Bertolt Brecht** has its premiere in Zurich on Feb. 4.

1943 *The Little Prince*, a story by French aristocrat writer **Antoine de Saint-Exupéry**, is published on April 6 in New York.

1943 Swiss chemist **Albert Hofmann** accidentally discovers the **drug LSD** on April 19 while experimenting on himself.

1943 The first solo exhibition by American painter **Jackson Pollock**, the founder of **Action Painting**, opens on Nov. 9 in New York.

1944 The most recent major **eruption of Vesuvius** (near Naples) to date occurs on April 4.

1944 At a conference in Bretton Woods, USA, from July 1–22, 44 nations agree to the introduction of a worldwide **fixed exchange rate centered on the U.S. dollar**. As part of this, the **World Bank** (IBRD) and the **International Monetary Fund** (IMF) are created.

1944 *Double Indemnity*, the film noir masterpiece by American director **Billy Wilder**, starts on Sep. 6 in New York.

1945 The first **"Pippi Longstocking"** story by children's book author **Astrid Lindgren** is published in Sweden on Sept. 1.

1945 The Americans set off the **first atomic bomb for test purposes** (Trinity Test) in the desert of New Mexico on July 16.

1943 — 1944 — 1945

1943 At the **Casablanca Conference** of Jan. 14–26, President Roosevelt and Prime Minister Churchill agree to demand Germany's unconditional surrender.

1943 On Jan. 31, **the German troops in Stalingrad surrender**. Over 90,000 soldiers are taken captive. The German defeat marks the turn of the war in the East.

1943 In a speech on Feb. 18, German Propaganda Minister **Joseph Goebbels** incites the German people to **"total war."**

1943 On Feb. 22, Sophie and Hans Scholl, members of the resistance movement **"White Rose,"** are executed in Munich.

1943 On April 19, an **uprising** breaks out in the **Warsaw ghetto** that takes the German occupiers a month to crush.

1943 The **war in North Africa** ends with the **surrender of the German-Italian army** on May 13.

1943 The **great offensive against Japan** is launched on June 30 with the **landing of Allied troops** on the Solomon Islands and New Guinea.

1943 On July 25, **Mussolini**, the Italian **"Duce,"** is arrested by order of King Victor Emmanuel III.

1943 On Sept. 15, after Hitler has had **Mussolini released**, the Duce places himself at the head of the Fascist **"Republic of Salò."**

1943 From Nov. 22–26, **Roosevelt** and **Churchill** confer with Chinese President **Chiang Kai-shek** over the progress of the war against Japan in the Pacific.

1943 **Roosevelt**, **Churchill**, and **Stalin** meet in Teheran, Iran, between Nov. 28 and Dec. 1 to discuss military strategy and **postwar order**.

1944 On March 19, Hitler orders the **occupation of Hungary by German forces**.

1944 The first **Hungarian Jews** arrive in the **Auschwitz-Birkenau extermination camp** in May. Despite spectacular rescue efforts by Swedish diplomat **Raoul Wallenberg**, up to 500,000 people are sent to their death in the following months.

1944 **D-Day:** Under the command of U.S. General Eisenhower, **Western Allied troops land on the coast of Normandy** on June 6.

1944 **Adolf Hitler** survives an **attempted bomb assassination** by German officers led by **Claus von Stauffenberg** on July 20. A nationwide wave of executions follows.

1944 **Allied troops** enter **Paris** without a fight on Aug. 25. General de Gaulle forms a provisional government.

1944 **British forces occupy Athens** on Oct. 13. Communists in the north of Greece attempt a power grab.

1945 On Jan. 12, a **Soviet large-scale offensive** is launched on the **German eastern front**. The advance of the Red Army into the German Reich's eastern territories triggers a **mass flight of the German population**.

1945 Soviet troops liberate the **Auschwitz-Birkenau concentration and extermination camp** on Jan. 27.

1945 **Stalin**, **Churchill**, and **Roosevelt** meet in **Yalta** on Feb. 4–11 for a second **summit meeting**. They agree on a common postwar policy for Germany.

1945 In the final months of the war, the German city of **Dresden** is completely destroyed by a series of Allied firebombing **air raids** on Feb. 13–14.

1945 Surrounded by the Red Army in Berlin, **Adolf Hitler commits suicide** on April 30.

1945 The **German Reich unconditionally surrenders** on May 7–9.

1945 The **United Nations** (UN) is constituted on June 26 in San Francisco.

1945 At the **Potsdam Conference** from July 17 to Aug. 2, the victorious Allied powers settle the **post-war order in Europe**.

1945 On Aug. 6, the U.S. Air Force drops the **first atomic bomb** on the Japanese city of **Hiroshima**. It is followed three days later by a second bomb on **Nagasaki**.

1945 On Sep. 2, **Japan declares unconditional surrender** onboard the U.S. battleship *USS Missouri*, ending the Second World War.

1945 The first in a series of military trials against leading Nazis begins in the city of **Nuremberg** on Nov. 14.

1945 In costly fighting lasting from Feb. 19 to Mar. 16, **U.S. armed forces** capture **Iwo Jima**, a strategically important island south of Japan.

1941 The **musical** *Arsenic and Old Lace* has its premiere in **New York** on Jan. 10.

1941 The film *Citizen Kane* by Orson Welles has its premiere on May 1 in New York.

1941 German inventor **Konrad Zuse** unveils his Z3 calculator on May 12, the **first functioning digital computer**.

1942 American jazz musician **Glenn Miller** receives the first gold record in music history on Feb. 10.

1942 American art patron **Peggy Guggenheim** opens the **Art of This Century Gallery** in New York on Oct. 20.

1942 The *Royal Game*, a novella by the exiled Austrian writer **Stefan Zweig**, is published posthumously at the end of the year in Buenos Aires.

1941 The **world's first fighter jet** (HE 280), with two turbojet engines, takes off in the German Reich on April 2.

1941 On May 15, the **European P.E.N. in America**, a society of European writers in exile in America, is founded in New York.

1942 The world's **first long-range missile**, the German V2 rocket, lifts off from Peenemünde on the Baltic island of Usedom on Oct. 3.

1942 The film *Casablanca* starring **Humphrey Bogart** and **Ingrid Bergman**, has its premiere in New York on Nov. 26. It becomes a worldwide blockbuster.

1941 — **1942**

1941 **German troops** commanded by **Lieutenant General Erwin Rommel** arrive in **North Africa** on Feb. 11 to support the Italians.

1941 **Lend-Lease Act:** The program to supply Germany's enemies with **armaments** without direct payment is passed in the USA on March 11, effectively ending American neutrality.

1941 The **German campaign against Yugoslavia and Greece** begins on April 6. Four days later, the Fascist "Independent State of Croatia" is proclaimed in Zagreb.

1941 Without prior declaration of war, **German forces invade the Soviet Union** on June 22. The German units are able to advance rapidly until October. On Dec. 5, however, a Soviet counteroffensive turns back the German advance just outside Moscow.

1941 To avenge the destruction of a British battle cruiser, the Royal Navy sinks the **Bismarck**, Germany's most modern battleship, on May 27. **German naval forces are increasingly forced on the defensive.**

1941 **Commissar Order:** On June 6, the German Wehrmacht High Command orders that all Red Army political commissars captured during the course of the war with the Soviet Union be put to death.

1941 On July 4, successful uprisings led by Communist **Josip Tito** begin in **Yugoslavia** against the German occupiers.

1942 In the **Washington Pact** on Jan. 1, 26 nations pledge adherence to the principles of the Atlantic Charter of Aug. 14, 1941.

1942 On Jan. 2, **Japanese forces** occupy the capital of the Philippines, **Manila**, which had been under American sovereignty until now.

1942 Japan has conquered all of **Dutch East India** (Indonesia) by March 8.

1942 On March 17, the first Jews are deported to the Belzec extermination camp. This is the start of the **systematic mass murder of the Jewish population** in the Nazi death camps in German-occupied Poland.

1942 SS Obergruppenführer **Heydrich**, one of the organizers of the Holocaust, **is assassinated** on June 4 in Prague. In retaliation, the village of Lidice is leveled on June 10 and all the male inhabitants are killed.

1942 The **opening of a second front in Europe** is decided upon at the close of the **Second Washington Conference** on June 26.

1942 The USA takes the initiative in the **Pacific War** and lands troops on the Japanese-occupied **Salomon Islands** east of New Guinea on Aug. 7.

1942 On Nov. 11, after the French troops of the Vichy government join the Allies, **German units** move into the **parts of France that were unoccupied** until now.

1941 The **Soviet Union** signs a **neutrality pact** with **Japan** on April 13.

1941 On April 17, German troops force **Yugoslavia to capitulate**. The government flees to London. Five days later, **Greece** is evacuated by British troops and must surrender as well.

1941 By May 18, **British forces have liberated Ethiopia** from its Italian occupiers. Emperor Haile Selassie I returns from exile.

1941 **Great Britain** and the **Soviet Union** sign a **military alliance** on July 12.

1941 British Prime Minister Churchill and U.S. President Roosevelt announce the **Atlantic Charter** on Aug. 14 that defines the **principles of the post-war order**.

1941 Soviet and British forces invade Iran simultaneously from the north and south on Aug. 25 and force **Shah Resa Pahlevi to abdicate**.

1941 SS Gruppenführer Reinhard Heydrich is appointed chief executor of the **"Final Solution to the Jewish Question."** He presents his plan at the **Wannsee Conference** in Jan. 1942.

1941 On Oct. 18, **General Hideki Tojo** becomes **Japanese Prime Minister**.

1941 Japanese airplanes attack in a surprise military strike on the **U.S. naval base in Pearl Harbor** in Hawaii on Dec. 7. The following day, the USA declares war on Japan. The war expands into a **world war**.

1942 The **British Air Force** begins its **carpet bombing of major German cities** with the destruction of Lübeck on March 28–29 and Cologne on May 30–31.

1942 The Allies stop Japan's advance to Australia at the **Battle of the Coral Sea** in the South Pacific from May 4–8.

1942 Allied naval forces defeat the Japanese for the first time in the **Battle of Midway** in the North Pacific from June 3–7.

1942 In their counter-offensive, the **Red Army** encircles the German forces at Stalingrad on Nov. 22. Despite their hopeless position, Hitler will not let them surrender.

HISTORICAL EVENTS

The Battle for Britain
The failed invasion of Great Britain in 1940–1941 halted the victorious German advance for the first time.

At the beginning of the Second World War, the German army seemed to advance wherever it desired. After occupying Poland and almost all of Scandinavia, the Blitzkrieg of **July 1940** brought France under German control as well. Only Great Britain stood in the way of Hitler's absolute conquest of Europe. When the British government refused to negotiate an armistice that Germany wished to obtain, the Luftwaffe launched air strikes in **August 1940** to soften the island for invasion. Despite massive attacks, such as the carpet bombing that almost completely leveled the city of Coventry in November 1940, the resistance of the Royal Air Force could not be broken. After suffering heavy losses of their own, the Germans ended the air campaign. As the only European power to withstand German aggression at that time,

Battle of Britain: German bombers in an air strike over London in 1940

Great Britain did everything in its power to organize a global fight against the German Nazi regime.

German Wehrmacht soldiers executing Jews in occupied Poland

Ideological War in the East
During their invasion of the Soviet Union, the German Nazi leadership attempted to implement their racist program.

To some extent, the Germans solicited support from the populace of the countries they occupied in Western and Northern Europe. With regard to Eastern Europe, however, the Nazi leadership defined the war from the beginning as a "struggle for German living space" and a campaign against "Slavic subhumans" and the "Jewish-Bolshevik" system. On **June 6, 1941**, prior to the Russian campaign, Hitler issued an order, instructing the Wehrmacht to shoot all captured political officers of the Red Army. Other prisoners of war were often deliberately starved to death. Even during the invasion of Poland on **Sept. 1, 1939**, SS units had systematically murdered "racially inferior" persons. The objective was to Germanize Eastern Europe. However, the Nazi acts of barbarity were retaliated when the Red Army marched into Germany in **January 1945**, taking revenge on the German civilian population.

Entrance to the infamous Auschwitz-Birkenau extermination camp in present-day Poland

Holocaust – Shoa
The systematic mass murder of European Jews in the Second World War marks a moral low point in the history of modern civilization.

Auschwitz-Birkenau, Majdanek, Treblinka, Belzec, Sobibor, and Chelmo—these are the sites of terror that have been burned into our collective memory as symbols of man's inhumanity to man. These are the camps where Jews and other "undesired people" were systematically murdered. At the onset of the Russian campaign in **July 1941**, the Nazi leadership made the decision to exterminate the Jews in German-occupied territories. At the beginning, special SS commandos operated behind the front lines to kill the Jewish population. Later, death camps were constructed for reasons of "efficiency." As the murder campaigns were completed and the Russian troops closed in, the Nazis began dismantling the camps, hoping to cover up evidence of their crimes. On **Jan. 27, 1945**, the Red Army liberated Auschwitz-Birkenau, the largest of the extermination camps. It is estimated that six million Jews alone perished in the Nazi death factories.

Attack on Pearl Harbor: The War in the Pacific
After the Japanese attack on the U.S. naval base on Hawaii in 1941, the European war turned into a world war.

After the Germans had taken the Netherlands and France in **1940**, Japan intensified its course of expansion in East Asia and annexed the Dutch and French colonies. The USA saw their territories in the Pacific region threatened and reacted with effective boycott measures. The situation came to a head on the morning of **Dec. 7, 1941**. Without any declaration of war, squadrons of Japanese planes attacked the U.S. naval base at Pearl Harbor, killing more than 2,400 Americans and sinking eight battleships. After the surprise attack by the Japanese, the USA mobilized for war. By **March 1942**, the whole western Pacific region, from the borders of India to Australia, was in Japanese hands. It was not until the naval battle of Midway in **June 1942** that the USA was able to turn the tide of the war. The now superior U.S. forces conquered island after island and drove the Japanese into retreat. The cost in lives was high. For instance, during the invasion of the small Japanese island of Iwo Jima, completed on **March 16, 1945**, every third G.I. was wounded or killed.

Japanese attack on Pearl Harbor

Allied Summit Conferences

The "Big Three"—Roosevelt, Churchill, and Stalin—had settled the fundamentals of the European post-war order while the war was still raging.

After the German invasion of the Soviet Union on **June 22, 1941**, the ideological and political differences between the USA, Great Britain, and the USSR temporarily diminished. The three great powers united in an anti-Hitler coalition to oppose further German aggression. Despite the Japanese attack on Pearl Harbor, they directed their collective efforts on ending Nazi tyranny, as stated in the Atlantic Charter of **1941**. At the Casablanca Conference in **1943**, the Allies called for the unconditional surrender of the Axis powers. When a military victory was in sight, attention was given to post-war planning. At the end of **1943**, the "Big Three" gathered in Tehran and agreed upon the manipulation of the Polish border. In **Feb. 1945**, they met again in Yalta, devoting special attention to the partitioning of Germany into four occupation zones under the supervision of an Allied Control Council while the Soviet Union was given a free hand in the political reordering of Eastern Europe.

The Big Three, Churchill, Roosevelt, and Stalin, in 1943 in Yalta on the Crimean Peninsula

D-Day

In June 1944, the USA opened a second front against the Germans in northern France with the largest combined naval, air, and land operation in military history to date.

Ever since its defeat at Stalingrad in **1943**, the German army had been in retreat. Germany was ultimately doomed, when a massive Allied military force landed on the French Atlantic coast on **June 6, 1944**. Within five days, 50,000 ships brought 3.5 million soldiers from southern England to the beaches of Normandy while 10,000 fighter planes provided cover. The German army was unable to prevent the advance of the Allies. On **Aug. 25, 1944**, Paris was liberated. Germany's last attempt to break the Allied stranglehold in the Ardennes failed. Aachen became the first major German city to fall on Oct. 21, 1944. Despite the hopeless situation, the Nazi leadership continued to propagate resistance at all costs.

American soldiers landing in Normandy

The Battle for Berlin

Although the war had been lost for Germany, Hitler ordered his troops to stand their ground and defend Berlin to the last bullet.

The last great battle of the war began on April 6, 1945. The Red Army, with a total of 2.5 million soldiers and 9,000 tanks, marched into Berlin. Hitler and his staff took refuge in an underground bunker under the German Chancellery. Although the situation was hopeless and the German troops, consisting of youth and old men, were undermanned and too ill-equipped, the Nazi leadership called for further resistance. The battle for the Reich's capital proved to be the most costly of the Second World War. Tens of thousands of Red Army soldiers and Germans, contesting every street and house, lost their lives in an inferno that lasted almost three weeks. On **April 30**, the day of Hitler's suicide, a red flag finally waved over the destroyed Reichstag. On **May 7–9**, the German Wehrmacht declared unconditional surrender.

The red flag on the Berlin Reichstag as a symbol of the Soviet Union's victory

Hiroshima

The most costly war in history to date ended with the deployment of a new type of weapon with unimaginable capabilities for destruction: the atomic bomb.

On **Aug. 6, 1945**, the American bomber *Enola Gay* dropped the world's first atomic bomb on the Japanese city of Hiroshima. Its destructive power was so devastating that it even unsettled the plane's crew. "My God! What have we done?" the pilot later wrote down. Within seconds, the whole city was engulfed in flames. Up to 70,000 people died instantly. The number of casualties later increased to a hundred thousand succumbing to long-term complications. U.S. President Truman had ordered the mission hoping to convince Japan to surrender and thus avoid total destruction. Ever since rumors of a new German super weapon had emerged, nearly a quarter of a million people, some of the most brilliant physicists and chemists of the 20th century amongst them, had worked feverishly on the secret program to develop the atomic bomb. After the second bomb was dropped on Nagasaki on Aug. 9, Japanese emperor Hirohito finally agreed to unconditional surrender on **Sept. 2, 1945**, officially ending the

The mushroom cloud over Nagasaki after the dropping of the atomic bomb

Second World War. At the same time, the first use of the atomic bomb also marked the beginning of the age of nuclear armaments. The following decades were overshadowed by the awareness of the new super powers, the USA and Soviet Union, and that each was capable of obliterating the other.

1946 French automobile engineer and fashion designer **Louis Réard** invents the **bikini bathing suit** for women and provokes worldwide outrage.

1947 The book *Dialectic of Enlightenment* by German philosophers **Theodor W. Adorno** and **Max Horkheimer** is published in Amsterdam.

1948 The **Vatican** places all the works of **Jean-Paul Sartre** on its Index to spare the faithful from putting "faith and good conduct in danger."

1948 The Japanese city of **Fukui** suffers serious damage on June 28 during a severe **earthquake**.

1948 The **first vinyl records** appear on the music market.

1949 Arthur Miller's drama *Death of a Salesman* has its premiere on Broadway on Feb. 10 in New York.

1949 French philosopher **Simone de Beauvoir** publishes *The Second Sex* in Paris. Her book becomes a standard work of feminist literature.

1951 The definitive study of Nazi and Stalinist totalitarianism, *The Origins of Totalitarianism*, by political theorist **Hannah Arendt**, a German Jew, is published in the USA.

1952 The **USA** detonates a **hydrogen bomb** on Nov. 1 as part of its nuclear testing program.

1952 The premiere of the western *High Noon* starring **Gary Cooper** on April 14 launches a successful wave of western movies in the theaters. *High Noon* is considered to be one of the best films of all time.

1945 — **1950**

1946–1949 A **civil war** rages in **Greece** between Royalists and Communists.

1947 **Truman Doctrine:** On March 12, U.S. President Harry S. Truman urges support for every country whose freedom is "under threat" from Communists.

1947 **U.S. Secretary of State George Marshall** introduces the **Marshall Plan** on June 5. It is designed to aid Europe in restoring its economy.

1947 On Aug. 15, Great Britain grants **India** its **independence**. The country splits into two states, India with a Hindu majority and Pakistan with a Muslim majority.

1947–1949 Chiang Kai-shek's nationalist government forces a fight against the Communists, led by **Mao Zedong**, in the **Chinese civil war.**

1946 Military officer **Juan Péron** is elected the next **president of Argentina** on Feb. 24.

1946 Under pressure from the USA, **Japan ratifies a new constitution** on Nov. 3, put into effect on May 3, 1947. The Emperor loses all influence in political affairs and suffers the loss of his deity-like status.

1946 **Communist resistance fighters led by Ho Chi Minh** launch a war against **French colonial power in Indochina** on Dec. 19.

1948 Soviet occupation forces begin blocking access to **West Berlin** on June 24. General Lucius Clay organizes an **airlift** ("Candy Bomber") to fly in supplies for the population.

1948 The **Republic of South Korea**, headed by President Rhee, is proclaimed in the south of Korea on July 20. Shortly afterwards, the **Communists** proclaim the **People's Republic of Korea** in the north.

1948 After the withdrawl of British troops from Palestine, **Ben Gurion** proclaims the **state of Israel** on May 14 in accordance with the UN's partition plan. A coalition of Arab states refuses to recognize the truce and attacks Israel.

1948 After an election victory in **South Africa** on May 26, the Boer's National Party introduces a systematic **apartheid policy** against the Black population.

1950 The **Korean War** begins on June 25 when North Korean forces invade the territory of South Korea. The intervention of the **USA** on the side of South, and **China** on the side of North, give the conflict international meaning. It becomes the first "hot war" in the **"Cold War of ideologies."**

1950 The **House Committee on Un-American Activities,** originally established in 1937, is revived by Republican Senator **Joseph McCarthy.** Anticommunist hysteria, known as the **"Red Scare,"** has reached its zenith.

1949 The **North Atlantic Treaty Organization** (NATO), under the leadership of the USA, is formed in Washington on April 4. Most European nations become members.

1949 Great Britain, Ireland, France, Italy, Denmark, Sweden, and the Benelux countries found the **Council of Europe** on May 5.

1949 With the formal approval of its Basic Law on May 8, the **Federal Republic of Germany** is constituted on the territory of the three western occupation zones. Konrad Adenauer is chosen the first Federal Chancellor of the new republic.

1949 **Israel** and the **Arab League** finally sign a **general armistice agreement** in Egypt on June 20. Israel emerges with new territorial gains.

1949 The nations within the Soviet bloc join together to form **The Council for Mutual Economic Assistance** (Comecon).

1949 After the Communist victory in China, **Mao Zedong proclaims the People's Republic of China** on Oct. 1.

1949 On Oct. 7, the **German Democratic Republic (GDR) is proclaimed** in the Soviet Occupied Zone with East Berlin as its capital.

1951 On May 23, **China** pledges broad **autonomy** to the **annexed region of Tibet.**

1951 **ANZUS Treaty: Australia**, **New Zealand**, and the **USA** sign a **mutual defence agreement** in San Francisco on Sept. 1.

1951 **Italy grants Libya independence** on Dec. 24. King Idris I becomes head of the new state.

1953 Head of Soviet State and Party **Josef Stalin dies** on March 5 in Moscow. **Nikita Khrushchev** becomes his successor.

1951 France, West Germany, Italy, the Netherlands, and Luxemburg come to agreement on the founding of **The European Coal and Steel Community** (ECSC) on April 18. It is the first step toward an economically united Europe.

1952 On March 10, **General Fulgenico Batista** overthrows the governing Cuban president and establishes a **military dictatorship in Cuba.**

1952 France, Italy, Belgium, and West Germany agree to place their armed forces under a **European Defence Community** (EDC) on May 26–27, but the plan is never brought into effect.

1952 **King Farouk** is overthrown by army officers during the Egyptian Revolution on July 23. Two years later, Colonel **Gamal Abdel Nasser** takes control of the state.

1945-1970

*The ideological conflict between
Capitalism and Communism that had
been smoldering since the Russian
Revolution of 1917 was put on hold
during the Second World War. After
the victory over the Nazis in 1945,
however, the conflict could no longer
be supressed. The Soviet Union
pursued an imperialistic course and
installed repressive regimes in their
Central and Eastern European satellite
states while the USA used predomi-
nately economic means to expand
its reach of influence. The two super
powers faced each other irreconcilably
in a race for military, technological,
and cultural superiority. Several times,
the East-West rivalry threatened to escalate into a serious conflict, but faced
with the prospect of a third world
war, the USA and Soviet Union stayed
on a diplomatic path to mitigate the
crisis. The war remained "cold."*

An American astronaut on a "spacewalk" in
1965

HISTORICAL FIGURES

Mao Zedong (1893-1976) After years of civil wars, the Chinese revolutionary leader united the country in 1949 under the banner of Communism.

Mao had strengthened the Communist movement in the civil war of the 1920s and had built
up a military base in the northeast of China in
1935. His troops began to conquer the entire
country in 1945. The People's Republic was
proclaimed in **1949** and the Communist restructuring of society launched. Re-education
camps, the nationalization of industry, and
the forced collectivization of agriculture cost
the lives of millions of people but did not provide protection against economic failures. In
1966, Mao initiated the "Cultural Revolution"
to enforce socialism. His policies were only
revised after his death in **1976**—but his
political reputation remains untouched
in China to this day.

Willy Brandt (1913-1992) Willy Brandt, a Social Democrat and former resistance fighter against the Nazis, came to power in West Germany in 1969. For his "Ostpolitik" he was honored with the Nobel Peace Prize in 1971.

After Hitler seized power in **1933**, Brandt tried
to establish opposition to the Nazi regime from
his exile in Norway and Sweden. The charismatic visionary returned to Germany after the
war and joined the Social Democratic Party in
1947. From 1957–1966, he gained worldwide
esteem as governing mayor of the divided city
of Berlin. In **1969**, Brandt was the first Social
Democrat to become chancellor. Domestically, he sought to modernize German society
and urged his countrymen to "risk more democracy." To ease tension with neighboring
Communist states, he pursued an accomoda-
tionist policy toward Eastern Europe and the
Soviet Union and signed two treaties in **1970**
to achieve this goal. In the wake of a spy affair,
he resigned from office in 1974 but remained
active in politics for the rest of his life.

John F. Kennedy (1917-1963) The 35th President of the USA embodied the hope of a new beginning and change for a whole generation. His assassination in 1963 shocked millions worldwide.

Kennedy, a Democrat, came from a long Irish
line of politicians. At 43, the Roman Catholic
narrowly won the **1960** presidential election
with his vision of a "New Frontier." He pursued
a modern style of government and developed
far-reaching social reforms. However, his time
in office was overshadowed by the Cold War. He
supported the South Vietnamese against the
Vietcong and unsuccessfully attempted to intervene against Cuba in **1961**. The Cuban Missile Crisis that began in October **1962** brought
the world to the brink of a nuclear war. On
Nov. 22, 1963, Kennedy was shot in Dallas
under mysterious circumstances.

Ernesto "Che" Guevera (1928-1967) The Argentinean revolutionary fighter became the idol of the leftwing protest movement and remains to this day a symbol of the struggle against injustice.

Outraged over the social inequality in Latin
America, Guevara joined the exiled Cuban revolutionaries led by Fidel Castro in 1955. He was
trained in guerrilla combat and became instrumental in overthrowing the Batista dictatorship in Cuba in **1959**. He was rewarded with
the post of president of the national bank in
Castro's revolutionary government. From 1961,
he served as Minister of Industry and sought to
establish a socialist economy and society. With
the goal of initiating revolutionary uprisings in
other countries, Guevara disappeared from the
public eye in 1965. On Oct. 9, 1967, he was murdered in Bolivia by the military.

1962 **Marilyn Monroe**, American actress and worldwide sex symbol, dies on Aug. 5 in Los Angeles allegedly from an overdose of sleeping tablets.

1962 The **first James Bond film** *Dr. No* celebrates its premiere in London on Oct. 5. This launches the most successful film franchise of all time.

1962–1965 Catholic bishops from all over the world gather in Rome for the **Second Vatican Council** and decide on **liberal reforms** in the Church.

1964 Boxer Cassius Clay, who later takes the name **Mohammed Ali**, gains the **world heavyweight title** for the first time in Miami Beach on Feb. 25.

1964–1966 The British rock group *The Beatles* create a storm of excitement among teenagers all around the world.

1966 On March 1, after a flight of three months, a **Soviet space probe** becomes the first manmade object to land on the **planet Venus**.

1967 South African surgeon **Christiaan Barnard** performs the **first successful heart transplant** in Cape Town on Dec. 3.

1968 Pop artist **Andy Warhol** is badly injured in an assassination attempt on June 3.

1969 On July 20, American astronauts **Neil Armstrong** and **Edwin Aldrin** become the first men to land on the moon.

1969 The **Woodstock Festival** takes place on Aug. 15–17. It becomes a legend of the Hippie generation.

1965   **1970**

1960 On Nov. 8, the 43-year-old Democrat **John F. Kennedy** is **elected president of the USA,** narrowly beating Republican contender Richard Nixon.

1962 After an eight-year war, **Algeria** gains its **independence** from France. A truce had been previously signed on March 18 between France and the Algerian nationalists.

1965 General **Suharto** seizes power in Indonesia with a coup in March. He establishes a pro-Western, authoritarian regime that takes extreme measures against any opposition.

1967 The **European Economic Community** (EEC) of France, Italy, the FRG, and the Benelux countries comes into operation on July 1. In addition, the formation of a **Council of Ministers** is decided upon.

1967–1969 A **student protest movement** rapidly spreads in Western countries. It had emerged in the **USA**, particularly in reaction to the Vietnam War, questioning traditional authority and values.

"No one has any intention of building a wall."

Walter Ulbricht, Chairman of the Council of State of the GDR, on June 15, 1961

1965 **Singapore** secedes from the Malaysian Federation on Aug. 9 and **becomes an independent city-state**.

1966 **Indira Ghandi** is sworn in as India's **Prime Minister** on Jan. 24.

1968 American civil rights activist **Martin Luther King is murdered** by a White supremacist in Memphis on April 4.

1961 **South Rhodesia** is **expelled from the Commonwealth of Nations** on March 15 because of its Apartheid policy.

1962 **Adolf Eichmann**, a central figure in organizing the Holocaust, is **executed** on May 31 **in Israel**. He had been condemned to death in 1961 after a months-long trial that had attracted worldwide attention.

1966 On Feb. 24, **Ghana's President**, Kwame Nkrumah, is overthrown by a military coup while on a state visit to Vietnam.

1968 On Aug. 20–21, Soviet troops march into **Czechoslovakia** and end the **"Prague Spring."** The government of Alexander Dubcek had been following a course of liberal reform since January.

1961 **The Bay of Pigs Invasion:** From April 14–20, the USA tries, in vain, to overthrow Fidel Castro with the help of Cuban exiles. As a result, Cuba becomes more closely linked to the Soviet Union.

1963 The **March on Washington** in August marks the highpoint of the **Black Civil Rights Movement** in the USA led, by Martin Luther King Jr.

1966 Party Chairman Mao Zedong calls for a **Great Proletarian Cultural Revolution** in **China** on May 16. It is meant to strengthen Mao's position and to accomplish the objectives of the class struggle.

1970 To normalize relations, the **FRG** concludes treaties with the **Soviet Union** and **Poland** on Aug. 12 and Dec. 7, renouncing the use of force.

1961 On the initiative of India, Egypt, and Yugoslavia, the **first conference of non-aligned states** is held in Belgrade from Sept. 1–6. The 25 participating states demand disarmament and direct negotiations between the USA and the Soviet Union.

1963 U.S. President **John F. Kennedy is assassinated** in Dallas on Nov. 22.

1967 On Jan. 27, the USA, the Soviet Union, and Great Britain sign an agreement on the **peaceful use of outer space**.

1969 On Sept. 1, a small group of military officers led by **Muammar Gaddafi** overthrow King Idris I and proclaim a republic in Libya.

1970 **Salvador Allende** is elected **president of Chile** on Sept. 4. His socialist administration attempts to reshape society and the economy in a democratic manner.

1962 The USA and the Soviet Union come to the brink of nuclear war in October over the **stationing of Soviet missile bases in Cuba**.

1964 On Aug. 7, the U.S. Congress passes a joint resolution requested by President Johnson to give military support to the government of South Vietnam **against guerrilla attacks by the Communist Vietcong**.

1967 After a coup in **Greece**, the rightwing military, led by **Colonel Papadópoulos**, establishes an authoritarian military regime on April 21.

1964 The participants in an Arab summit meeting (Sept. 5–11) recognize the **Palestinian Liberation Organization** (PLO) as the official representatives of the Palestinian people.

1967 In the **Six-Day War** (June 5–11), Israel annexes West Jerusalem, the Golan Heights, the West bank, the Gaza Strip, and the Sinai.

1969 When Tage Erlander resigns from office as **Prime Minister of Sweden, Olof Palme** takes his place on Oct. 9.

1970 **Black September:** Bloody clashes erupt between the **army of King Hussein and militant units of the PLO in Jordan** between Sept. 16–27. The PLO is driven out of the country.

1953 On May 29, New Zealand mountain climber **Edmund Hillary** and Tenzing Norgay become the first to climb the highest mountain in the world, **Mount Everest**.

1955 American actor **James Dean** dies at the age of 24 in an automobile accident on Sept. 30 in California. He posthumously becomes a **teenage idol**.

1956–1958 The popularity of the "King of Rock'n Roll," **Elvis Presley**, reaches its peak.

1957 French philosopher, novelist, and journalist **Albert Camus** is awarded the **Nobel Prize for Literature** for his oeuvre.

1960 The **first birth-control pill** is introduced to the U.S. market.

1953 The **first color television** is introduced in the **USA**.

1954 On July 15, the prototype of a **Boeing 707** takes off in the USA. The modern plane subsequently becomes the most used passenger aircraft.

1957 The philosophical work by **Karl Popper**, *The Open Society and Its Enemies*, is published in German.

1957 On Oct. 4, the **Soviet Union** places **Sputnik**, the first artificial satellite, in orbit around the earth.

1958 On July 29, the **National Aeronautics and Space Administration** (NASA) is established.

1961 Soviet pilot and **cosmonaut Juri Gagarin** becomes the **first man in space to orbit the earth** on April 12.

1955 **1960**

1953 **Elizabeth II** is crowned **Queen of Great Britain** in Westminster Abbey in London on June 2.

1953 **Workers stage an uprising in a number of East German cities on June 17**. However, the strikes and demonstrations for free elections are violently suppressed by Soviet military forces.

1955 At a conference in **Bandung**, Indonesia, held on April 18–24, 29 non-aligned African and Asian states **demand the end of colonial rule**.

1955 **West Germany** (FRG) gains its **sovereignty** when the General Treaty goes into effect on May 5. Four days later, the FRG is given a **seat in the UN**.

1957 To further Western Europe's economic integration, France, the Benelux countries, and the GFR join together to form the **European Economic Community** (EEC) and **European Atomic Energy Community** (Euratom) on March 25.

1957 The UN General Assembly unanimously elects former Swedish Foreign Minister **Dag Hammarskjöld Secretary General of the United Nations**.

1959 On Jan.1, after years of guerrilla fighting, **social revolutionary Fidel Castro seizes power in Cuba**. Establishing socialist reforms, he expropriates the big land owners and nationalizes foreign assets.

1959 In March, a nationalist uprising in **Tibet** is bloodily suppressed by Chinese troops. The **Dalai Lama** is forced to flee into exile to India.

1960 During the **"Year of Africa,"** 17 European colonies are granted **independence**, among them Cameroon, Congo, and Nigeria.

1960 To safeguard their economic interests, the oil exporting countries, **Iran, Iraq, Kuwait, Saudi Arabia,** and **Venezuela**, found the **Organization of Oil Exporting Countries (OPEC)** on Sept. 14.

1953 **Hostilities** in the **Korean War** are **ended** by an armistice on July 27. A peace treaty is not signed.

1953 **Shah Resa Pahlevi** seizes back **power in Iran** with the aid of the American Secret Service in August and ousts Prime Minister Mohammad Mosaddegh from office.

1954 After a military defeat at the hands of the Viet Minh militia on July 21, **France is forced to give up its colony in Indochina**.

1954 On Nov. 1, the **Nationalists** in **Algeria** begin their **struggle against French colonial power** that continues until 1962.

1955 The Roman Catholic **Ngo Dinh Diem** becomes the first president of **South Vietnam** on Oct. 26. He later establishes a dictatorship.

1956 Within the context of **de-Stalinization**, Khrushchev condemns the personality cult of and tyrannical misuse of power by dictator Stalin in his "secret speech" during a CPSU congress meeting.

1956 An **uprising** against Soviet rule flares up in **Hungary** on Oct. 23. The country leaves the Warsaw Pact. In a large-scale military offensive, Soviet troops crush the revolution in November.

1955 As a **counterweight to NATO**, the Soviet Union and its eastern European satellites join together to form a military alliance, the **Warsaw Pact**, on May 14 in the Polish capital of Warsaw.

1956 **Suez Crisis:** Following Egypt's nationalization of the Suez Canal on Oct. 29, the French, British, and Israeli attack the country, but are forced to withdraw a short time later, bowing to pressure from the Soviet Union and the USA.

1957 The independent **Republic of Ghana** is created out of the Gold Coast and British Togo on March 6. It is the **first Black African country to gain independence** from the European colonial powers. Its first president is Kwame Nkrumah, a proponent of Pan-Africanism.

1958 **Industrialization** and **mandatory collectivization** are forcibly implemented in **China**. The **"Great Leap Forward"** leads into a famine catastrophe that costs millions of people their lives.

1958 France adopts a new constitution on Sept. 28, in which the president's position is strengthened. On Dec. 21, **Charles de Gaulle** becomes the first president of the **Fifth Republic**.

1961 On Aug. 13, the **East German (GDR) leadership in Berlin** begins sealing off the borders to the Western sector by **building a wall** through the center of the city. It is meant to stop the flow of refugees into the western zones.

HISTORICAL EVENTS

Khrushev Thaw
The de-Stalinization that began in the Soviet Union under Communist Party leader Khrushchev in 1953 raised false hopes in the Eastern Bloc.

Nikita Khrushchev's "secret speech" at the 20th Congress of the Communist Party of the Soviet Union in 1956 elicited incredulous astonishment at home and abroad. Its content was a sensation because Stalin's former protégée distanced himself from his regime and condemned the terror and personality cult as a "criminal" deviation from socialism. Right after Stalin's death in **March 1953**, the new Soviet leadership under Khrushchev began to mitigate the repressive nature of domestic politics. Amnesties were granted, production of consumer products increased, and liberalizing measures introduced. The half-baked reforms, however, were stalled and never challenged the dictatorial Soviet system as such. Moreover, the Soviet Union continued to assert absolute authority over its puppet states. In November **1956**, Soviet troops crushed a political uprising in Hungary, and Imre Nagy's reformed Communist government was replaced by more loyal cadres. Later, during the Prague Spring in **1968**, the Soviet leadership mercilessly suppressed any attempt at political emancipation by its satellite states.

President Eisenhower receives Nikita Khrushchev in the USA in 1959.

Suez Crisis
With the military occupation of the Suez Canal in 1956, Great Britain and France attempted to force Egypt to her knees by exercising colonial tactics, but failed miserably.

When Arab Nationalist Nasser came to power in Egypt in 1954, he established military ties with the Soviet Union and supported independence movements in Africa. In **1956**, Egypt nationalized the strategically important Suez Canal, prompting Britain and France to attack in protection of their economic interests. Their ally, Israel, occupied the Sinai Peninsula. Although the military operation was successful, the aggressors were forced by the USA and the Soviet Union to withdraw their troops from the region by 1957. The canal territory was placed under UN protection. The political winner was Nasser, who was able to present himself as a champion of anti-colonialism.

An Indian UN soldier on the Suez Canal

Congolese celebrating their independence

The Year of Africa
17 African colonies gained their independence in one year, 1960.

Following the Second World War, strong nationalist movements emerged on the African continent that led to the independence of most colonies after **1960**. With the exception of Kenya, where the Mau Mau uprising cost many lives between 1950 and 1957, and Algeria, where the National Liberation Front waged a bitter war against the French between **1954** and **1962**, the decolonization process proceeded relatively peacefully in all countries. Beginning with Ghana, under the charismatic pan-African leader Kwame Nkrumah in 1957, the British colonies became, in quick succession, sovereign members of the Commonwealth—like Nigeria in **1960**. In the same year, France granted independence to a majority of its possessions in Western and Central Africa as well. Portugal alone fought long wars to retain its colonies. It was not until 1975 that Angola and Mozambique gained independence. To this day, the former colonies suffer from the consequences of ruthless exploitation and the arbitrary drawing of borders by the European powers.

A Soviet and an American warship in the Atlantic in November 1962.

Cuban Missile Crisis
The Cold War boiled into a hot conflict, when the USA and the Soviet Union clashed over Soviet missile bases in Cuba in October 1962.

Fidel Castro's regime on Cuba had been a thorn in America's side since **1959**. Economic blockades and a military intervention in **1961** did not stop the Communist regime from drawing closer to the Soviet Union. The situation escalated when the CIA discovered launching sites for Soviet medium-range missiles on Cuban soil in October **1962**. President Kennedy publicly demanded the withdrawal of the Soviets. A sea blockade was imposed around Cuba, and the military was placed on red alert. Unperturbed, the Soviet leadership sent a naval fleet toward Cuba. The world was on the brink of a third world war. Only after tense negotiations did Khrushchev remove the rockets and call the ships back. In turn, the USA later withdrew its missiles from Turkey. Eventually, the crisis led to first efforts to diffuse tension between the governments of both countries.

Injured South Vietnamese children fleeing from their village after an American napalm attack.

The Vietnam War
America's open military intervention in the Vietnam conflict from 1964 developed into a military and moral disaster for the superpower.

Ever since Ho Chi Minh had proclaimed a people's republic in North Vietnam in 1945, the unity and political direction of the country had been the subject of harsh dispute. The partitioning of Vietnam in 1954 began to be undermined in 1957 by Communist guerrilla forces successfully waging war in the pro-West South. Since the USA wanted to prevent the spread of Communist regimes in the region, they directly intervened in the conflict on the side of the South in **1964**. Despite technological superiority and massive military operations, the Americans were unable to gain a decisive victory. Instead, their war crimes, like the massacre in My Lai or the use of napalm, sparked increasing outrage, especially in the West. By **1973**, American troops had been pulled out of South Vietnam, whereupon the South Vietnamese army finally collapsed. By **1975**, all of Vietnam was under Communist rule.

Student Movements
Protest movements that formed in the mid-1960s led to permanent cultural changes and a fundamental liberalization in many Western societies.

The USA's deepening military involvement in the Vietnam War spawned a student protest movement in the 1960s that quickly spread to other countries, particularly to Western Europe, and eventually led to a fundamental opposition to the existing political conditions. The students in the USA allied themselves with the Black civil rights movement. In Europe, the protesters demanded a democratization of society under the banner of socialism. Protests against the "establishment" and the "ruling authoritarian structures" were successful in launching processes of social liberalization in many places in the 1970s. Non-conformist clothing and music symbolized resistance to traditional values, and the pacifist "Hippies" lived the credo of "sex, drugs and rock 'n' roll."

Students from the Sorbonne in Paris protesting against conditions in Western society.

Prague Spring
Soviet troops marched into Czechoslovakia in August 1968, putting a brutal end to Alexander Dubcek's attempt to establish "socialism with a human face."

In the course of the 1960s, economic problems and the extreme ossification of state and society sparked reform efforts within Czechoslovakia's Communist Party. In **1968**, Alexander Dubcek was elected head of the party and state. He immediately launched a comprehensive democratization process—without leaving the socialist path. With the large backing of the Czech population, his government introduced liberalizing reforms. The Soviet Union was alarmed. Dubcek's refusal to rescind the measures prompted Moscow to decide on military intervention. In order to "protect socialist society," Soviet forces and other Warsaw Pact contingents invaded Czechoslovakia on **Aug. 20–21, 1968** and occupied the country. The reforms were repealed and Dubcek was removed from office in April 1969.

Demonstrators attempting to stop the advance of Soviet tanks in Prague.

Neil Armstrong saluting the American flag on the moon.

Space Race
Eager to win the competition for supremacy in space, the Soviet Union sent the first man into orbit. The USA, however, was able to land the first man on the moon.

"That's one small step for man, one giant leap for mankind." Over 500 million people huddled around their television sets on **July 20, 1969**, as Neil Armstrong stepped onto the moon and planted an American flag in the lunar dust. Soviet television was silent about the American triumph. The shame was too great for a nation whose ambitious space program had always been a step ahead of the USA and seemed to demonstrate the superiority of the Communist system. On **Oct. 4, 1957**, the Soviet Union had launched the world's first satellite, the *Sputnik*, into orbit and a short time later had sent the first living creature, a dog named Laika, into space. On **April 12, 1961**, Yuri Gagarin became the first man to orbit the earth. Then, in May 1961, President Kennedy announced a new *Apollo* space program and plans to send astronauts to the moon by the end of the decade. By 1972, the Americans had undertaken another five space flights to the moon.

1970 Jimi Hendrix, one of the most influential rock guitarists, dies on Sept. 18 at the age of 27.

1971 The **first ATMs (automatic teller machine)** are put into operation in the USA.

1971 Stanley Kubrick's film, *A Clockwork Orange*, opens.

1972 For the forth time, Belgian professional cyclist **Eddie Merckx** wins the **Tour de France**, the world's most important bicycle race.

1973 British rock group **Pink Floyd** releases their most famous album *Dark Side of the Moon,* on March 24.

1973 The **World Trade Center** is opened in Manhattan on April 4. The "Twin Towers" are for a short time the tallest buildings in the world.

1974 On April 6, Swedish pop group **ABBA** wins the **Eurovision Song Contest** with *Waterloo*, marking the start of their extraordinary international career.

1974 In a spectatcular fight on Oct. 30 in Kinshasa, boxer **Mohammed Ali** beats the undefeated George Foreman by a surprise knockout and **gains the World's Heavyweight title** for a second time.

1975 Punk becomes popular in the **youth culture** of the mid-1970s. Among the best-known punk bands are the Sex Pistols.

1970

1975

1971 On March 26, **East Pakistan splits from West Pakistan** and is internationally recognized in December as the independent, sovereign **Republic of Bangladesh**.

1971 On May 3, **Walter Ulbricht** steps down from his office of First Secretary in **East Germany**. His successor is **Erich Honecker**.

1971 Envoys from France, Great Britain, the USA, and the Soviet Union come to terms **over the special legal status of Berlin** in a **Four Power Agreement** on Sept. 3.

1971 On Dec. 2, **six sheikhdoms** on the Persian Golf join in a federation, the **United Arab Emirates,** and give themselves a constitution.

1972 Soviet Party Chief **Leonid Brezhnev** and U.S. President **Richard Nixon** sign the first **SALT Agreement** in Moscow on May 26, which limits strategic nuclear armament.

1972 On Jan. 30, **"Bloody Sunday,"** 13 unarmed civilians are killed by the British military during a demonstration in **Derry, Northern Ireland.** The British government takes over direct administration of Northern Ireland in March.

1973 Great Britain, Ireland, and **Denmark** join the **European Economic Community** on Jan. 1.

1973 Following a **truce agreement with North Vietnam** on Jan. 28, the **USA pulls its troops out of Vietnam**, while the war between North and South Vietnam continues.

1973 On April 26, the **Soviet Union** launches its **first heavy aircraft carrying cruiser**, the Kiev, in the Black Sea, expanding its armament race with the USA over all the world's seas.

1973 The first meeting of the **Conference on Security and Co-operation in Europe** convenes in Helsinki on July 3.

1973 **Oil Crisis:** In protest of the pro-Israeli policies of Western nations, the **Arab OPEC states** curb oil production in October and spark a deep recession in the industrialized countries.

1974 **Watergate Affair:** Due to his involvement in spy operations targeting political foes, **U.S. President Richard Nixon** offers his **resignation** on Aug. 9. His successor is Gerald Ford.

1974 **Carnation Revolution:** With the large backing of the general public, military officers overthrow the dictatorial regime in **Portugal** on April 25 and launch a process of democratization.

1975 A **new constitution** comes into effect in **Sweden** on Jan. 1. The king no longer has parliamentary head of state functions, but is limited to a representative role.

1975 The **Khmer Rouge** conquer the capital of Cambodia, Phnom Penh, on April 17. **Pol Pot** establishes a bloody regime of terror in 1976. Hundreds of thousands of people lose their lives on the "Killing Fields."

"The Games must go on."
IOC President Avery Brundage on September 6, 1972, after the hostage-taking at the Olympic Games in Munich

1974 After failing in an attempted coup in **Cyrus** on July 25, the military regime in **Greece** falls. The country develops into a democracy under Prime Minister **Konstantin Karamanlis**.

1975 **South Vietnam surrenders unconditionally** on April 30 when North Vietnamese troops march into Saigon. On July 2, 1976, both parts of the country are united in the Socialist Republic of Vietnam.

1972 On Feb 21, **Richard Nixon** becomes the **first American President to visit the People's Republic of China**, an important step by both sides to normalizing relations.

1972 **West Germany** and **East Germany** mutually recognize each other's national sovereignty on Dec. 21 in the **Basic Treaty of 1972**. One year later, both German states are given seats in the United Nations.

1972 Members of the Israeli team are taken captive by **Palestinian terrorists** on Sept. 5 during the **Olympic Games in Munich**. The terrorists demand the release of fellow activists held in **Israel**. 16 people, 11 of them captives, die in the botched rescue attempt.

1973 On Sept. 11, a military junta led by General **Augusto Pinochet** and aided by the American secret service, overthrows the socialist government of **Salvador Allende** in Chile.

1973 **Jom Kippur War:** A coalition of Arab states led by **Syria** and **Egypt** stage a surprise attack on **Israel** on Oct. 6, but are repelled far back into their own territory by Israeli troops. A truce is negotiated by the great powers on Oct. 26.

1974 **Guillaume-Affair:** German Chancellor **Willy Brandt** steps down on May 6 because one of his personal assistants, Günter Guillaume, turned out to be a spy. His successor is **Helmut Schmidt**.

1975 35 European and North American states, including the Soviet Union and the USA, sign the **Final Act of the Helsinki Accords** on Aug. 1 in Helsinki.

1975 Dictator **General Franco dies** on Nov. 20 in Madrid. The new **King of Spain, Juan Carlos I,** announces the **democratizatio** of the country.

Between East and West

1970–1990

The intense political tension that had gripped the world since the end of the Second World War relaxed noticeably at the beginning of the 1970s. Although the USA remained far superior to the Soviet Union economically, the nuclear armaments race had led the two super powers into a military stalemate. Since a nuclear attack would inevitably result in self-annihilation, a keen interest in a policy of global détente grew on both sides. Intensified diplomatic relations as well as countless armament protocols and economic treaties give proof to a change in thinking that became manifest in the increasing multipolarity of global politics. Under the shadow of the two superpowers, other countries such as China, France, and even West Germany were gaining international significance. Economic mismanagement as well as political and social inflexibility at all levels increased the pressure for reform in almost all of the Eastern Bloc countries by the 1980s and resulted in a wave of revolutionary upheavals at the end of the decade.

A relic of the Cold War: North and South Korean soldiers, eye to eye, at the Panmunjeom border crossing

HISTORICAL FIGURES

Deng Xiaoping (1904–1997) The pragmatic Communist ruled over China from 1979 to 1997 and opened up the country's economy to the West.

A companion of Mao in the civil war, Deng quickly rose in the ranks after **1949**. In 1955, he became a member of the Politburo. At times, Deng fell out of Mao's favor as he expressed criticism about the excesses of the Cultural Revolution. With Mao's death in **1976**, however, he became the most influential politician in the country. In order to stabilize China, he began to liberalize the economy in 1979. The resulting upswing naturally did not entail a renouncement of the Communists' claim to sole political authority. Deng was mainly responsible for the crushing of the democracy movement on **June 4, 1989**. Even after his retirement from politics in 1990, he retained control over China.

Indira Gandhi (1917–1984) For almost twenty years, the Indian Prime Minister had a decisive influence on the destiny of the world's largest democracy.

Two years after the death of her father, Jawaharlal Nehru, the first prime minister of independent India, Gandhi was sworn in as head of state in **1966**. She continued India's policy as a non-aligned state, but maintained good relations with the Soviet Union. She militarily supported Bangladesh's independence in 1971. Domestically, she sought to modernize the economy and foster social understanding in religiously divided India. Since the mid-1970s, her governance took on authoritarian traits. After an election defeat in 1977, Gandhi was forced to step down but returned to office in 1980. On **Oct. 31, 1984**, she was assassinated.

Olof Palme (1927–1986) Tireless in his efforts to promote disarmament, the Swedish Social Democrat won admiration far beyond Sweden's borders for his non-aligned peace policies.

Palme was born into a conservative upper-class family, but became a committed Social Democrat at an early age. As prime minister from 1969–1976 and 1982–1986, he played a major role in shaping the Swedish welfare state. As "advocate" of the Third World, Palme criticized the imperialism of the superpowers. He was the UN's special mediator in the Iran-Iraq War of **1980–1988** and established Sweden's long-lasting image of neutrality. Between 1980 and 1982, he led the UN disarmament commission named after him. On **Feb. 28, 1986**, Palme was killed in Stockholm by an unknown assailant.

Mikhail Gorbachev (born 1931) The Soviet Party Chief intended to reform the socialist state and social system, but unwillingly triggered the collapse of the Soviet Union.

There can be no doubt about Gorbachev's place in history. In **1985**, he unintentionally set a process in motion that led to the destruction of the Soviet Union. When the party careerist took office as head of state, he called for transparency and more democracy in the inflexible state apparatus. He liberalized the economy, released political prisoners, and promoted public dialogue. He also abandoned the Soviet's position of supreme power within the Eastern Bloc. What was meant to revitalize socialism, however, led in blinding speed to an overall social revolution. The Communist regimes in Central and Eastern Europe fell like dominos in **1989** and the Soviet Union disintegrated. When Gorbachev stepped down on **Dec. 25, 1991**, he had failed as a reformer in his own country, but had liberated many other states.

1983 Luc Montagnier and Françoise Barré-Sinoussi identify the Human immunodeficiency virus (**HIV**) as the cause of **AIDS**.

1984 Archbishop **Desmond Tutu** is awarded the **Nobel Peace Prize** for his non-violent involvement against the apartheid regime of South Africa.

1984 With four gold medals, **American track athlete Carl Lewis** becomes the most outstanding athlete at the 23rd Olympic Summer Games in Los Angeles.

1985 **Boris Becker**, a 17-year-old German, is the surprise winner of the Tennis World Championships in **Wimbledon** on July 7.

1986 The **U.S. space shuttle** *Challenger* explodes one minute after takeoff on Jan. 28; all seven astronauts on board are lost.

1986 On April 26, a **nuclear reactor** explodes in the Ukrainian nuclear power plant in **Chernobyl**. It is the worst disaster in the history of the peaceful use of nuclear energy.

1987 Artist **Andy Warhol**, co-founder and a main representative of **American Pop Art**, dies on Feb. 22 in New York.

1988 On Dec. 21, an onboard **bomb explosion** causes Pan Am Flight 103 to crash into the Scottish village of **Lockerbie**. A total of 270 people die as the result of the terrorist attack.

1989 A **glass pyramid** by Chinese-American architect **Ieoh Ming Pei** is unveiled in the inner courtyard of the **Louvre** in **Paris** on March 29.

1989 Herbert von Karajan, one of the **most famous conductors** of his day, dies on July 16 in Anif near Salzburg.

1985 ———————————————— **1990**

1983 On July 23, a **civil war** breaks out in **Sri Lanka** between Buddhist Singhalese and Hindu Tamils.

1983 On Aug. 10, **France**, the former colonial power, intervenes in the **civil war** in **Chad**; the country is de facto divided.

1983 On Oct. 25, **American forces** occupy the Caribbean island-state of **Grenada**.

1983 **Military rule ends in Argentina** on Dec. 10 when democratically elected president, Rául Alfonsíns, takes office.

1984 The death of Yuri Andropov elevates the ailing **Konstantin Chernenko** to leadership of the Soviet Communist Party on Feb. 13.

1984 Indian Prime Minister **Indira Ghandi** is shot to death by radical Sikhs in New Delhi on Oct. 31. Religious tension in the country intensifies.

1984 After eleven years of military rule, **free elections** are held in **Uruguay** on Nov. 25.

1985 The eleven-year military dictatorship in Uruguay ends with **Julyo María Sanguinetti**'s victory in the presidential election.

1985 When **Chernenko dies** on March 10, 54-year-old **Mikhail Gorbachev** becomes the new Party Chief in the **Soviet Union**. He launches a comprehensive program of social and economic liberalization.

1985 Under pressure from a **popular democratic movement**, the 21-year military dictatorship in **Brazil** ends on Jan. 15.

1986 **Spain** and **Portugal** become members of **EEC** on Jan. 1.

1986 Unrest causes Philippine Dictator **Ferdinand Marcos** to flee on Feb. 25. **Corazón Aquino** becomes president.

1986 Swedish politician **Olof Palme is assassinated** on Feb. 28 in Stockholm. The perpetrator is never apprehended.

1986 By lauching air strikes on the **Libyan cities of Tripoli** and **Benghazi** on April 15, the **USA** retaliates for Libya's support of terror attacks.

1986 Due to his Nazi past, the election of **Kurt Waldheim** as **president of Austria** on June 8 sparks a governmental crisis.

1987 On July 4, **Nazi collaborator Klaus Barbie** is sentenced to life imprisonment in Lyon.

1987 **First Intifada: A Palestinian uprising** erupts in December in the Israeli-occupied West Jordan territory and the Gaza Strip. Israel responds with armed force. In 1988, **PLO leader Yasser Arafat** proclaims the autonomous state of Palestine.

1987 On Dec. 8, Soviet Party Chief **Gorbachev** and U.S. President **Reagan** sign the INF Treaty on the complete elimination of intermediate-range and shorter-range missiles.

1988 The **Soviet Union** begins its **withdrawal of troops from Afghanistan** on May 15, which is completed nine months later.

1988 Reform-orientated **Károly Grósz** is appointed **prime minister in Hungary** on May 22.

1988 The warring parties in **Angola** agree to a **truce** in August after 13 years of **civil war**.

1988 **Iran** and **Iraq** lay **down their weapons** on Aug. 20, thus ending the Iran-Iraq War that had been raging since 1980.

1989 The **Chinese democratic opposition movement**, primarily supported by students, is bloodily crushed in Tiananmen Square in **Beijing** on June 4.

1989 On June 4, Solidarnosc, the Polish workers' union, wins the majority in the **first free elections held in Poland** since the Second World War.

1989 The **East German leadership opens the borders** to West Berlin and West Germany on the night of Nov. 9. A few weeks later, the **Socialist Unity Party's dictatorship collapses**.

1989 On Dec. 25, **Romanian State President Ceausescu** is sentenced to death by a military court and executed.

1989 On Oct. 23, **Hungary declares itself a Democratic Republic**. After the country had opened its borders to Austria in May of the same year, the flight of East German citizens to the West reaches epic proportions.

1975 Film director **Pier Paolo Pasolini**'s confrontational Fascist film parable, *The 120 Days of Sodom*, provokes worldwide controversy because of its open depiction of violence.

1976 On April 1, **Steve Jobs** and **Steve Wozniak** found the **Apple** computer company in the USA.

1977 On May 25, *Star Wars* celebrates its premiere in New York. The **science fiction saga** by **George Lucas** becomes an icon of pop culture.

1977 Greek soprano **Maria Callas dies** in Paris on Sept. 16. She is considered the most important opera singer of the 20th century.

1978 Following the death of Pope Paul VI, Polish Bishop **Karol Wojtyła** is **elected pope** on Oct. 16. He chooses the name **John Paul II** and is the first non-Italian Pope in 455 years.

1979 The **first World Climate Conference** meets in Geneva from Feb. 12–23.

1980 In protest of the **Soviet invasion of Afghanistan in late December 1979**, the USA leads a boycott of Western nations of the **22nd Summer Olympic Games in Moscow**.

1981 The musical *Cats* has its premiere on May 11 in London.

1981 Over 750 million people worldwide witness the televised **royal wedding** of **British Crown Prince Charles** and **Lady Diana Spencer** at St. Paul's Cathedral in London on July 29.

1982 The **Nobel Prize for Literature** is awarded to the Columbian **Gabriel José García Márquez**.

1982 **Michael Jackson** releases the world's best selling album, *Thriller*, on Nov. 30.

1980

1976 On March 24, Argentine President **Isabel Péron** is ousted and placed under house arrest. A military junta, led by General Jorge Videla, takes over power in **Argentina**.

1976 An **uprising** against the **apartheid regime** that started on June 16 in Soweto spreads across **South Africa**.

1976 **Mao Zedong dies** on Sept. 8 in China. The new Party Chief, Hua Guofeng, cautiously begins to de-radicalize the party's policies.

1976 On Sept. 19, **Thorbjörn Fälldin** becomes the first **non-Social Democrat** in 40 years to be elected **prime minister** in Sweden.

1976 Democrat **James Earl "Jimmy" Carter** wins the U.S. presidential elections on Nov. 2.

1977 The terror of the **Red Army Fraction (RAF)** reaches its zenith in West Germany with the murder of several high-ranking businessmen, like Hanns-Martin Schleyer.

1977 The Spanish lawyer and politician **Adolfo Suárez** is elected prime minister on June 15 **in the first free elections in Spain** in over 40 years.

1977 On July 5, **General Mohammed Zia ul-Haq** seizes power in **Pakistan** in a bloodless coup.

1977 On Dec. 4, the president of the **Central African Republic**, **Jean-Bédel Bokassa**, crowns himself emperor.

1978 Following a military putsch in **Afghanistan** on April 27, a left-wing Democratic Republic is proclaimed.

1978 **China** and **Japan** sign a treaty of peace and friendship on Aug. 12.

1978 After thirteen days of acrimonious debate, **Egyptian President Anwar El Sadat** and **Israeli Prime Minister Begin** sign a **peace agreement** negotiated by American President Jimmy Carter in **Camp David** on Sept. 17. The two nations take up diplomatic relations.

1979 Vietnamese forces capture the Cambodian capital Pnom Penh on Jan. 8, **ending the terror regime of Pol Pot**. The followers of the **Khmer Rouge** go underground.

1979 When **Shah Resa Pahlevi flees Iran**, Iranian religious leader **Ayatollah Khomeini** returns to Teheran from his exile in Paris on Feb. 1. On April 1, he proclaims an **Islamic Republic** in Iran.

1979 **Margaret Thatcher** becomes **British prime minister** on May 3. She is the first woman to hold the office.

1979 **Direct elections to the European parliament** are held for the first time from June 7–10 in the member states of the EEC.

1979 On July 16, **Saddam Hussein** takes over power in Iraq and proceeds to establish a dictatorial regime.

1979 **Deng Xiaoping**, who has gained the leading position in China's Communist State Party, **opens the country's economy to the West**. The Party's sole supremacy over China remains untouched.

1979 On Dec. 27, **Soviet troops march into Afghanistan** to prevent a seizure of power by Islamic-oriented militias and keep the country pro-Communist. Resistance fighters, particularly the Muslim **Mujahideen**, involve the Soviet troops in a costly guerrilla war over the next couple of years.

1980 The **leftist government** junta in **El Salvador** declares martial law in the country on March 7.

1980 The South African state of **South Rhodesia** officially gains independence from Great Britain on April 18 and is renamed **Zimbabwe**. **Robert Mugabe** is elected the first president.

1980 On Sept. 12, General Staff Chief Kenan Evren takes power in **Turkey** after a **military putsch**.

1980 The **Iran-Iraq War** erupts over border disputes, political differences, and religious schisms on Sept. 22 when Iraqi troops march into Iran.

1980 **Solidarnosc** (Solidarity), the first freely organized Polish workers' union led by **Lech Wałesa**, is founded in Oct.–Nov. Advocating non-violence, it becomes the focal point of political opposition against the Communist regime in Poland.

1981 **Greece** becomes a member of the EEC on Jan. 1.

1981 **Ronald Reagan**, a staunch anticommunist, is sworn in as **U.S. President** on Jan. 20. At first, he pursues a policy of military might vis-à-vis the Soviet Union.

1981 The **civil war in El Salvador** between the military regime of José Duarte and left-wing guerrilla fighters escalates.

1981 On Oct. 6, **Egyptian President Anwar El Sadat** is murdered in Cairo by opponents of his policy of rapprochement with Israel. **Hosni Mubarak** follows him as president.

1981 Under Soviet pressure, head of state General **Jaruzelski** declares martial law in **Poland** on Dec. 12. The workers' union Solidarnosc is banned.

1982 Argentine forces capture the British-ruled **Falkland Islands**, an archipelago in the South Atlantic Ocean, on April 1 but are forced to withdraw after a successful British military operation in June.

1982 Israeli forces march into **Lebanon** on June 6 and destroy PLO military bases in Beirut. The Israelis pull out again in May 1983.

1982 The **Socialists**, who have won the parliamentary elections of Oct. 28, form a government in **Spain** for the first time in 40 years. Prime Minister Felipe González remains in office until 1996.

1982 Soviet head of state and party chief **Leonid Brezhnev** dies on Nov. 10 in Moscow. Yuri Andropov takes his place.

HISTORICAL EVENTS

Political Terrorism
The use of terror for political or ideological ends has increased since the late 1960s and continues to be a threat to the social order worldwide.

At the onset of the media age, groups with little or no direct power used acts of violence to bring their political demands to public attention. The Palestine Liberation Organization (PLO) led by Yasser Arafat, for example, began staging spectacular acts of terror and airplane hijackings in 1968. The terrorist attack during the Olympic Games in Munich in **1972** in which 16 people lost their lives, including 11 Israeli athletes, gained tragic notoriety. The PLO actually earned recognition as representing the interests of the Palestinian people in 1974. The actions of other political groups, however, usually remained ineffective. The attempts by splinter groups like the RAF to destabilize the "capitalistic system" in Germany and Italy in the 1970s were unsuccessful. So was the terror being perpetrated

Police securing the Olympic Village in 1972

by ETA, a Basque nationalist organization, in their fight for an autonomous homeland separate from the rest of Spain.

Kissinger, Brezhnev, Ford, and Gromyko at the Helsinki Accords in Finland

Helsinki Accords-Final Act
The Final Act of the Helsinki Accords signed in 1975 marks the highpoint of détente during the East-West conflict.

Parallel to the start of the disarmament talks, a conference initiated by the Warsaw Pact on security and cooperation in Europe (Helsinki Accords) was held in **1973** in an attempt to improve relations between the Communist bloc and the West. On **Aug. 1, 1975**, the governments of 32 European countries as well as the USA, Canada, and the Soviet Union signed the Final Act of the Helsinki Accords in Finland. By contemporaries, its contents were initially in-

terpreted as a success for the Eastern Bloc as the signatories had agreed upon a deepening of economic cooperation and the inviolability of existing borders. The postwar borders had been officially recognized for the first time. Even more significant was the affirmation of human rights and national self-determination by the Warsaw Pact states. However, the accords were not binding and no institutions were established to monitor the agreements.

Followers of Ayatollah Khomeini cheering his coming to power in Teheran

The Iranian Revolution
After the overthrow of the Shah's regime in the spring of 1979, the religious leader Ayatollah Khomeini established an Islamic theocracy in Iran.

In the mid-1970s, the government of Iran suffered a legitimation crisis. The economic and cultural modernization, essentially guided by the USA and implemented by Shah Mohammad Resa Pahlevi over the objections of conservative religious circles, ignored cultural traditions and deepened social antagonism. The Shi'ite clergy surrounding the charismatic Ayatollah Khomeini, who was exiled in Paris, took the lead of a heterogeneous opposition

movement. The Shah was finally forced to flee the country in **Jan. 1979**. The following month, Khomeini installed a dictatorial system in Iran that passed virtually unlimited political power to the religious leaders. Bit by bit, public and private life was subjugated to Islamic fundamentalism. The change had severe consequences as the cultivated country once allied with the West became a radical theocracy in bitter opposition to the USA.

Camp David Accords
Egypt became the first Arab country to sign a peace accord with Israel on March 26, 1979.

Following the Jom Kippur War in October **1973**, the fronts between Israel and the Arab states in the Near East conflict began to crumble. Egypt, led by Anwar El Sadat, was leaning to the West and cautiously seeking a conciliation with Israel through U.S. Secretary of State Henry Kissinger. On **Sept. 17, 1978**, after twelve days of negotiations in Camp David, the country retreat of U.S. President Carter, a breakthrough was achieved. The peace accord provided for the withdrawal of Israeli forces from the Sinai and the opening of diplomatic relations. For their commitment, Sadat and Israeli Prime Minister Begin were both awarded the Nobel Peace Prize in 1978. However, for breaking ranks with the anti-Israel coaltion, the Egyptian president had to pay with his life. On **Oct. 6, 1981**, he was murdered by an Islamist. Although his successor, Hosni Mubarak, sought to achieve a rapprochement with the other Arab states and a reinstatement of Egypt's leadership position in the Arab camp, he continued the pragmatic peace policy toward Israel until he was deposed in 2011.

Carter, Begin, and Sadat in Camp David in 1978

Solidarnosc
In 1980, striking workers in Poland gained permission for the first time to establish unions free and independent of the Communist state authority.

In the summer of **1980**, Polish workers nationwide laid down their work and demanded the right to establish free unions. The Communist state party was on the defensive. The economic situation had dramatically worsened, and the new pope, a Pole by birth, had given an enormous boost to the reform movement in the Catholic population during his visit in 1979. In hopes of calming the situation, the Communists recognized Solidarnosc, an independent union led by Lech Wałesa. When the throng of workers joining the organization did not subside and the Soviet Union threatened with military intervention, Prime Minister Jaruzelski declared martial law in Poland on **Dec. 12, 1981**, outlawed the union, and arrested its leaders. However, the democratic movement could no longer be stopped. Official negotiations between government and opposition led to political change in the summer of 1988.

Demonstrators holding a banner for Solidarnosc, Poland's first free workers' union.

Chernobyl
The rupture of a reactor vessel in an outdated nuclear plant in the Soviet Union unleashed a devastating catastrophe in 1986.

The worst reactor accident to date happened on **April 26, 1986**. A block of the Chernobyl nuclear plant 80 miles north of Kiev had exploded during a poorly conducted test and enormous amounts of nuclear material were released. Information about the disaster was withheld from the public at first. The Soviet Union only initiated rescue operations after a radioactive cloud had spread over Scandinavia toward Western Europe. Thousands of disaster aid workers died from high doses of radiation, but the long term effects of the accident remain unclear even today. A restricted area is still maintained around Chernobyl. The catastrophe added strength to the position of the opponents of nuclear energy and in turn the green movement that has become increasingly popular since the oil crisis of **1973**. In view of the limited availability of natural resources, environmental topics have gained significance.

Chernobyl nuclear plant's reactor destroyed by a super-GAU in present-day Ukraine

INF Treaty
On Dec. 8, 1987, U.S. President Ronald Reagan and Soviet General Secretary Mikhail Gorbachev signed the first real disarmament treaty in history.

When Ronald Reagan was inaugurated in **1981**, hardly anyone could have foreseen the the role he would play in the disarmament process. On the contrary, the strict anticommunist at first pursued a policy of confronting the Soviet Union with military strength. In this vein, he proposed the Strategic Defense Initiative (Star Wars) in 1983 and had the new U.S. medium-ranged missiles (Pershing-II) stationed in Europe. That signaled the next round in the arms race. It was not until Gorbachev, the new Soviet Party leader, took office in **1985** that a change in thought occurred. When Gorbachev suggested far-reaching disarmament measures to take pressure from the process of domestic political reform, he came a long way in accommodating the USA. The INF Treaty of **1987** was a milestone in armament control.

For the first time, not just limits to the number or deployment of the weapons were agreed upon but their actual destruction. By May 1991, all land-based nuclear medium-range missiles in Europe had been systematically destroyed.

Ronald Reagan and Mikhail Gorbachev signing the INF Treaty

Thousands of Germans celebrating the fall of the Berlin Wall in front of Brandenburg Gate

1989 – The Year of Change
The fall of the Berlin Wall on Nov. 9, 1989, was the symbolic high point of the democratic revolution that had toppled Communist regimes in Eastern Europe since summer.

When Gorbachev introduced a reform course in the Soviet Union in 1985, the people in the Eastern Bloc nations became emboldened enough to demand democratic change from their governments. Poland, where the Communists had given up their monopoly of power in April 1989, was at the vanguard of the revolution. On **Aug. 24, 1989**, Tadeusz Mazowiecki became the first non-Communist head of government in a Warsaw Pact state. A multiple-party system was established in Hungary in **Oct. 1989**. The Communist leadership in Czechoslovakia, Bulgaria, and Albania quit after November in the face of mass protests. The brutal Ceausescu dictatorship in Romania was overthrown in Dec. 1989. Prior to that, on **Nov. 9**, the Berlin Wall, the symbol of a divided Europe, had fallen. Ever since Hungary had begun to dismantle the fortifications along its border to Austria in May of the same year, thousands of East German citizens had been taking this path to the West, forcing the East German leadership, unwilling to reform, to open their borders. The Iron Curtain was history.

1990 The **Internet,** whose origins reach back to the 1960s, begins to revolutionize information exchange and the way people communicate. By 2008, more than a **billion people** worldwide are using the World Wide Web.

1993 On Jan. 1, the agreement on a single **economic zone** within the **European Community (EC)** between member states goes into effect.

1993 The **Hassan II Mosque** is opened in Casablanca on Aug. 30. It has the highest minaret in the world.

1994 The Mabo Law of Jan. 1 entitles **Aborigines,** Australia's original inhabitants, to file **claim to ownership** of traditional tribal lands.

1994 *Schindler's List,* Steven Spielberg's Holocaust film drama based on historical facts, wins seven Oscars on March 22.

1994 The **train tunnel** beneath the **English Channel** linking England and France is opened with a celebration on May 6.

1995 The **Japanese Aum Shinrikyo sect** carries out a lethal gas attack in the Tokyo subway on March 20, killing twelve people.

1995 After a massive protest by the environmental organization **Greenpeace** and European-wide boycotts against gas stations, the **oil company Shell** decides on June 20 to dispose the Brent Spar oil storage and tanker loading platform on land instead of the sea.

1990   **1995**

1990 William de Klerk's reform government in **South Africa** introduces the **end of apartheid** on Feb. 11. **Nelson Mandela,** the black civil rights activist imprisoned for the last 27 years, is released, and the African National Congress (ANC) made legal again.

1990 On March 21, **Namibia** becomes the last African state to gain **independence**.

1990 In the Russian Soviet Republic, **radical reformer Boris Yeltsin** leaves the Communist Party on July 12. One year later, he becomes the first freely elected **president of Russia**. He initiates the transition to a **market economy**.

1990 Iraqi dictator **Saddam Hussein marches his troops into Kuwait** on Aug. 2 and annexes the emirate.

1990 The **GDR joins the Federal Republic of Germany** on Oct. 3. The restored German national state recognizes the existing borders and receives full rights of sovereignty.

1990 The **Baltic states of Lithuania and Latvia** declare their **independence** from the Soviet Union; Estonia follows in 1991.

1990 **Charta of Paris:** At a meeting of the Organization for Security and Cooperation in Europe (OSCE) in Paris on Nov. 21, the member states commit to democracy and human rights. They declare an **end to the Cold War.**

1991 The Iraqi troops begin to withdraw from **Kuwait** on Feb. 25. Supported by a **UN mandate,** a multinational force led by the USA had been taking action against Iraq since Jan. 17.

1991 The **Warsaw Pact is dissolved** on July 1.

1991 The socialist military regime of **Mengistu Mariam** in **Ethiopia** is overthrown on May 21.

1991 **Disintegration of multinational Yugoslavia:** On June 25, **Slovenia** and **Croatia declare their independence**. Serbian President Milosevic orders the Serbian-dominated Yugoslav federal army to march into the former member states.

1991 Gorbachev steps down on Dec. 25; the **Soviet Union is dissolved,** and the satellite states gain full sovereignty. Eleven former Soviet republics join to form the **Commonwealth of Independent States (CIS)**.

1992 **European Union:** The EC member states agree to the implementation of an **economic union** with a common currency and a common foreign and security policy in **Maastricht** on Feb. 7.

1992 On April 16, the Muslim **Mujahideen** emerge as victors of the thirteen-year **civil war in Afghanistan.**

1992 On Nov. 3, **Bill Clinton** becomes the first Democrat to be elected U.S. president in twelve years.

1992–1995 Serbian, Croatian, and Muslim ethnic groups fight for **supremacy** in the independent **Republic of Bosnia and Herzegovina**.

1993 The **Czechoslovakian state** splits into two independent republics, **Czechia** and **Slovakia,** on Jan. 1.

1993 **Islamic fundamentalists** perpetrate a bomb attack against the **World Trade Center** in New York on Feb. 26.

1993 After a long-running civil war, **Eritrea** declares its **independence** from Ethiopia on May 24 and proclaims a republic.

1993 Israeli Prime Minister **Yitzhak Rabin** and PLO leader **Yasser Arafat** witness the signing of the **Oslo Accords** in Washington on Sept. 13. It grants the Palestinians staged autonomy in the Israeli-occupied territories.

1994 In civil war-shattered **Rwanda,** members of the Hutu majority commit **genocide against the Tutsi minority** between May and September. At least 500,000 people are murdered in the process.

1994 The election of **Nelson Mandela** as president in **South Africa** on May 9 ends the **apartheid regime**, and the Black majority population gains full political participation.

1994 On July 8, **Kim Il-sung** dies in **North Korea** after ruling for almost 50 years. By 1997, his son, **Kim Jong-il,** is able to establish himself as supreme leader.

1994 **Forces of the Russian Federation** march into the independence-seeking **republic of Chechnya** on Dec. 11. Hostilities end with an armistice in 1996.

1995 **Sweden, Finland,** and **Austria** become members of the **EU** on Jan. 1.

1995 The last **UN soldiers** pull out of **Somalia** on March 3 without having brought peace to the country ravaged by civil war and famine.

1995 On Nov. 4, a far-right-wing **orthodox Jew murders Prime Minister Yitzhak Rabin,** whose Oslo Accords with the PLO provoked violent protests in sections of the population.

1995 On Dec. 14, the **Dayton Accords** end the war in Bosnia following a military intervention by the NATO forces. Under UN supervision, **Bosnia-Herzegovina** is divided into a Bosnian federation and a Serbian Republic.

1996 **Necmettin Erbakan** becomes the **first Islamist prime minister of Turkey** on June 7. He is forced to step down by the military on June 18, 1997.

1996 **Taliban militia** capture Kabul, the capital of **Afghanistan,** on Sept. 27 and establish a strict **Islamic regime** in major portions of the country.

1990–2010

With the fall of the Soviet Union, the USA became the sole remaining world power. Liberal democracies and market economies were being established in many parts of the world. Innovations in the field of information technology and the opening of markets in the former Eastern Bloc sparked worldwide economic growth, benefiting emerging economies such as China and India. The vulnerability of global economic interdependency became evident in the recent financial crisis. However, national borders are increasingly losing their significance, not only in economic terms but in political matters as well. Overriding issues like environmental protection and climate change, international terrorism, the spread of AIDS, and the ever-widening gap between the rich and the poor can only be effectively combated on a transnational level.

Between tradition and modernity: Japanese women in the Tokyo megatropolis

HISTORICAL FIGURES

Nelson Mandela (born 1918)
The first Black President of South Africa is the personification of the Black population's victorious struggle against the apartheid regime.

Mandela, the son of a Xhosa chief, had fought against apartheid in South Africa as a member of the African National Congress (ANC) since 1947. After the organization was banned in 1961, he went underground. In 1964, he was sentenced to life imprisonment, but his unwavering commitment to social justice made him a symbol of a free Black South Africa and the "world's most famous prisoner." Finally, the de Klerk administration legalized the ANC and released Mandela on **Feb. 11, 1990**. For their joint efforts in ending apartheid, Mandela and de Klerk received the Nobel Peace Prize in 1993. On **May 9, 1994**, Mandela was elected president with a great majority. Five years later, he voluntarily left office and has since dedicated himself to the fight for human rights.

Yitzhak Rabin (1922–1995)
Rabin was awarded the Nobel Peace Prize in 1994 for his efforts to establish peace with the Palestinians.

The military officer had played a major role in Israel's successful wars against its Arab neighbors and was long considered a proponent of hard line tactics against the Palestinians. However, in his second term in office as president, beginning in 1992, he sought to end violence through dialogue. In 1993, against opposition in his own country, Rabin recognized the PLO led by Yasser Arafat as a negotiating partner, stopped the building of Jewish settlements in occupied territories, and conceded partial autonomy to the Palestinians in the two Oslo Accords of 1993/95. In 1994, he concluded a peace treaty with Jordan. For his policy of rapprochment Rabin paid with his life. On **Nov. 4, 1995**, he was shot by a radical Israeli in Tel Aviv.

Aung San Suu Kyi (born 1945)
For decades the Burmese opposition leader has been fighting unswervingly for democratic change in her homeland.

The fate of her father determined Aung San Suu Kyi's political life. Shortly after being elected the first president of an independent Burma in 1947, General Aung San was murdered. To this day, Suu Kyi has been fighting for his political legacy and is an advocate of human rights and nonviolence in the mold of Mahatma Gandhi. She returned home in 1988 after decades in India and Great Britain and became a symbolic figure of the democratic opposition movement against the military dictatorship in Burma. Although her party won the 1990 election, the military prevented her from taking over the government. In 1991, Suu Kyi received the Nobel Peace Prize for her struggle for democracy, yet had to live under house arrest until 2010.

Hugo Chávez (born 1954)
Venezuela's president represents South America's shift to the left at the beginning of the 21st century.

Chavez, an admirer of Bolivár and Cuban revolutionary leader Castro, founded a left-wing nationalist movement in 1983 to fight poverty and corruption. His putsch in 1992 against the Pérez government failed, but endeared him to the impoverished population. Since taking office in **1999**, he has established an increasingly autocratic regime —against the resistance of the opposition but legitimized by elections and referendums. His social and state nationalization policies, as well as his attacks against the "imperialistic" government of former U.S. President George W. Bush, amplified his popularity in left-wing circles worldwide. He is seeking the integration of the Latin American continent to contain North American influence.

2002 The **SARS virus** spreads from China to Southeast Asia in September. By Dec. 2003, the serious disease has claimed the lives of almost 1,000 people.

2003 The **Three Gorges Dam** spanning the **Yangtse River** in China begins operation on June 1.

2004 A severe earthquake off the coast of Sumatra on Dec. 26 triggers a devastating **tsunami** that destroys the whole **coastal region of the Indian Ocean**. In total, the tidal wave claims the lives of almost 300,000 people.

2005 On July 24, American cyclist pro **Lance Armstrong** wins the **Tour de France** for the seventh time in a row.

2005 Pope John Paul II dies in Rome on April 2 after one of the longest pontificates in history. 17 days later, German Cardinal Joseph Ratzinger is elected pope and takes the name **Benedict XVI**.

2008 NASA's Phoenix **space probe** lands in the north polar region of **Mars** on May 25. It sends pictures to earth that prove the existence of water on the red planet.

2009 American pop icon **Michael Jackson dies** in Los Angeles on June 25. No musician has sold more recordings worldwide.

2005 — **2010**

2003 In spring, the **Israeli government** begins building a security wall to isolate the **autonomous Palestinian region of West Jordan**.

2003 Based on the alleged possession of weapons of mass destruction, the **USA** begins a **war against Iraq** on March 20 without the agreement of the UN and topples the regime of **Saddam Hussein** within a few weeks.

2003 Swedish Foreign Minister **Anna Lindh** is **stabbed** in a department store on Sept. 10 and dies a short while later.

2004 On June 28, the U.S. **occupiers in Iraq** turn over power to a **transitional government**.

2004 191 people die in **bomb attacks** in trains and at several train stations in the Spanish capital of **Madrid** on March 11.

2004 The EU heads of state and government draft a **European constitution** on June 18–19. It remains unratified after being **rejected by popular referendum** in France and the Netherlands.

2005 Following the death of Yasser Arafat on Jan. 9, the chairman of the PLO, **Mahmoud Abbas**, is elected the **new president of the Palestinian National Authority**.

2005 Conservative mayor of Teheran, **Mahmoud Ahmadinejad**, wins a surprise election victory in June and becomes new president of Iran.

2005 A series of four closely-timed **bombs** explode on July 7 in underground stations and on a bus in **London**. A total of 56 lives are lost in the attack.

2005 Christian Democrat **Angela Merkel** is elected the new **German chancellor** on Nov. 22. She is the first woman to hold this office, first heading a Christian-Social coalition and then a Christian-Liberal government since 2009.

2006 A **caricature of the Prophet Muhammad** published in **Denmark** sparks a rage of protest in the Muslim world and isolated attacks on Western embassies in January and February.

2006 Socialist **Evo Morales** is sworn in as president of **Bolivia** on Jan. 22.

2006 On July 12, **Israel** launches a **military offensive** against Islamist **Hisbollah** operating in Lebanon. Hostilities end in August with a truce.

2006 Former Iraqi Dictator **Saddam Hussein** is found guilty of crimes against humanity and **sentenced to death** in a special court on Nov. 5. The sentence is carried out on Dec 30.

2007 Conservative **Nicolas Sarkozy** is elected president of **France** on May 6.

"Yes we can"

Barack Obama's 2008 election campaign slogan

2007 Between June 6–8, the government heads of the eight **major industrialized nations** meet in Heiligendamm, Germany, for the 33rd **G8 summit**.

2007 On June 27, **Gordon Brown** replaces Tony Blair as **British prime minister**.

2007 **Cristina Fernández de Kirchner** is elected **president of Argentina** on Oct. 28.

2007 On Dec. 27, the former Pakistani prime minister and opposition leader, **Benazir Bhutto**, is **murdered**.

2008 **Israel** begins a military offensive against **Hamas** in the **Gaza Strip** on Dec. 27.

2008 **Dmitry Medvedev** is elected Russian president by a large majority on March 2. However, his predecessor, **Vladimir Putin**, continues to be a powerful government official.

2008 On Aug. 7, a short war breaks out between **Russia** and **Georgia** over **South Ossetia**, a rebellious autonomous Georgian province.

2008 The collapse of the **U.S. investment bank Lehman Brothers** on Sept. 15 exacerbates the **financial crisis** that broke out in 2007 and shakes the world economic system; only massive government intervention is able to prevent the system's collapse.

2008 On Nov. 4, **Barack Obama** becomes the first African-American to be elected **U.S. president**. There is worldwide hope that he can contribute to easing the tense relations between the West and Islam.

2009 Incumbent **Ahmadinejad** is accused of **manipulating the Iranian presidential elections** of June 12, causing an outbreak of unrest.

2009 Ratified by all 27 **EU** member states, the **Treaty of Lisbon** becomes law on Dec. 1.

2010 On April 10, Poland's president, **Lech Kaczynski** dies in a **plane crash**, along with many other members of the country's political leadership,

2010 Beginning in December, the **Jasmine Revolution** in Tunisia sparks the **Arab Spring**, a wave of civil protests against authoritarian regimes ruling in the Arab world.

2011 A **nuclear power plant accident** takes place in **Fukushima**, Japan, on March 11.

1996 On July 5, the first **cloned** mammal is born, **Dolly** the sheep.

1997 On June 26, British writer **Joanne Rowling** publishes the first of a total of seven *Harry Potter* **novels**. All over the world, the fantasy series about the adventures of a young wizard breaks all sales records.

1997 **Princess Diana**, the ex-wife of British Crown Prince Charles, dies on Aug. 31 in an **automobile accident** in Paris. The world reacts with shock and grief to the death of the "Queen of Hearts."

1998 **attac** is founded in France on June 3. The network, active worldwide, criticizes the **negative results of globalization** and claims to now have over 90,000 members in 50 countries.

1999 On July 10, some 1.5 million techno fans celebrate at the **Love Parade** in **Berlin**, the world's largest open-air dance event.

2000 A **Concorde** crashes shortly after taking off from the Paris airport on July 25, killing 113 people.

2001 Despite worldwide protests, the **Taliban** regime in Afghanistan destroys the monumental **Buddha statues of Bamiyan** on Mar. 9.

1995 The Internet platform **ebay** is founded in San José, California, in September. It develops into the world's largest **Internet auction house**.

2001 An international team of scientists is able to largely **decode the human genome**.

2002 On Jan. 1, the **euro** becomes legal tender **in twelve EU countries**, replacing the national currency.

2000

1996 The warring parties end the 36-year **civil war** in Guatemala on Dec. 30 with a peace treaty.

1998 **Good Friday Agreement:** Great Britain, Ireland, and the **warring parties in Northern Ireland** agree upon a peace plan on April 10.

2000 Participation in the Austrian government by the **right-wing Populists** led by Jörg Haider on Feb. 4 is met with harsh criticism both at home and abroad.

2001 Troops of the oppositional **North Alliance** overthrow the Islamist **Taliban regime** in **Afghanistan** in November. Taliban positions had been under aerial attack by U.S. forces since October.

1998 Social Democrat **Gerhard Schröder** is elected Chancellor of the **Federal Republic of Germany** on Oct. 27. In a coalition with the Greens, his party takes over from Helmut Kohl's Christian-Liberal government.

2000 **Sunshine Policy: South Korea**'s policy of of engagement towards the north reaches its zenith during President Kim Dae Jung's visit to the **North Korean** leader, Kim Jong-il, in Pyongyang on June 13.

1997 **Kim Dae Jung** is elected **president of South Korea** on Dec. 18. This sets off a process of democratization in the country, which experiences a massive economic upswing. Kim Dae Jung seeks to create greater political contact with North Korea with his "Sunshine Policy."

1998 An ultimately unsuccessful **impeachment process for perjury** is initiated against **President Clinton** on Dec. 19.

2000 The **visit** by Israeli politician **Ariel Sharon** to **Temple Mount** in Jerusalem on Sept. 28 is seen as a provocation by the Palestinians, who launch the **Second Intifada** in Israeli-occupied territories.

2000 Republican **George W. Bush** wins by a slim margin over his Democratic contender Al Gore in the **U.S. presidential elections** on Nov. 7.

2002 Dutch **right-wing populist Pim Fortuyn** is **assassinated** because of his purported anti-Islamic views shortly before parliamentary elections in May. The first political murder in over 400 years shocks the Dutch nation.

1997 Communist economic reformer **Deng Xiaoping** dies in **China** on Feb. 19. President Jiang Zemin announces the will to continue the policy of a **"socialist market economy."**

1999 The **Turkish secret service** apprehends **Abdullah Öcalan**, the leader of the militant Kurdish workers' party, **PKK**, on Feb. 15. In August, the PKK announces the end of the decades-long guerrilla battle in the north of the country.

2001 President **Kabila** of the **Democratic Republic of Congo** is assassinated on Jan. 16.

2001 Italian media mogul **Silvio Berlusconi** wins **parliamentary elections** for a second time on May 13. He is the leader of a central-right coalition.

2002 The Southeast Asian island-state of **East Timor** officially **becomes independent** on May 20. Its first president is José Gusmão.

1997 After 18 years of Conservative rule in Great Britain, the Labour leader **Tony Blair** is elected Prime Minister on May 1.

1999 The threatening **escalation of violence in Kosovo** prompts NATO to launch an **air war against Serbia** on March 24 without approval of the UN. The attacks are suspended in June following the withdrawal of Serbian troops from Kosovo.

1999 **Hugo Chávez** takes office as president in **Venezuela** on Feb. 2. An amendment to the constitution strengthens his authority.

2002 A **bomb attack** by Islamist terrorists on the holiday island of **Bali** on Oct. 12 claims 189 lives. Among the victims are many tourists.

1997 Great Britain loses its last important colony when, on July 1, Hong Kong is handed back to China.

1999 The democratically-elected prime minister of **Pakistan**, **Sharif**, is **ousted** on Oct. 12 by the military. He is succeeded by General Musharraf.

2001 Islamist terrorists carry out devastating **attacks** in the USA on Sept. 11. **Airplane attacks on the World Trade Center in New York** and the Pentagon in Washington claim lives of more than 3,000 people.

1998–2002 **Argentina** suffers from a **severe economic crisis**.

1999 On Dec. 20, **Portugal** returns **Macao** to **China**, the last remaining European colony in the Far East.

HISTORICAL EVENTS

The Reunification of Germany
Less than a year after the fall of the Berlin Wall, the GDR merged with the "old" Federal Republic of Germany to become a fully sovereign German national state.

The dictatorship of the East German Socialist Unity Party collapsed shortly after the Berlin Wall fell on **Nov. 9, 1989**. The first free elections in the German Democratic Republic held on March 18, 1990, were won by the Christian Democrats, who formed a government with Lothar de Maizière as president. The two German governments agreed upon a social and economic union, making the D-mark the official currency of the GDR on July 1. On Aug. 23, the East German parliament resolved to join the Federal Republic on **Oct. 3, 1990**. Prior to that, the four allied victors of the Second World War had reached an agreement with both German governments over the general framework of the union's foreign policy. In mid-July 1990, the Soviet government accepted the membership of a united Germany in NATO in return for financial concessions. With the concluding of the Two Plus Four Agreement on German reunification on Sept. 12, 1990, the Federal Republic gained its full sovereignty.

Thousands of Germans celebrate German reunification at Brandenburg Gate on Oct. 3, 1990. The gate has become a symbol for both the division and unity of Germany.

The Disintegration of Yugoslavia
The desire for independence drove the various ethnic groups in the multiethnic Yugoslavian state to lead several wars in the Balkans after 1990.

The Yugoslavian multiethnic state began to disintegrate with the death of President Tito in 1980. The Serbian Communist leader Slobodan Milosevic had already been fighting for the unity of his country since 1986 and annulled the autonomy of Albanian Kosovo in 1989. In the course of the democratic upheavals in the Eastern Bloc in **1989–90**, nationalistic forces gained ground and the federation began to crumble. In 1991 Slovenia and Croatia became the first to declare their independence, followed later by Bosnia-Herzegovina and Macedonia. Since the leadership surrounding Milosevic in Belgrade did not want to accept the disintegration, they mobilized the Serb-dominated federal army. A civil war broke out that was brutally waged, particularly in Bosnia and in Kosovo, leading to genocide being committed by the various warring ethnic groups. The violence ended in **1995** after a military intervention by NATO. The country was divided into a Bosnian-Croat part and a Serbian part. NATO forces occupied Kosovo in **1999**, which has gained the status of a UN protectorate.

Post-Soviet Russia
Between pretensions to the status of a Great Power, autocracy, and democracy: Post-Soviet Russia has been struggling with its domestic and foreign image.

Russia emerged from the dissolution of the Soviet Union on **Dec. 25, 1991**, as the mightiest of the successor states. During his term in office, Boris Yeltsin, the first democratically elected head of state in the history of Russia, sought to economically align with the West and introduced radical market reforms. He strengthened the position of the president, but his impaired ability to exercise his office due to health problems, mismanagement, and organized crime in all areas of public life drove Russia to the brink of national ruin after 1997. Yeltsin finally resigned at the end of 1999. Vladimir Putin took over the presidency and began stabilizing the country in 2000—often employing authoritarian means. His concept of a "guided democracy" greatly encroached upon the freedom of the press and culture. After **Sept. 11, 2001**, Putin moved closer to the USA in its war against terror and used that approach to justify his harsh measures in Chechnya, where guerrilla groups had been fighting against Russia's controlling power since **1994**. Added to that, Russia is now more openly seeking to exercise hegemonial rights over former Soviet republics like the Ukraine and Georgia, where it became militarily involved in 2008.

A Bosnian Muslim praying at the grave of his son who was killed in the massacre of Srebrenica.

Boris Yeltsin and his successor Vladimir Putin at celebrations in 2004

The signing of the EU treaty in Lisbon on Dec. 13, 2007

European Unification
The founding of the European Union in 1992–93 was an important step toward the unification of Europe.

The process of European unification accelerated at the end of the Cold War in **1990**. The Maastricht Treaty of **1992** on the European Union created the basis for a common foreign and security policy as well as closer cooperation in legal and domestic policies. On **Jan. 1, 2002**, the euro replaced the national currency in eleven countries. By 2007, the EU's economic appeal had increased the membership to 27. This growth made structural reforms necessary to ensure the Union's efficiency and ability to act. Unlike the reform treaty of 2004, the Treaty of Lisbon was implemented on **Dec. 1, 2009**.

Globalization
Groundbreaking innovations in the field of communication have brought the world closer together, both economically and socially—and increased mutual dependency.

Since the early 1990s, modern communications and information technology have fundamentally changed the world. The World Wide Web allows immediate access to information from almost any location, contributing to the globalizing of the once regional marketing potential of services, goods, and finance. Since the mid-1990s, there has been an accelerated growth in world trade that has also benefited emerging economies like Brazil, India, and China, where more favorable conditions like low labor costs and a large domestic demand attract more investors. The reverse side of the closely interdependent, deregulated world economy became evident in **2008** when unbridled speculation brought a collapse of banks in the USA, triggering a worldwide financial crisis.

The media revolution is also making inroads in India: internet cafés are widespread.

September 11th
The suicide attacks by Islamist terrorists in New York and Washington in 2001 had a seismic effect on America.

The terrorist attacks of **Sept. 11, 2001**, sent a shock wave around the world. About 9 o'clock in the morning, two hijacked aircrafts hurtled into the World Trade Center, and within a short time brought the symbol of American economic strength to fall. Half an hour later, a third plane was piloted into the Pentagon, the headquarters of the U.S. Department of Defense. Another plane, allegedly targeting the White House, crashed near Pittsburgh. The day's attacks claimed more than 3,000 lives. In the aftermath, President Bush proclaimed a "War on Terror." At the end of 2001, an internationally supported military strike brought an end to the radical Taliban regime in Afghanistan that had provided a safe haven for Osama bin Laden, the alleged mastermind behind the attacks. International forces led by NATO are still in the country today trying to prevent the radical Islamists from regaining power.

The burning Twin Towers in New York after the terror attacks on Sept. 11, 2001

Genocide victims of the Tutsi minority in Rwanda

Crisis Hotspot Africa
Even though democracy has been established in many countries, millions of Black Africans continue to suffer from poverty and civil wars.

Due to a lack of access to modern technologies, sub-Saharan Africa has benefited little from the world economy that has been booming since the 1990s. Poverty still dominates many regions. Additionally, the AIDS epidemic has spread explosively on the continent since the early 1980s. Unresolved ethnic and religious conflicts continually escalate into extreme acts of violence, such as the genocide of the Tutsi minority in Rwanda in **1994** or the constant fighting in the Darfur region of Sudan since 2003. Nevertheless, the continent is slowly going through a process of democratization, except in isolated countries like Zimbabwe or Sudan, where authoritarian regimes still continue to rule, and backward structures characterize the social systems in many places. However, countries like Ghana, Botswana, Namibia, and particularly Senegal have developed into relatively stable democracies that have been able to exhibit considerable economic growth.

USA – The last super power
Since the end of the Cold War, the USA has been the world's leading nation culturally, militarily, and economically. However, it remains dependent on multilateral cooperation.

The USA assumed the leading role in world politics after the collapse of the Soviet Union. In **1991**, President George H. W. Bush forged an international alliance that, with a UN mandate, drove Iraqi troops out of Kuwait. Under Democrat Bill Clinton, who took office in **1992**, the USA increasingly used its power to deal with regional conflicts, such as the Near East conflict in **1993**. Following the failed peace mission in Somalia in **1995**, the USA backed away from further multinational coop- eration in UN missions. After the attacks of 9/11, President George W. Bush, who was elected in **2000**, became primarily guided by national security interests that were also a rationale for pre-emptive strikes. U.S. forces attacked Iraq in March **2003** without UN sanction and smashed the regime of Saddam Hussein. Since Barack Obama's election in **2008**, the USA, conscious of the global nature of problems like terrorism and climate change, is again relying heavily on international cooperation.

30,000/20,000 B.C. The **first humans** reach the American continent across the region known today as the **Bering Strait**. The earliest surviving evidences of human life were found north of the Rio Grande.

13,000 B.C. The **Clovis culture** spreads out in North America.

700 The **highly developed Native American Mississippi culture** spreads out in the Midwest, East, and Southeast of present-day USA.

1507 The term "**America**" —after Italian navigator **Amerigo Vespucci**—is first used to describe the New World.

1619 A day of **Thanksgiving** is codified in the founding charter of Berkeley Hundred in Charles City County, Virginia.

1636 **Harvard University**, the earliest institution of higher learning in the United States, is established in Cambridge, Massachusetts.

1636 In the **Rhode Island colony**, church and state are kept **separate** for the first time and religious tolerance is practiced.

1660 For the first time, statute law declares Blacks imported from Africa as **slaves**. Prior to this, the **legal status** of slaves was uncertain.

1692/93 The **Salem witch trials** are the first in a series of arrests, prosecutions, and executions for witchcraft in New England.

1743 The **American Philosophical Society**, the hub of American enlightenment, is founded in Philadelphia.

30,000 B.C. — **1500** — **1600** — **1700**

9000 B.C. The **culture of the big game hunters** spreads from North America across Central Mexico to South America.

1000 **Pueblo Indians** settle the **Mesa Verde** area in present-day Colorado and build apartment-like structures made of adobe.

1000 **Vikings** associated with **Leif Eriksson** are the first Europeans to cross the Atlantic. They colonize the North American coastline near Newfoundland.

1492 The Italian explorer **Christopher Columbus** lands on a small island in the Bahamas and starts Europe's race of colonizing the New World.

1497 The Italian explorer **John Cabot** (Giovanni Caboto) becomes the **first European to reach the North American mainland** and thereby establishes a claim to North America.

1534 The French explorer **Jacques Cartier** is the first to explore the North American continent. On a total of three expeditions, he explores the area around Quebec and Montreal and establishes the French claim to the region.

1565 The Spaniards found **St. Augustine**, the first permanent European colony in the present-day state of **Florida**.

1570 The **Iroquois Confederacy** is founded to eliminate intertribal warfare. During the 17th and 18th centuries, it plays a strategic role in the struggle between the French and British for mastery of North America.

1585 **Sir Walter Raleigh** establishes the first colony on **Roanoake Island,** off the coast of modern-day North Carolina. The Roanoake settlement becomes known as the **lost colony** because the outpost was mysteriously deserted by 1590. The fate of its settlers has never been determined.

1607 With the aid of the British crown, English merchants found **Jamestown**, the **first permanent British colony in Virginia**.

1608 The French found **Quebec**, which becomes the **center of the French colonial territories** in North America.

1614 The **Dutch East India Company** establishes a trading post on the Hudson River.

1619 The **House of Burgesses**, the first **representative government** in North America, is established in Virginia.

1620 The **Pilgrim Fathers** found the **Plymouth Plantation** in present-day Massachusetts. They had already committed themselves to a democratic self-government while crossing over on the *Mayflower*.

1624 The **Dutch East India Company** founds "**New Amsterdam**," which is captured by the British in 1664 and renamed "**New York**."

1630 The establishment of a Puritan colony by the **Massachusetts Bay Company** launches a **massive wave of Puritan immigration** to New England, which leads to the founding of many new colonies.

1675–1676 The Native American Wampanoag led by Metacomet (King Philip) fight in the two-year-long **King Philip's War** against the expansion of the British colonists in New England.

1682 **William Penn** founds **Pennsylvania**, the **first proprietary colony.**

1732 **Georgia is founded** as the last of the 13 British **North American colonies**. These 13 colonies later become the first 13 states of the United States.

1739 On Sept. 9, an **armed uprising of slaves** near the **Stono River** in the British colony of South Carolina is bloodily crushed by white militia. The remaining rebels are executed.

1754–1760 **French and Indian War:** As a result of the conflict France is forced out of the North American continent (and its territories are divided between England and Spain). **Great Britain becomes the leading power on the continent.**

1765/1766 **Stamp Act Crisis:** A stamp tax law ignites coordinated resistance against English colonial rule ("**No taxation without representation**").

1770 The first bloody confrontation between British military and colonial resistance takes place in the **Boston Massacre**.

1771 In the **Battle of Alamance** on May 16, the **Regulators**, an armed rebellion of backcountry farmers from **North Carolina**, fight against royal militia in a conflict over taxes, dishonest sheriffs, and illegal fees imposed by the British Crown and are decisively crushed.

1750 Benjamin Franklin invents the **lightening rod**.

1764 William Brown and Thomas Gilmore publish **Quebec's first newspaper**, the dual-language *Quebec Gazette*.

1776 In his pamphlet *Common Sense*, **Thomas Paine** demands independence and liberty for the colonies, fashioning a blueprint for the Declaration of Independence.

1787/1788 Alexander Hamilton, James Madison, and John Jay defend the federal constitution in the *Federalist Papers*. The papers are still considered to be an important contemporary aid in interpreting the **U.S. constitution**.

1793 **Eli Whitney** invents the **cotton gin**, which makes the large scale cultivation of cotton in the South possible.

1800 The **Library of Congress** is founded in Washington D.C.

1804/06 **Lewis and Clark Expedition:** An expeditionary force succeeds for the first time in **crossing the country to the Pacific West Coast**.

1813 Boston merchants establish the **first fully mechanized textile factory**, launching the rapid **industrialization of New England**.

from 1830 Introduced by Irish immigrants, **Halloween** becomes one of the USA's most important festivities.

1848 The **gold rush** in California lures a massive stream of adventurers and fortune seekers to the West.

1851 **Herman Melville** publishes *Moby Dick*, one of the most celebrated works in world literature.

1750 — **1800** — **1865**

1773 **Boston Tea Party:** In protest of the British tax on tea, rebels in Boston dressed as Indians throw hundreds of crates of tea into the sea. The confrontation escalates.

1775 The American **War of Independence** between the colonists and the British army begins on April 19 with armed clashes in Lexington and Boston.

1775 On May 10, **George Washington** is named **commander-in-chief** of the newly-founded **American Continental Army**.

1776 With a reference to man's inalienable **right to liberty**, the 13 colonies declare their independence from Great Britain as the **United States of America** on July 4.

1776–1780 The **republican constitution**, which is often amended with a separate **declaration of human rights**, is ratified in the individual states.

1781 The **capitulation of the British army** at **Yorktown**, Virginia, is the virtual end of the **War of Independence**.

1783 Great Britain officially recognizes the **sovereignty of the USA** in the **Treaty of Paris**.

1789 After years of debate, a **new constitution** that provides for a republican democratic federal state comes into force in the USA.

1789 **George Washington** is elected the **first president of the USA**.

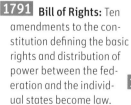

1791 **Canada Act:** On June 10, the Province of Quebec is divided into the predominantly British Upper Canada (Ontario) and the predominantly French Lower Canada (Quebec).

1791 **Bill of Rights:** Ten amendments to the constitution defining the basic rights and distribution of power between the federation and the individual states become law.

1793 **Fugitive Slave Act:** The fugitive slave laws are passed by the United States Congress to provide for the return of slaves who escape from one state into another state or territory.

1800 **Thomas Jefferson**, the leader of the anti-federalist Democratic-Republicans, is elected third **president** of the USA.

1803 **Louisiana Purchase:** Napoleon sells the **Louisiana territory** to the USA, doubling the size of the USA in a single stroke.

1808 A **federal law** officially **bans** the **importation of slaves**.

1812 Due to a **British naval blockade,** the USA declares **war** on Great Britain. The conflict ends two years later with a return to the status quo.

1820 The **Missouri Compromise** regulates the balance in the Union between the individual slave-owning and non-slave-owning states.

1823 Introduced on December 2, the so-called **Monroe Doctrine** specifies a **policy of neutrality regarding foreign conflicts** but also condemns all attempts by European powers to further colonize the western hemisphere.

1828 The election of **Andrew Jackson** marks the beginning of political change. He establishes a **democratization of society** and political structures (Jacksonian Democracy). He easily wins his re-election in 1832.

1831 **Nat Turner**, an American slave, leads a slave rebellion in Virginia on Aug. 21, that results in 60 white deaths and at least 100 black deaths.

1837 **Battle of Alamo:** Mexican troops under President General Antonio López de Santa Anna launch an assault on the Alamo Mission near San Antonio de Béxar. All but two of the Texan defenders are killed.

1846–1848 In a **war against Mexico**, the USA seizes the territories of the later states of New Mexico, Arizona, Nevada, Utah, and California.

1854 **Opponents to the spread of slavery** form the **Republican Party** in the North and Midwest.

1860 The **Republican Abraham Lincoln** is elected president on Nov. 9, which causes the southern slave states to secede from the Union. On Feb. 8, 1861, the rebel states form the **Confederate States of America,** adopt their own constitution, and later elect their own president, Jefferson Davis.

1861 The four-year **American Civil War begins** with the Confederate attack on Fort Sumter near Charleston.

1863 **Emancipation Proclamation:** On Jan. 1, President Lincoln declares all slaves living in Confederate territory to be free.

1830 **Indian Removal Act:** Tens of thousands of **Native Americans** from the southern states are forcibly relocated to the far West (Trail of tears).

1865 The **capitulation of the Confederate states** on April 9 ends the **Civil War**. The Union is restored and slavery is officially abolished in the 13th amendment to the American constitution.

1865 On April 14, **John Wilkes Booth**, an actor and proponent of slavery, **attempts to assassinate President Lincoln**, who dies one day later.

1866 The racist **Ku Klux Klan** is founded in Tennessee.

1867 The **first transcontinental railroad** is completed.

1872 **Yellowstone** in Montana is declared a **National Park**. It is the world's oldest nature reserve.

1875 **Alexander Graham Bell** constructs the **first functioning telephone** in Boston.

1879 **Thomas Alva Edison** makes the first public demonstration of his **light bulb** on Dec. 31.

1886 The **Statue of Liberty**, a gift from the French nation, is dedicated in New York on Oct. 28.

1900 A new genre of music originally centered in **New Orleans** develops out of the gospel tradition: **jazz**.

1903 **Henry Ford** builds his **first automobile factory** in Dearborn, Michigan. In 1909, he becomes the first to use an **assembly line method** to produce cars.

1920 The production and sale of alcoholic beverages becomes officially illegal. The **Prohibition** is not lifted until 1933.

1927 *The Jazz Singer*, the **first sound film**, has its premiere in New York.

1927 **Charles Lindbergh** flies solo non-stop from **New York to Paris.**

1928 **Walt Disney** creates his animated film figure *Mickey Mouse*.

1929 The first **Oscars** for special achievement in the film industry are awarded by the **Academy of Motion Picture Arts and Science**. The worldwide success of **Hollywood films** makes the Oscar the most coveted film prize in the world.

1866 — **1900** — **1920** — **1945**

1867 The Canadian provinces are united in the **Confederation of Canada**, which gains relative independence as a **British Dominion**.

1867 The USA purchases the territory of **Alaska** from Russia. This concludes the **western continental expansion**.

1867 **Reconstruction** begins in the South, which remains under Northern military occupation until 1877.

1868 African-Americans are granted **civil rights** in the **14th Amendment** to the American constitution.

1870 **John D. Rockefeller** founds the **Standard Oil Company**, the first trust in the USA, and becomes a symbolic figure of the economic boom triggered by the discovery of oil.

1876 On June 25, Native American tribes led by Chief **Sitting Bull** gain a spectacular victory over the U.S. cavalry in their struggle for independence.

1886 **Trade unions** are organized for the first time under an umbrella organization (American Federation of Labor).

1890 The **Sherman Antitrust Act**, the first attempt to restrict the power of the trusts in order to prevent anticompetitive monopolies, is made a statute.

1890 The **U.S. cavalry's victory over the Sioux at Wounded Knee** on Dec. 29 ends the Indian Wars. Most of the Native Americans are forced onto reservations.

1893 **Overspeculation by the trusts** and the **collapse of foreign markets** trigger one of the first serious economic crises.

1896 **"Separate but equal":** The Supreme Court justifies the constitutionality of racial segregation in public transport and schools in **Plessy v. Ferguson**.

1898 **Spanish-American War:** The USA becomes an imperial power and gains control over Cuba, Puerto Rico, Guam, and the Philippines.

1904 **Roosevelt Corollary:** On Dec. 6, President Roosevelt formulates the right of the USA to counter threats to U.S. security and interests in the Pacific region and Latin American through intervention.

1906 An **earthquake** destroys the city of **San Francisco** on April 18.

1910 21 American nations under the leadership of the USA meet in Washington to form the **Pan American Union**.

1913 **Woodrow Wilson**, a Democrat and proponent of social reform, becomes **president**.

1914 The **Panama Canal**, which links the Atlantic and Pacific, is formally opened.

1917 On April 6, after the declaration of unrestricted submarine warfare, **U.S. President Wilson** formally **declares war on Germany** and enters the conflict in Europe.

1918 On Jan. 8, **President Wilson** formulates an idealistic peace plan in his **"14 Points."**

1920 The U.S. Senate refuses to ratify the **Versailles Peace Treaty**. The **USA does not join** the newly-founded **League of Nations** that is part of the treaty.

1920 **Women's right to vote** is **adopted** on Aug. 26.

1921 On March 4, **Warren G. Harding**, a Republican, becomes the new **president**. He stands for a withdrawal from world politics.

from 1922 **Modernizations of the economy and in the area of technology** result in growing prosperity and a general feeling of optimism. Women's emancipation and a belief in a better future set the tone for the lifestyle of the **"roaring twenties."**

1928 **Kellogg-Briand Pact:** On Aug. 27, a **general treaty for the renunciation of war**, initiated by Secretary of State Frank Billings Kellogg and his French colleague Aristide Briand, is initially signed by 15 nations.

1929 On Oct. 25, the prices on the **New York Stock Exchange** fell dramatically for the first time. This is followed by a worldwide economic crisis of unprecedented severity.

1931 **Statute of Westminster:** Canada gains independence and equality within the framework of the **British Commonwealth of Nations**.

1933 **New Deal:** On March 4, President Franklin D. Roosevelt announces an active **social and economic policy to overcome the Great Depression**.

1935 A strict **neutrality law** bans the USA from selling weapons to warring nations.

1935 **Social Security Act:** The introduction of a system of old-age benefits on Aug. 14 marks the beginning of federal welfare legislation in the United States.

1941 The **surprise attack by the Japanese on the U.S. naval base at Pearl Harbor** on Dec. 7, 1941, officially forces the USA into the war. Four days later, Germany and Italy declare war on the USA.

1942 The victory in the **Battle of Midway** at the beginning of June **turns the Pacific War against Japan** in favor of the USA.

1944 **D-Day:** The **second front against Germany** is opened with the **landing of Allied forces** on the coasts of **Normandy** on June 6, signaling Germany's ultimate defeat in the Second World War.

1945 Japan unconditionally surrenders on Aug. 10 after the USA drops atom bombs on Hiroshima and Nagasaki. **The Second World War is over.**

1936 Margaret Mitchell publishes her epic novel of the antebellum and postbellum South, *Gone with the Wind*. The film version starring Vivien Leigh and Clark Gable becomes one of the most successful films of all time.

1942 Rosie the Riveter, a cultural icon of **working women during the Second World War**, is first mentioned in a song by Redd Evans and John Jacobs.

1961 The Nobel literature laureate **Ernest Hemingway** commits suicide.

1969 More than 500,000 concert goers attend the legendary outdoor music festival **Woodstock** near Bethel, New York. The event is considered the culmination of the **Hippie movement**.

1969 The **first landing on the moon** by U.S. astronauts Neil Armstrong, Edward Aldrin, and Michael Collins is the crowning achievement of the 1960s' space program initiated by President Kennedy.

1977 **Elvis Presley**, the King of Rock 'n' Roll, dies at only 42 in Memphis.

1987 **Andy Warhol**, the most important representative of **Pop Art**, dies on Feb. 22.

1993 **Toni Morrison** is the first African-American female writer to get the Nobel Prize.

1999 For the first time, more **e-mails** are sent in the USA than letters.

2009 **Michael Jackson**, the most successful and extravagant popstar of the 20th century, **dies** on June 25.

2011 **Steve Jobs** dies of cancer on Oct. 5. He had turned Apple into the most innovative and influential company in the global computer industry.

1975 — *2000* — *2010*

1947 **Truman Doctrine:** President Truman announces **military and economic aid** to all peoples threatened by Communism.

1950 Republican Senator **Joseph McCarthy** begins a four-year campaign against the supposed infiltration of Communists in the American government.

1954 In the case **Brown v. Board of Education**, the Supreme Court declares segregation in public schools to be unconstitutional.

1957 The *Sputnik* shock results in increased efforts in space exploration and sparks a **race between the USA and the Soviet Union for dominance in space**.

1961 The election of charismatic President **John F. Kennedy** is accompanied by the hope for **reforms** and positive change, above all by the younger generation.

1962 **Cuba Crisis:** The attempt by the Soviets to station nuclear weapons on Cuba in October brings the world to the brink of a **nuclear war** between the USA and the Soviet Union.

1963 **"I Have a Dream":** **Martin Luther King Jr.** pleads against racial discrimination and for non-violence at the **"March on Washington,"** a peaceful demonstration of the African-American civil rights movement.

1963 On Nov. 22, **President Kennedy is assassinated** during an election campaign tour in Dallas. The motives behind his murder remain unclear to this day.

1964 A **civil rights law** is signed by President Johnson on July 2, officially **banning racial discrimination**. Despite the legal guarantee of equal rights, racial unrest occurs regularly in the poorer sections of the major cities until 1968.

1965 **Vietnam War:** Without a constitutionally mandated declaration of war, close to half a million American soldiers are sent to Vietnam to support the pro-American government of South Vietnam against Communist rebels.

1968 **Year of political violence:** In short succession, civil rights leader **Martin Luther King Jr.** and the Democratic nominee for president, **Robert Kennedy**, are murdered.

1972 **Beginning of the Détente:** In February, President **Nixon visits the People's Republic of China** for the first time. In May, the first nuclear **arms limitation treaty** is concluded with the Soviet Union.

1973 On Jan. 27, the **last U.S. soldiers are withdrawn from Vietnam**. The war ends for the USA in political and moral disaster.

1974 President **Richard Nixon resigns from office** in the wake of the **"Watergate Affair."**

1976 **Jimmy Carter**, a Democrat, is **elected president** and makes human rights the cornerstone of American foreign policy.

1981 On Jan. 20, the Republican **Ronald Reagan** becomes president. He ensures years of economic boom by massively cutting social expenditures, lowering taxes, and greatly increasing defense spending.

1987 On Dec. 8, President **Reagan** and the Soviet head of state, **Gorbachev**, sign the **first treaty** in history **to eliminate weapons**.

1991 Under a **mandate by the UN**, an international coalition led by the USA **liberates Kuwait from Iraqi occupation**.

1992 In April, **Los Angeles** and other major cities are shaken by severe **racial riots**.

1993 **Bill Clinton**, a Democrat, becomes **president** on Jan. 20. During his time in office, the economy booms and the budget deficit is reduced enormously.

1999 The **killing frenzy** of two students at **Columbine High School** near Denver on April 20 ignites an ongoing debate about federal gun control laws.

1999 An **impeachment process** that is brought against **Bill Clinton** because of the **"Lewinsky scandal"** fails in the Senate in February.

2000 After a historically close presidential election, the Republican **George W. Bush**, former governor of Texas, becomes the 43rd president of the USA on Dec. 12.

2001 Over 3,000 people die in a **terror attack** on the **World Trade Center** and the **Pentagon** on September 11. The attacks lead to American military intervention in Afghanistan. President Bush declares **"war on international terrorism."**

2002 On Nov. 25, President Bush approves the creation of a **"Department of Homeland Security"** for protection against domestic terror.

2003 In the name of the **war on terror**, the USA launches **a military strike against Iraq** on March 20. After a few weeks, the **regime of Saddam Hussein** has fallen.

2005 In August, **Hurricane Katrina** causes horrific destruction. New Orleans is almost completely under water.

2008 Following the bankruptcy of the American investment bank **Lehman Brothers**, the **international financial market** is on the **verge of collapse**.

2009 In times of severe economic upheaval, the first African-American is elected president in the USA: **Barack Obama**.

2010 On March 25, historic **health care reform legislation is passed**, expanding compulsory health insurance to all U.S. citizens.

2011 On May 2, the mastermind behind the attacks of Sept. 11, 2001, **Osama bin Laden**, is killed by a U.S. special strike force in Abbottabad, Pakistan.

Milestones in World History

70,000 B.C. **Modern man** leaves East Africa and **populates the world**.

9000 B.C. Beginning in the Near East, humans start to settle and practice animal husbandry and agriculture during the **Neolithic revolution**.

480 B.C. In the **Sea Battle of Salamis**, the Greeks, led by Themistocles, defeat the Persian fleet.

333 B.C. **Alexander the Great** decisively defeats the Persian king, Darius III, in the **Battle of Issus**.

410 **Visigoths** led by King Alaric I capture Rome on Aug. 24 and plunder the city for three days.

451 In the **Battle of the Catalaunian Plains**, the Franks, Visigoths, and other Germanic tribes in alliance with the Romans under Aëtius defeat the Huns and force them to retreat.

1431 French folk hero, **Joan of Arc**, is burned at the stake as a condemned heretic.

1620 Puritan religious refugees from England, the **"Pilgrim Fathers"** onboard the *Mayflower* land in Massachusetts and found the colony of Plymouth.

1618 The conflict between the confessions in the Holy Roman Empire escalates with the **Defenestration of Prague**; the **Thirty Years' War** begins.

---

ca. 70,000   **500**   **1600**

3000 B.C. The first territorial state in world history is created through the **union of Upper and Lower Egypt**.

1285 B.C. Ramses II fails in his attempt to seize northern Syria from the Hittites in the **Battle of Kadesh**.

1200 B.C. The **"Sea people"** crush the Hittite Kingdom and settle in the Syrian-Palestine coastal region.

753 B.C. According to tradition, Romulus founds the city of **Rome** on April 21.

539 B.C. The 50-year **"Babylonian exile"** ends for many Jews with the Persian conquest of Babylon.

508/07 B.C. **Cleisthenes introduces reforms** that make Athens the first democracy.

221 B.C. King Zheng of Qin unites the various parts of China for the first time and founds an **emperorship in China**.

218 B.C. Carthaginian general **Hannibal marches** his army from Spain, **across the Alps**, and invades northern Italy. The Second Punic War has begun.

44 B.C. **Julius Caesar** is stabbed to death by conspirators on the **Ides of March**.

9 In the **Battle of Teutoburg Forest**, Arminius, a chieftain of the Germanic Cherusci, wipes out three legions of Roman Governor Varus.

312 In the **Battle of the Milvian Bridge** outside Rome, Emperor Constantine I defeats Maxentius, his rival in the West, forcing his recognition as Roman Emperor.

375 Huns, nomadic horsemen from China, invade Eastern Europe and displace the Goths living in the Balkans, triggering the **Migration Period** that lasts until 800 A.D.

622 **Hijra:** Muhammad travels with his followers from Mecca to Medina, where he builds up an Islamic polity.

793 The raid by Scandinavian seafarers at the Abbey of Lindisfarne, off the northeast coast of England, marks the start of the **Age of the Vikings**.

800 The Frankish king, **Charlemagne**, is crowned Emperor of the Romans by Pope Leo III in Rome.

850 The classic **Maya civilization** goes into decline on the Mexican peninsula of Yucatán.

1066 **William the Conqueror**, Duke of Normandy, lands in England and defeats the Anglo-Saxon King Harold II at the **Battle of Hastings**.

1099 **Crusaders** under the command of Godfrey of Bouillon capture **Jerusalem** and kill more than 70,000 Muslims and Jews.

1206 Prince Temujin unites the Mongolian tribes and takes the title of **"Genghis Khan."**

1215 King John Lackland is forced to guarantee the rights and liberties of the English aristocracy in the **Magna Carta**.

1348 The **plague** rages in Europe until 1351.

1453 The Ottoman Turks **conquer Constantinople** (Istanbul), putting an end to the Byzantine Empire.

1492 The last Muslim bastion on the Iberian Peninsula falls with the Spanish **conquest of Granada**. The **Reconquista** is completed.

1492 Genoese navigator **Christopher Columbus** lands on an island in the Bahamas and unknowingly discovers a new continent: **America**.

1498 Portuguese **Vasco da Gama** becomes the first European to reach India by sea.

1517 The German monk **Martin Luther** voices public criticism of the Pope's selling of indulgences and thereby ignites the **Reformation**.

1572 During the French Wars of Religion, thousands of Huguenots are killed by fanatic Catholics in the **St. Bartholomew's Day massacre**.

1588 The **destruction of the Spanish Armada** by an English fleet leads to the decline of Spain as the supreme Catholic power in Europe.

1661 **King Louis XIV**, the "Sun King," begins his reign in France and rules as an unrestrained absolute monarch until his death.

1683 In the **Battle of Vienna** at Kahlenberg, a German-Polish army defeats the Ottoman Turks. The victory ends the two-month siege of Vienna.

1703 Russian Tsar Peter I the Great founds the **city of St. Petersburg**. It becomes the new Russian capital in 1713.

1776 The **USA** comes into being in Philadelphia with the Declaration of Independence by the 13 North American colonies.

1789 A mob storms the Bastille, the Paris city prison. The **French Revolution** has begun.

1815 Napoleon Bonaparte is defeated once and for all in the **Battle of Waterloo** by a British-Prussian coalition.

1814/15 After the defeat of **Napoleon Bonaparte**, the European powers agree upon a reorganization of the continent at the **Congress of Vienna**.

1830 The **July Revolution** in France results in the overthrow of the Bourbon monarchy, leading to the dominance of the bourgeoisie under the liberal King Louis Philippe of Orléans.

1942 At the **Wannsee Conference**, SS Gruppenführer Reinhard Heydrich discusses the plan for a "final solution for the Jewish problem" with leading officials of the Nazi Regime.

1944 **D-Day:** Western Allied forces land on the beaches of Normandy under the command of U.S. General Eisenhower.

1963 The **March on Washington** marks the highpoint of the Black civil rights movement in the USA led by Martin Luther King Jr.

1965 The military intervention of the USA in the conflict between the government of South Vietnam and the Communist North escalates into the **Vietnam War**.

1979 After the Shah Reza Pahlavi flees, religious leader Ayatollah Khomeini proclaims the Islamic **Republic of Iran**.

1989 The **Fall of the Berlin Wall** heralds the end of East Germany and the collapse of Communism in Eastern Europe.

1992 In Maastricht, the member states of the EC agree to join together in the **European Union** (EU).

1994 The reform government of William de Klerk takes a first step toward **ending Apartheid** with the release of the Black civil rights activist **Nelson Mandela** from prison.

1900 · **1950** · **2011**

1848 The **overthrow of the French "Citizen King," Louis Philippe**, and the proclamation of the Second Republic inspires popular uprisings in almost all of Europe.

1861–65 The conflict over the open question of slave ownership escalates into the American **Civil War** between the Northern and Southern states.

1868 A new **process of rapid reform** begins in Japan when Emperor Mutsuhito (Meiji) takes power.

1885 With the signing of the **Congo Act**, the general act of the Berlin Conference, the great powers come to an agreement over the colonial division of Africa.

1914 The assassination of the Austrian heir apparent, **Archduke Franz Ferdinand**, by the Serbian nationalist Gavrilo Princip in Sarajevo triggers the **First World War**.

1917 A continuing economic crisis leads to social upheavals in Russia. In the **October Revolution**, the Bolsheviks led by Lenin seize power and launch a Communist reorganization of society.

1919 The **Treaty of Versailles** between the Allies and the German Reich ends the First World War and results in a reorganization of Europe.

1929 The **Crash of the New York stock exchange** (Black Tuesday) triggers a severe worldwide economic crisis.

1930 To protest the British salt monopoly, the leader of the Indian struggle for independence, **Mohandas K. Gandhi**, organizes the **Salt March**.

1933 **Adolf Hitler is appointed chancellor** by Hindenburg and establishes a National Socialist (Nazi) dictatorship in the German Reich.

1936–39 The **Spanish Civil War** between Republicans and Nationalists begins with a coup by the right-wing General Francisco Franco.

1939 The **Second World War** begins with Germany's invasion of Poland.

1941 In the aftermath of a **Japanese surprise attack on the U.S. naval base in Pearl Harbor** on Hawaii, the USA declares war on Japan.

1945 The U.S. Air Force drops the first **atomic bomb** on the Japanese city of Hiroshima. It is followed three days later by a second one on Nagasaki.

1948 After British troops have been withdrawn from Palestine, Ben Gurion proclaims the **state of Israel**.

1949 Following a Communist victory, **Mao Zedong** proclaims the **People's Republic of China**.

1950–53 Intervention by USA and China turns the **conflict between North and South Korea** into the first "hot" war in the "Cold War of the systems."

1959 After years of guerilla fighting, social revolutionary **Fidel Castro seizes power in Cuba**.

1961 The East German (GDR) leadership in Berlin seals off the borders to the Western sector by building the **Berlin Wall**.

1962 The **conflict between the USA and the Soviet Union** over missile bases in **Cuba** becomes the boiling point of the Cold War.

1968 Soviet troops march into Czechoslovakia to end the liberal reform movement of the **"Prague Spring."**

1968 A **student protest movement** starts in the USA in reaction to the American intervention in Vietnam and rapidly spreads all across Western Europe. The protesters question traditional authority and values.

1969 U.S. astronauts Neil Armstrong and Edwin Aldrin become the **first humans to land on the moon**.

1973 In protest of the Western nations' pro-Israeli policies, the Arab OPEC states throttle oil production and trigger an **oil crisis** in the industrial world.

2001 In the USA on **Sept. 11**, Islamist terrorists perpetrate devastating attacks on the World Trade Center in New York and the Pentagon in Washington.

2003 Based on the alleged possession of weapons of mass destruction, the USA begins a **war against Iraq** without the consent of the UN and topples the regime of **Saddam Hussein**.

2008 **Barack Obama** becomes the first African-American to be elected U.S. President.

2008 The collapse of the U.S. investment bank **Lehman Brothers** exacerbates the **financial crisis** that broke out in 2007 and shakes the world economic system. Only extensive government interventions are able to prevent its total collapse.

2010/11 The **Jasmine Revolution** in Tunisia triggers a wave of civil protests against authoritarian regimes ruling in the Arab world.

First edition published in 2012 for North America by Barron's Educational Series, Inc.

All inquiries should be addressed to:
Barron's Educational Series, Inc.
25 Wireless Boulevard
Hauppauge, NY 11788
www.barronseduc.com

ISBN: 978-0-7641-6565-8

Library of Congress Control Number: 2012936060

Author: Christoph Marx
Editor: Detlef Berghorn
Assistant Editors: Christin Knop, Natalie Lewis
Translator: David Andersen
Translation Editors: Anja Kesper, Natalie Lewis
Graphic Design: Burga Fillery
Package Design: Dirk Brauns

All images © akg-images Berlin/London/Paris; dpa Deutsche Presse Agentur, Hamburg; Corbis Images, Düsseldorf; Shutterstock Images, New York.
For detailed credits and picture captions please visit our website
www.theKnowledgePage.com

Printed in Thailand

10 9 8 7 6 5 4 3 2 1